THE UNHOLY LEGACY
OF ABRAHAM

THE
UNHOLY LEGACY
OF ABRAHAM

G. M. WOERLEE

Matador
9 De Montfort Mews
Leicester LE1 7FW, UK
Tel: (+44) 116 255 9311 / 9312
Email: books@troubador.co.uk
Web: www.troubador.co.uk/matador

ISBN 978-1906221-652

Printed in the UK by Biddles Ltd, King's Lynn, Norfolk

Matador is an imprint of Troubador Publishing Ltd

*Judaism, Christianity, and Islam are three religions
divided by the same God.*
The Author
(with apologies to George Bernard Shaw)

Contents

Preface

More than four thousand years ago, a covenant was made between God and a man called Abraham. In exchange for belief in, and total obedience to the one and only God, as well as circumcision of all males as a sign of their faith, God would multiply his descendents to as many as the stars in the heavens and grant them the land of Canaan in which to live (Bible, Genesis 12:1-7, 17:1-13, 21:12, 26:3-5). Abraham had a total of eight male children. His firstborn son was Ishmael, a child by Hagar, the slave of his barren wife Sarah (Bible, Genesis 16:1-15). When Ishmael was fourteen years old, the previously barren Sarah wondrously gave birth to Isaac, the second son of Abraham, when she was at the ripe old age of 90 years (Bible, Genesis 21:1-7). Ishmael and Hagar were subsequently banished by order of Sarah, who was jealous that Ishmael might claim the inheritance of Abraham, but God promised Ishmael that he would become the arch-father of a great nation (Bible, Genesis 17:21, 21:9-18). And indeed, Ishmael had twelve sons who settled and founded tribes all over the Middle-East up to the borders of Egypt, which is why many in the Middle-East believe him to be the arch-father of the Arabic people (Bible, Genesis 25:13-18). Many followers of Islam even believe the prophet Mohammed to be a lineal descendent of Ishmael. Isaac eventually became the arch-father of the Jewish peoples through the twelve children of his second son Jacob (Bible, Genesis 21:12, Exodus 32:13), who by lies and trickery deceived his older brother Esau out of his rightful inheritance as firstborn son (Bible, Genesis 27:1-40). Abraham's remaining six male children were by his concubine Keturah whom he acquired later in life (Bible, Genesis 25:1-2). The monotheism preached and practised by Abraham eventually evolved into the three great world religions of Judaism, Christianity, and Islam. Accordingly, these three religions are also termed Abrahamic religions after their arch-founder, and may rightly be considered the legacy of Abraham.

But what has become of this legacy of Abraham in Europe? Europe has a long tradition of uneasy coexistence between the followers of these religions – an uneasy coexistence which has arrived at a new crossroad because of the profound demographic and social changes Europe is now undergoing. Record low birth rates mean that the populations of the original European inhabitants are declining. At the same time, Islamic immigrants with high birth rates form an increasingly larger proportion of the populations of these same European countries. Bat Ye'Or, an Egyptian-Jewish writer, once proposed that these ongoing demographic changes may eventually result in a future overwhelming and subordination of the original Judeo-Christian cultures of European countries by the steadily increasing proportion of these Islamic inhabitants such that Europe would be better termed Eurabia (Bat Ye'Or 2005). This is a truly frightening thought. It would be an association between cultures of quite different philosophies as well as a historical unwillingness to communicate. Worse yet, increasingly vociferous fundamentalist Jewish, Christian, and Islamic groups – all with very literal interpretations of the holy texts of their religions – exert a disproportionate effect on the ways members of these disparate communities perceive and interact with each other. Subjugation of European cultures to the degrading horrors of Islamic fundamentalist dominion, combined with a return to the dark spiritual terrorism exerted by an increasing trend to Judeo-Christian fundamentalism noticeable in some parts of the world, is something no-one would ever wish to experience. Europe and the Middle-East would revert to thought and socio-cultural patterns more appropriate to the Middle-Ages.

Accordingly, much of this book is a study of how the "God-given" ancient systems of thought revealed in the fundamental holy texts of the three Abrahamic religions can generate frighteningly evil forms of narrow-minded religious fanaticism. Such terrifying forms of fundamentalism may truly be said to be the unholy legacy of Abraham. So what are the holy texts of Judaism, Christianity, and Islam?

- The Bible is the paramount religious text of the followers of Christianity. It is actually a collection of books, 39 books in the part of the Bible called the Old Testament, and 27 books in the part of the Bible called the New Testament. This book quotes mainly from the American Standard Version of the Bible published in 1901 CE. This translation corrects many inconsistencies and errors in the text of the King James Authorized Version of the Bible, while retaining the grandeur of the language used in this old version of the Bible.

- The 39 books of the Old Testament of the Christian Bible are also the holy books of the Jewish faith, and the followers of Judaism call this collection of books the Tanakh. Genesis, Exodus, Leviticus, Numbers, and Deuteronomy are the first five books of the Tanakh. These five books comprise the most fundamental part of all these Jewish religious texts, the Pentateuch, and are known more commonly as the Torah. The five books of the Torah contain the laws of God as revealed to the Israelite peoples, while the remaining 34 books of the Tanakh describe the workings of these laws and the relationship of God to humankind. For many followers of Judaism, the five books of the Torah as written in Hebrew, are the literal message of God as directly revealed to Moses during his sojourn on Mount Sinai sometime about the year 1280 BCE. Accordingly, many followers of Judaism believe that to understand the message of the Torah is to understand the relationship of God with humankind. This book mainly uses the translation of the Old Testament in the American Standard Version of the Bible, because this differs in no significant way from other English translations of the Tanakh and Torah made for followers of Judaism.

- The paramount Islamic holy text is the Koran, or Qur'an. According to the followers of Islam, the Koran is a literal revelation of the word of Allah, the one supreme God, to the founding prophet of Islam, Mohammed (570-632 CE). Accordingly, the followers of Islam believe the original Arabic language version to be the only clear and untainted revelation of God. This is stated several times in the Koran (Koran 12:1-3, 39:1, 55:1-2). Indeed, followers of Islam claim a person can only begin to grasp the true revelation of God to humankind by reading the original Arabic text, because this was the language in which God revealed the Koran to Mohammed. But this is an antique local Arabic dialect from the Mecca region, with ancient idioms, and equally ancient ways of thought. No one except scholars speaks or reads this dialect any more. Asking a follower of Islam to read the Koran in the original Arabic dialect is a bit like asking a Christian to read the Bible in the original dialects of Sumerian, Egyptian, Aramaic, Hebrew, Greek, and Latin in which it was written. Except for scholars of these languages, no Christians can do this, any more than most followers of Islam can read the Koran in the original Arabic dialect in which it was written. So the Koran has been capably translated into many other languages. This is no blasphemy, for God also says in the Koran that: 'And We never sent a messenger save with the language of his folk, that he might make (the message) clear for them (Koran 14:4).' Except where otherwise stated, this book quotes from the capable English translation of the Koran made by Marmaduke Pickthall (1875-1936 CE), and first published in 1930 CE.

- All followers of Islam consider the Koran to be the paramount holy text of Islam, but there are also several compendia of the sayings and deeds of the prophet Mohammed called the Sunnah. The reasoning behind the Islamic desire to compile the known deeds and sayings of Mohammed is as follows – Mohammed was a man inspired and guided by God, so all he said, and all he did were very likely also guided by God. Indeed, this is confirmed in the Koran where we read that the deeds and words of Mohammed are an example to all followers of Islam: 'Verily in the messenger of Allah ye have a good example for him who looketh unto Allah and the last Day, and remembereth Allah much.' (Koran 33:21) This is indeed fortunate for the followers of Islam, because the Koran is unclear on some subjects, so the Sunnah forms an invaluable supplementary body of knowledge as to the will of God. About 85% of all followers of Islam belong to the Sunni sect of Islam, and Sunnites regard the Sunnah as second only to the Koran in religious importance. The most important Sunnah was compiled by the scholar Sahih Al-Bukhari (809-869 CE), and elegantly translated into English by Dr. Muhammad Muhsin Khan (1927-? CE). This is the translation of the Sunnah of Al-Bukhari referred to in this book.

Superficial analysis of the literal meanings of these holy texts does indeed provide divine justification for the most extreme manifestations of fundamentalism. 'Aha!' say many people. 'But no-one ever interprets these holy texts literally any more. After all, these holy texts may actually be fraudulent, corrupted during transcription in the ages before the coming of the printing press, or defectively translated. So who takes any notice of them, or even believes enough to interpret them literally, or say that we should live as the people writing these holy books lived?' Unfortunately, many Jewish, Christian, and Islamic sects or communities do just this. They consider the texts of these books to be the literal and unchangeable word of God. So they live devout but gloomy lives, fearing that the least infringement of the God-given laws in their holy texts may endanger their chances of an eternal life in the paradise promised to the faithful after death. A sad situation, for by so doing they deny themselves the chance of living happy and fulfilled mortal lives – the only life of which any mortal can be certain. 'Ah ... But this is just your fantasy,' say some people. I tell these people to look around them at the believers in "intelligent design" madness, as well as the innumerable fanatical Christian sects around them. Think of the fanatical Jewish sects determining aspects of current Israeli political policy with a philosophy expressed in the words, 'Praise God and pass the bullets!' Think of the fundamentalist Islamic sects who consider the most ideal form of existence is to live in primitive squalor, just as their prophet Mohammed lived. Think of fanatical Islamic suicide bombers, and Islamic terrorists. All these are people with simple beliefs and exceedingly literal interpretations of their holy texts. Even worse, many of these fanatics have an irrepressibly zealous desire to enforce their interpretations and beliefs upon others. It is unfortunate, but such sects and belief systems appear to thrive in an increasingly vociferous and public opinion determining manner.

I cannot determine whether the holy texts these fanatical fundamentalists, or so-called religious people, use to defend their beliefs and justify their depravities are corrupt or not. This is an almost impossible task of scholarship. Even if I were to complete such a task, the explanation would be so detailed, so abstruse, and so difficult to follow, that it would change nothing. The holy texts, and the beliefs associated with them would remain. What then? How then to reveal the unspeakable horridness and abominations resulting from total belief and subjugation to simplistic, very literal interpretations of the texts in these holy books? This book does this by illustrating just these simplistic, very literal interpretations of the texts of the holy books of Judaism, Christianity, and Islam. After all, the holy texts of these religions are so full of inconsistencies and appalling vileness, that mere disclosure of these texts reveals them to be no longer relevant to this day and age. Some people may say the citations from holy texts used in this book are passages torn out of their proper context. To those people I can only say, 'Read these texts and be convinced that these citations have most definitely not been ripped from their proper context, except where explicitly stated.'

Much of this book also discusses another important aspect to any serious study of the Abrahamic religions. This is the question of why the followers of Judaism, Christianity, and Islam actually believe in things such as: God, angels, devils, the human soul, and an eternal life after death. None of these things are visible, able to be touched, or detected with any of the senses of the body. Nor are these things able to be detected with any apparatus known to man. Even so, faith in the truths of these beliefs has thrived for thousands of years, and continues to thrive. This means there must be some sort of proof supporting these beliefs, otherwise they would simply fade away, and the associated religions die. Fortunately for many believers, examination of the holy texts of Judaism, Christianity, and Islam, reveals many apparent proofs for these beliefs. Furthermore, the functioning of the human body and the natural laws of the universe in which we live, appear to confirm the reality of God, the reality of miracles, the reality of prophecy, as well as confirming the almost universal belief in the reality of a soul and a life after death. This is the proof sought and found by all believers! However, all these proofs are no more than apparent proofs, because these apparent proofs are all explained by natural laws and the functioning of the human body. So this book explains the truly fascinating ways natural laws and the workings of the human body apparently confirm the reality of God, miracles, prophecies, the reality of a soul, and belief in a life after death. Insights derived from understanding these aspects of the functioning of the human body reveal much about the basic perceptions driving people into the arms of religious faith, and totally remove the fundamental proofs for any faith in such beliefs. This is truly fascinating knowledge understandable to all with a good basic schooling. Such knowledge enables us to understand our basic drives, the apparent confirmation of religious beliefs, as well as providing a true understanding of ourselves, of others, and of human societies.

This is a somewhat different approach to just exposing the many logical inconsistencies in the very idea of a God, angels, a life after death etc. There are several outstanding books employing logic and common sense to totally demolish belief in the reality of God, an immaterial soul, and an eternal life after death (e.g. Dawkins 2006). And these books do indeed provide a plethora of outstanding logical arguments as to why these beliefs are illogical delusions. However, they fail to take the reality of personal human experience into account. After hearing all these logical arguments, a true believer will say these logical arguments are all very interesting ... Then without even pausing for breath, a true believer will proceed to say these very same logical arguments are absolute nonsense, because they totally ignore the totality of true proof for the reality of God, an immaterial soul, as well as an eternal life after death. By true proof, the believer means evidence provided by paranormal phenomena, out-of-body experiences, near-death experiences, and the genuine feeling that there is a God. So this book describes how the functioning of the human body and natural laws generates these direct and indirect apparent proofs of the ancient human belief in God, the human soul, and an eternal life after death. This method reveals the apparently paranormal to be a perfectly normal part of human existence and experience. Such an approach supplements logical argument and reason by explaining how it is we humans come to believe in the reality of these things.

But does discussion of all these things and especially of the excesses of Judaism, Christianity, and Islam mean I despise these Abrahamic religions? Absolutely not! In spite of the many negative aspects associated with these religions – aspects such as bigotry, suppression of freedom of thought, suppression of freedom of expression, intolerance, pogroms of unbelievers, etc – religions of all types have in the past conferred enormous benefits upon their believers. Judaism welded the twelve disparate and primitive tribes of Israel into a single proud people with a single identity and purpose, enabling them to survive as a socio-cultural entity despite isolation, persecution, as well as pogroms throughout their history. Christianity gave the peoples of the benighted and brawling postage stamp sized nations of Europe a single cultural identity during the Middle-Ages. This uniform cultural identity and philosophy culminated in the rapid technological development and welfare now existing in these nations. Islam transformed an ignorant rabble of disparate desert tribes into proud nations with a single cultural identity, ultimately enabling them to develop grand philosophical, cultural, and aesthetic works. These are but some of the benefits conferred upon believers in all great and good religions. And indeed, Judaism, Christianity, and Islam are great religions, for they generated systems of thought ennobling and empowering their believers.

This book is set in a fictitious, possible near future in the ancient Dutch university city of Leiden. It is a future in which the tenets of Islam are increasingly being applied to everyday European life. The sounding of church bells on Sundays is forbidden because it offends the sensitivities of the followers of Islam. Serving alcohol outside on a terrace during Islamic prayer times is forbidden. Other religions such as Christianity are also undergoing an Islam-approved fundamentalist resurgence. Finally, church bells are only permitted to ring on the eve of the Islamic Feast of Sacrifice to celebrate a legend common to all three Abrahamic religions – the near-sacrifice of Isaac, (or Ishmael), by Abraham (Bible, Genesis 22:1-18). This is the setting for Socratic dialogues between the two main characters: a cynical, wine-loving older physician, and a naive young student of theology. Their free-ranging discussions cover all the subjects mentioned in this preface, finally coming to the conclusion that faith in the three Abrahamic religions is supported by apparent evidence generated by the laws of nature and the functioning of the human body. Furthermore, these same discussions emphasize the fact that literal interpretations, as well as strict application of the laws in the religious texts of all Abrahamic religions, can give rise to fanatical, evil, and abhorrent systems of thought and laws akin to the worst ever experienced in Europe during the Middle-Ages.

The ultimate purpose of this book is to imbue readers with a realization of the cruel insanities and dark abominations inherent in literal interpretations of the texts of these religions, together with a sense of wonder at the very fact of their personal sentience, of wonder at the very fact of life, of wonder at the very fact of existence, and a sense of wonder and awe for the universe we all share. It is my hope that the very fact of understanding the truths of all these things, an understanding of the biological basis of many human belief systems and our being, as well as an understanding of the impermanence of existence, will imbue the reader with a respect for all things animate and inanimate – a respect founded upon factual knowledge of the biological, physical, and spiritual nature of our being. Such an understanding can only aid and further the fruitful integration of cultures on our increasingly smaller planet – a sorely needed integration – for no culture exists alone.

G.M. Woerlee, 2007

Chapter 1

Bread and abrogation

'God is real! God is there for you, God is there for me, God is there for all of us!' declaimed the pale, greying little man in front of the Hartevelt Church. The group of men listening to these words shifted restlessly. Some yawned. A few wandered off in search of coffee, a kebab, or other entertainment.

It was a sunny market day in the ancient Dutch university city of Leiden, and as usual the main shopping street was filled with a lively bustle of Saturday shoppers. The speaker continued enthusiastically, seemingly oblivious to the boredom of his restive audience. 'Proof of God's reality, God's works, and God's mercy are all about us. They are revealed by the wonders of the world about you, and in the perfect functioning of this world. It is like a perfect machine made by a master machine maker. Only in the situation of our universe and our world, the machine and its workings are infinitely more complex – too complex for human understanding. Yet we are here. We are part of it. Somehow all this perfection came to be. It is inconceivable that such perfection "just somehow" evolved from nothing. Such perfection had to be created by some perfect intelligence! It is inconceivable that it could be otherwise. Truly, these wonders we see and experience, and of which we each are insignificant parts – truly these things are proof of a design, a plan far above anything we mere mortals can conceive. These things, these wonders, all add up to undeniable proof of God, the architect of all these things. This is true proof for all who see, observe, and think. God is all about us, God is all powerful, and God knows and understands all that happens in our hearts, even our most secret thoughts.'

Evidently many of his listeners thought otherwise, or simply did not engage in too much thinking at all. Some yawned and looked bored, while

1

yet others began walking away. An expression of desperation appeared on the face of the speaker who redoubled his efforts to win the attention of the remaining few bored souls. 'Here in this very city is proof of all I say. It is proof that our God, the one and only true God, is concerned with the wellbeing of each and every one of us. The miracle of Leiden reveals all these things, and it happened only a few streets away from this place, in one of the meaner streets of this fair city, in the Miracle Alley.'

'What! A miracle here in Leiden? Go on, you're pulling our legs. Get real! Nothing ever happens here in Leiden!' called one of the listeners.

'It is true; God did indeed work a miracle here in this very city. I must warn you though, although this miracle may sound trite and insignificant to us in these modern times as we approach the celebrations of the 2000th anniversary [2030 CE] of the start of the glorious ministry of our Lord and Saviour, Jesus of Nazareth (peace be upon him). Nonetheless it is a true miracle, and as such is proof of the reality of God.'

'Come on, get to the point,' heckled another listener.

'Okay, okay, I was just about to start. The year 1315 CE was a famine year in Leiden. One day a well-to-do woman purchased a loaf of bread. Fearing that others less fortunate might ask to share this loaf, she ate one half secretly in her home, afterwards locking the other half in her provision box. Her hungry poor sister came to her house and begged her for some bread. The wealthier sister vehemently denied having any bread in the house. Finally, exasperated by the entreaties of her sister, she said, "If there is any bread in this house, may God turn it into stone!" Later, she went to her provision box, opened it, and found the remaining half loaf had indeed been turned into stone. God had punished her for her mean-spirited behaviour!' He looked triumphantly towards his listeners. Incontrovertible proof! At least so he thought.

'Rubbish,' called one of the listeners. 'Have you ever tried eating day-old French bread? Hard as stone – like rock! You don't need miracles to make quick-hardening bread – just a French baker!'

Another listener, a distinguished, tall older man with a thick bush of unkempt greying dark hair added in a querulous and exasperated tone, 'Call a 700 year old fable proof? If this story is even half true, then why couldn't the cause of the rapid hardening of the bread simply be due to an indecent amount of sawdust added to the flour by the miller or the baker?

After all, if grain is in short supply such as during a famine, then either the miller, or the baker, or both, may well have eked out their meagre supply of flour with something else. And here you're talking about a time when adulteration of food was commonplace.'

'Oh men of little faith! Doubters in the mercy and reality of God!' thundered the speaker. 'I can prove what I say. This very half-loaf has been preserved all these years. First it hung in a red box on a pillar in the Saint Peter's Church, but was lost for many years after the Catholics were driven out of the church. However, the wondrous and mysterious ways of God ensured it was found during a recent renovation. Now it is displayed for believers and unbelievers alike in the Lakenhal Museum nearby here. Each and every one of you can see it for yourself, and be awed by this proof of the reality of God.' He warmed to his subject, and white foam began forming in the corners of his mouth, 'This proof may seem trivial to you, but it is a manifestation of God's supreme power in this universe, a manifestation of God's presence everywhere in this universe, and a manifestation of God's knowledge of all that happens in this universe. Indeed, this is proof of the word of God as expressed in the one and only true holy book – a book truly written under the divine inspiration of God – the Bible. Laugh, joke, demean and belittle, but ultimately you and I are all subject to the judgment of God. Deride such proofs at your own peril! For the prophets have warned us of God's ultimate judgment on us all!'

For God will bring every work into judgment, with every hidden thing, whether it be good, or whether it be evil. (ASV Bible, Ecclesiastes 12:14)

'Come on now,' heckled the distinguished older man, 'you're not going to try and sell that hoary old story again about Christianity having a monopoly on the truth about God. After all, the Koran says exactly the same.'

And the earth shineth with the light of her Lord, and the Book is set up, and the Prophets and the witnesses are brought, and it is judged between them with truth, and they are not wronged. And

3

each soul is paid in full for what it did. And He is best aware of what they do. (Koran 39:69-70)

The few remaining listeners suddenly aroused from their indifferent torpor. They began listening attentively in expectation of a rousing theological argument. This was what they wanted to hear. This was more enjoyable than buying food in the market, more fun than drinking coffee, and certainly much more fun than looking at clothes with their wives.

'I hear unbelief. I hear vile and filthy perversions coming from your mouth. Are you a closet Moslem? Are you an atheist, or even worse – a humanist?' ranted the speaker. 'For it is written in ...'

Whatever he wanted to say was drowned by the thunderous and strident call to noon prayer from the nearby Mare Mosque. *'Allahu Akbar Allah, Allahu Akbar Allah, Allahu Akbar Allah, Allahu Akbar Allah ...'* echoed through the streets and alleyways of Leiden. All conversation became impossible as the muezzin turned up the volume of the sound emitted by the loudspeakers installed in the recently constructed minaret of the Mosque. The remaining listeners dispersed to continue their Saturday shopping. *'Ashhadu an la ilaha illa Allah, Ashhadu an la ilaha illa Allah,'* rang through the streets around the Hartevelt Church. The distinguished man walked into the nearby Madhouse Alley, followed by a pale and serious-looking young man.

The younger man caught up with the older man and began, 'Excuse me, but you gave that poor man rather a hard time. After all, he was only expressing his sincere belief in his religion. So why ridicule him?'

'Who are you young man?'

'My name is Thomas. I study theology at the university here. I was interested in what you had to say because you seem to know a lot about Islam and Christianity.'

'Humph! Theology ... You look pale. Must be all that prayer and serious thought. I'm Ben. I'm on my way to the Lakenhal Museum to see this miraculous half loaf. You want to tag along? Should be entertaining as well as instructive to actually see this petrified bread.'

'I'd like that,' was the equally curt rejoinder from Thomas.

They walked together in silence through the winding alleys of the old inner city pursued by the sounds of the call to Islamic prayer. Some years before, the city council had sold the increasingly dilapidated Mare Church for use as a mosque. The Islamic community had leapt at the opportunity to buy this central location for a peppercorn price, rapidly refurbishing the church, together with building an adjacent minaret in a cheap modern style. Opinions on the style and appearance of the new minaret were divided, but everyone was unanimous regarding the incredible power of the public address system installed inside the minaret, and enthusiastically employed to summon the faithful to prayer five times a day. The muezzin apparently delighted in using it at maximum power, especially on Sunday mornings since the predominantly Moslem city council had forbidden the ringing of church bells so as not to offend the sensibilities of the Islamic community. Ben was not religious, but he did miss the familiar ringing of church bells on Sunday mornings. It was a sound remembered from his youth – a sound signifying home and a safe and familiar world. He sighed with some relief as the call to prayer finally ceased.

Thomas began, 'You seem to be a very critical person. You appear to know about the Bible as well as the Koran, and yet seem to be impressed by neither, nor do you seem to be impressed by the wonders all around us quite evidently proving the truth of the existence of God. I'm puzzled. Are you a believer in any religion, an apostate, an atheist, or simply a humanist?'

'I'm certainly not a devout follower of any creed or brand of religion. I'm also not an atheist, because that requires just as much belief as a belief in God. You could say I'm a sort of humanist, because I do believe in humankind and a belief in the rewards of a true understanding of the human condition, as well as an understanding of our individual place in the universe.'

'But God, and especially his only Son, Jesus, have taught us all these things.'

'Read my lips and listen young man, I'm not particularly interested in whatever creed or brand of religion, you or the speaker we were given the opportunity to escape are trying to peddle.'

Thomas began to splutter; 'Now just a moment, I didn't count on being insulted about my beliefs.'

'I'm not insulting, just explaining a point of view. I once had a devout Jewish colleague, yet he was very liberal and understanding towards believers in all other religions. Judaism suited him because that was the way he was brought up. He once told me a wonderful analogy about how he viewed different religions.'

> *Different religions are like witnesses at a traffic accident. You have the basic physical facts of the traffic accident itself, but each of the witnesses will tell a different story. Religions are a bit like that. Each tells the story of what believers hold to be a fundamental fact – a belief in God – a God present throughout the universe, a God who knows all, and a God who is ultimately powerful. Nearly all major world religions acknowledge this as a fundamental belief, but express this belief in different ways.*

'Aha! So you do believe in God!' was the quick rejoinder.

'No, I'm just fascinated by the individual ways people express their belief in God.'

The exhibit of the miracle loaf in the Lakenhal Museum was soon found. It was somewhat disappointing – a single smooth, brown coloured stone that admittedly did vaguely resemble a half loaf of bread, if you assumed the loaf had been petrified and polished by some supernatural miracle. The description next to it stated that it was a stone typical of the type used as ballast for ships trading between Holland and Sweden at the time of the miracle.

'Disappointing …' said Ben in a tone redolent of a very different emotion. 'Another miracle explained and banished. It couldn't be the original in any case, otherwise it would have looked like a shrivelled up piece of organic material. Even then it wouldn't have survived all those hundreds of years, because it would have either rotted away, or rats and mice would have eaten it. It's very likely that some church functionary replaced the remaining crumbs of the original loaf with a stone to keep the story of the miracle alive. After all, during the Middle-Ages in Europe, relics, and the wonders associated with them were big business, generating a good income from pilgrims for any place with a particularly popular relic. Think of relics such as the bones of saints, mummies of saints and holy men, powdered breast milk of the mother of Jesus, samples of the blood of Jesus, splinters of the cross upon which Jesus was crucified, the shroud of Turin, and even more bizarre relics such as the Holy Prepuce.'

'Prepuce? What is a prepuce?'

'A prepuce is the foreskin of the penis, and the Holy Prepuce was the foreskin of Jesus. After all, Jesus was brought up as a Jew, and all male Jews were circumcised as babies. Apparently someone in the Middle-Ages managed to get hold of the foreskin of Jesus.'

'Do you really mean to tell me that the foreskin of Jesus was actually considered a religious relic?' queried Thomas in a tone of utter amazement.

'Christians in the Middle-Ages were obsessed with relics, and the Holy Prepuce was just another relic in this religion-crazed period of European history. The Holy Prepuce was first recorded as being present in the abbey of Charroux in France sometime in the early twelfth century – more than 1000 years after Jesus lived on this world. I can't believe it really was the foreskin of Jesus, because traditionally the foreskin is buried after a Jewish circumcision ceremony, and somehow I don't believe the parents of Jesus preserved it for posterity. So I think some person claimed their church had the foreskin of Jesus as a relic in an attempt to attract pilgrims, or they were cheated by someone who sold them the relic. After all, during the Middle-Ages there were several churches claiming they had the one and only true Holy Prepuce.'

'Oh, which churches then?'

'Aside from the abbey of Charroux, there was also the abbey of Coulombs in France, the Lateran Basilica in Rome, the cathedral of Santiago de Compostela in Spain, Onze Lieve Vrouwe Kerk in Antwerp, Belgium, as well as other churches in the cities of Besancon, Metz, and Hildesheim. Amazing isn't it? Pilgrims in the Middle-Ages sometimes made dangerous journeys through bandit infested regions, endured hunger and thirst, exposure to the weather, lack of shelter, as well as many other deprivations and discomforts. Some pilgrims even added a variety of wondrous and fantastical self-inflicted discomforts or torments upon themselves, such as self-flagellation, walking on their knees, stuffing stinging nettles inside their shirts, or fasting. These discomforts and torments had a purpose; they supposedly increased the amount of celestial credit gained from such a pilgrimage. What is more, these pilgrims nearly always made these journeys by foot, sometimes walking thousands of kilometres, enduring all these many hardships in order to worship at places imbued with a religious significance transcending that possible in their home districts. The mind boggles at the idea of such pilgrims kneeling to worship at a shrine holding a shrivelled up ancient foreskin.'

'Er, yes ...' responded Thomas in a hesitant tone. 'Luckily Christian churches these days no longer actively encourage the use and adoration of relics.'

They paused at the entrance to the Lakenhal Museum. Outside it was warm. The sun shone. People wore bright and cheerful summer clothing. It was turning into a beautiful summer day. Ben looked appraisingly at Thomas for a moment before asking, 'Would you like to share some lunch with me? I'd enjoy your company. My treat.'

'Thank you. I'd like that very much.'

'Okay. Let's go to one of the restaurants on the High Street. I always enjoy it there in the summer, and we're early enough to avoid the lunchtime rush.'

As they walked towards the High Street, they passed the Hartevelt Church where the same preacher had recommenced preaching: 'It is good we no longer use church bells to summon the faithful as we did in the past. For the use of church bells to summon the faithful is ostentatious vanity – vanity leading straight to the hell promised the vain and the self-seeking. This sharing of a common call to prayer by the muezzin is also a sign of consideration for our fellow Islamic countrymen, for by so doing we cause no offence to Islam by ostentatious display of Christian symbols. God needs no such ostentation, for he knows what is in your heart, knows what is in your minds, and knows what is in your most secret thoughts. God knows the honour we so deeply feel and express in our hearts, minds, and thoughts.'

'Cockroach!' yelled Ben as he walked past, continuing to Thomas, 'I can't stand it when a fanatic like that supposedly professing his faith actually tries defending the injustices visited upon him – in this situation, the recent ordinance totally banning the use of church bells. This is a regulation redolent of those in Islamic lands such as Saudi Arabia, where no religious symbols other than those of Islam are allowed to be displayed in public. Yet in this country, those professing other religious beliefs are permitted to display the symbols of their beliefs, as well as to publicly practice their beliefs. Just try that in some other fundamentalist Islamic countries such as Sudan or Saudi Arabia. And here you have this fellow, this Christian fanatic, this cockroach, this low-life heel-licker, justifying an intolerance foisted upon us. It's almost enough to make me intolerant myself.'

'Do you detest Islam?'

'Not at all! I have the greatest respect for what it did for the advancement of the peoples professing this faith. And when you look at it carefully, it's no worse or better than Christianity in many regards. Aha, here we are, and there's an unoccupied table. Wonderful! I like it here in the summer. Let's order first, and then I'll explain my problems with religion, and why I may seem rather iconoclastic to you.'

They sat themselves at a table on the pontoon forming the restaurant. The pontoon moved gently up and down in the wake of a boatload of tourists passing under the bridge into the New Rhine Canal. Service was quick, and the requested French-fries with saté and cold beer appeared rapidly. Ben sipped his beer, leaned back in his chair, felt the sun pleasantly warm his body, and looked around him. Colourful crowds thronged the market along the canal. He sighed contentedly.

'Thomas, this is paradise. This is the way people were meant to live – a place in the sun, good food, delicious cold beer, and all around – happy people.'

Thomas sipped his beer and looked appraisingly at Ben. 'I agree wholeheartedly. But what about your attitude towards religions? We were just coming to that when we arrived here.'

'Such haste ... Now Thomas; you seem a nice fellow, a fellow who wants to learn, even though you do study theology ...'

'Now just a minute ... There's absolutely nothing wrong with studying theology. It's a difficult study, one that I've always wanted to do, because it teaches me more about the nature of God, the purpose God has with our world and for each of us as individuals, as well as teaching me more about my own small part in the grand plan of God.'

'That's precisely what I mean. By saying what you just said, you've already stated you believe in a God, although to me the reality of a God is very disputable.'

'How can you say the reality of God is disputable? Just as that preacher quite correctly said, God is manifest everywhere, and we learn can more about God by studying the word of God as revealed by the prophets and Jesus in the Bible.'

'Hmmm ... Followers of many other religions such as Islam, Buddhism, Hinduism, and countless others say the exactly the same things about their religions and their holy books. Let's examine this idea that the intentions of God are only revealed in the Bible. To begin with, would you agree that the followers of the Jewish, Christian, and Islamic faiths believe in the very same God?'

'Well ... Yes, it is the same God, but religions other than Christianity do not have the true and final revelation of God. They have glimpse of the truth, but it is incomplete as in Judaism, or was distorted at a later date by Islam. As Christians we know we have the true revelation of God, because we know Jesus was the Son of God. The word of God could not have been delivered in a more direct and personal manner than through the Son of God. It is through Jesus, the true Son of God, that we know the true word of God, whereas only human prophets revealed the word of God to all other religions. These prophets were undoubtedly inspired by God, but they misinterpreted many of these revelations.'

'An interesting idea Thomas. But if the prophets misinterpreted some revelations, then some revelations may actually be totally incorrect. So how can we differentiate the false and corrupted revelations from the true and uncorrupted revelations?'

Thomas took a sip of beer, leaned back in his chair, felt the soft sunlight warm his face and body. He felt good. A slight smile appeared upon his lips. This argument was elementary. 'That's easy. We know Jesus of Nazareth, the founder of the ideas of Christendom, was the Son of God. Accordingly his revelations must be true and uncorrupted. So all we need do is compare the revelations of all other prophets in the Bible for consistency with the revelations of Jesus. When you do this, you realize the revelations of the prophets in the Bible are consistent with the revelations of Jesus. This is not altogether surprising, because as the Son of God, Jesus confirmed and fulfilled the divine revelations of the prophets (Bible, Matthew 5:17).'

'So you really believe Jesus of Nazareth was the Son of God?

'Definitely. The Bible tells us this.'

'Do you also believe that the revelations of the ancient prophets of

Israel in the Old Testament of the Bible are consistent with the revelations of Jesus?'

'Yeees ...' and Thomas began sitting straighter. This was evidently building up to something Ben might attempt calling a counter-argument.

'Then I'm curious as to how many sons God has. After all, I read in the Bible that God has several sons (Bible, Genesis 6:2, Job 1:6, Job 38:7). Long before Jesus was born, other evidently unruly and fun-loving sons of God had sexual relations with human women from which children were born (Bible, Genesis 6:4). These children were called Nephilim, and were said to be unmanageable evildoers, which is why God caused the earth to be flooded so as to kill all evildoers, including the Nephilim.'

'Disputable ... You must have read those parts of the Bible incorrectly. I'll look it up.' Thomas pulled a copy of the Bible out of the shoulder bag lying next to his chair, looked at Ben enquiringly, 'Which chapter was it?'

'Genesis 6, verse 1 onwards.'

And it came to pass, when men began to multiply on the face of the ground, and daughters were born unto them, that the sons of God saw the daughters of men that they were fair; and they took them wives of all that they chose. And Jehovah said, My spirit shall not strive with man for ever, for that he also is flesh: yet shall his days be a hundred and twenty years. The Nephilim were in the earth in those days, and also after that, when the sons of God came unto the daughters of men, and they bare children to them: the same were the mighty men that were of old, the men of renown. And Jehovah saw that the wickedness of man was great in the earth, and that every imagination of the thoughts of his heart was only evil continually. And it repented Jehovah that he had made man on the earth, and it grieved him at his heart. And Jehovah said, I will destroy man whom I have created from the face of the ground; both man, and beast, and creeping things, and birds of the heavens; for it repenteth me that I have made them. (ASV Bible, Genesis 6:1-7)

Ben leaned back in his chair, a pawkish glint in his eyes, 'These Nephilim as well as the people among whom they lived were evildoers whose actions, speech, and thoughts were in conflict with the will of God. So why couldn't Jesus of Nazareth simply be one of these Nephilim, and his so-called "fulfilment" of the revelations of the prophets be no more than a mischievous trick of a fundamentally evil Nephilim?'

'What a cheap argument! Rubbish! A sophistry!' spluttered Thomas. 'I'm quite sure many capable theologians demolished that idea long ago.'

'Even so, it's an interesting thought. But for me it makes the idea that Jesus is the Son of God rather less tenable. So let's just regard Jesus of Nazareth as a major prophet. There are also many other prophets, and the religions founded by their revelations are dedicated to the same God. Let's take the example of the Koran. Followers of Islam say the Koran is the eternal, the final, and the definitive revelation of the will of God for this world. Who knows? They may even be correct. After all, Mohammed, the prophet of Islam, received his revelations from God about 600 years after the passing of Jesus and other Christian prophets, and more than 2000 years after Abraham, the arch-father of the tribes of Israel first received his revelations from God. So it may well be that the revelations of the prophet Mohammed are superior to those of Jesus and the prophets of the Old Testament. After all, God had an extra 600 years after the death of Jesus to refine his arguments and perfect his wishes for humankind.'

Thomas was aghast. This was heresy. This was honeyed evil. This was a method of argument suited to contemptible apostates, to despicable humanists, to evil philosophers, and even worse – to loathsome sophists – degraded creatures for whom truth has no meaning as long as they are believed. 'Utter nonsense! God is eternal. God is the creator of the universe and all within. God is eternal, infallible, all-powerful, all-pervading, and all-knowing. So God cannot give revelations at one moment, change and give other totally different revelations at a later time. God is eternal, so a time span of 1000 years is as a day to God, for time is a property of our universe, and as the creator of our universe, God is the creator of time itself! There is proof of this in the Bible!'

Lord, thou hast been our dwelling-place in all generations. Before the mountains were brought forth, or ever thou hadst formed the earth and the world, even from everlasting to everlasting, thou art God. Thou turnest man to destruction, and sayest, Return, ye children of men. For a thousand years in thy sight are but as yesterday when it is past, and as a watch in the night. (ASV Bible, Psalms 90:1-4)

'And Saint Peter emphasized this even further in one of his letters,' continued Thomas opening his Bible at another passage and shoving it across the table.

Ben leaned over the Bible, a French-fry between the fingers of one hand and a glass of beer in the other. He took a sip, engulfed the French-fry, and burped softly as he started to read.

But forget not this one thing, beloved, that one day is with the Lord as a thousand years, and a thousand years as one day. (ASV Bible, 2 Peter 3:8)

'Well Thomas, it looks like you've given me even more compelling reasons not to believe in Judaism, Christianity, or Islam.'

'Huh! What do you mean?'

Ben stabbed in the air with another French-fry. 'Just this – you tell me that God is all-pervading, all-powerful, and all-knowing – but I happen to disagree with this belief. Let's start with Judaism. The first five books of the Old Testament form a group of books called the Torah, which is one of the main holy texts of the Jewish faith. Even a cursory examination of the Torah reveals a number of inconsistencies totally incompatible with the idea of an all-knowing and all-pervading God.'

'Oh … Prove it if you can.'

'Just look at the last bit of the passages from Genesis we looked at before.'

Thomas opened the Bible, and they read:

And Jehovah saw that the wickedness of man was great in the earth, and that every imagination of the thoughts of his heart was only evil continually. And it repented Jehovah that he had made man on the earth, and it grieved him at his heart. And Jehovah said, I will destroy man whom I have created from the face of the

13

ground; both man, and beast, and creeping things, and birds of the heavens; for it repenteth me that I have made them. (ASV Bible, Genesis 6:5-7)

'Just a moment Thomas. Waiter! Two more beers please!' Ben turned towards Thomas. 'Now Thomas, just tell me, is the fact of God repenting having created humans because they acted against the wishes of God a sign of an all-knowing entity?'

'Aha, but God gave humans the capacity of free will and choice. They all chose to be wicked of their own free will. Such massive, all-encompassing wickedness and evil is irreversible, and cannot be corrected. It is an affront to the will of God, and must be expunged so that God's grand plan for humankind can come to fruition. So God had no choice but to exterminate them all.'

Ben laughed. 'Good try Thomas, but not good enough. The big question raised by this passage is why God created humans with the ability to exercise free will in the first place. After all, if God really only wanted grovelling worshipers, God would have created them that way. Instead God created humans with the capacity for free will. Then, because these people exercised this free will in ways not meeting with God's approval, God considered them evil, and decided to destroy them all. This is really strange. God is the all-knowing and all-powerful creator of our universe. This universe is vast beyond comprehension, filled with countless billions of suns and planets. Our world, and all the peoples living upon it, is but one miniscule part of an incomprehensibly vast universe full of grand wonders. This same all-knowing and all-powerful God also created these wicked peoples on this one insignificant planet. So this same God could have changed their behaviour into more God-approved forms of unctuous sycophancy without them ever knowing anything of the change, after which the necessity to destroy them would disappear altogether. This passage actually implies that God requires worship from beings with free will, rather than worship from unthinking drones without the capacity for free will. The implication is evident; God wants adoration and worship, and is prepared to destroy those who do not give it of their own free will. If you ever want an example of imperfection and conceit on an awe-inspiring and grand scale, then here you have a perfect example!'

Thomas was at a loss, and could only respond with a lame, 'But Noah and his family were permitted to survive the total destruction of mankind by the flood.'

'They were probably the most zealously fanatical God worshipers of all humankind. The survival of Noah and his one wife, together with his three sons and their three wives, meant a total of eight people survived the destruction of humankind (Bible, Genesis 6:13). This means there was very little human genetic diversity remaining after the flood destroyed the rest of humankind, because they were all survivors of one tribe. But look at the diversity of peoples now living on our world. So either the area where Noah's family lived after the flood subsided was a teratogenic disaster zone, which is one possible explanation of how the current human genetic diversity came into being, or did this all-powerful God subsequently induce the human genetic diversity present on our world today? If the latter is true, then why didn't God correct the behaviour of all the people beforehand, instead of taking the easy way out by just killing everyone, and starting again?'

Thomas looked slightly crestfallen as he sipped his beer, but brightened as another thought came to mind. 'Most of the stories in the book of Genesis are allegorical and not intended to be interpreted literally.'

'Another good try. But again, not quite good enough. Why then do people talk about what amounts to fallibility, in a supposedly infallible, eternal, all-knowing, and all-powerful God? Let's look at another example from the Torah. After their charismatic prophet and leader, Moses, led them to freedom from serfdom and oppression in Egypt, the ancient tribes of Israel wandered for several years through the deserts of the Middle-East. They were subject to thirst, hunger, and the other harsh privations of nomadic existence in a desert. Many had fond memories of the much easier life they had in Egypt as serfs of the Egyptians (Bible, Exodus 16:2-3, Numbers 11:4-6). At one point during their wanderings they paused at the foot Mount Sinai while Moses ascended to the top to commune with God. Moses communed with God for forty days and nights, receiving the laws written in the five books of the Torah, which are also the first five books of the Old Testament. During these forty days and nights, the waiting peoples of the tribes of Israel melted their gold ornaments and made an image of a golden calf, which they proceeded to worship with much

15

feasting, dancing, and a really good orgy (Bible, Exodus 32:1-6). God told Moses of this, and told him to go down at once from the mountain to his people (Bible, Exodus 32:7). As Moses descended the mountain, God told Moses of his intention to destroy the tribes of Israel because of their idolatry, yet changed his mind after speaking with Moses.'

> *And Jehovah said unto Moses, I have seen this people, and, behold, it is a stiffnecked people: now therefore let me alone, that my wrath may wax hot against them, and that I may consume them: and I will make of thee a great nation. And Moses besought Jehovah his God, and said, Jehovah, why doth thy wrath wax hot against thy people, that thou hast brought forth out of the land of Egypt with great power and with a mighty hand? Wherefore should the Egyptians speak, saying, For evil did he bring them forth, to slay them in the mountains, and to consume them from the face of the earth? Turn from thy fierce wrath, and repent of this evil against thy people. Remember Abraham, Isaac, and Israel, thy servants, to whom thou swarest by thine own self, and saidst unto them, I will multiply your seed as the stars of heaven, and all this land that I have spoken of will I give unto your seed, and they shall inherit it for ever. And Jehovah repented of the evil which he said he would do unto his people. (ASV Bible, Exodus 32:9-14)*

'So Thomas, here you have a tribe of refugees having a bit of fun, dancing, singing, feasting, and in general having a wonderful time worshipping a golden idol during a boring moment in a seemingly endless journey through an equally endless and inhospitable desert. This tribe of Israel not only happened to be God's chosen people, but God had created these very people as well! So why didn't this all-knowing and all-powerful God foresee and correct this penchant for idolatry in a people God not only created, but also chose for special treatment? Furthermore, God is supposedly all-pervading and all-knowing, so God knew what was happening from the very moment these people decided to build this golden idol and have a good time. Yet this all-pervading and all-knowing God did not warn Moses of the infidelity of the tribes of Israel at this point. Instead, this all-pervading and all-knowing God only told Moses of the infidelities of his followers after Moses had spent forty days and nights on top of Mount Sinai, and only after the Israelites had well and truly begun their feasting. Even more incredible, after deciding to destroy these sinners, why did this eternal, and supposedly all-knowing, super-intelligent God, undergo a change of mind on the basis of a really very simple discussion with his chosen leader of these peoples. Just look at the level of argument used by Moses to change God's intentions. All Moses did was to remind God he could not destroy these people, because of an old promise made by God to multiply the population of Israel to as many as the stars in the heaven, as well as giving them a really quite insignificant area of desert land in the Middle-East to inhabit. Such a level of argument would be appropriate when speaking with an ignorant itinerant goatherd, or a half-crazed desert rat, but would be totally inappropriate when addressing an awesome all-knowing and all-powerful God, who not only created these people God was about to destroy, but also created the incredible vastness and wonder of the universe in which these very same people existed. That Moses would use such an argument is even more surprising. After all, Moses was raised as a prince by the daughter of the Pharaoh in the sophisticated royal court of ancient Egypt, and had undoubtedly received an excellent education (Bible, Exodus 2:1-11).'

'Oh ...'

'You understand what I mean Thomas. Regardless of the historical accuracy of the story, here you have a supposedly eternal, infallible, all-pervading, all-knowing, and all-powerful God being described as something quite different altogether. Here you have God being described as changeable, petty even, concerned with the transgressions of an insignificant few thousand people on one of the countless billions of planets in the universe, all of which were creations of this very same God. The level and nature of the argument used by Moses, and the response of God to this argument, is so trivial, and so petty compared with the awesome greatness of such a God, that this passage is actually quite insulting in its depiction of God as having less than superhuman intelligence and power. For example, this very same all-powerful and all-knowing God did not want to correct these people, instead this God just wanted to destroy them – a very simple punishment indeed when you compare it to the elegant options available to such a God. All these things indicate God is neither all-knowing nor all-powerful, or that the God of Moses is a different God to that of the Christians. Pretty wild hey? And there are a lot more of these contradictions and inconsistencies in the Old Testament.'

'I'll speak with my tutors. We've never had any lessons on these things yet. But you have to consider this is the Old Testament of the Bible, and Jesus brought us a new covenant in the New Testament, so revealing the true nature of God.'

'That's strange. I thought we were speaking about writings regarded as being inspired by the same eternal and all-knowing God, regardless of whether they are in the Old or the New Testament of the Bible. Okay, let's examine one very evident change in attitude between the Old and the New Testaments. In the books of the Old Testament we read that God communicated directly with Moses, giving laws to Moses to guide the ancient peoples of Israel. One of these laws was the well-known "eye for an eye, tooth for a tooth" law.'

And he that killeth any man shall surely be put to death.

And he that killeth a beast shall make it good; beast for beast.

And if a man cause a blemish in his neighbour; as he hath done, so shall it be done to him;

Breach for breach, eye for eye, tooth for tooth: as he hath caused a blemish in a man, so shall it be done to him again.

And he that killeth a beast, he shall restore it: and he that killeth a man, he shall be put to death.

Ye shall have one manner of law, as well for the stranger, as for one of your own country: for I am the LORD your God. (KJV Bible, Leviticus 24: 17-22)

'When you think about it Thomas, you realize this was actually a very good law, because it limited the level of revenge and recompense injured people could claim. This means it was also effective in minimizing the chance of feuding resulting from injuries due to accident or intention.'

'But no one uses that law any more. In fact, Jesus did away with this law, replacing it with a philosophy of mercy and peace.'

Ye have heard that it was said, An eye for an eye, and a tooth for a tooth: but I say unto you, resist not him that is evil: but whosoever smiteth thee on thy right cheek, turn to him the other also. And if any man would go to law with thee, and take away thy coat, let him have thy cloak also. And whosoever shall compel thee to go one mile, go with him two. Give to him that asketh thee, and from him that would borrow of thee turn not thou away. Ye have heard that it was said, Thou shalt love thy neighbor, and hate thine enemy: but I say unto you, love your enemies, and pray for them that persecute you; (ASV Bible, Matthew 5:38-44)

'Just my point Thomas. Moses was born sometime around 1390 BCE, and God communicated these laws directly to him. Jesus was born about 1300 years later, and many Christians believe he was the Son of God. As the Son of God, Jesus may well have had more direct communication with God than other prophets. According to many Christians, Jesus taught a different message to that of Moses. Yet Moses was also directly inspired by God – a God who created the universe, including time itself! To such a God, time means nothing, and 1000 years is as a day. So why does God, the all-knowing, eternal creator of this universe, as well as the creator of time, tell one thing at one moment, and then after an insignificantly short period in the existence of God, tell totally the opposite? If you want inconsistency, then here is a perfect example!'

'But this is not inconsistent at all. Jesus, the Son of God brought an undiluted message of love uncorrupted by misinterpretation by the hate-filled and selfish emotions to which humans are prone. For God, is a God of meekness and love, a God who understands human frailty, and a God who is forgiving of error and sin. So Jesus revoked this hatred-filled human interpretation of God's message to humanity.'

'Ahhh, so human frailty and inaccuracy is the reason why Saint Paul misinterpreted the loving message of Jesus. Paul said that people should forgive sinners on this world so that God can torture them forever in a life after death!' retorted Ben.

'Saint Paul would never have said that!'

'But he did. Read this!' and Ben pushed the opened Bible over to Thomas.

Bless them that persecute you; bless, and curse not. Rejoice with them that rejoice; weep with them that weep. Be of the same mind one toward another. Set not your mind on high things, but condescend to things that are lowly. Be not wise in your own conceits. Render to no man evil for evil. Take thought for things honorable in the sight of all men. If it be possible, as much as in you lieth, be at peace with all men. Avenge not yourselves, beloved, but give place unto the wrath of God: for it is written, Vengeance belongeth unto me; I will recompense, saith the Lord. But if thine enemy hunger, feed him; if he thirst, give him to drink: for in so doing thou shalt heap coals of fire upon his head. Be not overcome of evil, but overcome evil with good. (ASV Bible, Romans 12:14-21)

Thomas was silent for a moment as he digested the impact of Ben's interpretation of this passage. He drank a bit more beer. 'I'll have to think a bit more about this one. You've certainly given me some knotty problems to solve. But I'm sure there are no inconsistencies in the New Testament.' He looked at Ben. 'Or are there?'

'Certainly are ...' replied Ben with some gusto. 'I'll only deal with the most fascinating example, but there are a lot of others if you look carefully enough. During the initial period of his ministry, Jesus wandered the land of Judea, preaching, teaching, performing miracles, and training his twelve apostles to continue and further his ministry. During this time he commanded them to only spread his teachings among Jewish peoples.'

These twelve Jesus sent forth, and charged them, saying, Go not into any way of the Gentiles, and enter not into any city of the Samaritans: but go rather to the lost sheep of the house of Israel. (ASV Bible, Matthew 10:5-6)

'He very specifically excluded Samaritans, a people living in a region to the north of Judea, the land where the Jewish nation lived at the time Jesus was alive. Samaritans were despised and shunned by Jews living in Judea as a race of loathsome half-breeds. Even worse, they committed the unpardonable crime of heresy, because although they practiced Judaism, it was a different form of Judaism to that practiced by the pureblood Jews in Judea. And Jesus was a pureblood Jew, born and raised in Judea. Gentiles were not descended from the twelve tribes of Israel, nor did they practice any form of Judaism at all. Accordingly they were not deemed worthy of the same consideration as Jews, which is why the message of Jesus was not intended for them either. That's the background to this command of Jesus of Nazareth to his apostles.'

'I know all that Ben. But where's the inconsistency in all this?'

'I'm coming to it. Patience, patience. All will become clear. This is just the build-up. Some undetermined time after giving this command, Jesus was crucified for being a rabble-rouser and general troublemaker. The Bible tells us he rose from the dead three days afterwards, and told the women visiting his empty tomb that he wanted to meet his apostles on a specific hill in Galilee. Jesus appeared to his apostles there, and made a surprising statement.'

And Jesus came to them and spake unto them, saying, All authority hath been given unto me in heaven and on earth. Go ye therefore, and make disciples of all the nations, baptizing them into the name of the Father and of the Son and of the Holy Spirit: teaching them to observe all things whatsoever I commanded you: and lo, I am with you always, even unto the end of the world. (ASV Bible, Matthew 28:18-20)

'Nothing surprising there. It's the basic statement of Jesus enjoining all Christians to spread his teachings to all peoples of the world.'

Ben paused to drink some more beer. 'I'm surprised you don't realize the truly stunning nature of what Jesus told his apostles in Galilee after his resurrection from death. While still alive and physically present on this world, Jesus told his apostles specifically not to spread his teachings among Samaritans and Gentiles. Yet when appearing to his apostles after his resurrection, these prejudices are all gone, and he told them to spread his teachings to all peoples. This is an astounding and truly dramatic change of attitude!'

Thomas looked thoughtfully at Ben, 'You're quite right when you view it that way. It is a definite inconsistency in the teachings of Jesus. However, this is almost certainly a simple textual mistake, a "slip of the pen" on the part of the author and reviewers of the book of Matthew, because Jesus was a prophet of love whose message was for all peoples.'

'I'd agree with you if this was the only instance of this type of statement from Jesus. However, the facts simply do not support your belief that the mortal Jesus said his message was for all peoples. In this very same book of Matthew, there is another instance of the prejudice of the mortal Jesus against people who were not pureblood Jews.'

'I don't believe you! Prove it to me!'

'Okay, you asked for it. When Jesus and his disciples were in the district of Tyre and Sidon, a Canaanite woman begged, beseeched, and implored him in a loud and insistent voice to cure her daughter of demonic possession. The first reaction of Jesus was to ignore her totally. Finally, his disciples implored him to send her away, presumably because her loud cries and entreaties were annoying them. The response of Jesus to the Canaanite woman was simple and blunt – his message was only for Jews (see also Bible, Mark 7:24-30).'

> *Leaving that place, Jesus withdrew to the region of Tyre and Sidon. A Canaanite woman from that vicinity came to him, crying out, "Lord, Son of David, have mercy on me! My daughter is suffering terribly from demon-possession."*
>
> *Jesus did not answer a word. So his disciples came to him and urged him, "Send her away, for she keeps crying out after us."*
>
> *He answered, "I was sent only to the lost sheep of Israel."*
>
> *The woman came and knelt before him. "Lord, help me!" she said.*
>
> *He replied, "It is not right to take the children's bread and toss it to their dogs."*
>
> *"Yes, Lord," she said, "but even the dogs eat the crumbs that fall from their masters' table."*
>
> *Then Jesus answered, "Woman, you have great faith! Your request is granted." And her daughter was healed from that very hour. (NIV Bible, Matthew 15:21-28)*

'This fascinating passage clearly reveals Jesus comparing Canaanites and other non-Jewish peoples to dogs – really quite astounding bluntness and rudeness. However, this woman's quick wit and belief resulted in the desired miraculous cure for her daughter. So here you have a second instance of Jesus discriminating against non-Jews. This is a passage which is extensive enough not to be a simple "slip of the pen" on the part of the writers and reviewers of the book of Matthew. In any case, I am not a scholar of ancient Bible texts. All I and all others know is that this passage is in a standard version of the Bible, and as such this version has been used and studied for more than 1700 years to guide people in the ways of Jesus. When you look at the literal wording of these two passages, you might even say they prove Jesus was a sort of Jewish "red-neck" who considered Samaritans, Canaanites, and all non-Jews in general as inferior scum unworthy of receiving his teachings ...'

Thomas was visibly disturbed and irritated. He was silent for a moment before responding emphatically, 'Jesus was a prophet preaching love, peace and tolerance, and not a prejudiced "red-neck" as you insultingly propose. Even so, I'm at a loss to explain the difference between the literal wordings of these passages and the message of tolerance and love I know Jesus preached. How would you explain them?'

'I really haven't a clue. But these inconsistencies do give rise to fascinating speculations. Are these inconsistencies merely reflections of the prejudices of the writer and reviewers? If this is the case with the book of Matthew, then how can you trust what is written in other parts of the same book, or even other books of the Bible?'

The response of Thomas was rapid and emphatic, 'One thing I know for certain is that the Bible is directly inspired by God, and therefore cannot be inaccurate. After all, Saint Peter told us this.'

And we have the word of prophecy made more sure; whereunto ye do well that ye take heed, as unto a lamp shining in a dark place, until the day dawn, and the day star arise in your hearts: knowing this first, that no prophecy of scripture is of private interpretation. For no prophecy ever came by the will of man: but men spake from God, being moved by the Holy Spirit. (ASV Bible, 2 Peter 1:19-21)

'Hmmmnn ...' continued Ben. 'Very well, let's assume the writings in the Bible are accurate. In that case, we are confronted with the very definite inconsistency, or rather the question of for whom Jesus intended his message. How could this inconsistency arise? God interacts with human prophets by inspiring them to communicate the teachings of God to other humans. This single basic fact means these divine inspirations and teachings must first undergo translation within the brains of these prophets to something understandable to the prophets themselves. Human prophets are made of material flesh, which means they can only make their divine inspirations and teachings known to others by means of the mechanisms of their material brains and material bodies – by means of speech, writings, and deeds. The mechanisms of the material human body are wondrous, but sometimes function imperfectly. This means errors of interpretation, as well as in the communication of the teachings of God by human prophets are possible. Jesus, whom many Christians say is the Son of God, recognized the basic fact of the fallibility of the mechanisms of the material human body (Bible, Matthew 26:41). Saint Paul even emphasized that the erratic and sinful character of human nature is a natural consequence of the functioning of the material body.'

Those who live as their human nature tells them to, have their minds controlled by what human nature wants. Those who live as the Spirit tells them to, have their minds controlled by what the Spirit wants. To be controlled by human nature results in death; to be controlled by the Spirit results in life and peace. And so people become enemies of God when they are controlled by their human nature; for they do not obey God's law, and in fact they cannot obey it. Those who obey their human nature cannot please God. (GNB Bible, Romans 8:5-8)

'Now, even though Jesus was the Son of God, and presumably had a rather more direct communication with God than other humans, he still had a material human body with resulting human nature. Jesus was raised as a material child made of flesh and blood in an environment surrounded by the normal prejudices current in Judea at that time. So his first command issued to his apostles, while he was still incarnated in a physical body before his crucifixion, was presumably a misinterpretation of the wishes of God made while under the influence of his human nature, which is why he told them his teachings were not intended for Samaritans and Gentiles. After he rose from the dead, his body was no longer physical, and accordingly no longer subject to errors of interpretation due to the imperfect functioning of his material body, so he was able to give the correct and true message of God to his disciples when they met on the hill in Galilee. This is why he then told his apostles to spread his teachings to the peoples of all the nations of the world.'

'Fascinating reasoning Ben, but it is reasoning fraught with far-reaching consequences. If your reasoning is correct, then it applies to all prophets of flesh and blood. It means we can't trust anything in the Bible, because all human writers of the books of the Bible might have made errors writing the messages of God, and all human prophets may have made errors interpreting the revelations they received from God. This idea is a malignant cancer in the very heart of Judaism and Christianity. I cannot believe it's true. I'm going to speak with some of my tutors about this.'

'Sounds like you and your tutors are going to do a lot of talking next week. But now it's time for Islam.'

'Are you also saying that Islam is also plagued by the same inconsistencies?'

'Indeed I am, because although the followers of Islam believe the prophet Mohammed (570-632 CE) was directly inspired by God, Mohammed was also a material human being made of very material flesh and blood. But I'll first start with a definition. What we are actually talking about are not just inconsistencies and contradictions, but also abrogation of earlier texts by newer texts. Abrogation is where a newer ordinance, law, or statement nullifies a previous statement. The Bible has a number of abrogations. We've already discussed one example – where Jesus first says that the apostles must not spread his teachings among Samaritans and Gentiles, but later abrogates this by telling the apostles to spread his teachings among all peoples.'

'Isn't this discussion a sort of legalistic exercise in splitting hairs?'

'I'll admit that is true to some degree. Even so, these contradictions, inconsistencies and abrogations are important, because as we've already discussed, they indicate one of two possibilities. Firstly, that God changes

25

opinions within a time span totally inconsistent with the idea of an eternal, all-powerful, all-knowing creator of the universe, and the creator of time itself. Secondly, that misinterpretation of the teachings and inspirations of God by the fallible material brains of human prophets introduced inconsistencies and abrogations into the holy texts. So now let's start with Islam, but not before we've had another beer. This is thirsty work. Waiter!'

They waited in silence, basking and warming themselves in the pleasant sunlight. Around them a colourful bustle of shoppers in the stalls of the Saturday market along the canal. It was truly a rare and magical summer day. Their reverie was broken by the arrival of their beer. The waitress looked at Ben, hesitated, but finally spoke, 'Excuse me for asking, but you look very familiar. Have we met before?'

'Quite possibly. I'm a doctor, so I see a lot of people. I work in a lot of different places too, filling in for people on holiday, or for people who are sick. So it is very possible that you have seen me before.'

'Ah ... that's it. Now I know where I saw you.'

'I hope I managed to help you with the problem for which you came to me.'

'You did. Oh it wasn't anything major, but I was very pleased with the way you treated me. Nice to see you in a different way. Do you want to order anything else?'

'No thanks. This will do for the moment.'

Thomas looked quizzically at Ben.

'Yes Thomas,' was Ben's reaction. 'It's my work. I'm a medical doctor.'

'How is it that you know so much about the Bible and the Koran if you're a doctor?'

'Years ago, while studying some of the lesser known aspects of the functioning of the human body for a book I was writing, I discovered to my amazement that the functioning of the human body actually forms the basis of most religious experience. This realization that changes in body function can result in experiences generating profound philosophies moving whole peoples and nations fascinated me, driving me to study ever more aspects of the relationship between body and religion.'

'But God and religion are spiritual, intangible, and not of this world!

The functioning of the human body has nothing whatsoever to do with religion or any of these things!'

'I disagree entirely. Body function has everything to do with these things and these beliefs. The holy books of most religions form an enormous body of knowledge and thoughts written down and studied over many centuries, and it is from a study of these that I came to this conclusion about the role of the functioning of the body in the development of religious thought. And it is also from this study that I learned something about the holy books of these religions.' Ben raised his glass, 'Anyway, here's to this magical day. Look about you. Feel the sun. See how this same sun brightens and cheers all the people around you. Experience the effects of two bottles of beer. This is all bodily pleasure. Enjoy it. Enjoy the way these things modify your thinking. And now, if you want, I'll explain why the holy texts of Islam are as full of errors as the Bible.'

Thomas sipped his beer, and gave Ben another quizzical glance, 'Please do. Islam is so obviously an inferior religion when compared to the true enlightenment offered by Christianity, that I'm not at all surprised to hear Islamic holy texts are riddled with errors.'

Ben laughed, 'Actually, Islam is no better or worse than Judaism or Christianity. These three religions espouse almost exactly the same philosophies and laws. But one thing is certain, just as you do, just as all Jews, and all Christians do, the followers of Islam also claim their religion is the one and only true religion. They also claim the Bible and the Torah are full of discrepancies and error.'

Will they not then ponder on the Qur'an? If it had been from other than Allah they would have found therein much incongruity. (Koran 4:82)

'I'm amazed they even dare utter such self-evident drivel, when the light of Christianity is there as a shining beacon to lead them to the true belief,' responded Thomas.

'Well Thomas, that's your opinion, hundreds of millions believers in Islam would disagree with you though.' Ben paused to rinse his parched throat with beer. 'The prophet Mohammed lived from 570 to 632 CE, a miniscule period of time to an eternal God. And just like Christians and

Jews, the followers of Islam also believe God not only created this universe, but also time itself, which is why time is irrelevant to God. This is why followers of Islam also say one day to God is as thousands of years to humankind (Koran 22:47, 32:5, 70:4). So you could even say Islam is another attempt by God to get an uncorrupted message across to humankind, only now using the prophet Mohammed as an earthly receiver and transcriber of the message of God. The message of God in the Bible and the Torah is certainly untrustworthy and full of errors, while the Koran, the message of the very same God to humankind, may well be free of error. Indeed, just as Christians and Jews each claim their holy texts are the perfect and true messages of God, followers of Islam also claim the message of God expressed in the Koran is the perfect and ultimate message of God. Several passages in the Koran even tell us this (see also Koran 6:115, 18:27).'

Theirs are good tidings in the life of the world and in the Hereafter. There is no changing the Words of Allah that is the Supreme Triumph. (Koran 10:64)

'However, just like Jews and Christians who often only select the passages they want to hear, believers in Islam also conveniently neglect to say these passages are contradicted, abrogated, or simply made untrustworthy by later revelations where God replaces earlier revelations with new revelations (see also Koran 16:101).'

Such of Our revelations as We abrogate or cause to be forgotten, we bring (in place) one better or the like thereof. Knowest thou not that Allah is Able to do all things? (Koran 2:106)

'In other words, this eternal, all-powerful, all-knowing God, for whom one thousand years is as a day, continually changes and improves on the revelations made to the prophet Mohammed. Personally, I would say these passages seriously undermine the infallibility of the Koran. Mohammed got around this inconsistency by saying that some revelations were made in stages, and that this is apparently the will of God. But why does God not reveal the true and full revelation at once? If God is capable of leading people onto the paths of righteousness (Koran 14:4), then this same God was certainly more than capable of instantly inducing the first few followers of Islam to accept the revelations of God at once without introducing them by stages. After all, this eternal, all-pervading, all-powerful, all-knowing God created these very same first few followers of Islam. Moreover, the truths of Islam are supposedly self-evident. But perhaps God only wants to make it seem that people have a measure of free will. This is the only possible explanation for these passages I can think of.'

'Just a moment,' interrupted Thomas, 'sura 2 was surely revealed at an earlier time than sura 10 which it you say it replaces.'

'Actually sura 2 was revealed at later time than sura 10 (Edgecomb 2002). This is one of the confusing things about the Koran; the sura's are not numbered in the chronological order in which they were revealed. In general, the order of sura's in the Koran is by length, the longer sura's first and the shortest last (Encyclopaedia Britannica). This is confusing to most people. On the other hand this might be just the correct God-given way of organizing these sura's. Who knows? After all, it is said in the Koran that God is the ultimate guide to truth for humankind.'

> Say: Is there of your partners (whom ye ascribe unto Allah) one that leadeth to the Truth? Say: Allah leadeth to the Truth. Is He Who leadeth to the Truth more deserving that He should be followed, or he who findeth not the way unless he (himself) be guided. What aileth you? How judge ye? (Koran 10:35)

Ben continued his discourse, 'But then we read in a passage in a later sura, that it does not matter what a good believer in Islam does, it is God who ultimately decides whether a person is led astray or not, or whether a person finds grace in the eyes of God or not (see also Koran 7:178, 7:186).'

> And We never sent a messenger save with the language of his folk, that he might make (the message) clear for them. Then Allah sendeth whom He will astray, and guideth whom He will. He is the Mighty, the Wise. (Koran 14:4)

'Wow!' was the only reaction of Thomas as he gulped a mouthful of beer.

'I agree. This is truly amazing! It's the ultimate in fatalism. The Koran tells us that we humans have no control over our destiny. So regardless of what we do, however hard we may strive, it is ultimately God who determines whether we stray from the paths of righteousness or not. This same merciful and just God who causes people to stray from righteousness, also torments them eternally in a life after death for straying from righteousness. Our paths in life are determined beforehand, or to use other words, are predetermined or predestined. Predetermination, or predestination, is a truly repulsive philosophy. It saps all personal initiative from some believers, leaving them with only one passive and fatalistic response to life expressed in the words: "It is all in the hands of God. I don't have to do anything. God will decide whether I am rich or poor, whether I am hated or loved, whether I am evil or good, whether I will go to everlasting torment in Hell or dwell eternally in paradise" (see also Koran 6:2, 11:6).'

Naught of disaster befalleth in the earth or in yourselves but it is in a Book before We bring it into being Lo! That is easy for Allah (Koran 57:22)

'Thank God I'm a Christian,' was the only response of Thomas as he digested these words together with another refreshing gulp of cool beer. 'At least as a Christian, if you believe in the message of Jesus with all your heart, and do your best for your fellow man, you will achieve the reward of heaven.'

'Don't you believe it!' was the firm reaction from Ben. 'Fatalism and predestination, or predetermination was no new philosophy at the time Mohammed received his revelations from God. It was even ancient when Jesus espoused this same philosophy of predestination to his followers (Bible, Psalms 139:16), saying that only the chosen would truly be able to accept his teachings.'

But there are some of you that believe not. For Jesus knew from the beginning who they were that believed not, and who it was that should betray him. And he said, For this cause have I said unto you, that no man can come unto me, except it be given unto him of the Father. Upon this many of his disciples went back, and walked no more with him. Jesus said therefore unto the twelve, Would ye also go away? (ASV Bible, John 6:64-67)

Ben continued, 'This fascinating passage implies that Jesus once had more than twelve disciples. Then he tells these disciples that it really doesn't matter how profound they feel their belief in his message to be, God his Father, had already determined whether they would receive eternal life in heaven. Accordingly, these other disciples left upon hearing these words of Jesus. They realized from these words that their ultimate fate in a life after death was neither dependent upon the profundity of their belief, nor upon what they said or did, but was solely determined by God irrespective of their belief or deeds. So they decided they may as well have a comfortable life on earth, instead of drifting around homelessly with Jesus and living on charity, because ultimately God had already determined whether they would receive eternal life anyway. It was all predestined. This is Christian-style fatalism.'

Thomas appeared to be very uncomfortable. He looked appraisingly at Ben, searching for any hint of mockery. 'Actually this passage just tells us that the followers who left Jesus really did not truly believe deep within their hearts that Jesus was the Son of God. They realized this, and left. This is the only true meaning of this passage.'

'I don't entirely agree with you Thomas. What Jesus was saying in this passage is very clear. He was asking those who did not truly believe to leave, as well as giving them the glad tidings of predestination. You cannot interpret this passage in any other way. Moreover, the great Saint Paul, the founding father of the Christian church, also confirmed this same perfidious philosophy of predestination.'

Blessed be the God and Father of our Lord Jesus Christ, who hath blessed us with every spiritual blessing in the heavenly places in Christ: even as he chose us in him before the foundation of the world, that we should be holy and without blemish before him in love: having foreordained us unto adoption as sons through Jesus Christ unto himself, according to the good pleasure of his will, to the praise of the glory of his grace, which he freely bestowed on us in the Beloved: (ASV Bible, Ephesians 1:3-6)

'In other words Thomas, at the very creation of this universe, a long, long time before we were born, God determined whether our souls are destined for everlasting suffering in the fires of hell, or for eternal life in heaven in a state of bliss (Bible, Matthew 25:34, Acts 13:48, Romans 8:28-30 & 9:11-13, Ephesians 1:11, Revelation 13:7-8). The only thing you and I can do is hope we are among those chosen for a life after death in heaven. And for Christians, the only way they even have a chance of being among of the chosen, is to believe in the message of Jesus.'

He that is not with me is against me, and he that gathereth not with me scattereth.. (ASV Bible, Matthew 12:30)

'And,' added Ben with an impish smile, 'Saint Paul also confirmed that those who did not follow the teachings of Jesus would certainly suffer the everlasting torments of hell.'

Seeing it is a righteous thing with God to recompense tribulation to them that trouble you;
  And to you who are troubled rest with us, when the Lord Jesus shall be revealed from heaven with his mighty angels,
  In flaming fire taking vengeance on them that know not God, and that obey not the gospel of our Lord Jesus Christ:
  Who shall be punished with everlasting destruction from the presence of the Lord, and from the glory of his power; (KJV Bible, 2 Thessalonians 1:6-9)

'This is frightening stuff Thomas. These passages reveal Christianity to be an evil and tyrannical sect using supernatural terror to keep its followers in line with doctrine, because Christians know that God has already decided at the beginning of the universe whether they will receive eternal life in heaven. They know they cannot do anything about the choice of God, but they do know they will certainly be tortured forever in hell if they do not follow the teachings of Jesus. So they really have only one choice – follow the teachings of Jesus, and they may possibly be rewarded with eternal life in heaven. Of course this raises the question of what happens to good and decent people who never heard of Christianity, or were born before the time of Jesus. Do these people – people living good lives, people who are good to their families and neighbours, people who are good and kind to others – do these people merit eternal torment in hell because they happened to be born at a time, or in a place where they never had the opportunity to hear the message of Jesus?'

'I'm sure what you are saying about the reasons to be Christian are unmitigated nonsense. People follow the teachings of Jesus because they know within their hearts that these teachings are the truth, a truth filling a vacuum in their lives, a truth enabling a full and complete life with the surety of eternal life in the hereafter. This is what I understand, and have been taught is the true message of Jesus, and the true nature of God, regardless of what all these passages you've trotted out say, as well as your even more tendentious reasoning. However, as regards kind and good people who never had the opportunity to hear the message of Jesus, I agree it hardly seems fair that a just and merciful God would condemn fundamentally good people to eternal anguish in hell. It's a difficult problem, and I don't know the answer. This is another interesting problem for my tutors.'

'Okay, enough fascinating digressions,' said Ben. 'Let's continue and consider what was revealed to Mohammed about other religions. Initial revelations to Mohammed stated that Islam permits all peoples to practice other religions freely and without any compulsion whatsoever.'

There is no compulsion in religion. The right direction is hence-forth distinct from error. And he who rejecteth false deities and believeth in Allah hath grasped a firm hand hold which will never break. Allah is Hearer, Knower. (Koran 2:256)

'Indeed, one passage in the Koran states that Christians and Jews also go to heaven together with believers in Islam.'

Lo! those who believe (in that which is revealed unto thee, Muhammad), and those who are Jews, and Christians, and Sabaeans whoever believeth in Allah and the Last Day and doeth right surely their reward is with their Lord, and there shall no fear come upon them neither shall they grieve. (Koran 2:62)

'But these passages are abrogated by subsequent revelations telling that Christians and Jews, (known as People of the Scripture), are also condemned to eternal torment in hell after death (see also Koran 5:51-53, 5:72-73, 9:30-35).'

Lo! those who disbelieve, among the People of the Scripture and the idolaters, will abide in fire of hell. They are the worst of created beings. (Koran 98:6)

'And,' continued Ben, 'it goes without saying that those who do not believe in the God of Abraham at all, always go to hell.'

And whoso seeketh as religion other than the Surrender (to Allah) it will not be accepted from him, and he will be a loser in the Hereafter. (Koran 3:85)

'These later revelations of God to Mohammed reveal an increasing intolerance towards other religions. Yet this increasing intolerance was limited to the life after death in these revelations. However, subsequent revelations also extended Islamic intolerance to this mortal world (see also Koran 8:12-13, 9:5).'

Fight against such of those who have been given the Scripture as believe not in Allah nor the Last Day, and forbid not that which Allah hath forbidden by His messenger, and follow not the religion of truth, until they pay the tribute readily, being brought low. (Koran 9:29)

'In other words, the Koran is just as inconsistent, untrustworthy, and intolerant of other religions as are the Bible and the Torah. So the sad truth is that this attempt by God to correct the mistakes in the Torah, and the Bible, by inspiring the prophet Mohammed with new revelations of the true word of God as expressed in the Koran was ultimately unsuccessful. This is why I cannot believe in any of these religions. If there truly is a God, perhaps this God will inspire other prophets, and eventually another religion may succeed in revealing the true word of God.'

'That's some speech. I'm impressed. However, I've experienced the awe, power, and the wonder of God in my prayers. So I'm still not convinced you're correct.'

'That's your good right. But beware of holy books, for they are full of contradictions and inconsistencies. Followers of Judaism, Christianity, and Islam, can choose passages they want and disregard others they do not want. "Cafeteria Religion" is the name given to religious philosophies based upon such selective choices of passages in holy books. It is called cafeteria religion, because people can choose from a wide variety of passages in these holy books, just like choosing from a wide variety of dishes in a cafeteria. Selective choices of passages in this way can result in the holy texts of all these religions becoming instruments of the vilest and most perverted forms of human behaviour; justifying discrimination by race, sex, and religion; justifying oppression of women, slavery, torture, murder, and genocide; stifling all that is good and wonderful in people; crushing all advance and betterment, while forcing the followers to follow a benighted and primitive life style.'

'Do you hate religion that much?'

'Not at all,' was Ben's passionate reply. 'In spite of the many negative aspects associated with religion – aspects such as bigotry, suppression of freedom of thought, suppression of freedom of expression, intolerance, pogroms of unbelievers, etc – religions of all types have in the past conferred enormous benefits upon their believers. Judaism welded the twelve disparate and primitive tribes of Israel into a single proud people with a single identity and purpose, enabling them to survive as a socio-cultural minority despite isolation, persecution, as well as pogroms throughout their history. Christianity gave the peoples of the benighted and brawling postage stamp sized nations of Europe a single cultural identity during the dark and Middle-Ages. This uniform cultural identity and philosophy ultimately culminated in the rapid technological development and welfare now existing in these nations. Islam transformed an ignorant rabble of poverty-stricken, warring desert tribes into proud peoples with a single cultural identity, ultimately enabling them to develop grand cultural and aesthetic works. These religions unify and empower their believers. And these benefits are not just limited to a unification of socio-cultural identities, or empowerment of peoples, because selectively reading the "cafeteria" of the holy texts of these religions provides the followers of these religions with wonderful philosophies for betterment of the human condition.'

'Well Ben, I'm impressed. I've never heard of Judaism, Islam, or Christianity discussed in this way before. But why do you mainly emphasize the negative sides of these holy books?'

'Very simply, because the most vociferous proponents of these religions are often those making the most evil, darkest, and violently literal interpretations of basically very good philosophies. The strident yells, harsh shrieking and overly loud voices of this regrettably vociferous and often violent minority, drown the quiet voices of reason expressed by the larger majority of all believers in these religions, people who only want to live good lives in harmony with their fellows and families. Only by understanding how such horrors and vile perversity arise, can you begin the process of banishing them into the abyss in which they truly belong. Knowledge of these things, and understanding of how the functioning of the human body drives and reinforces religious belief, enables those who understand these things to be understanding of other people and other cultures, as well as providing true insights into the meaning of our existence. These things fascinate me, and drive me to study the things we've just talked about.'

'I'll have to think about what you've told me, pray, and discuss it with my tutors.'

'I'd do that if I were you. I must admit I enjoyed our talk and our lunch here. How about lunch together next weekend? What do you say?'

'Sounds good to me. I'd like that.'

'Okay, I'll give you a telephone call next week.' And with these words they parted, disappearing in the Saturday crowds.

Chapter 2

The fleshy veil

'Ahh … That hit the right spot,' sighed Ben, placing his half empty glass on the table.

'You're not wrong there,' was the equally satisfied response from Thomas. 'What a good idea to meet here. I've always liked this café.'

A contented silence descended upon the two men as they sat at their table on the terrace on the Boisotkade. Warmed by the sun, they were happy, at ease, calmly observing the people walking and cycling into and out of the old city centre of Leiden. It was another one of those magically bright and warm summer days – a day guaranteed to even raise the spirits of the dour denizens of the dank alleys of this ancient Dutch city. They drank beer, talked about the latest world and local news, about their tastes in beer and wine, about their favourite places in the region, as well as about the indifferent reactions of Thomas's tutors to his questions about what he had heard from Ben the previous Saturday. His tutor's reactions were strikingly similar, summed up by the statement made by one of them, 'All products of an overheated imagination, of twisting the meanings of Biblical passages, as well as the use of inaccurate Bible translations.' Much to the frustration of Thomas, the reactions of his fellow students were similar. They simply waved his questions away as insignificant and irrelevant noise, or ignored them altogether.

As they talked, a portly, bearded young man wearing a white dishdasha and kufi passed. He flicked the beads of a rosary in one hand, and carried a shopping bag in the other. Following him was a slim woman clad in a voluminous black abaya and niqab that failed to totally conceal her strikingly graceful bearing and beautiful large, dark, and doe-like eyes.

'Look before you Thomas, underneath that mass of black cloth is an houri, a woman answering the description of one of the companions of the faithful in paradise as described in the Koran – only we are privileged to see this vision here on earth.'

And We shall wed them unto fair ones with wide, lovely eyes.
(Koran 44:54)

Thomas reacted quite differently to this vision of beauty, 'That may be … But look at her! It's scandalous the way Islamic women are treated by their men and their religion. See this unfortunate woman wearing black, hot, uncomfortably stuffy clothing covering her entire body on a day as warm and wonderful as today. She is graceful, has striking eyes, and is probably an exceptionally beautiful woman. She may even long for a life with freedom to enjoy light and airy clothing outside the house, freedom to show herself to others, freedom to enjoy the enjoyment and confirmation of her beauty by others, freedoms such as are enjoyed by Christian women.'

Upon noticing the two men observing her, the unknown woman quickly turned her eyes to the ground.

'Ah Thomas, you can't do anything about things like that. She's a prisoner of her culture, her family, her upbringing, and her mind. All we can do is observe, and enjoy the sight of her veiled beauty. See how she averts her eyes. She is a true embodiment of the teachings in the Koran instructing women how to behave in front of strange men.'

And tell the believing women to lower their gaze and be modest, and to display of their adornment only that which is apparent, and to draw their veils over their bosoms, and not to reveal their adornment save to their own husbands or fathers or husbands fathers, or their sons or their husbands' sons, or their brothers or their brothers' sons or sisters sons, or their women, or their slaves, or male attendants who lack vigour, or children who know naught of women's nakedness. And let them not stamp their feet so as to reveal what they hide of their adornment. And turn unto Allah together, O believers, in order that ye may succeed. (Koran 24:31)

'As you see Thomas, just like the Bible, the Koran is also a complete book, because it also gives instructions on clothing and behaviour. There is one other passage in the Koran giving supplementary clothing advice.'

O Prophet! Tell thy wives and thy daughters and the women of the believers to draw their cloaks close round them (when they go abroad). That will be better, that so they may be recognized and not annoyed. Allah is ever Forgiving, Merciful. (Koran 33:59)

'Really? All those two passages you've trotted forward say, is that women should behave and dress modestly, and not to make a show of their bodies, clothing, or jewels, but they don't instruct women to cover themselves totally by dressing in clothing such as a burka, abaya, or a niqab.'

'Actually they do, albeit rather indirectly. Many followers of Islam say that the physical beauty of a woman is also an adornment, and as was stated in the first of these two citations, a woman should cover her adornments. This makes the idea of a niqab or burka more logical.' Ben paused to sip his beer. 'Another line of reasoning is that if a woman is to obey God by covering most of her body, she can express her love of God even better by taking no chances of making a mistake about which parts she should cover, and cover everything by wearing a niqab or burka.'

'That sounds reasonable,' said Thomas. 'It certainly provides a logical and sacred justification for such clothing, although I still feel that it goes against the natural instinct of young women to display their beauty and finery.'

'Islam originated in the Middle-East, but veiling of women in this region of the world is a custom older than Islam, and older than Christianity. It originated as a practical measure to protect delicate female skin against the ravages of the hot sun in this region. However, veils were impractical items of clothing for hardworking slave girls, female servants, and peasant women. Accordingly, it was only women in wealthier families who had sufficient leisure to wear veils protecting them from the sun. So veiling even developed into a sign of status. In the situation of Islam, there was an additional reason. Most of the Arabian Peninsula was a primitive backwater during the lifetime of Mohammed, and as is revealed in the Sunnah of Bukhari, sewage processing technology was equally primitive.'

Narrated 'Abdullah bin 'Umar: People say, "Whenever you sit for answering the call of nature, you should not face the Qibla or Bait-ul-Maqdis (Jerusalem)." I told them. "Once I went up the roof of our house and I saw Allah's Apostle answering the call of nature while sitting on two bricks facing Bait-ul-Maqdis (Jerusalem) but there was a screen covering him." (Bukhari 4:147)

'Wow!' exclaimed Thomas. 'That's expressive! You hear this, and you're immediately transported back in time. You can vividly visualize the situation – a man sitting on two large sun-baked bricks answering the call of nature. I like it.'

'Thomas, Thomas,' said Ben shaking his head, 'I never realized you could get so excited about ancient sanitary facilities. However, I do admit it is a colourful passage. It hammers the reality of the human nature of the prophet Mohammed into the awareness of people, telling us that even though Mohammed was chosen by God as an instrument of divine revelation, he was just as human as you or I. These very same primitive sanitary facilities also provided a stimulus for veiling the female followers of Islam. The wives of Mohammed would often answer the call of nature in a large open field near their house in Medina. Presumably many other people also did the same. But Mohammed was a public figure, so his prying neighbours spoke to his wives when they went outside, and also asked Mohammed to get them to wear veils to prevent their being recognized while relieving themselves. These facts almost certainly hastened the coming of the divine revelation of an instruction to wear veils covering the whole body.'

Narrated Aisha: The wives of the Prophet used to go to Al-Manasi, a vast open place (near Baqia at Medina) to answer the call of nature at night. 'Umar used to say to the Prophet "Let your wives be veiled," but Allah's Apostle did not do so. One night Sauda bint Zam'a the wife of the Prophet went out at 'Isha' time and she was a tall lady. 'Umar addressed her and said, "I have recognized you, O Sauda." He said so, as he desired eagerly that the verses of Al-Hijab (the observing of veils by the Muslim women) may be revealed. So Allah revealed the verses of "Al-Hijab" (A complete body cover excluding the eyes). (Bukhari 4:148)

Thomas was silent for a moment. 'What a fascinating concept – primitive sanitation as a stimulus for divine revelation – and to think this all happened fourteen hundred years ago.' He continued in a rather more passionate tone, 'However, I still can't understand why only Islamic women must wear veils, and cover themselves partially or totally, while Islamic men need not cover their heads at all. Both men and women would wear veils if modesty resulting from primitive sanitation was the only reason for wearing veils. So veiling is only one aspect of the socio-cultural justification for segregation and oppression of women in some Islamic communities. There are even several Islamic proverbs about women confirming this (Schipper 2004).'

A girl must not leave the house more than twice: on the day of her marriage, on the day of her death. (Arabic, Maghreb/West Sahara)

A woman should come to her husband's house in a veil, and leave it in a burial shroud. (Persian)

A woman belongs either in the house or in the grave. (Afghanistan)

Ben smiled, 'Aha Thomas, two can play this game. You'll have to do a lot better than that to beat me in an argument. What makes you think these attitudes of the followers of Islam are unique to Islam? In fact, these same attitudes, and these very same proverbs are also found in developed Christian countries (Schipper 2004).'

A woman may leave her house three times; when she is christened, married and buried. (English, UK)

The men and dogs for the barn, the women and cats for the kitchen. (English, USA)

Women and cats at home, men and dogs in the street. (Catalan/French)

Women and cows do not go abroad. (Italian)

Thomas was silent for a moment, 'Hmm ... Those proverbs certainly seem to imply that Christians have much the same attitude towards women as the followers of Islam. Even so, at least Christians don't degrade their women by denying them opportunities outside their homes. Nor do Christians use socio-cultural pressure, or even the law to enforce the wearing of veils. Yet the Koran states all these things in one short passage.'

Men are in charge of women, because Allah hath men the one of them to excel the other, and because they spend of their property (for the support of women). So good women are obedient, guarding in secret that which Allah hath guarded. As for those from whom ye fear rebellion, admonish them and banish them to beds apart, and scourge them. Then if they obey you, seek not a way against them. Lo! Allah is ever High Exalted, Great. (Koran 4:34)

Thomas was visibly upset as he continued. 'This passage also indirectly instructs women to veil themselves, "... guarding in secret that which Allah hath guarded." Furthermore, this same passage states that women are inferior to men, and need a good beating if disobedient, or even potentially disobedient. This is religious approval of oppression and violence against women!'

'Well Thomas, I agree with you on this passage. It certainly does give divine approval for female veiling and oppression. However, when you examine the two matters you seem to think are intertwined – veils and oppression of women – you find that Christianity is just as oppressive towards women, as well as requiring them to wear veils or cover their heads. Think of the custom of Christian nuns wearing veils. No-one complains about them wearing veils, yet they do complain about followers of Islam wearing veils. Strange ... In fact, until about one hundred years ago, social pressure enforced the wearing of hoods, hats, and even veils upon Christian women, especially when worshipping God. This was a result of literal interpretation of the instructions of one of the founding fathers of the Christian church, Saint Paul. He very clearly and indisputably stated that women were inferior and subject to men, as well as stating they should either shave their hair, or cover their heads.'

Every man praying or prophesying, having his head covered, dishonoreth his head. But every woman praying or prophesying with her head unveiled dishonoreth her head; for it is one and the same thing as if she were shaven. For if a woman is not veiled, let her also be shorn: but if it is a shame to a woman to be shorn or shaven, let her be veiled. For a man indeed ought not to have his head veiled, forasmuch as he is the image and glory of God: but the woman is the glory of the man. For the man is not of the woman; but the woman of the man: for neither was the man created for the woman; but the woman for the man: for this cause ought the woman to have a sign of authority on her head, because of the angels. (ASV Bible, 1 Corinthians 11:4-10)

'Okay, Okay,' responded Thomas. 'Those verses make it quite obvious why Christians once required women to veil themselves while in church, and why nuns are required to wear veils. However, Christianity does not recommend beating women. In fact, there is no passage in the Bible recommending the beating of women.'

'That is certainly true, but the Bible does tell us very clearly that women are inferior to men, as well as telling us that God seems to have a diseased predilection for forms of female repression far more degraded than mere scourging of disobedient women (see Chapter 9, "Holy misogyny"). A truly bizarre example of this divine misogyny, was the decree of God that the concubines of King David be publicly raped as punishment for the crimes he committed against God!'

'Huhhh!' was the only reaction from a flabbergasted Thomas.

'Yes indeed. King David was an ancient Jewish hero. He was the slayer of the giant Goliath and incredible numbers of Philistines, (which was apparently a very good deed in the eyes of God), as well as being the father of King Solomon. This same King David once saw Bathsheba the wife of Uriah, one of his most loyal captains. David lusted after Bathsheba, and had an intense, adulterous sexual relationship with her. Accordingly, he arranged for Uriah to die a hero's death in an attack upon a city with which David was at war. Uriah was duly heroically killed in battle, and Bathsheba became one of David's wives. They even had a son (Bible, 2 Samuel 11:14-26). But God was not pleased with these crimes of King David, and told him he would punish him by having his wives and concubines raped in public.'

> *Wherefore hast thou despised the word of Jehovah, to do that which is evil in his sight? Thou hast smitten Uriah the Hittite with the sword, and hast taken his wife to be thy wife, and hast slain him with the sword of the children of Ammon. Now therefore the sword shall never depart from thy house, because thou hast despised me, and hast taken the wife of Uriah the Hittite to be thy wife. Thus saith Jehovah, Behold, I will raise up evil against thee out of thine own house; and I will take thy wives before thine eyes, and give them unto thy neighbor, and he shall lie with thy wives in the sight of this sun. For thou didst it secretly: but I will do this thing before all Israel, and before the sun. (ASV Bible, 2 Samuel 12:9-12)*

Ben continued, 'And indeed, Absolom, one of the sons of King David, eventually drove his father out of the Kingdom of Israel, and usurped control over the land. Incidentally, this was the same Absolom who killed his brother Amnon for raping their half-sister Tamar (Bible, 2 Samuel 13:1-29). Yes Thomas, King David and his children certainly did their best to uphold low moral standards. Anyway, returning to our subject again: after driving his father out of the kingdom and annexing the capital city, Jerusalem, Absolom asked advice from the courtier Ahithophel.'

> *Ahithophel answered, "Go and have intercourse with your father's concubines whom he left behind to take care of the palace. Then everyone in Israel will know that your father regards you as his enemy, and your followers will be greatly encouraged." So they set up a tent for Absolom on the palace roof, and in the sight of everyone Absolom went in and had intercourse with his father's concubines. (GNB Bible, 2 Samuel 16:21-22)*

'So you see Thomas, God is cruel and perverted, and God is sometimes incredibly unfair by punishing innocents for the crimes of others. Just think – this is the same eternal, all-pervading, all-powerful, and all-knowing God who created the vast universe in which we live. Our universe is at least 26 billion light years in diameter. A light year is the distance light travels in one year at a speed of 300,000 kilometres per second. So our universe is unimaginably vast, filled with countless billions of suns and planets, as well as many different life forms. Yet the creator of this inconceivable vastness, the creator all these wonders and grandeur, the very creator of time itself, instigated the public rape of some concubines abandoned by the petty king of an unimportant and primitive tiny kingdom on an insignificant planet in the outer rim of one of countless millions of galaxies in the universe. You may well ask yourself about the logic behind this strange divine punishment for the crimes of adultery and murder committed by King David. To begin with, the concubines of King David evidently meant no more to him than employees whose purpose was to give him pleasure when required. After all, he clearly demonstrated his lack of affection for these women by leaving them behind to maintain the royal palace when he fled Jerusalem before the army of his usurping son Absolom. The concubines of King David were not involved in his adultery with Bathsheba, nor were they involved in the murder of her husband Uriah. They were totally innocent of these crimes, yet God punished King David for his crimes by having these innocent women raped in full view of the people of the city of Jerusalem! Monstrous and incredible injustice! Worse yet, only one man violated these women in public. And this one man, this sexually potent instrument of God's chastisement, was none other than King David's own degenerate son, a man who not only killed his brother, but also a son who tried killing his father after usurping his throne (Bible, 2 Samuel 17). God is supposedly all-knowing, all-powerful, and just. Nonetheless, in this story the Holy instrument of God's cruel so-called justice, was as pitiless, criminal, and perverted as the person supposedly being punished. This is really strange. Or is the rape of innocents by degenerates the true nature of divine justice? If so, the ways of God are indeed mysterious.'

Thomas looked uncomfortable, but managed to reply, 'I never thought about this story in this way before, and I'm not sure whether your interpretation is correct. All I know is that the ways of God are inscrutable to mortals such as we. Even so, I have faith, and I do trust in the infinite love and mercy of God.'

'Well said! Spoken like a true product of Christian indoctrination,' cheered Ben. 'However, regardless of how fascinating these depravities and diversions are, we are digressing from the subject of Islamic veils, and veils in general. When you consider the subject of veiling, you realize that one other result of wearing an all-enveloping veil is to hide the distraction of the physical appearance, so that all that is revealed are the personality and mind of the person under the veil.'

'Yes, that's certainly true,' responded Thomas thoughtfully.

'I always think this relationship between a veil and the person underneath is similar to the relationship between the invisible soul and the visible flesh of the body. You cannot see the person under the veil, but you are confronted by the mind and personality generated by the combination of visible veil and invisible person. In the same way, you cannot see the soul inside the physical body, but if the soul really is the generator of mind and personality, you are confronted by the mind and personality generated by the combination of physical body and invisible soul. At least that's the way I view these things. How do you view the idea of an invisible and immaterial soul? Do you believe each person has a soul? And if each person has a soul, what are the properties of this soul?'

'Really Ben, need you ask? Of course each individual person has a soul. People have believed in the reality of the individual human soul for countless millennia. This belief is so rooted in our minds, and so ancient that it must be based upon reality. And when you think about it, proofs of the reality of the human soul abound in experiences familiar to each and every living person. No thinking person can deny the reality of the human soul, and religion merely confirms its reality. The human soul is real – it exists!'

'Ah, Thomas. Such passion and such belief! I hadn't realized you were such a good demagogue. And now Thomas, explain these proofs of the reality of the soul to me. Give me details. I want to know the reasons for your belief.'

'You sound a bit like one of my examiners, but first some beer. My throat is dry.'

They were silent for a moment. Thomas slowly sipped from his glass as he ordered his thoughts. Ben settled himself in a more comfortable position, basking in the sunlight. This was paradise: sunlight, beer, conversation, and stimulating argument.

Thomas began, 'I'll summarize what I know and what I've been taught are the proofs of the reality of the human soul. To begin with, everyone has a feeling there is more to life than the physical reality in which we live. I know this is only a feeling, yet it is a feeling everyone has experienced at some point in life. This feeling is so universal, that it cannot be ignored, even though it is such a vague emotion. And because this feeling is about something we cannot see, smell, touch, or measure in any way, it seems to indicate there may be something invisible and intangible with which we sometimes come in contact. However, I must admit that such an emotion by itself is proof of nothing. This emotion only attains real significance when considered in conjunction with other proofs.'

'Okay Thomas, that's your proof number one, but a very vague one at that, if you can even call it a proof.'

'I know, but it gets more convincing. Every now and then when you look in a mirror and see your reflection, you wonder if the reflection staring at you really is yours. This feeling of dissociation is also similar to the feeling of dissociation some people have at times, when they feel as if they are living in a dream and their bodies are acting automatically without any real control from themselves. These experiences imply a dissociation between mind and body, a sensation corresponding more with the idea that mind and body are separate, rather than that the mind is a product of the functioning of the body.'

'That's number two, but you're still very vague.'

'Now comes something which you're much more likely to be familiar with. When a person dies, and you have seen them before and after their death, you notice an indefinable absence of something in the deceased person, yet you have seen nothing depart. Nothing measurable or detectable has departed, yet all that remains is an empty husk of decaying flesh. It is as if with the passing of life, that an invisible and intangible something has departed from the body. This invisible and intangible something must be the soul, a concept which becomes more likely when taken in conjunction with the other two situations.'

'Number three, and still very vague Thomas …'

'You really can be irritating Ben. Is it a natural gift, or did you have to study hard to acquire this ability? But now we come to another proof. These are the reports of people who were actually clinically dead, and yet came back to life. Some of these people tell of surprising experiences they underwent while they were dead. They tell of consciously viewing their bodies from a position outside their physical bodies, actually viewing what was happening to their bodies at the same time as they were clinically dead, yet invisible to all the people in the room, and now possessing the wondrous ability to pass through ceilings, walls, as well as other solid objects. Upon arousing from this period of clinical death, many of these people can quite accurately report what was said, what happened to them, and what happened around them during the period they were clinically dead – a period during which they could not possibly have observed the things they report, because they were dead at the time. Furthermore, some people even tell of passing into another world where they meet with deceased relatives, God, angels, and saints, during such periods of clinical death.'

'I agree with you, such near-death experiences as you describe are certainly very profound, and may even be life-changing for the individuals undergoing them. But what makes you think these reports prove the reality of the human soul? After all, these experiences may be just halluci-nations aroused by the severe illnesses or conditions causing these episodes of so-called clinical death.'

Thomas looked at Ben, surprise written large on his face, 'I would have thought that was very evident. These people were clinically dead. As a doctor you must know what that means.'

'I know very well what death is, but I'm interested in hearing what you think the term clinical death means.'

'Clinical death is when people are pronounced dead by a doctor.'

'Interesting, but how do you think the doctor defines death.'

'A deceased person does not move, is totally unresponsive and uncon-scious, does not breathe, and has no heartbeat.'

'Well Thomas, I will agree that all deceased persons certainly exhibit all these properties. However, not all apparently unconscious people without detectable breathing or heartbeat are dead. I can give you many examples illustrating this point. Nonetheless, unconsciousness, together with absence of heartbeat and breathing is a practical definition of death covering most situations quite well. But we are digressing again. Tell me more about why you think these near-death experiences prove the reality of the human soul.'

Thomas was momentarily at a loss for words, and sipped his beer as he collected his thoughts. 'Okay, aside from your hair-splitting about the definition of clinical death, one fact is very evident from these near-death experience reports – many people undergoing them found themselves to be outside their physical bodies. They describe their disembodied selves standing next to, or floating above their dead material bodies. They describe seeing their material bodies being resuscitated, or simply lying dead. They describe hearing and seeing what people in the vicinity of their bodies said and did to them. Some of them can even accurately describe the room, the place, the situation, the appearances, and even the clothing of people involved in treating them. Yet they were dead at the time, unconscious, unmoving, unseeing, and unhearing. At the same time, their disembodied selves were invisible to people in the vicinity of their bodies, as well as being able to float, fly, and even move through solid walls. All these things add up to a definite and logical conclusion – human consciousness is invisible, immaterial, and separable from the physical human body.' Thomas paused, and looked at Ben.

'Interesting reasoning Thomas. There is even a certain logic to it. So please do continue,' was the response delivered with an irritatingly self-satisfied look.

Undeterred, Thomas continued, 'Now we come to the matter of how consciousness is transported, or housed. Is it something vague, such as an essence, or is it housed in a separate spiritual body? As a doctor you know that some people who undergo amputation of a leg or an arm develop the sensation of a phantom limb which feels identical to the limb they lost. You cannot see, photograph, or touch these phantom limbs, but amputees with phantom limbs feel them to be as real as the physical limbs they lost: they perceive the presence of the phantom limbs, they sense the positions of their phantom limbs, and even feel pain in their phantom limbs. Yet these phantom limbs are invisible, because you cannot see them. Furthermore, phantom limbs are immaterial, because you cannot touch them, and they can pass through solid substances. All these things mean phantom limbs may well be part of the invisible and immaterial spiritual body we call the soul.'

'Well I can help you there a bit Thomas. People don't just sometimes develop phantom limbs after amputation: medical experience teaches that almost all amputees develop sensations of phantom limbs (Ramachandran 1998, Stone 1950). Even more surprisingly, some people who were born without limbs can perceive phantom limbs identical to the limbs they never had (Brugger 2000). As for phantom limbs being part of an invisible immaterial aspect of the spiritual body ... Hmm ... But don't let me discourage you, please do continue.'

'What you just told me about people born without limbs is amazing! It's all coming together! Now combine the reality of phantom limbs with the fact that some people reporting near-death experiences tell of meeting their deceased relatives in a world inhabited by the souls of the dead. Sometimes they meet with a family member from whom one or more limbs were amputated during life, but in this world inhabited by the souls of the dead, the bodies of these deceased relatives are whole again. You can read about this in one of the near-death experiences reported by a cardiologist called Maurice Rawlings, where a man described meeting his deceased parents in the life after death.'

> *There was a background of music that was beautiful, heavenly music, and I saw two figures walking toward me and I immediately recognized them. They were my mother and father, both had died years ago. My mother was an amputee and yet that leg was now restored! She was walking on two legs! (Rawlings 1979, page 80).*

Thomas continued with an ever-increasing enthusiasm. 'See how the pieces of the puzzle all join together to form a logical whole. Amputation of a physical limb does not affect the substance of the invisible and immaterial soul. So the fact that people who were born with missing limbs can have sensations of phantom normal limbs, as well as the fact that almost all people sense a phantom limb after amputation, combined with the fact that the spirits of the dead in a life after death seen by those reporting near-death experiences appear the same as in life – all these things logically combine to indicate that consciousness is an aspect of the human soul, and that the human soul has an appearance identical to the human body!' Thomas animatedly continued his chain of reasoning, 'And consciousness and the human soul are separable from the human body as is clearly demonstrated by out-of-body experiences and near-death experiences. Here you have it Ben – fact and logic prove that every person has a separable, invisible, and immaterial human soul, the vehicle of individual consciousness, which has a form identical to the visible material body!'

'I'll agree that to a believer you've provided a very good, rigidly logical proof for the reality and form of the human soul. Of course, I can shoot holes in your reasoning as big as China, because there is a provable physical explanation for all these phenomena you've trotted forward as proof. No invisible, immaterial and spiritual phenomena or human soul are required to explain any of these phenomena at all. However, I am interested in hearing more of how you think about the human soul, because even though I consider your proof of the invisible and immaterial soul to be a wild fantasy generated by an overheated brain, it is a fantasy with its own rigid logic, and you've expressed it extremely well. So tell me Thomas, does the human soul in which you believe, and which you are trying to tell me I also possess, live for an eternity after death?'

'Ben, I can't understand why you still refuse to believe you have a soul. The evidence is quite clear, even to a sceptic like you. However, as regards the question of whether the soul is eternal, the answer is simple. The breath of life animating the flesh, which is the soul, comes from God. We know this from the holy books of Judaism and Christianity.'

And Jehovah God formed man of the dust of the ground, and breathed into his nostrils the breath of life; and man became a living soul. (ASV Bible, Genesis 2:7)

Thomas continued enthusiastically, 'We know God is eternal, so the breath of life – the human soul – is also eternal because it comes from God. So the soul lives eternally after death. This is no fantasy, because it is confirmed by the near-death experiences of people who describe meeting their deceased relatives in an immaterial world inhabited by the dead, and the souls of these relatives are very much alive in this world.'

'Amazing ...' said Ben as he sipped his beer. 'Do continue.'

'We cannot directly see or sense the souls of the dead, or the world they inhabit. Accordingly, the souls of the dead and the world they inhabit are invisible and immaterial, although none the less real for that. Furthermore, the near-death experiences of people who visited this world inhabited by the souls of the dead confirm that Christianity is the one true religion, because these people describe meeting Christian saints and Christian holy people in the afterlife. They never describe seeing Moses or Mohammed, nor do they describe seeing other Jewish or Islamic religious figures. This is positive proof of the truth of the message of Jesus as expressed in Christianity!'

'Well done Thomas! You've managed to present me with a logical masterpiece proving the reality and appearance of the invisible and immaterial soul, the truth of a life after death in some invisible and immaterial universe, as well as the fundamental truth of the Christian religion. Wonderful, wonderful! However, your proof is nonsense, even though it is nonsense with a very sound and rigid internal logic. Unfortunately for you, and all others like you, the basic premises forming the foundations of your logic are incorrect, totally destroying the edifice you constructed with your logic, because as I said earlier, each of these things has a much more logical and provable physical explanation. But I won't digress further, except to say your information about near-death experiences is also incorrect: followers of Islam have Islamic near-death experiences, followers of Judaism have Jewish near-death experiences, just as followers of Hinduism have Hindu near-death experiences (Evans Wentz 1960, pages 33-34). This totally destroys the idea of near-death experiences being proof of any one particular religion. But don't be discouraged, one day I'll explain the true nature of the basic premises forming the foundations of your arguments, and you'll eventually learn other ways of viewing these things. But now we've arrived at an interesting moment. You've proven the reality and the nature of the human soul to your satisfaction, you've proven each of us has an invisible and immaterial soul, you've proven the soul is the vehicle of our consciousness and mind, and you've proven the soul lives for an eternity after death. So tell me, other than existing and living for an eternity after death, why does the soul need a corruptible physical body, and what is the interaction of the soul with the body?'

'I can't explain these things in a few words. It's impossible.'

'Well you managed to do just that with your proof of the existence, form, and lifespan of the soul, so why not for these properties?'

'I just can't. But how do you view these same questions? You seem to have an opinion on a lot of things, and you're rather scathing about the validity of what I conclusively proved about the soul. So you tell me.'

'Hmmn ...' grunted Ben as he looked carefully at Thomas, searching for evidence of sarcasm. 'Okay, let's get on with it. Just for the sake of argument, I'll put myself in your shoes, and continue with your logic, arguing as if I actually believe in the reality of the human soul. Let's first start with the reason for a corruptible physical body, even though the soul itself is incorruptible. Only one explanation fits the facts. The soul is a product of the biological process of fertilization and generation of an embryo. Somehow this very biological and physical process also generates an invisible, immaterial, and immortal soul, the vehicle of the conscious mind. This is alluded to in the passage in the book of Genesis you used to prove the soul was immortal (Bible, Genesis 2:7), and indeed, this idea is current in mainstream Judaism and Christianity. Followers of Islam have much the same idea, saying also that the soul returns to life at the time of judgment of the souls of the dead.'

> *Verily We created man from a product of wet earth;*
> *Then placed him as a drop (of seed) in a safe lodging;*
> *Then fashioned We the drop a clot, then fashioned We the clot a little lump, then fashioned We the little lump bones, then clothed the bones with flesh, and then produced it another creation. So blessed be Allah, the Best of Creators!*
> *Then lo! after that ye surely die.*
> *Then lo! on the Day of Resurrection ye are raced (again).*
> *(Koran 23:12-16)*

'Ben, I understand these religions have identical thoughts on the matter, but why do you say this is the reason a soul is associated with a corruptible physical body?'

'I say this, because this is the only way to explain why the behaviour of people during this physical life determines their fate in a life after death. Consider the situation where an egg is fertilized, and God imbues it with an immortal soul which has existed billions of years since the creation of the universe. The physical body lives for but a moment, a few short years in comparison to eternity, yet the religious texts of Judaism, Christianity, and Islam, all tell us that the fate of a soul in an eternal life after death depends upon the behaviour of the physical body during a relatively insignificant few short years of life. This is not logical, because the character of each soul would be known to God at the moment of creation of that soul, as well as in the eons between creation and imbuement of a fertilized egg with that soul. After all, God is all-knowing and so would certainly know all these things about each soul. You also tell me that the immaterial soul is unaffected by the things affecting the material body. Accordingly, a very few short years of life on this material world would not affect the soul at all, meaning that eternal punishment or reward of an immortal soul for thoughts, words, or deeds performed by the physical body during a very insignificant few years of life in a physical body would be very illogical indeed. Are you following me here?'

'Hmmm ... Yes. What you're saying is logical up till now. But what is the most logical way for the soul to come into being according to you?'

'I would reason in this way. If the soul is acquired, or generated as a product of fertilization, then the newborn individual would have a soul that develops together with that individual during growth to adulthood. This would explain why the appearance of the soul is the same as that of the physical body. At the end of life, the soul associated with the body would have developed as much as was possible, and would pass into a life after death. If the soul came into being and developed in this way, then it would be logical that the thoughts, speech, deeds, and development of the soul during its sojourn in the mortal body would determine the fate of that soul in an eternal life after death – and indeed, this latter belief is a basic tenet of Judaism, Christianity, and Islam. These three religions even express this concept in a similar fashion. The first ideas about punishment and reward in a life after death were expressed in the Jewish holy book of Daniel in the Old Testament of the Bible.'

And many of them that sleep in the dust of the earth shall awake,

*some to everlasting life, and some to shame and everlasting
contempt. (ASV Bible, Daniel 12:2)*

Ben continued, 'But Jesus, the just and merciful prophet of
Christianity, apparently considered everlasting contempt to be far too mild
a punishment for sinners. So in the New Testament of the glorious
Christian Bible we read his solution to the problem of how best to chastise
sinners. And indeed, the new punishment for sinners prescribed by Jesus
was a profoundly satisfying improvement upon everlasting contempt –
from now on these loathsome sinners would suffer everlasting torment in
the blazing fires of hell!'

*Then shall the King say unto them on his right hand, Come, ye
blessed of my Father, inherit the kingdom prepared for you from
the foundation of the world:*
   *For I was an hungred, and ye gave me meat: I was thirsty, and
ye gave me drink: I was a stranger, and ye took me in:*
   *Naked, and ye clothed me: I was sick, and ye visited me: I was
in prison, and ye came unto me.*
   *Then shall the righteous answer him, saying, Lord, when saw
we thee an hungred, and fed thee? or thirsty, and gave thee
drink?*
   *When saw we thee a stranger, and took thee in? or naked, and
clothed thee?*
   Or when saw we thee sick, or in prison, and came unto thee?
   *And the King shall answer and say unto them, Verily I say
unto you, Inasmuch as ye have done it unto one of the least of
these my brethren, ye have done it unto me.*
   *Then shall he say also unto them on the left hand, Depart from
me, ye cursed, into everlasting fire, prepared for the devil and his
angels:*
   *For I was an hungred, and ye gave me no meat: I was thirsty,
and ye gave me no drink:*
   *I was a stranger, and ye took me not in: naked, and ye clothed
me not: sick, and in prison, and ye visited me not.*
   Then shall they also answer him, saying, Lord, when saw we

*thee an hungred, or athirst, or a stranger, or naked, or sick, or in
prison, and did not minister unto thee?*

*Then shall he answer them, saying, Verily I say unto you,
Inasmuch as ye did it not to one of the least of these, ye did it not
to me.*

*And these shall go away into everlasting punishment: but the
righteous into life eternal. (KJV Bible, Matthew 25:34-46)*

Ben really began to warm up to his subject. 'About 600 years elapsed
between the passing of Jesus and the revelations of God to Mohammed.
This was evidently a time filled with intense effort by God, and the
helpmeets of God, to further improve the torments provided for sinners in
hell. Old-fashioned concepts of merely punishing sinners with eternal
contempt and everlasting torment in the flames of hell were evidently
deemed insufficient. Divine improvements in torture techniques meant
that each time sinners' skins were consumed by fire, they would now be
miraculously regenerated, enabling these degraded creatures to suffer the
torment of fire afresh with new skins full of wonderfully sensitive new
nerves.'

*And of them were (some) who believed therein and of them were
(some) who disbelieved therein. Hell is sufficient for (their)
burning.*

*Lo! Those who disbelieve Our revelations, We shall expose
them to the Fire. As often as their skins are consumed We shall
exchange them for fresh skins that they may taste the torment.
Lo! Allah is ever Mighty, Wise. (Koran 4:55-56)*

'As if this were not gratifying enough, other forms of suitably horrific
heavenly chastisement were developed during these scant few, but
evidently very productive 600 years. We know this because the Koran
reveals that God, and the denizens of hell, had fruitfully employed these
few short years to develop new torments for sinners, such as: dragging the
souls of the damned into hell with manacles and chains (Koran 40:71,
73:12, 76:4), beating them with hooked iron rods (Koran 22:21), showering
them with scalding water as hot as molten brass (Koran 18:29, 40:72,

55:44), giving them boiling pus to drink (Koran 14:16), or forcing them to drink boiling water while cramming their stomachs with the evil fruits of the Zaqqum tree, the horrid tree of hell (Koran 37:62-68). When you learn of these things, you realize God can torment sinners in any manner of ways – precisely tailoring these torments to the nature of their sins and their vile depravities. And knowing these things, who can doubt the truth of the mercy and justice of God!' finished Ben with an expression of unspeakably false piety.

Thomas looked decidedly unhappy, but Ben ignored him, continuing enthusiastically, 'So Thomas, the very fact that the soul is supposed to undergo punishment or reward in a life after death for deeds and speech of the physical body, means it is very likely that each individual soul comes into being at the moment of fertilization. This is logical, and explains the concept of punishment and reward in a life after death very well. However, if we are going to believe in explanations derived from holy texts like these, then you also have to believe in other passages out of these same holy texts of Judaism, Christianity, and Islam, in which the prophets tell us that God sometimes purposely deceives people, and then tortures their souls for an eternity in a life after death for thoughts, speech and deeds resulting from this divine deception (see also Bible, Ezekiel 14:9 & Koran 14:4).'

And for this cause God shall send them strong delusion, that they should believe a lie:
That they all might be damned who believed not the truth, but had pleasure in unrighteousness. (KJV Bible, 2 Thessalonians 2:11-12)

'So Thomas, when you look at passages like these, you begin to realize this God is a decidedly untrustworthy deity. After all, God may well be deceiving you, leading you astray from true obedience to God during this mortal life, so that this same God can spend eternity torturing you in a life after death. This is evidently a deity stooping to low and dirty tricks such as entrapment to get extra people to torment in hell for all eternity! Personally I would want nothing whatsoever to do with such a God.'

'Oh ...' was Thomas's only comment.

'Anyway, enough vague speculation,' continued Ben. 'Now it's time for something about the relationship of the soul to the body which is demonstrable in this physical world. After all, we cannot prove with absolute certainty that the soul lives for all eternity, we cannot prove when the soul enters the physical body, and we cannot prove whether the soul causes the body to live. All we know for certain is that if we have an invisible and immaterial soul that is punished or rewarded in a life after death, then this soul must somehow interact with the physical body to control the thoughts, speech, and deeds of the physical body. This is a fascinating concept – interaction of the immaterial soul with the material body. How can something immaterial like the soul interact with something material like the human body? Actually, just like all people who have studied this problem since the time of Rene Descartes (1596-1650 CE), I have absolutely no idea how such an interaction could occur. But it is certain that such an interaction must occur if we have souls with the properties we've been discussing. What is more, if such an interaction between the immaterial soul and the material body does exist, it should be observable in the material body on this material world.'

'Oh?' was heard again. 'How can you do that?'

'By opening our eyes, and observing the human body while assuming each person has an immaterial soul controlling their every thought, word, and deed. I'll give an example. You have undoubtedly seen people who are confined to a wheelchair because they are paralyzed from the waist down.'

'Yes ...' said Thomas cautiously. 'But what has this got to do with the soul?'

'Everything. Some of these unfortunate people have had an accident which has totally severed their spinal cord at the level of their lower chest vertebrae. As a consequence, the nerves going to their legs have been severed, and so they cannot move their legs. If a normal healthy person wills a leg to move, then the leg moves according to the will of the normal person. But when a person paralyzed from the waist down tries to move a leg, the leg will not move, no matter how hard the person wills that leg to move, because the nerves conducting the commands from the brain to the muscles of the leg have been severed, and the appropriate nerve impulses do not arrive at the muscles of the leg to cause movement. This indicates quite conclusively that the soul must use the mechanisms of the body to exert control over the actions of the body.' Ben looked enquiringly at Thomas.

'That's very clear. Do you have another example?'

'Indeed I do,' said Ben. 'Here we are – you and I. We're sitting here drinking beer, a weak solution of alcohol. The effect of a small amount of alcohol is to relax people, enabling a more fluid form of social interaction. If we drink a large amount of alcohol, we will become drunk. As we all know, some drunken people become violent and abusive. Consider what happens when a kind and religious man who normally never drinks alcohol goes to a party with some friends. These friends play a foolish practical joke on him by spiking his non-alcoholic fruit juice with a taste-less form of strong alcohol. Being unaccustomed to alcohol, the man soon becomes very drunk. While drunk, he becomes violent and abusive, saying and shouting the most horrible things, as well as mouthing the vilest heresies imaginable. To make matters even worse, let us imagine this drunken man then gets into his car, and drives home, but on the way collides with, and severely injures a child crossing the street. This man is so drunk that he ignores the impact of his car with the child, and leaves the severely injured child to die on the street. Normally this man would shudder at the very thought of such things – yet he committed them all while drunk. The body of this man was affected by the chemical effects of the alcohol on his material brain, but his immaterial soul would certainly be unaffected by the alcohol. Here we have a man whose behaviour while drunk was totally different to that desired by his soul. Evidently the immaterial soul of this man was unable to control his material body while it was under the influence of alcohol. This example raises the fascinating question of whether the soul of this man should be tortured for all eternity for acts performed by the body while his soul was unable to control his body. Furthermore, this example is yet another illustration that the soul can only control the body through the mechanisms of the body. What do you think of this example Thomas?'

'It certainly is a knotty problem Ben. His so-called friends should go to hell in any case, because they were the ones who made him drunk. As for the man himself, I would say he was innocent. But then again, I'm not God. In any case I am sure God would be merciful.'

'Oh Thomas, what have we discussed before? God is not merciful.

God sometimes even predestines people to go to hell, regardless of how religious and kind they may be (see Chapter 1). However, let's get onto another example. General anaesthesia is usually administered by injecting a sleep-inducing drug into a vein. After injection into a vein, the drug flows with the blood into the heart which pumps it to all parts of the body, including the brain. Once a sufficient quantity of the drug flows with the blood into the brain, it causes a degree of brain malfunction sufficient to cause loss of consciousness. Some people say they don't believe the injection of this drug will cause them to lose consciousness. They even emphatically claim they will stay conscious. But within a few seconds after sufficient anaesthetic drug arrives within their brains, all these people lose consciousness, even though they try their best not to lose consciousness. This phenomenon also indicates that the soul must use the mechanisms of the body to generate consciousness, or at least to manifest consciousness. I can go on and on, but each example indicates the same thing – if the soul exists, then the soul must use the mechanisms of the physical body to exert control over the body. This is an important consideration when determining the reality of the soul.'

Thomas thought for a moment, 'This means there are manifestations of the presence of the soul that you can detect in this material world?'

'Oh yes indeed.'

Thomas was ecstatic, 'So there is physical proof for the reality of the human soul after all! How then can you deny the reality of God, and the message of Jesus?'

'Easily,' was the terse response. 'You've got to realize there are two ways of thinking about the properties you ascribe to the soul. To the believer, the soul is the controller of the body, the generator of consciousness and mind, the generator of all thoughts, the generator of personality, the generator of free will, and the resulting thoughts, speech, movements and deeds. However, to the materialist, all these properties you ascribe to the soul are products of the functioning of the body and the brain. An incredible amount of research performed during the last century is beginning to reveal the functioning of the brain. This research reveals that the functioning of the brain and its parts generates all the properties of mind that theologians and believers alike ascribe to the invisible and immortal soul. There is however one big difference between the idea that the mind and all its properties are manifestations of the invisible and immaterial soul, and the idea that the functioning of the brain generates all the qualities ascribed to the human mind: the functioning of the brain is measurable, while that of the soul is only speculation and faith. When you examine the functioning of the body and the mind in relation to these two beliefs, you find you cannot distinguish between these two hypotheses: because regardless of whether free will is a product of brain function, or whether free will is a property of the soul, the mechanisms of the body are required to exert actions determined by free will in either situation. So all that can be done to differentiate between the two, is to demonstrate that the soul is less likely, simply because the physical mechanisms of the body explain all the attributes ascribed to the soul.'

'Oh,' was the somewhat crestfallen response of Thomas, 'and just as I thought there was physical evidence for the soul.'

Suddenly Ben looked at his watch, 'Is that the time? I'm sorry that this is a bit sudden, but I really do have to go to an appointment. Let's telephone this coming week and arrange to meet on Saturday when there is a paranormal fair I want to visit. I do believe you might find it instructive. Do you want to come?'

'Yes, I'd like that.'

'Okay, we'll see each other then.' Ben drained the rest of his beer, leapt on his bicycle, and disappeared in the direction of the inner city.

Chapter 3

Windows of the Soul

'Your soul will be doomed! Don't condemn yourself to eternal hellfire!' were but a small sample of the cries and slogans on placards and banners wielded by a group of pale complexioned, self-professed Christians accosting all those entering the Groenoord Hall parking area.

A girl with a serious expression offered Thomas a pamphlet describing the insidious and corrupting evil inherent in the belief, and practice of the paranormal. 'Don't go inside,' she entreated. 'Your soul will be damned! So few people are able to withstand the vile and sinister temptations of the paranormal. Save yourself! Don't expose yourself to this evil! Even those who say they are immune to this evil compromise themselves by entering.'

Thomas looked at the pamphlet, seriously read most of the first page, and looked at Ben. Ben smiled, and also scrutinized the pamphlet he had received. 'Yes ... You've got all the correct citations from the Bible. Well done young lady. But we're still going inside. Come on Thomas, this is a good paranormal fair. Let's go and expose our immortal souls to the vilest and most insidious forms of spiritual poison offered by what these people consider to be wicked devil-worshipers. At the same time we'll learn a lot about the functioning of the human body and its relation to spiritual belief systems.'

Ben walked resolutely further. Thomas looked uncertain, carefully folded the pamphlet, put it in a pocket, and followed Ben.

'I must admit, I never go to these paranormal fairs because they really are against my belief. After all, the Bible tells us in no uncertain terms that the use of paranormal abilities is forbidden by God.'

There shall not be found with thee any one that maketh his son or his daughter to pass through the fire, one that useth divination, one that practiseth augury, or an enchanter, or a sorcerer, or a charmer, or a consulter with a familiar spirit, or a wizard, or a necromancer. For whosoever doeth these things is an abomination unto Jehovah: and because of these abominations Jehovah thy God doth drive them out from before thee. (ASV Bible, Deuteronomy 18:10-13)

'And,' continued Thomas, 'Christian Holy texts confirm this, telling that those who practice these paranormal arts are doomed to suffer eternal punishment in hell after death.'

He that overcometh shall inherit these things; and I will be his God, and he shall be my son. But for the fearful, and unbelieving, and abominable, and murderers, and fornicators, and sorcerers, and idolaters, and all liars, their part shall be in the lake that burneth with fire and brimstone; which is the second death. (ASV Bible, Revelations 21:7-8)

A mischievous glint appeared in Ben's eyes, 'So you mean that Saint Peter, the foremost apostle of Jesus, and the first leader of the fledgling Christian church in Rome, is doomed to burn forever in hell?'

Ben looked flabbergasted. Surprise and amazement were terms woefully inadequate to describe his expression. 'Huhhh!!' was the only sound to emanate from his lips. 'Huhhh!' came from his lips again as he stopped walking, and looked at Ben.

'Go "huhhh" all you like Thomas, but according to the Bible passages you just quoted, the condition of the soul of Saint Peter in the life after death is very problematical indeed.'

Thomas recovered his composure sufficiently to ask, 'How could you even say such a thing? Saint Peter was a great and holy man. Ridiculous!'

'Okay let's examine the facts we know about Saint Peter. Saint Peter was not the Son of God. Saint Peter was not continually inspired by God to perform miracles. True he was the first and foremost disciple, or apostle of Jesus, a champion of Christianity, and the first leader of the church in Rome. He was a great man, but not a prophet continually inspired by God.

Would you say that's a fair summary of his contribution to Christianity?'

'Yes ...' was the cautious reaction.

'Now here is why I consider the position of the soul of Saint Peter to be decidedly problematical. Shortly after the death of Jesus and his ascension to heaven, a community espousing and practicing the teachings of Jesus arose in Jerusalem under the leadership of Saint Peter (Bible, Acts 2: 37-47). Some members of this community of proto-Christians sold possessions and donated the proceeds to support the works of the followers of Jesus, as well as the less fortunate members of their community (Bible, Acts 4: 31-37). A man called Ananias and his wife Sapphira were members of this proto-Christian community. They sold a plot of land with the expressed intention of donating all the proceeds to the church (Bible, Acts 5:1-11). But instead of donating the total sale proceeds to the church, they decided to keep some of the money for themselves. So Ananias handed Peter only part of the sale proceeds, claiming this was the full sum received from the sale. Saint Peter was enraged by this deceit. He confronted Ananias, telling him he had sinned by lying to him, sinned by lying to his fellow church members, and worse still, he had sinned by lying to God. Ananias was stunned by Saint Peter's knowledge of his deceit, and aghast at the vicious browbeating he received. He suddenly fell to the ground and died. Some young men in the church wrapped him in a cloth, carried him outside, and buried him. Saint Peter seems to have been really angry about the basic principle underlying this deceit. This couple said they were giving the whole of the sale price of a piece of land to the church, yet agreed with each other to lie about the sale price so as to keep some of the money for themselves. Several hours later, Sapphira began to get worried about the whereabouts of Ananias. She went to Saint Peter, and the following events transpired.'

> *About three hours later his wife came in, not knowing what had happened. Peter asked her, "Tell me, is this the price you and Ananias got for the land?"*
>
> *"Yes," she said, "that is the price."*
>
> *Peter said to her, "How could you agree to test the Spirit of the Lord? Look! The feet of the men who buried your husband are at the door, and they will carry you out also."*

At that moment she fell down at his feet and died. Then the young men came in and, finding her dead, carried her out and buried her beside her husband. Great fear seized the whole church and all who heard about these events. (NIV Bible, Acts 5:7-11)

'Nowhere does this passage say that God intervened to tell Saint Peter about the missing money. Nor does this passage say that God, or Saint Peter, struck this couple dead for their avarice or lack of faith. Instead, we only read that Ananias fell dead when confronted with his deceit, and that Saint Peter predicted the immediate death of Sapphira. But how did Saint Peter know about the deceit of Ananias and Sapphira, and how did he know Sapphira would die? This is the use of paranormal abilities to learn of unknown things in the present, and the use of paranormal abilities to foretell the future. God expressly forbids the use of paranormal abilities on pain of death in this life (Bible, Exodus 22:18), as well as punishment with eternal torment in the afterlife (Bible, Revelations 21:7-8). This is why I said earlier that the situation of Saint Peter in the afterlife is decidedly problematical. So has Saint Peter now undergone almost 2000 years of the eternity of torment promised those who use paranormal arts? However, regardless of his present possible unhappy situation in the fires of hell, Saint Peter must have been very pleased at the time with the salutary example provided by the deaths of this unlucky couple, because the rest of the church members were awed and afraid afterwards. This episode in the history of the early Christian church reveals the opportunistic use of coincidence at its best. No one would ever dare withhold money from the church again after such an example of the true power and wrath of God! Saint Peter also revealed himself in this episode as an evil and ruthless exploiter of superstitious terror to bind and control the followers of his new cult – Christianity.'

'I think it's very offensive and insulting to a man as great as Saint Peter. How could both Ananias and Sapphira suddenly drop dead at Peter's feet if it wasn't the punishment of God? This is too coincidental to be due to anything else except divine intervention.'

'I don't think it was divine intervention at all,' laughed Ben. 'It was more likely a wonderful opportunity for Peter to establish his authority. I imagine the unlucky Ananias and Sapphira were sickly people with heart conditions, or both very opportunely developed what is called a "vasovagal cardiac arrest" during the really vicious browbeating they received from Saint Peter. A vasovagal cardiac arrest is a situation where the heart stops beating for a shorter or longer time as a result of pain or strong emotion (Cantanzaro 2006, Kinsella 2001, Suzuki 2004). Sometimes the heart does not resume beating of its own accord, and the person dies unless resuscitated. People lose consciousness within five to twenty seconds after the heart suddenly stops beating (Rossen 1943), which would explain why both Ananias and Sapphira suddenly collapsed at the feet of Peter. Peter really put the fear of Peter and God into them, so there was certainly emotion enough to induce a vasovagal cardiac arrest. Cardiac resuscitation was simply unknown in ancient times, so if these people fell down with a cardiac arrest, then they would simply remain dead. However, if they had not developed a true cardiac arrest, a period of just ten seconds of absent heartbeat during such a vasovagal reaction has been known to cause a period of unconsciousness lasting about ten minutes (Cantanzaro 2006). A longer period of absent heartbeat, or a longer period with a very slow heartbeat, will cause an even longer period of uncon-sciousness which might well be considered death in some ancient cultures. This is the most likely explanation of why they both appeared to fall dead at the feet of Saint Peter. The speed with which they were buried was indecently fast, even when you consider that Jewish religious law requires people to be buried before sunset on the day of death (Bible, Deuteronomy 21:23). The fact that Peter actually dared to bury Ananias without first attempting to contact his wife Sapphira is truly astounding! This fact indicates the unfeeling disrespect with which he regarded this couple – two people who had supported his church with their faith and their money. And then, after Sapphira also dropped dead at his feet, he also dared to bury her with equal haste, as well as a total absence of any attempt to contact any of their family members who would normally have performed the necessary funeral rites. These facts indicate the profound contempt with which Peter regarded these two unfortunate people. What is more, these facts also indicate that Ananias and Sapphira were easy prey for this wicked man. They were very evidently a lonely couple completely in the power of this clearly incredibly evil sect leader, who would never have acted in this way unless he knew they had no family or friends in the city to exact vengeance for such behaviour. Peter also had very practical reasons for these indecently rapid burials. Burying them at once made sure they remained dead, and their sudden deaths, as well as their equally rapid burials would strike terror in the minds of other members of his sect, binding them to him with mind-numbing shackles of fear. He certainly knew how to exploit a situation.'

'Ben, I've never heard of such a loathsomely cynical and insulting explanation of this story before. Okay, I must admit to being somewhat puzzled by this story too. It's so out of character for a man as holy as Saint Peter. I'm sure yours is only one of several possible explanations. Perhaps what we read in the Bible is only a coloured story, and God really did inspire many of the deeds and statements of Saint Peter.'

'Unfortunately most people are not scholars of ancient scripts and texts. All they have to go on is the Bible as it now is. No more than that – and this is what the Bible says about Peter and the way he dealt with Ananias and Sapphira.'

'I'll take it up with one of my tutors next week,' was the somewhat harried response of Thomas. And he fell silent.

They recommended walking to the entrance of the Groenoord Hall. At the side of the entrance was a group of placard wielding Moslems, each of whom was reading or clutching a copy of the Koran. Their placards and banners were covered with inspirational texts such as, 'Allah forbids the paranormal! Save your soul – don't enter! Entry is apostasy! Roast in hell Satan-loving dogs!'

'Ah Thomas, just look at those placards ... There you see a wonderful example of a religion more evolved than Christianity.'

'Now Ben, that really is going too far,' responded Thomas unhappily, as he began to think he had made a mistake coming to this paranormal fair with Ben.

'I'll tell you why I said that Thomas. Jewish and Christian holy texts merely say that the use of paranormal abilities such as sorcery, foretelling the future, etc, is an abomination in the eyes of God. Christian holy books then simply go on to say that practitioners of these arts must be killed (Bible, Exodus 22:18), after which their souls will be tortured for an eternity in a life after death (Bible, Revelations 21:7-8). No reasons – just statements as from a father to his children. Do you follow me?'

'Yes ...'

'Now in the viewpoint of Islam, only God, the eternal and all-powerful creator of the universe, is all-knowing (Koran 27:65). Accordingly, to learn more than is possible by means of the normal physical senses is to assume some of the all-knowing qualities of God, which is quite evidently heresy amounting to apostasy, because no one can presume to assume such powers (Al-Fozan 1997, pages 38-50). So instead of simply being forbidden to use paranormal abilities, the followers of Islam are told why their use is forbidden. This is evolution in religious thought!'

'Hmmmn ... Interesting,' was the terse response.

'Such enthusiasm Thomas! These are really fascinating similarities between Islam, Judaism and Christianity, and you fob it all off with one word – interesting ... But there are also other fascinating things to observe here too. Look at these devout followers of Islam, and observe what they do. See how tightly they clasp copies of the Koran to their breasts! Observe how fervently they read from the Koran! In their viewpoint they are braving eternal damnation in hell from the insidious satanic evil permeating and polluting the surroundings of the Groenoord Hall (Koran 2:102). Even so, they courageously continue trying to save fellow followers of Islam from the horrors of heresy by deterring them from entering the fair. Notice I only said followers of Islam, and not Christians. They don't speak to Christians.'

'Now you mention it – you're right.'

'Yes Thomas, these followers of Islam won't try stopping us, because as followers of different religions we are automatically doomed to an eternity of agony in hell after we die anyway (Koran 5:51-53, 5:72-73, 9:30-35, 98:1-6). Entering only makes our doom more certain, and our future sufferings in hell even more horrid. So why bother trying to stop us.'

With this cheering thought in mind, they entered the main concourse of the Groenoord Hall, once the local cattle market, now a multifunctional event centre. Incense perfumed the air, there was soft music, occasionally chimes and gongs sounded, and through all this were the sounds of many people talking and walking between the stands of the numerous sellers of paranormal services, courses, books, and paraphernalia. Thomas, confronted with the unfamiliar, looked uncertainly at Ben, whose only response to his enquiring glance was to say, 'Enjoy yourself. I enjoy paranormal fairs like this because they really are fantastic exhibitions of how the functioning of the body can mislead people into believing in immaterial, paranormal, and spiritual forces. And this looks like being one of the better ones.'

'Even though I am beginning to understand your fascination with the theological aspects of belief in the paranormal, I'm still not quite sure how a draughty old hall filled with deluded superstitious people could be described as "better". These people would be better off in their respective synagogues, churches, or mosques. After all, as we discussed earlier, engaging in activities related to the paranormal such as visiting this fair, is potentially a form of spiritual suicide, because all the holy books of the Jews, the Christians, and even the Moslems forbid the use of paranormal abilities.'

'So so Thomas,' laughed Ben. 'Are you saying you aren't superstitious? After all, you believe in the reality of invisible paranormal beings and powers, such as God, Satan, angels, and evil forces. If you didn't believe in these things, you wouldn't be so serious about the risk of eternal damnation of the immaterial and immortal souls of these people. So are you really any better than these people?'

'Okay, okay, point taken. But what's so fascinating about this type of fair then?'

'Let's just look around and see what's being offered. I particularly want to look at the people claiming to see an aura of light around the human body, because I've recently developed a new theory about how people can see halo's of light around the heads of people as depicted in Middle-Ages European paintings of holy people. So let's look around and enjoy ourselves. We can talk afterwards and compare notes on what we saw and observed.'

They walked slowly through the aisles. There were people selling semiprecious stones and crystals with healing powers, others sold Tibetan musical bowls, yet others sold many different types of incense for as many different purposes. There were people with divining rods and pendulums. One man claimed to receive messages from the dead at the beginning of empty magnetic tapes. Tarot card readers, palm readers, and clairvoyants abounded. There were practitioners of Reiki, practitioners of iris diagnosis, and there were regression therapists claiming to be able to help people remember incarnations in previous lives. Many stands sold books on a simply enormous range of subjects related to paranormal abilities. Ben spent most of his time studying those people able to see auras. Some of these people made drawings of the auras of paying customers, and Ben devoted special attention to these people.

Thomas observed all these things. His initial emotion was of careful assessment and some slight trepidation, because his immortal soul might well be at risk. After a while, he began to understand the nature of the people at the paranormal fair, the quality of the explanations, and the evidence for all these things. Soon he began to feel a sense of amazement at the gullibility of the people in the stands, and especially of their customers. So it was that his initial feeling of trepidation for his immortal soul was soon replaced by an emotion akin to supercilious scorn. 'How could such a pathetic event, such gullibility, and such largely foolish superstition be of interest to a man as intelligent and developed as Ben?' he thought. He began observing what Ben observed, only to be surprised by the apparent trivia interesting him, and frustrated by his lack of understanding as to why these things could possibly be of any interest to Ben.

After three quarters of an hour, Ben turned towards Thomas. 'I hope you've enjoyed yourself as much as I have. I've seen enough here. Do you want to look any further?'

'Not really. I'm beginning to get bored. I can't understand why those Christians and followers of Islam tried stopping people at the entrance. Letting them enter would be an almost certain way of driving most sensible people away from the superstitious nonsense presented here.'

'Hmm … it sounds like you didn't learn much here. A pity, because there were some beautiful examples of how the functioning of the human body can give people the illusion of paranormal perceptions.'

'You saw examples of that here?'

'Indeed I did. Let's have lunch at the cafeteria here, and I'll explain what I observed,' said Ben as he picked up a tray. He looked at the food offered by the cafeteria, and continued, 'After looking at all these anaemic, rabbit-food eating believers in the paranormal, I'm going to have a solid meal of meat and alcohol. I'm going to drink lots of beer, and eat French fries with meatballs. What about you Thomas?'

Thomas grinned, replying in an incredibly fake tone of shocked piety, 'Oh Ben, but Saint Paul actually advised against eating meat and drinking alcohol.'

It is good not to eat flesh, nor to drink wine, nor to do anything whereby thy brother stumbleth. (ASV Bible, Romans 14:21)

'Ha! That old one again!' laughed Ben. 'That passage is one of the reasons why many so-called Christians are vegetarian, teetotal, bloodless, and boring. Saint Paul was only repeating a teaching in the Old Testament book of Proverbs about eating and drinking to excess. He didn't actually forbid meat and alcohol – just excess consumption.'

Be not among winebibbers, among gluttonous eaters of flesh:
    For the drunkard and the glutton shall come to poverty; and drowsiness will clothe a man with rags. (ASV Bible, Proverbs 23:20-21)

'So Thomas, are you saying that you want to eat rabbit-food?'

'Absolutely not! I want the same as you. I also enjoy eating irresponsibly every now and then.'

Service was quick, and soon the pair began devouring French fries and meatballs with some considerable relish and gusto, every now and then washing their food down with beer.

Ben wiped his mouth, 'Good French fries. Wish I could say the same for the meatballs. Ah well, at least the beer is good. So Thomas, if I understood your comments correctly, you weren't overly impressed with this paranormal fair. You saw everything I saw, yet you only saw ignorant superstition and nothing else.'

'That's certainly true. As I said earlier, I still can't understand why you found this pitiful demonstration of human gullibility so interesting.'

'You saw me spending most of my time observing the people who claim to see an aura of light around the human body. This aura they claim to see is similar to the golden aureoles that medieval painters depicted around the heads of saints, only with more colours, and surrounding the whole body. These aura gazers claim to be able to determine personality and state of health from the aura of light they claim they see around the human body. I've developed the idea that this perception is based on a misinterpretation of quite normal aberrations in the function of the human eyes. That's why I spent most of my time observing these aura gazers, and found to my satisfaction that my observations confirmed my theories.'

'I always wondered about those golden aureoles. I thought it was simply a fashion amongst medieval painters to distinguish holy from ordinary people. I'd be fascinated to hear your explanation.'

'Before I can explain that, you first have to know something about the functioning of the human eye. To begin with, the human eye is no more than an organ to perceive light, which is a form of electromagnetic radiation in the wavelength range from 400 to 700 nanometres [1 nanometre = 0.000,000,001 meter = 10^{-9} meters]. Light with a wavelength of 400 nanometres is violet, and as the wavelength increases, the colour changes from violet to blue, to green, to yellow, to orange, and finally to red which has a wavelength of 700 nanometres. The eye is unable to perceive any other wavelengths of electromagnetic radiation, or other forms of radiation. An important fact to remember is that what can be seen with the eyes can be photographed. So a person claiming the ability to see something no-one else can see or photograph, is either hallucinating, or the eyes of that person are malfunctioning.'

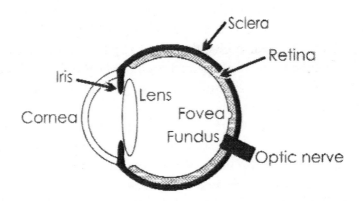

Figure 3.1 Elements of the human eye in cross-section.

'Oh, and what about the "third eye" many of the people in this paranormal fair claim each of us possesses?'

'It simply doesn't exist as an anatomical entity,' was Ben's very categorical reply. 'Centuries of painstaking anatomical studies have never revealed anything even resembling a third eye. It is simply a fantasy devised by people who fail to understand the sometimes quite wondrous ways the eyes and the brain function together. Here, I'll draw a picture of the basic structure of the eye.' Ben pulled a pen from a pocket and proceeded to draw a picture of a cross-section of the eye on a scrap of paper (figure 3.1). 'Now look at this Thomas. Light enters the eye through the transparent cornea in front of the pupil. The cornea not only functions as a window, letting light into the eye, but is also a powerful lens focusing light onto the back of the inside of the eyeball. Light passes through the cornea, but is only able to enter the rear of the eyeball through the opening in the iris called the pupil. Light does not enter the rear part of the eyeball other than through the pupil. Having passed through the pupil, light then passes through the lens of the eye which performs the fine focusing of incoming light onto the back of the eyeball. The cornea and lens form a double lens optical system, where the cornea does the majority of the focusing of light onto the retina, (about 70%), while the lens performs the fine focusing. This lens system focuses light entering the eye onto the back of the eyeball, onto the network of light-sensitive nerve cells covering the inside of the eyeball called the retina. Each of the light sensitive nerve cells of the retina forms a picture element. Nerve impulses generated by light activating the many tens of thousands of light sensitive nerve cells of the retina are transmitted along the nerve fibres forming the optic nerve into the brain where they undergo filtering and processing, as well as unconscious and conscious interpretation. This is the structure and function of the human eye in a nutshell.'

'That's all basic stuff Ben. Everyone knows that.'

'Do they? I sometimes wonder. For instance, when you look at people, you look to see their eyes. Are their eyes normal, or beady, do they bulge, are they deep? You observe their eyes to get an idea of their personality and their interest in you. Are their eyes hard, cold and calculating, sharp and perceptive, warm and interested, or lying? And what you lightly dismiss as the very simple and basic structure and function of the eyes explains all these expressions, as well as the so-called paranormal perception of the human aura.'

'You're bluffing,' said Thomas. 'You can't explain all these things with simple anatomy. But I'm listening – do continue.'

'Okay,' replied Ben. 'Here it comes. I'll begin with the basic elements first, and the first thing I want to talk about is the way you look at other people. Mostly you do this totally unconsciously, saying they had narrow eyes, bulging eyes, or whatever … But what do you actually mean by statements such as these?'

'Just those things.'

'That's precisely what I mean. You can't define these observations in precise terms. Let's begin by defining the normal position of adult eyes. Now Thomas, the eyelids are kept open by the action of an involuntary muscle called the muscle of Müller pulling the upper eyelid upwards. The normal position of the upper eyelid is half-way between the upper edge of the iris and the opening of the pupil, while the edge of the lower eyelid also covers a bit of the iris. Look around you, and you will see the truth of this. The eyelids of a person with narrowed eyes are narrowed, covering more of the iris than normal in the same way as you look towards bright light. So you only see a narrow slit of eye white, iris, and pupil. On the other extreme, you have a person with bulging or wide open eyes. Here the eyelids are wide open, and do not cover the iris or pupil at all. This gives the appearance of eyes bulging forward, something which actually does happen as a result of one particular type of thyroid disease. Are you following me so far?'

'You certainly do define these expressions exactly, but what about the others?'

Ben sipped his beer. 'Ahhh … That was the easy bit. Now for the next bit. Pupil diameter has quite a profound effect upon the optical performance of the eyes, as well as determining how we react to a person, a picture of a person, or how we describe a person. Depending upon the context in which we observe someone, a person with narrow pupils may be described as cold and calculating, as a person with sharp and piercing eyes, or as just plain disinterested. This is quite the opposite to the description of a person with widened pupils. A person with widened pupils is often described as attractive, or as interested in the observer (Hess 1966, Hess 1975). Usually we make judgments based on pupil diameter quite unconsciously, but some people train themselves to specifically observe the pupil diameter of people with whom they come into contact, for example, shop owners, policemen, and so on. The reason for ascribing these properties to differing pupil diameters is actually based upon the optical properties of the eyes.'

'Oh, how is that?'

'The best way of visualizing the effect of pupil diameter is to look at photographs. A good portrait photograph has the person being photographed sharply in focus while the background is blurred. This type of photograph is taken with a wide open camera lens diaphragm, which is a situation similar to looking at the same scene with wide open pupils. A person with wide open pupils can focus clearly on a person being looked at, but everything else behind or in front of that person is blurred and out of focus. This is why a person with widened pupils appears to display interest in the person being looked at, and accordingly is considered more attractive, or as having a warm personality. There are also photographs of scenery, or of buildings where everything in the foreground and background is in focus. These types of photographs are taken with a narrow camera lens diaphragm, which is similar to looking at the same scene with narrowed pupils. A person with narrowed pupils can clearly see the person at whom they are looking, as well as everything in front and behind that person. This is why a person with narrowed pupils is described as being disinterested, as having sharp and piercing vision, or as having a cold, calculating, or hard glance.'

'Wow! I do believe I'm going to observe pupils more carefully from now on!' was the enthusiastic reaction from Thomas.

'Don't get too excited, I'm only just warming up. Everyone knows the expressions: everything's rosy, looking at the world through rose-colored glasses, looking through rose-colored spectacles, or seeing red. The structure and functioning of the eyes also explains these expressions. The surface of the retina at the back of the eyeball is covered by a network of blood vessels radiating all over the surface of the retina from a single point called the fundus (figure 3.2). This network of blood vessels lies on top of the retina, and light must pass through this network of blood vessels before it impinges on the layer of light-sensitive nerve cells of the retina. So tell me Thomas, what is the colour of blood?'

Surface of retina

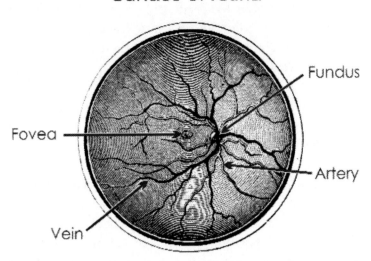

Figure 3.2 A view of the back of the eyeball, as if looking into the eyeball through the pupil at the rear surface of the eyeball. The view shows the retina, the light-sensitive membrane at the back of the eyeball, and the various structures of, and on the retina. The fovea is the focal point of the cornea and lens, while the fundus is the point where blood vessels enter and leave the eyeball.

'Ohhh ... Now I understand what you're trying to tell me. So you mean this network of blood vessels on top of the retina acts as a sort of red coloured filter, imparting a pinkish red colour to the light we normally see. But then why don't we normally see white light as pinkish or red in colour?'

'Because the layer of blood is too thin to have much effect on the colour of the light we see, and we compensate for it anyway. But there are situations when the blood vessels of the retina are more engorged than normal, making this normal layer of red blood thicker than usual. For example, hanging upside-down and swinging violently, can cause massive engorgement of the blood vessels of the retina at the point of maximum downwards acceleration. This means these blood vessels are thicker than normal, and so the network of blood vessels through which incoming light must pass before activating the light-sensitive cells of the retina is thicker than normal. The resulting effect is that you see red. Sometimes these wild manoeuvres cause loss of consciousness, and is called a red-out in distinction to the much more common black-out. Human emotions can also increase the thickness of the layer of blood flowing in front of the light-sensitive layer of the retina. The flow of blood to the head of a person in love, or an ecstatically happy person is increased, as is the flow of blood to their eyes, so increasing the thickness of the layer of blood in front of the retina, and as a result they see everything through rose-colored glasses, or spectacles. The veins in the heads and necks of enraged persons are visibly swollen, or engorged, as are the veins inside their eyes. The resulting massive engorgement of the blood vessels on the surfaces of the retinas of enraged persons causes them to see red.'

'Fascinating stuff, but you still haven't explained any paranormal phenomena with normal eye function,' was the response of Thomas as he finished his last French fry.

Ben sipped his beer, 'First the basics, then I'll get to the more interesting things. One of the more interesting aspects of the functioning of the retina is that per gram of tissue, the flow of blood to the retina is about five times that to the brain (Strang et al 1977), effectively swamping the light sensitive cells of the retina with oxygen. This may sound excessive, but the light sensitive nerve cells of the retina consume oxygen at a rate faster than the nerve cells of the brain, so they need all the oxygen they can get.'

'Just a minute Ben,' interrupted Thomas, 'but what have blood flow and the oxygen consumption of the light sensitive cells in the retina got to do with the paranormal?'

'Everything Thomas, everything. Tell me, what do you consider the function of blood and oxygen to be?'

'Everyone knows you need oxygen to stay alive, and your blood has to flow around your body too. But these are things needed for your physical body, and I can't see them having any relation to paranormal observations.'

'In other words Thomas, you don't have a clear idea of the function of blood and oxygen in the body. I'll enlighten you. The heart is just a pump, only it's made of meat instead of metal, and its function is to pump blood around the body – no more than that. The heart has two sides – a left side and a right side, and they work in tandem, each pumping exactly the same amount of blood. The left side of the heart pumps blood into the arteries going to all organs and tissues of the body. Arteries are actually no more than tubes transporting blood to all organs and tissues of the body. Within these organs and tissues, the arteries divide and divide until they form microscopically blood vessels called capillaries. Oxygen, nutrients, and many other substances within blood diffuse out of these capillaries into the cells surrounding them. At the same time, carbon dioxide, waste products, many other substances diffuse out of the surrounding cells into the capillaries. The capillaries re-unite, and re-unite, forming ever larger blood vessels called veins. Veins return blood to the right side of the heart, which then pumps this blood through the lung capillaries, where oxygen diffuses into the blood, and waste carbon dioxide diffuses into the lungs where it is exhaled. Blood then flows into the left side of the heart where the whole process is endlessly repeated. This is the circulation. Normally an adult body contains about five to six litters of blood, and the heart of a resting adult pumps about four to six litters of blood per minute. Blood is no more than a transport fluid, and the function of blood and the circulation is to transport substances around the body: transporting oxygen, nutrients, and other substances to the tissues of the body, as well as removing waste products from these same tissues. The body grows, is sustained, and stays alive because of thousands of chemical reactions occurring within the cells of the body. Most of these chemical reactions require energy, and oxygen is an absolutely vital ingredient in these energy generating chemical reactions. But there is no reserve supply of oxygen in any of the tissues of the body, so any reduction or interruption to the supply of oxygen to the cells of the body has a rapid effect on the functioning of the affected parts of the body. Are you still following me Thomas?

'Yes, that's all quite clear. But how rapidly do body parts start to malfunction when the supply of oxygen is interrupted?'

'Very rapidly indeed. Suddenly stopping the flow of blood to a body part, an organ, or tissue, suddenly stops the supply of oxygen to that body part, organ, or tissue. There is no reserve supply of oxygen in any tissues of the body, and some organs need more oxygen than other organs. The brain needs a lot of oxygen to generate consciousness and all other attributes of the mind, which is why people lose consciousness within five to twenty seconds after the heartbeat stops (Rossen 1943, Aminoff 1988). And this brings us back to the functioning of the eyes and the paranormal. The common experience of fainting, as well as the experiences of those who have survived sudden cessation of heartbeat, all reveal that the eyes are more sensitive to the effects of oxygen starvation than the brain.'

'How can you say that?' asked Thomas.

'Fainting is a common experience. It is actually an experience of a short period of loss of consciousness caused by a temporary extreme slowing, or actual cessation of heartbeat. People reporting their experiences of fainting often report that everything went dark, grey, or black, just before they lost consciousness. This is often called a black-out, and is used incorrectly by some people as an expression for loss of consciousness. What these people are actually saying is that everything went black because their vision failed before they lost consciousness due to oxygen starvation of their heads. This is hardly surprising, because the light sensitive cells of the retina need more oxygen than do the cells of those parts of the brain needed for perceiving the sensation of light, or those parts of the brain generating consciousness. This experience is the same as the experience of darkness reported by people who tell of their near-death experiences due to cardiac arrest, a situation where the heart either stops beating altogether, or beats so abnormally that it no longer pumps blood. A woman once reported a near-death experience caused by a cardiac arrest where she also described loss of vision before loss of consciousness.'

> Suddenly, 1 was gripped by squeezing chest pains, just as though an iron band had been clamped quickly around the middle part of my chest and tightened. My husband and a friend of ours heard me fall and came running in to help me. I found myself in a deep blackness, and through it I heard my husband, as if he were at a great distance, saying, "This is it, this time!" And my thoughts were, "Yes, it is." (Moody 1976, page 27)

'This woman's experience of darkness was a good example of what we were just talking about.'

'But I always thought that people undergoing near-death experiences always saw tunnels, or passed through tunnels.'

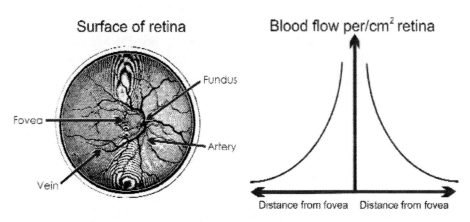

Figure 3.3 Blood flow per unit area of retina tissue is related to the inverse square of the distance from the fovea.

'Most people only see darkness, or pass through darkness, but some do see tunnels. And the explanation for the experience of passing through a tunnel, or seeing a tunnel, during a near-death experience is also rooted in the functioning of the eyes. Studies of the total flow of blood within the retina reveal the flow of blood to the tissues of the retina is highest in the central part of the retina called the fovea, which is also the focal point of the cornea and the lens, and decreases rapidly as the distance from the fovea increases (Alm 1973) (figure 3.3). But there are light sensitive nerve cells all over the retina, and all these cells consume equally large amounts of oxygen. The consequence of these two factors is that the central retina around the fovea is more resistant to the effects of oxygen starvation than are the parts of the retina further from the fovea. Tissue oxygen starvation is caused by either a reduction in the flow of blood to that tissue, or a reduction in the amount of oxygen within the blood flowing to that tissue, or a combination of both these factors. All studies on the effects of oxygen starvation reveal that with increasing degrees of oxygen starvation, a person first notices a narrowing of the visual fields due to oxygen starvation causing failure of the functioning of the outer parts of the retina. This causes an effect similar to looking through a tunnel, which is why it is called tunnel vision. Even more profound degrees of oxygen starvation cause failure of all the retina, and all the person sees is darkness. Recovery of normal retina function due to restoration of normal oxygen supplies to the retina occurs in the reverse order – the person first sees only darkness, then has tunnel vision, after which the visual field returns to normal again (Rossen et al 1943, Liere 1963, Duane 1966). A good example of this is revealed in the story of a man who nearly died.'

I knew I was dying. ... Then I was suddenly enveloped in this black cloud and went through this tunnel. I emerged from the other end in a white light which had a soft glow. There was my brother who had died three years previously. I attempted to go through a doorway, but my brother was blocking my view and wouldn't let me see what was behind him. Then I saw what was behind him. It was a bright angel. An angel of light. (Rawlings 1979, page 69)

Thomas had listened patiently up till now, but this last passage aroused him, 'Okay, if you tell me as a doctor that the myriad forms of oxygen starvation can give rise to a tunnel – darkness – tunnel – normal visual field experience, then I believe you. You've explained the mechanisms clearly and convincingly. But the man in this report saw an angel and his deceased brother. These visions were definitely something from the life after death awaiting this man. You can't explain this away. So the cause of this man's experience was most likely spiritual rather than the explanation you offered.'

'Sorry to disappoint you there Thomas,' said Ben with an insufferably smug look that said quite the opposite, 'but the functioning of the brain and the eyes explain his visions of an angel and his deceased brother extremely well too.'

'Oh?'

'Indeed. This man was dying, and suffered such a degree of oxygen starvation that even though he did not lose consciousness, his brain function was severely affected. The severe degree of oxygen starvation causing this man to nearly die caused his vision to fail before he lost consciousness. This was the blackness of which he spoke. Subsequent development of disorganized electrical activity in his brain due to epilepsy caused by brain oxygen starvation (Gastaut 1961) activated temporal lobe structures within his brain, arousing memories of his deceased brother (Gloor 1982), as well as the vision of an angel (Dewhurst 1970), together with activation of his visual cortex to arouse the experience of bright light (Dobelle 1974). Another explanation is that the bright light, and the angel, were possibly visions caused by his pupils being wide open at the time.'

'I realize that random electrical activity in the brain due to epilepsy is a bit like massive electrical shocks administered to the brain. So I can understand that epileptic activation of the temporal lobe could cause these visions of his deceased brother and the angel, and that epileptic activation of his visual cortex may have caused his experience of bright light. But how could you say that his vision of bright light as well as of the angel might also have been due to wide open pupils?'

'Oh that's easy. One of the effects of severe oxygen starvation is to cause widening of the pupils. Light can only enter the eyes through the pupils. The human pupil can be as small as one millimetre in diameter, or as large as ten millimetres. The pupil is a circle, so you can easily calculate the difference in the amount of light admitted into the eyes by these two pupil diameters.' Ben proceeded to perform a small calculation on a scrap of paper. 'See Thomas, a ten millimetre wide pupil will admit about one hundred times more light than a one millimetre wide pupil! This means a person whose pupils are much wider open than the pupils of other people in the same room will see everything bathed in bright light, simply because more light enters their eyes through their wide open pupils. This is the special bright and wonderful light, the bright light that does not hurt the eyes, that is sometimes described by people reporting their death-bed and near-death experiences!'

'I believe you. But what about the angels?'

'Easy. The focal depth of eyes with wide open pupils is small. This means people with wide open pupils can clearly see people upon whom they focus their eyes, but everything else is a blur. So a person with abnormal brain function and wide open pupils due to severe oxygen starvation will see everything bathed in a bright light, and persons upon whom they do not focus their eyes will be blurred and seen as vague beings of light, or angels of light. There is a good example of the seeing of bright light, as well as seeing wonderful beings of light, provided by a woman dying of heart failure after a difficult childbirth in the Mother's Hospital, in Clapton,

London, during 1923 CE. The obstetrician of this dying woman reported how the woman revived after a short period of unconsciousness.'

Suddenly she looked eagerly to one part of the room, a radiant smile illuminating her whole countenance. Oh, lovely, lovely, she said. I [the obstetrician] asked, What is lovely? What I see, she replied in low, intense tones. What do you see? Lovely brightness – wonderful beings. It is difficult to describe the sense of reality conveyed by her intense absorption in the vision.

Subsequently she had other visions among which a vision of a recently deceased sister.

But then she turned to her husband, who had come in, and said, You won't let the baby go to anyone who won't love him, will you? The she gently pushed him to one side, saying, Let me see the lovely brightness. (Barrett 1986, pages 10-17)

Ben continued, 'The hospital matron was also present, and reported further.'

Her husband was leaning over her and speaking to her, when pushing him aside she said, Oh, don't hide it; it's so beautiful. (Barrett 1986, pages 10-17)

Ben looked triumphantly at Thomas. 'These two passages reveal that the presence of her husband before her eyes blocked her vision of the lovely brightness, as well as her vision of wonderful beings, something which could only happen if the brightness was due to light entering her eyes. No-one else reported seeing a lovely brightness in the room, nor did anyone else report seeing wonderful beings. So the only way this woman could see a lovely brightness due to light entering her eyes under these circumstances, was due to her pupils being wider open than those of the other people in the same room, and the wonderful beings were merely the other out of focus people in the room!'

'Okay, okay … I'll admit you've explained it all again,' grumbled Thomas. 'Even so, I don't think you'll be able to explain the aureoles surrounding the heads of saints that easily.'

'I'll first define what most people mean by the human aura. Most people who believe in the reality of the human aura say they see an aura of light around every human. This aura has two main parts: a vague grey mist surrounding the body and extending to a distance one to three centimetres from the body surface, and a colourful aura of light surrounding and extending up to a meter from the surface of the body. This coloured aura is larger in sunlight, and shrinks in the dark. These are the properties of the human aura as determined by those claiming the ability to see this aura. And all these properties of the human aura are explained very well by the optical imperfections of the normal human eye.'

'I don't see how, when you consider that only very few people are able to see the aura.'

'Thomas, do you mean to tell me you actually believe some people are gifted with some wondrous ability to see aureoles of light, or auras of light surrounding the, human body?'

'Er, yes I do, but it's an extremely rare ability.'

'Then tell me how you explain the ability to see this aura.'

'I'm not entirely sure, but it must be due to an ability to sense and see a refined type of emanation from the human body.'

'Fascinating Thomas. But if these gifted people see the human aura with their eyes, then they are seeing the human aura with light. This would mean that everyone should be able to see this aura, and you should be able to photograph this aura, because these are normal properties of light seen with the eyes. Yet most people cannot see the aura, and you cannot photograph the aura, which means the aura has nothing to do with light which we see with our eyes. So how do these people perceive the human aura? Any other ideas?'

'Then they must perceive it with the third eye.'

'A third eye? We've spoken about that before. Unfortunately for that idea, people simply do not possess a third eye. As I told you before, anatomists have made extremely detailed and accurate studies of the human body for more than three hundred years. Yet nothing even resembling a third eye has ever been found.'

'Aha, but the third eye is a perceptive organ of the soul. As such it is immaterial, and hence invisible to anatomical studies.'

'An interesting idea Thomas. So if this third eye is an immaterial aspect of the soul, then it would be unaffected by diseases affecting the body, because the soul is unaffected by diseases and injuries affecting the body.'

'Yeees ... That's true,' responded Thomas cautiously.

'Now there are a lot of courses and books teaching people how they can train themselves to see the human aura. I've seen a lot of them here today at this paranormal fair. The paranormal departments of many bookstores also abound with such books. So the ability to see auras is apparently able to be acquired by training. Now if this is the situation, then why don't blind people train themselves to see auras with the abilities possessed by this third eye? After all, this immaterial, or spiritual third eye should be unaffected by the many eye diseases causing blindness. If blind people could train themselves to see human auras with their immaterial third eye, they would be able to see the auras of people. This would be wonderful. They would have regained a form of sight! But none of the millions of totally blind people alive today ever says they can see an aura, and none of the countless millions of totally blind people who lived in the past ever claimed this ability either. There are also no courses teaching blind people to see auras. So how do you explain this absence of an ability to see the human aura by blind people, when this ability is a supposedly trainable aspect of the functioning of the immaterial third eye?'

'I can't,' was the somewhat despondent reply. Suddenly Thomas had an idea. 'Perhaps people do use their physical eyes to see auras, but the eyes of some people are able to perform some subtle transformation of the immaterial and invisible energy of the aura into visible light. This would explain why blind people cannot see auras, why auras cannot be photographed, why not everyone can see auras, and also how it is possible to train yourself to see auras.' Thomas looked very pleased with himself and his answer, and rewarded himself with a large sip of beer.

'Well reasoned Thomas – for a believer in the paranormal that is. However, the functioning of the optical system of the human eye does all the things you described without any invisible and immaterial forces, subtle energies, or strange vibrations in higher spheres being required at all! I've already drawn the basic structure of the eye which also shows the optical system. The cornea does most of the focusing of images on the retina – about 70% – while the lens behind the pupil does the remaining

Spherical aberration with wide pupil

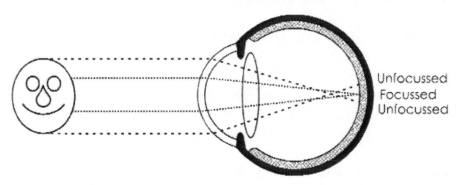

Figure 3.4 Light passing through the centres of the cornea and lens is focussed on the retina. Spherical aberration causes light passing through the edges of the cornea and lens to be focussed at a point before the retina. The result is that the centre of the face is seen clearly, and the outer edge of the face is seen as a hazy mist – the etheric aura.

finer adjustment. However the optical system of the human eye is an imperfect optical system. One of the main reasons for the imperfections of the human eye is the type of lenses in the optical system of the eye. The cornea and the lens are a type of lens called spherical lenses, which means they are shaped like a slices from the surface of a ball. Spherical lenses are prone to a number of optical aberrations, such as spherical distortion, chromatic aberration, and coma. These are the main causes of the perception of the human aura.'

As Ben paused to take a sip of beer, Thomas asked, 'What do you mean by spherical distortion, chromatic aberration, and coma?'

'I'll start with spherical distortion. A lens focuses light at a certain distance from the lens – this is the focal length of the lens. You would think that the focal length of a lens is the same for light passing through each part of the lens. But this is not true in the case of spherical lenses. Light passing through the edge of a spherical lens is focused at a shorter distance from the lens than is light passing through the centre of the same lens (figure 3.4).'

'Fascinating ... but what has that to do with seeing auras?' responded Thomas.

'Just this. When you look at something through a narrow pupil, light only enters the eye through the centres of the cornea and lens. The result is that both the centre as well as the edges of the image focused on the retina are sharp, and all parts of that which is being looked at are seen clearly. But when you look at something through a wide open pupil, light passes through the edges of the cornea and lens, as well as through the centres of these two lenses. Light passing through the centres of these lenses is focused sharply upon the retina, but light passing through the edges of these lenses is focused at a point before the retina. The result of these effects is that a person with wide open pupils sees that the image of what they are looking at is sharply focused in the centre, but has vague blurred edges – an effect similar to a vague mist surrounding these images. This mist is called the etheric aura by some people, but has nothing to do with the immaterial properties of the things being looked at. It is merely an effect due to the optics of the human eye (figure 3.4).'

'Hmmn ... I'm beginning to see what you mean about the human aura, and the optics of the human eye. But what about golden aureoles and multicoloured auras of light?'

'Golden aureoles ...' said Ben slowly. 'Yes, golden aureoles are also explained by spherical aberration together with chromatic aberration. Tell me Thomas, what happens when you pass a ray of white light through a prism?'

'The prism splits the light into the different colours of the rainbow, because glass and other transparent materials bend the different colours of light to a different degree. But what has that got to do with eyes and seeing golden aureoles?'

'Just this, the edge of a lens has much the same shape as a prism, which is why the edge of a lens also bends the different colours of light to a different degree (figure 3.5). This effect is less noticeable in the centre of the lens which is more or less straight on both sides. Now a prism and a lens bend violet light to a greater degree than indigo, than blue, than green, than yellow, than orange, than red light. When you look straight at something through narrow pupils, you mainly use the central part of the lenses of your eyes, and so most of the light is not split into its component colours. But when a person looks at something through wide open pupils, the light not only passes through the centres of their lenses, but also passes

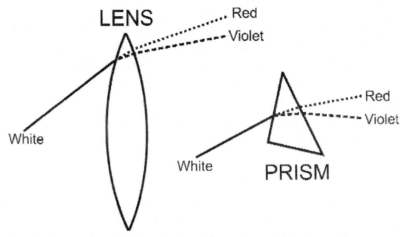

Figure 3.5 A prism shaped piece of glass splits light into its component colours, because violet light is bent more than indigo, than blue, than green, than yellow, than orange, than red light.

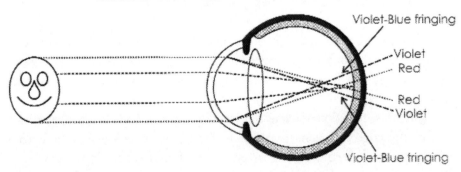

Figure 3.6 When looking at an object or face relatively far away, light enters the edge and centre of the cornea and the lens as parallel rays. But spherical and chromatic aberration causes light entering the edge of the cornea and lens to be focused and split into its component colours at a point in front of the focal point of light entering the centres of these lenses. The effect is a violet-blue fringe seen around objects and faces – the violet-blue aura of holiness.

through the edges of their lenses where it is split into its component colours. When you study this situation, you realize that a person with wide open pupils will most likely see relatively distant people and objects surrounded by a bluish-violet glow (figure 3.6). However, a person with wide open pupils will see relatively nearby people and objects surrounded by a reddish-yellow glow (figure 3.7). This latter is the golden aureole that may be seen around the heads of people, and this is the origin of the golden aureoles painted around the heads of saints and other holy persons by medieval painters.'

'I see what you mean,' was the enthusiastic reaction of Thomas. 'This explains the visions of the golden aureoles perfectly. But why do only some people see them, and how can you train yourself to see them?'

'Training is possible, and is directed to doing two things. The first priority is to relax and allow your pupils to widen, so as to make use of the

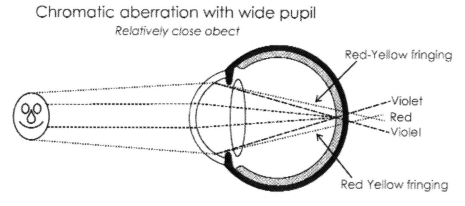

Chromatic aberration with wide pupil
Relatively close obect

Red-Yellow fringing
Violet
Red
Violet
Red Yellow fringing

Figure 3.7 When viewing a face or object relatively close to the eye, light passing through the central parts of the cornea and lens is focused on the retina. However, the different colours present in light passing through the edges of the cornea and lens is not only split into its component colours, but because the face or object is relatively close to the eye, light passing through the edges of the cornea and lens is focused at a point behind the retina. The resulting effect is that the face or object is seen clearly, but surrounded by a reddish-yellow fringe – the golden aureole of sainthood.

Chromatic aberration with wide pupil
Looking through corner of eye

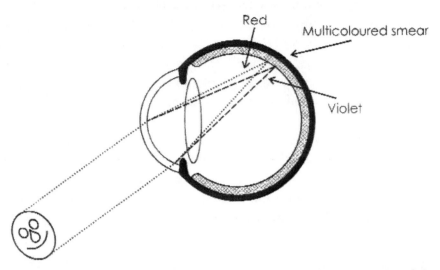

Figure 3.8 When looking at people or objects through the corner of the eye with widened pupils, chromatic aberration causes light entering the eyes from the edge of the image to be seen as a multicoloured smear surrounding the image focused on the retina – the multicoloured human aura.

spherical and chromatic aberration from the edges of the cornea and lens. The second objective is to gain some control over the ciliary muscle, which is a circle of muscle surrounding the circumference of the lens in the eye. When a person looks at an object or text close to their eyes, this muscle tightens, causing the lens to become thicker, so shortening the focal length of the optical system of the eye, allowing the person to read text, or see objects near to the eye. Tightening the ciliary muscle does not only cause the lens to become thicker to enable visual accommodation to view nearby objects, but also enhances the prism effect of the edge of the lens. Furthermore, tightening the ciliary muscle around the lens also lengthens the front-to-back visual axis of the eyeball (Drexler 1998, Mallen 2006), lengthening the path of light before it impinges upon the retina, so increasing the separation of the different colours of light before they impinge upon the retina. Pupil diameter and ciliary muscle function are normally totally unconscious, but a person can train themselves to gain a degree of conscious control of these muscles. People who train themselves to tighten their ciliary muscles at the same time as they widen their pupils, maximally exploit these deficiencies in the optical system of the human eye to better see halos and aureoles of coloured light. People born with abnormally shaped corneas, as well as nearsighted people, have eyes where these optical deficiencies are maximal without any training at all. This is why some of these people are born with a natural ability to see aureoles of coloured light.'

'Okay, okay, I believe you. But what about the large multicoloured auras with bands, jets, and rays of colour some people claim to see?'

'Oh that's a product of another property of lenses,' replied Ben. 'The ability to see coloured rays, jets, and bands of coloured light is an extension of what I've already told you. A narrow ray of light passing through the centre of a lens is focused to a point. But when a narrow ray of light passes at an angle through the edge of a lens, the ray of light is no longer focused to a point, but smeared out into a jet like the tail of a comet. The tail of a comet is also known as the coma of a comet, and coma is the name of this particular optical aberration of lenses. So if you look at something indirectly so that the light enters the eye through the edges of the cornea and lens, coma and chromatic aberration effects are maximal, causing the different colours to be smeared over the retina without overlaying much of the image of that which the person is observing through the centre of the lens (figure 3.8). This means multicoloured bands, jets, and rays of light due to coma effects can be seen, as well as aureoles and halos due to chromatic aberration. These effects are all enhanced in nearsighted people, in people born with abnormally shaped cornea's, and in people who train themselves to widen their pupils while at the same time tightening the ciliary muscles in their eyes. At this paranormal fair today, I particularly observed those people with an ability to see auras doing just these things. The nearsighted aura viewers had their glasses off, lying next to them on the table, while most of the aura viewers looked indirectly at the people whose aura they were viewing. You can reproduce every one of these effects for yourself by looking at people and objects through a large magnifying glass, moving it forwards and backwards, rotating it, and so on.'

'So that's why you paid special attention to the people looking at auras. I do believe you've explained multicoloured auras of light and aureoles of golden light very well. But if the human aura is just due to optical defects in the eyes, why don't we see auras of light surrounding people in photographs?'

'The answer is that manufacturers of photographic lenses work hard to eliminate all these optical aberrations from their lenses with special types of glass and lens shapes. This is why most good camera lenses never manifest these abnormalities, which is why you don't see auras of light surrounding people on photographs.'

'Oh ... After hearing all this, I can't believe there's anything magical or spiritual about the human aura, bright lights and tunnels any more. They're all just manifestations of the functioning of the eyes.' Thomas paused, looked somewhat despondent. 'Ah well, a few illusions less. Even so, I don't believe you can explain the paranormal away that easily.'

Ben grinned, 'Oh I don't know about that. But first things first. My throat is parched after all this talking. Let's have another beer.'

Chapter 4

Burn witch! Burn!

'Ah … that's cooled the overworked vocal cords down a bit,' sighed Ben as he placed his half-empty glass on the table. 'There's nothing like irrigating your throat with a cooling stream of ice-cold beer to revive the ability to speak.'

'You're right there,' responded Thomas with an equally satisfied sigh. 'It certainly helps you view this depressing cafeteria in a different light too. However, you dragged me to this paranormal fair with the evident intention of destroying my belief in the paranormal. I enjoyed the way you explained how the optical properties of the eyes and the functioning of the body explain all the emotional and paranormal properties attributed to the eyes. Nonetheless, I don't believe it's possible to explain all paranormal and supernatural phenomena with simple physical facts like you did with the eyes.'

'Now I hear you mixing terms such as paranormal and supernatural. So tell me Thomas, what do you exactly mean by these terms?'

'I believe I mean same things with these terms as you do. By the term paranormal, I mean events, phenomena, or perceptions which cannot be explained with natural laws. Things fitting this category are paranormal sensory phenomena such as telepathy, clairvoyance, seeing or foretelling the future, and seeing the past, as well as paranormally influencing events on this world with wondrous healings, the power of prayer, or force of mind. When I use the term supernatural, I generally mean things which are beyond, or originate on a different plane of existence than this physical or natural world, such as God, gods, angels, ghosts, evil spirits, demons, incubi and succubi, or the paranormal influence these entities exert on our world, and other paranormal forces in general.'

'Do you actually truly believe in all of these phenomena and entities?' asked Ben.

'Well, to be truthful, I'm not entirely sure I believe in them all,' was the uncertain reply.

'Why not?' asked Ben, 'Do you believe in an eternal, but invisible, immaterial, all-knowing, all-pervading, and all-powerful God, creator of this universe in which we exist?'

'Of course I do.'

'Do you believe in Satan, who is a fallen angel and the lord of all evil (Bible, Job 1:6-8, Mark 4:15 & Koran 2:208), as well as other malignant demons that are mentioned throughout the Bible and the Koran?'

'Yes.'

'Do you believe in the reality of the archangel Gabriel (Bible, Daniel 8:16-25, Luke 1:26 & Koran 19:17), as well as the reality of other angels also mentioned throughout the Bible and Koran?'

'Yes, the Bible tells me they exist.'

'Do you also believe each person has an eternal, invisible, and immaterial soul?'

'Yes,' replied Thomas equally rapidly, but now with a slight tone of caution in his voice.

'Do you also believe the soul somehow continues to exist for eternity in some sort of invisible, immaterial, universe inhabited by the souls of the deceased?'

'Yes ... ,' was the even more cautious response, 'but what's your point?'

'Just this ... We cannot see, smell, taste, touch, sense, or detect the reality of any of these things in which you believe, even though you say they are real and are all around us. This means you admit to believing in an invisible and immaterial universe thickly populated by any number of equally invisible and immaterial entities, such as the innumerable souls of deceased humans, God, angels, Satan, and demons. Moreover, this means you also admit to believing in all sorts of powers possessed by these entities, and in the supposedly inexplicable events resulting from their influence on this world. You claim these things are real and inexplicable by normal physical laws, which means they are paranormal. So what you have told me, is that you also believe in paranormal phenomena in general, such as: foretelling the future by paranormal means, telepathy, clairvoyance, psychokinesis, in witchcraft, sorcery, astrology, the evil eye, the power of prayer, miracles, and so on.'

'I guess so, although I wouldn't say I believe in all these things. However, there are a lot of things that cannot be explained by normal physical laws, and it's just these things that provide additional proof for the reality of God.'

'Oh dear, Thomas, it sounds dangerously like your God is a "God of the gaps",' laughed Ben.

'What do you mean by a "God of the gaps"?'

'It's a method of argument first used more than a hundred years ago by a Scottish evangelist and writer called Henry Drummond (1851-1897 CE). The argument is quite simple – if something cannot be explained by natural phenomena and the normal laws of physics, then God must have caused it. Examples of gaps in human knowledge are rife. For example, we cannot explain exactly how evolution of species occurs, or even how life came into being. In the past, meteorological and electrical phenomena were also inexplicable. Therefore, many people said, and sometimes even still say God is responsible for all these things. These were, and are gaps in our knowledge. But these gaps are disappearing at an ever increasing rate. Accordingly, to use God as an explanation for gaps in knowledge is increasingly nonsensical, because a gap, or a hiatus in knowledge of a particular subject, simply means we do not know the explanation as yet. So this argument neither proves nor disproves the existence of God in any way. In any case, God is supposedly unknowable, inscrutable, and inexplicable, implying that the reality of God is a matter of inspiration and faith rather than physical proof.'

'I agree wholeheartedly. The reality of God is impossible to prove by direct physical measurement,' was Thomas's firm reaction. 'Even so, that does not mean God is any less real. However let's return to the subject of paranormal phenomena. Supernatural entities and phenomena are proof of an impalpable immaterial reality co-existing with our world. Accordingly, because God, the angels, the souls of the dead, and the world inhabited by the dead are supernatural, this means that paranormal phenomena are also indirect proof of the reality of God. We also know that the use of these paranormal abilities is restricted to God, the angels, and the true prophets of God, because the Bible tells us that false prophets must be killed (Bible, Deuteronomy 18:20, Ezekiel 14:9-10). What's more, the laws given by

God to Moses are very definite on the matter of humans using paranormal abilities – those practicing paranormal arts such as sorcery or witchcraft, are disobeying the laws of God and must die (see also Bible, Leviticus 20:27)!'

Thou shalt not suffer a sorceress to live. (ASV Bible, Exodus 22:18)

'You're quite correct about the Old Testament. Even the Christians in the New Testament are very clear on this matter. Witchcraft is condemned along with many other crimes,' added Ben.

Now the works of the flesh are manifest, which are these: fornication, uncleanness, lasciviousness, idolatry, sorcery, enmities, strife, jealousies, wraths, factions, divisions, parties, envyings, drunkenness, revellings, and such like; of which I forewarn you, even as I did forewarn you, that they who practise such things shall not inherit the kingdom of God. (ASV Bible, Galatians 5:19-21)

'Ah, but this passage only means Christianity disapproves of witchcraft, sorcery, and the use of paranormal abilities, but does not condemn practitioners of these arts to death in this world as did the laws of Moses in the Old Testament!' said Thomas.

'That's what you think. Unfortunately for that idea, medieval Christian church fathers regarded witchcraft, sorcery, and the use of paranormal abilities in general as a form of turning away from Christianity, a form of heresy akin to apostasy, because practitioners of these arts no longer followed the teachings of Jesus. So they looked to the teachings of Jesus in the Bible on how best to protect good Christian society from these vile creatures. As you know Thomas, the Bible is a complete book with advice on every imaginable subject, so not surprisingly these good holy men found useful advice from an ever-merciful Jesus.'

Abide in me, and I in you. As the branch cannot bear fruit of itself, except it abide in the vine; so neither can ye, except ye abide in me. I am the vine, ye are the branches: He that abideth in me, and I in him, the same beareth much fruit: for apart from me ye can do nothing. If a man abide not in me, he is cast forth as a branch, and is withered; and they gather them, and cast them into the fire, and they are burned. (ASV Bible, John 15:4-6)

'The message in this passage was clear. It was a shining light in the darkness, giving guidance to those burdened with the onerous task of eradicating a depraved unwillingness exhibited by some people to follow the will of Jesus. Jesus said that those refusing to follow him were to be treated as withered vine branches, and cast into the fire! The merciful, but strict protectors of Christian religious virtue in the Middle-Ages were obedient servants of Jesus. They interpreted this passage literally to mean that not only false prophets, heretics and apostates, but also witches and sorcerers, as well as those who used other supposedly paranormal abilities, not only richly deserved death, but also that Jesus required them to be burnt to death! So it was that many tens of thousands of unfortunate wretches died painful and horrible deaths by being burnt alive during the witch hunting craze raging in Western Europe during the late Middle-Ages. The luckier ones died by other means, or were strangled by merciful executioners before burning. This attitude towards the paranormal is still prevalent in fundamental Christian practice, although it no longer extends as far as officially sanctioned killing of practitioners of paranormal arts.'

'I know. That's why they tried stopping us at the entrance. However, I've never heard of witch-hunting crazes in Islamic lands. Do you know anything more about the official Islamic attitude to the paranormal than what you told me earlier?'

'Well Thomas, it just so happens I do know something ...' Ben paused for effect as well as more beer. 'As I've said before, Islam is actually very similar to Judaism and Christianity in this regard. This is not really surprising when you consider it is the same God. So just as with these other religions, God also inspired the prophet Mohammed to tell the followers of Islam that those who practice paranormal arts are doomed to eternal torment in the life after death.'

And follow that which the devils falsely related against the kingdom of Solomon. Solomon disbelieved not; but the devils disbelieved, teaching mankind magic and that which was revealed to the two angels in Babel, Harut and Marut. Nor did they (the two angels) teach it to anyone till they had said: We are only a temptation, therefore disbelieve not (in the guidance of Allah). And from these two (angels) people learn that by which they cause division between man and wife; but they injure thereby no one save by Allah's leave. And they learn that which harmeth them and profiteth them not. And surely they do know that he who trafficketh therein will have no (happy) portion in the Hereafter; and surely evil is the price for which they sell their souls, if they but knew. (Koran 2:102)

'And the followers of Islam were warned of the evil perpetrated by some of the practitioners of the paranormal arts, such as witchcraft,' continued Ben.

*Say: I seek refuge in the Lord of Daybreak
From the evil of that which He created;
From the evil of the darkness when it is intense,
And from the evil of malignant witchcraft, (Koran 113:1-4)*

'So?' responded Thomas. 'All you've shown is that the followers of Islam believed in the reality of the paranormal, and were particularly afraid of witches and sorcerers who used their powers for evil ends.'

'Quite right,' said Ben. 'Only God also told the followers of Islam that there were some things only God was meant to know.'

Say (O Muhammad): None in the heavens and the earth knoweth the Unseen save Allah; and they know not when they will be raised (again). (Koran 27:65)

'I've mentioned this concept before, because it has such profound implications. Simply put, it means that to gain knowledge of things otherwise unseen and unknown, by means of fortune-telling, astrology, telepathy, clairvoyance, and so on, is to do something reserved for God alone, because only God can know the unseen and unknown. You may think this is trivial, but actually, this means practitioners of any of these and other paranormal arts are committing a serious form of heresy equivalent to apostasy by setting themselves up as equals to God (Al-Fozan 1997, pages 38-50). According to Islam, there is only one punishment for heretics such as these – death!'

> *Narrated Ikrima: Ali burnt some people and this news reached Ibn Abbas, who said, "Had I been in his place I would not have burnt them, as the Prophet said, 'Don't punish (anybody) with Allah's Punishment.' No doubt, I would have killed them, for the Prophet said, 'If somebody (a Muslim) discards his religion, kill him.'" (Bukhari 52:260)*

'This report from the words and deeds of Mohammed is really strange. God's final prophet, Mohammed, considered it presumptuous to the point of sacrilege to burn people alive, because the burning of heretics and other sinners in fire was a privilege reserved for God alone. Nonetheless, these odious and degraded heretics and apostates richly deserved death, and killing their mortal bodies was a holy task, because it meant the eternal torment of their souls in the fires of hell could begin that much sooner! However, Mohammed wanted them killed in ways less sacrilegious than by fire (Koran 5:33). Of course all true believers were glad to assist God in this divinely ordained duty, especially if it meant the possessions of these people were forfeit to those performing this holy work! Ah Thomas, the ways of God are inscrutable. Perhaps, as the Koran tells us, we were created only to worship God?'

> *I created the jinn and humankind only that they might worship Me.*
> *I seek no livelihood from them, nor do I ask that they should feed Me.*
> *Lo! Allah! He it is that giveth livelihood, the Lord of unbreakable might. (Koran 51:56-58)*

'Could it be Thomas that the sole purpose of humankind is to function as self-replicating biological devices generating worship for God? This concept begs the question of what strange and intangible benefit does God derive from worship from humans, regardless of whether they be Jewish, Christian, or Islamic? After all, most worship consists of paeans of praise to the power and glory of God – a nauseating form of grovelling and obsequious subservience detestable to all proud and independent persons. Viewed at this way, worship is a manifestation of monstrous conceit from God. You would expect God to be far above any desire for such loathsome fawning abasement as worship, because God is supposedly the eternal, all-knowing, all-pervading, and all-powerful creator of us all and the universe in which we live …'

Thomas looked unhappy, but brightened as he responded, 'Ah but you forget one important and basic fact – the mentality and nature of humankind. Even your mentality cannot be compared with that of God. After all, God is the eternal, all-knowing, all-pervading, and all-powerful creator of this universe. We are merely the lowly creations of God, given glimpses of the nature of God, but in no way comparable in mentality or power to God. So it is simply impossible to truly know why God requires us to worship. All we can do as believers in the reality of God is to follow the instructions of God as revealed to us by the prophets, and Jesus, the Son of God. But we, and in particular you, are digressing. What about the paranormal? Do you believe in the reality of the paranormal?'

'I'll be very blunt Thomas. I don't believe that any of the so-called paranormal abilities people claim to be real, are any more than manifestations of natural laws and the functioning of the human body.'

'That really is blunt, and very definite. But on what evidence do you base such a blunt and definite opinion? I can't think of a single civilization, population group, tribe, or race who have never believed in the reality of paranormal phenomena. Belief in the paranormal is so ancient, so deeply ingrained in the human psyche, that there must be some substance to this belief. So how can you just ignore millennia of belief, simply waving it away by saying it doesn't exist?'

'Really Thomas … The fact that many billions of people throughout millennia of human history believed in the reality of the paranormal is no proof of the reality of the paranormal. It's merely proof of their belief in the paranormal, but not proof of the reality of the paranormal. However, what you say is quite correct; belief in the reality of the paranormal is very widespread, even among people inhabiting the secular, modern, technologically advanced countries of North America and Western Europe. Nearly all people living in these countries believe in paranormal things such as God, ghosts, evil spirits, the human soul, survival of the human soul after death, as well as punishment and reward of the human soul after death (Taylor 2003). More than half of all people in these countries also believe in the reality of paranormal phenomena such as telepathy, clairvoyance, foretelling the future, astrology, premonitions, Tarot, precognitive dreams, out-of-body experiences, and so on (Utts 1991, Moore 2005, MORI 1998). What is more, even though the use of paranormal abilities is forbidden by God, at least one quarter of all people living in these countries claim to have personally experienced paranormal phenomena such as premonitions, extrasensory perception, telepathy, etc (Utts 1991, MORI 1998). So belief in, and actual experience of paranormal phenomena, are very widespread indeed. Furthermore, if you look at the number of books and courses teaching people to develop their paranormal abilities, you realize people not only believe in the reality of paranormal abilities, but also believe these paranormal abilities are latent in everyone, because they can be trained and developed. I think you'd agree with me on these things Thomas?'

'Yes I would Ben. But why don't you believe in the reality of the paranormal when confronted with all this evidence?'

'Well Thomas, I agree that people believe in the reality of the paranormal, and that experience of apparently paranormal observations and events is quite common. Nonetheless, as so many people before me have said; "If paranormal observations, experiences, and events are so common, then scientific study of these phenomena should easily and conclusively prove their reality to all sceptics." The Society for Psychical Research in London, England, was founded in 1882 CE, and the American Society for Psychical Research in Boston, USA, was founded in 1885 CE. Similar societies were also founded in other countries. For more than one hundred years, a simply enormous amount of intensive research by capable members of these societies, as well as by many outstanding scientists, has never proven the reality of paranormal phenomena, despite these phenomena apparently being so common and widespread (Utts 1991, Alcock 2003). In fact, the disappointing conclusion to more than a century of research is the equally disappointing realization that while many people believe in, and have experienced apparently paranormal phenomena, the reality of these phenomena remains unproven. Some people claim there may be something, an unexplained anomaly, which would explain paranormal phenomena, but even this is unproven (Utts 1991). Can you explain this?'

Thomas thought for a moment. 'Could it be that paranormal abilities and phenomena are so subtle, and so refined that they cannot manifest in the harsh and critical surroundings of sceptical scientific investigation? This is probably the most likely explanation for the failure to find evidence of these phenomena under the sceptical and unfriendly conditions of a scientific experiment.'

'Interesting idea Thomas. But it is not a new idea though. In fact this idea is commonly invoked by believers in the paranormal as an explanation for the total failure to find consistent experimental proof for paranormal phenomena. Yet we know these phenomena are apparently very common, and paranormal senses are apparently also able to be trained. So why don't people use paranormal senses in much the same way as we use sight, or hearing?' A mischievous glint appeared in Ben's eyes. 'If you could use paranormal phenomena in these ways you would always know what other people thought of you, language would become irrelevant, because you would always know what other people thought and wanted, you could always buy a winning lottery ticket, and you would never have an accident because you would be able to avoid it in time. In addition to these considerations, our world is actually an enormous natural laboratory for testing the reality of paranormal senses. After all, if paranormal abilities are so common, and people believe they can also be trained, then why don't blind and deaf people develop their possibly latent paranormal abilities to compensate for their sensory deficiencies. Consider this: there are about eight million totally blind people now alive on this world, as well as more than seven million totally deaf people now alive on this world (Woerlee 2003, appendix 2). If these people trained their paranormal abilities, then their handicaps would be nowhere near so serious. However, I've never heard of blind or deaf people being any more gifted in the use of paranormal abilities than other people. Nonetheless if paranormal abilities are so common and widespread, then why aren't they used in these, and many other even more unimaginable ways? After all, humans have had tens of thousands of years to develop societies in which the use of these supposedly common paranormal abilities would be commonplace. All these things indicate to me that paranormal phenomena and abilities simply do not exist.'

'There is another possible explanation Ben. Perhaps God prevents blind and deaf people developing these abilities, because God has forbidden the use of paranormal abilities to all except officially approved prophets. Accordingly, blindness and deafness are a trial which these people must undergo for the good of their immortal souls.'

Ben laughed, 'Oh no Thomas, not that old one again! Let's be logical. Even though God does forbid the use of paranormal abilities, about one quarter of the Western European population has experienced paranormal events. So it is quite evident that God does not prevent the manifestation of such abilities in normal humans, even though they are forbidden. This makes nonsense of the argument that God prevents blind and deaf people from using paranormal abilities to overcome their disabilities.'

'But Ben, all these things you talk about are uses of paranormal abilities for personal gain or benefit. Everyone knows that paranormal abilities are not supposed to be used for personal again or benefit!'

'That's strange, if you read the paranormal experiences most people report, then you realize they are nearly all very personal. Many paranormal experiences are dreams or premonitions of events, illnesses, or accidents occurring to the persons making these reports, or to their near family members. Many gamblers attribute a streak of luck to paranormal abilities, and gamblers most definitely work for personal gain. Throughout thousands of years, magicians, sorcerers, shamans, witch-doctors, astrologers, oracles, and fortune-tellers have exploited their paranormal abilities for very personal gain to earn a living, or even become very wealthy. And you tell me that you are not supposed to use paranormal abilities for personal benefit, financial or otherwise, when this is precisely what everyone does, and has done for tens of thousands of years. So tell me, who says you are not supposed to use paranormal abilities for personal gain? Is it God? This is very unlikely, because the God of the Jews, the Christians, and of Islam, permits one quarter of the Western European population to experience paranormal events for just these purposes of personal benefit or profit. Perhaps this ruling not to use paranormal abilities for personal gain comes from other gods, such as the gods of ancient Greece, from the gods of the Eskimos, the gods of ancient Persia, the gods of India, the gods of the Australian aboriginals, or those of the Aztecs? Do angels regularly descend to earth with flaming swords to order humankind not to use paranormal abilities for personal gain? Or is this simply good advice from little green men from outer space visiting our humble little planet? You tell me.' And Ben looked expectantly at Thomas as he took another sip of beer.

Thomas looked uncomfortable, but did his best, 'I understand what you mean about the use of paranormal abilities for personal purposes or personal benefit. I also don't know where this general knowledge about not using these abilities for personal gain came from. However, you can't deny that some things cannot be explained.'

'Tell me what things can't be explained?'

'For example, like dreams foretelling the future. Some people dream of something, and the next day it happens. Or they dream of something happening further in the future, and that something happens exactly in the way they dreamed. How do you explain things like that?'

'Oh, that ...' Ben looked unimpressed. 'Easily explained. A normal human lives to about 70 years of age, and dreams four to six times each night. Take the least number of dreams per night, then this means a person dreams four times a night, 365 days of the year for 70 years, which is 4 x 365 x 70 dreams: a total of at least 102,200 dreams during 70 years of life. This is a spectacular number, but most people don't remember all their dreams. When I examine how many dreams I actually remember, even temporarily, then I come to a figure of about one dream per three months which I partly or fully remember. If I extrapolate this to a period of 70 years, this means I fully or partly remember about four dreams per year, which is a total of 280 fully or partly remembered dreams during my life. This means I remember about one in every 365 dreams. For the sake of simplicity, I'll say I remember about one in every 400 dreams. Our world has a population of six billion people (6,000,000,000). Each of them dreams four times a night, which means a total of 24 billion (24,000,000,000) dreams per 24 hours. Let us assume each of them remembers only one in every 400 dreams, which means 24,000,000,000 divided by 400 dreams, or

60 million (60,000,000) dreams are remembered partly or fully each 24 hours. This is a very inflated figure, because it includes the dreams of babies and small children, isolated desert inhabitants, mad and demented people. These are people whose dreams are never heard, or told to others. So let's ignore two thirds of these dreams, which leaves a total of 20 million (20,000,000) partly or fully remembered dreams per 24 hours on this world. The subject matter of most dreams is quite random, or related to things affecting the dreamer. Pure statistical chance means that some of these 20 million remembered dreams per 24 hours will bear some relation to future events undergone by one of these dreamers, and that very rarely one or more of these dreams will correspond exactly to a future event. Dreams coming partly true are remembered because they predicted a future event. Those very rare dreams which exactly foretell a future event are considered wonders, and are told and retold, simply because they are so rare. As for dreams that never come true, human nature ensures they are quickly forgotten. All this means you don't need to invoke paranormal abilities to explain dreams foretelling future events, just enormous numbers of remembered dreams and chance.'

'Well, I must admit your explanation sounds plausible ...' said Thomas hesitantly. 'But what about the situation where you decide to telephone a certain person, and just as you are about to begin, that person rings you. I, and a number of people I know, have had this experience a number of times. The coincidence is so amazing at times that it can't have anything to do with chance. According to me, this is clear proof of telepathy, or another form of mutual subconscious paranormal contact resulting in a simultaneous wish to communicate with each other. How could you explain it otherwise?'

'As usual, with statistics,' was the rapid reply. 'Thomas, I assume you have a circle of family, friends, and acquaintances with whom you communicate by telephone every now and then?'

'Yes. I do.'

'Likewise, each of these persons you know also has a circle of family, friends, and acquaintances with whom they too communicate by telephone every now and then. Every now and then, for whatever reason, you may decide to make a telephone call to one of these persons. After all, you are more likely to think about making a telephone call to someone you know rather than to a total stranger. Such a circle of family, friends, and acquaintances with whom you are likely to make a telephone call is not composed of thousands of people, but is limited at most to about one hundred. The same is also true for each of the persons you know, and each of these persons may also decide to make a telephone call to one of the people they know. Occasionally two persons within such a circle of family, friends, and acquaintances decide to make a telephone call to each other at about the same time. The result is usually surprise and a feeling of wonder expressed at both ends of the telephone line. Nearly everyone has experienced this phenomenon at least once. But this experience isn't the result of some form of unconscious mutual paranormal communication, but the product of chance coincidence, simply because the chance of two people who know each other wanting to communicate with each other is quite high.'

'I must admit, your explanation does sound reasonable – again,' was the reluctant response of Thomas, 'although I must confess it leaves me with a gnawing sense of dissatisfaction. It's too cold, too sterile, too emotionally unsatisfying.'

'Statistics probably is a dissatisfying explanation for someone looking for wonders, even though it corresponds perfectly with the facts and requires no paranormal mediation. However Thomas, I do believe you're looking for paranormal wonders to support your belief in other paranormal beliefs such as God, the human soul, and life after death. Perhaps that's why this statistical explanation is so dissatisfying to you, even though I think it's perfect.'

'I guess so. Still, it remains unsatisfying. And then there's something else, I once read a book by an Israeli psychic called Uri Geller in which he told of a man called Michael Bentine who was an intelligence officer in the English Royal Air Force during World War 2. One of the tasks of Michael Bentine was to brief bomber crews about their missions prior to their departing. Sometimes during a briefing he saw the face of a crew member change into a skull, and knew the man would die on that mission (Geller 1987, chapter 13). How would you explain that observation with statistics?'

'Very simply – I won't,' and Ben continued, 'but I will surprise you with a revelation of my own. I know a woman who sometimes sees the actual faces of people she knows turn into skulls, or photographs of their faces change into skulls, and these people died shortly afterwards of serious illnesses. Yes, it's stories like these that almost make you believe in the paranormal.'

Thomas spluttered, 'How can you say almost, when you've got proof like this? Okay, it's anecdotal evidence, not experimental evidence from a laboratory, but if there's enough of it, and it's confirmed again and again, anecdotal evidence is also good evidence. So how do you explain the observations of these people?'

Ben smiled, drank some more beer, and replied in an irritatingly cheerful voice. 'I think I'll be insufferable again and explain these observations.'

'I'm listening ...'

'These stories require a bit of background, and are a bit different in some aspects. I'll start with the elements common to both stories – perception of dysfunction and disease, as well as the human sense of smell. When you look at people, you don't only notice the state and condition of their clothing, haircut, makeup, jewels and so on. You also look at how they walk, how they talk, how they sound, their intonation, and numerous other facets of their physical appearance and presence. You usually do this quite unconsciously to arrive at conclusions such as: this person is exhausted, this person is afraid, this person is sick, this person is happy, this person is clever, and so on.'

Thomas looked somewhat impatient, 'Yes, yes, I know all this ...'

'Tsk, tsk, such impatience,' said Ben in an irritating tone. He was enjoying himself with his long-winded explanation. 'To begin with, consider the situation of the Royal Air Force crews sent from England to bomb German cities and factories during World War 2 (1939-1945 CE). They flew their missions at night over well defended territory, with as a result one in twenty airplanes was shot down per bombing mission. The crew of shot down bombers had very little chance of surviving, because only one in ten bomber crew members survived being shot down. Each bomber crew member flew an obligatory 30 missions. So you realize that with a one in twenty chance of being shot down during each bombing raid, and a one in ten chance of surviving being shot down, the mortality among the aircrew of these nightly bombing raids was appallingly high. Records show that out of every 100 aircrew starting a 30 mission tour of duty: 55 were killed, 18 were injured or captured, and only 27 ever survived a tour of duty unscathed or without being captured (Davis 2006). The men flying for the Royal Air Force Bomber Command knew this. They knew they were likely to die, and were exhausted with the effort to keep functioning at a high level in spite of their fears. Michael Bentine knew that anxious and exhausted aircrew made more mistakes, and so were less likely to survive a mission. Experience and unconscious observation enabled Michael Bentine to select men whose level of anxiety and dysfunction was such that they were less likely to return. So it is not all surprising he eventually could unconsciously predict the likely demise of a crew member of one of these nightly bombing missions. This brings us to the observations of sick people made by the woman known to me. She evidently unconsciously realized from the appearance, gait, and behaviour of these people that they were unwell, even seriously ill. The details of such observations can be entirely unconscious, but the conscious interpretation is that the person they observe is seriously ill. So much for direct conscious and unconscious observation of people ... Now we can get onto the fascinating subject of human body odour, the human sense of smell, and the information we derive from our sense of smell. This really is fascinating.'

'Just a moment,' interrupted Thomas, 'but what has body odour got to do with this?'

'Everything young man, everything. We humans actually use our sense of smell to assess the bodily odours of our fellows more than we realize. When most people think of human odours, they think of primary odours such as of faeces, urine, grimy unwashed persons, bad breath, garlic, goat meat, the fishy smell of some women, and sweat. Many physicians go further. They recognize that some serious diseases are associated with typical body odours: the musty rat smell of people with liver failure, the uriniferous aroma of people with end stage kidney failure, the acetone (nail polish remover) odour of people with severe unregulated diabetes, the stench of pus on the breath of a person with a lung infection or a sinus infection, and so on. As a physician sometimes dealing with very sick people, I know you can smell a person who is seriously ill – they exhale a typical, but very evident odour – the odour of serious illness. I know of no other way to describe it, but it is typical.'

'Fascinating, but what has all this got to do with paranormal perceptions such as we're talking about?'

'Well here it comes. All I've spoken about up till now are conscious perceptions of odours. Humans can also consciously and unconsciously respond to body odours emitted as a result of anxiety or fear. For example, some people talk of the smell of fear, or actually say they can smell fear. Fascinating studies have been performed by asking volunteers to watch a frightening film during one session, and then to watch a neutral or happy film during another session. During these sessions the volunteers placed sweat absorbent pads in their armpits to absorb the sweat produced. These pads were collected at the end of each session and sealed in bottles. A set of totally unused pads were sealed in a third set of bottles. Volunteers were presented these three different bottles in a double blind manner, and requested to score whether the smell was from anxious or happy persons, or had no smell at all. The smell of sweat from anxious people was chosen correctly more often than not (Akerl 2002, Chen 2000), proving that some people really can smell the scent of fear in others. Even more surprisingly, other experiments show that inhaling air containing the sweat smells of anxious people actually improves human cognitive performance (Chen 2006), as well as exaggerating the normal human startle response to sudden random sounds (Prehn 2006), even though the experimental subjects could not even consciously perceive the scents causing these reactions! So we humans really are primitive creatures, and then we say in our arrogance that we are elevated above the base and primitive instincts of animals!'

'Amazing! I always thought that scent of fear story was just a popular myth. So you mean that Michael Bentine could predict the future demise of these unfortunate young men from their odour of anxiety and fear, as well as from their behaviour?'

'I think he actually used just their bodily appearance and behaviour, as well as his knowledge of the statistics of death among aircrew. After all, these intelligence briefings were done in cigarette smoke filled rooms, crowded with anxious aircrew, and at a time in English history when many people bathed only once or twice in the week. So I doubt very much whether he could ever have distinguished the odour of one particular man from another. However, he could have done this had he had personal talks with some of these men who subsequently died. All this demonstrates that people use a combination of behavioural signals, including body odour, to determine fear or anxiety. This brings us to the prediction of the imminent deaths of people by the woman I know.'

'Are you going to claim this woman could detect the smell of imminently lethal diseases?'

'Indeed I am,' replied Ben. 'A lot of research with an apparatus called a gas chromatograph, which is an apparatus to separate and analyze the different chemicals in gases, reveals that many diseases change the spectrum of chemicals present in exhaled air. This is why some people with sensitive noses can smell whether a person is sick by smelling their breath, something many doctors already know from their daily clinical practice. For example, bacteria are the cause of many lung infections. Each different bacterium causing a lung infection interacts with infected lung tissue to generate a spectrum of chemical products unique to that bacterium. Some of these chemical products are present in exhaled air, and this results in a spectrum of chemicals in the exhaled air of people with a bacterial lung infection unique for the type of bacteria causing the infection. You could call this unique spectrum of chemicals the chemical signature of that specific bacteria. These unique chemical signatures can be analyzed by an automated gas chromatograph – sometimes called a "chemical nose" – to accurately diagnose lung tuberculosis (Phillips 2007), as well as to diagnose and differentiate between various different bacteria causing lung infections (Lai 2002). Severe disease also changes the metabolism of the body such that the body starts breaking down fat and other tissues, so changing the spectrum of chemicals present in exhaled air from people with many different sorts of cancer (Hietanen 1994), heart disease (Weitz 1991, Mendis 1995, Phillips 2003), inflammatory bowel diseases such as ulcerative colitis (Sedghi 1994), or diabetes (Phillips 2004), into the characteristic odour of oxidative stress – the absolutely distinctive odour of sick people. So it is not surprising that many doctors can tell a person is severely ill simply by smelling the breath of a sick person. Particular types of cancer generate specific volatile chemicals which are also present in exhaled air. This brings us to the surprising fact that the presence, as well as the severity of lung cancer (Phillips 2003a, Natale 2003, Machado 2005, Poli 2005), and breast cancer (Phillips 2003b, McCulloch 2006), can be specifically diagnosed by analysis of the spectrum of chemicals present in the exhaled breath of persons with these diseases. And if you think this is really surprising, then listen to this! One group of doctors trained ordinary mongrel dogs to recognize the smell of lung or breast cancer in exhaled air samples collected from patients with these conditions. These dogs were trained to indicate which exhaled air samples were from people with lung or breast cancer, by lying down in front of the exhaled air samples from people with cancer. After training, these dogs were presented in a double-blind fashion with exhaled air samples from people totally unknown to them. Some exhaled air samples were from people with lung cancer, some were from people with breast cancer, and other exhaled air samples were from healthy persons. The accuracy of these dogs with the exhaled air samples from these unknown people was startling. They were 99% accurate in identifying the exhaled air of people with lung cancer, and 88% accurate in identifying the exhaled air of people with breast cancer (McCulloch 2006)! Now if dogs can detect these things, then some people may also be able to detect these things, either consciously or unconsciously.'

'There's only one possible reaction to that last snippet Ben ... Wow!'

'I do believe you're beginning to understand where I'm going with this rather lengthy explanation,' said Ben.

'You're obviously talking about the woman who saw the heads of some people she knew, or people she saw, change into death's heads, after which these people died shortly afterwards. From what you tell me, she could have realized these people had severe and rapidly lethal illnesses from both their behaviour, as well as their odour.'

'Exactly! And it gets even stranger ... One of the persons where she saw this happen, did not even know they were ill at the time! So this woman unconsciously made an accurate diagnosis of that person's lethal illness based on that person's behaviour and odour.'

'Even so,' was the pensive response from Thomas, 'why did Michael Bentine and this woman we're talking about, see the faces of people shortly to die transform into skulls? Such a transformation has nothing to do with what you've just been telling me.'

'Oh, that ... It's a phenomenon similar to synaesthesia. Synaesthesia is a curious neurological phenomenon where some people unconsciously translate one sensation into a totally different conscious sensation. For example, some people are able to see smells, hear light, smell sounds, taste colours, hear shapes, see vibrations, and so on and on (Ramachandran 2003). In the specific example of this woman, if she saw a man who would soon die of lung cancer, she would not consciously say to herself, "Hmm, this man has the unsteady gait of a sick person, his face shows evident signs of weight loss due to disease, his complexion reveals changes due to hormone production by cancer, his breath reeks of chemicals typical of those resulting from abnormal metabolism caused by severe illness, and I also smell other chemicals on his breath typical of lung cancer. Therefore this man has advanced lung cancer which will shortly cause him to die." Instead she would unconsciously perceive, integrate, and understand all the above. Her unconscious understanding of the information derived from her equally unconscious perceptions would express itself in the conscious vision of his head transforming into a death's head, and from this vision she would conclude that this unfortunate man would die very shortly. This is the mechanism by which she, and others like her translate their understanding of unconscious perceptions of something important but indescribable into their consciousness. It is similar to people having a "gut feeling" about something which later comes true. So these stories of faces transforming into death's heads is no more than a rather gruesome example of a sort of synaesthesia. I do believe this explains the death's head visions of these people very well.'

'I think so too,' said Thomas in a rather crestfallen tone. 'Amazing to see how something you believe to be convincing proof of the paranormal can also be explained with natural laws and the functioning of the human body. But what about all the other paranormal phenomena people speak of at this paranormal fair? Can they also be explained in this way?'

'They can,' was the very definite response. Ben continued, 'When you carefully examine each of all these phenomena thought to be paranormal, you always find you can explain them with just these things – natural laws and the functioning of the body. Now you might say that each of these individual explanations is not proof the paranormal does not exist, and you would be correct. However, when you can collectively explain all the phenomena believed to be paranormal with natural laws and the functioning of the body, the chance that paranormal phenomena really exist disappears altogether. What most people call paranormal, the things they believe are paranormal, and the experiences they believe are paranormal, are called paranormal simply because their causes are not understood.'

Thomas looked dissatisfied. 'So what you are actually saying is that the ages-old belief in the paranormal is simply a fantasy, a product of deficient understanding of natural laws and the functioning of the human body.'

'Absolutely!' was the immediate response.

'But God and the human soul do exist! They are also supernatural because they are unseen and intangible. And I know with a total and absolute certainty they do exist! They are real! How do you explain this?'

'I look at it this way Thomas – God is supposed to be the eternal, unseen, all-knowing, all-pervading, and all-powerful creator of the universe as well as humankind. All these things indicate the supernatural nature of God. But the total absence of proof for the reality of paranormal phenomena does not constitute proof of the non-existence of God, because such a God can continually change the nature of the universe, so making proof one way or the other impossible. So the absence of proof for the paranormal is not proof God does not exist. God may exist, even though what many people believe to be paranormal is no more than an ages-old collective fantasy!'

Thomas looked relieved. He looked at his watch, drank the rest of his beer, and said, 'I've seen enough here. Shall we go?'

'Good idea. I've also seen what I wanted to see.'

Outside the Groenoord Hall, the mid-afternoon sun shone brightly. It was even warm. The Christians protesting against the presence of the paranormal fair were gone, and in their place was a small vociferous group of young men waving Islamic Revival Brigade placards and banners. There were the usual slogans, "Burn in hell all apostates and sorcerers!" "Allah is great!" "Mohammed loathes Kaffirs!" A young man with a magnificent black beard declaimed loudly through a megaphone, and as they passed, Ben and Thomas heard him roar, 'The holy books of the Jews and the Christians are vile corruptions of the will of Allah as expressed to Abraham, Moses, and Jesus. Deranged scribes under the influence of evil jinn's perverted the pure will of Allah into books the Jews and the Christians call holy – books pandering to the filthiest tastes of pornography loving whoremongers!' The small group of listeners murmured. Some waved their fists, yelling, 'Infidel dogs! Allah is great!'

'Huh!' said Thomas and Ben in unison as they stopped to listen further.

The young man warmed up to his subject, 'Yes, whoremongers and incestuous pornographers! These "holy books" of the Jews and the Christians glorify prostitution, incest, and pornography, or at least regard it as quite acceptable. Firstly, they falsely slander Abraham, the first true follower of Islam, by saying he married his half sister Sarah (Bible, Genesis 20:12)! As true followers of Islam we know this to be an abominable and filthy travesty of the reality. Abraham was inspired by God. He could never have married his half sister. This would have been a gross transgression of the divine laws of marriage as revealed in the Koran, the true and eternal word of God (Koran 4:22-23)! I will give you another example of the degraded morals of followers of the false and aberrant religions called Judaism and Christianity. These vile creatures have a perverted version of the story of Lut (Koran 15:57-74, 29:26-35), whom they call Lot. Consider the horrid way they pervert the story of the family of Lot in their "holy books" (Bible, Genesis 19:1-38). They say that while living in the city of Sodom, Lot offered his two virgin daughters to a mob of inflamed homosexual rapists outside his house, saying they could do with them as they wished (Bible, Genesis 19:8). Unbelievable! Such a deed would be unthinkable for a normal loving and concerned Islamic father! Later, after Lot and his daughters escaped the destruction of Sodom, they claim these same daughters made Lot drunk, had sex with him, and even had children by him (Bible, Genesis 19:30-36). Mind-boggling! Jews and Christians write these nauseating slanders about Lot and his daughters, and then call him a holy man loved by God! They are actually proud of these filthy calumnies! Let us look at another example of Jewish and Christian degeneracy. Samson is a hero of the Jews and Christians, who also claim he was loved by God. He was actually no more than a violent psychopathic murderer, who besides performing "holy deeds" such as slaughtering inordinate numbers of Philistines – a race of people despised by the Jews – also killed and looted the possessions of 30 innocent people simply to pay his gambling debts (Bible, Judges 14, 19), as well as whoring in Gaza (Bible, Judges 17:1). Oh my brothers, not only do the Jews and Christians consider rape, incest, prostitution, and murder to be perfectly acceptable activities, but they also honour character traits such as the lowest forms of treason and betrayal. The high regard in which a treacherous prostitute called Rahab is held by Jews and Christians is a good example. They regard Rahab as a heroine, because she betrayed the city called Jericho in which she lived. Her treachery enabled the bloodthirsty Jewish army to slaughter all the inhabitants of Jericho: men and women, young and old, oxen, sheep and donkeys – all that lived. After completing this veritable orgy of slaughter, the holy army of Judaism plundered and razed the city to the ground (Bible, Joshua, chapters 2 and 6). Oh yes my brothers, all these are holy people – exemplary and proud pillars of virtue for Jews and Christians alike! Such a lust for murder and plunder! Such a high regard for rape, incest, and prostitution! All these things are inconceivable to true followers of Islam.' He paused, cleared his throat, and wiped flecks of foam from his beard and mouth. His listeners applauded enthusiastically, yelling, 'Whoremongering infidel dogs! Allah is great!'

'This fellow is really a good demagogue,' said Ben to Thomas in a soft tone. 'Let's listen to more of what he has to say. I'm enjoying this. Savage and inflammatory rhetoric. Good stuff. A real art form. He certainly knows his work.'

Thomas had no time to reply as the young man recommenced his tirade. 'This is more than enough to illustrate the perverted way Jews and Christians regard the modesty of their women, their tolerance of all manner of sexual perversions, as well as their love of violence. All these things are beyond the comprehension of peace-loving, modest, and chaste followers of Islam such as we. But if you think what I have told you is the sum of their depravities, steel yourselves, for the so-called "holy books" of these degenerate followers of deviant religions also contain, and even promote pornography! Yes, you heard me correctly – pornography! In fact, the most vivid and lasciviously pornographic descriptions of sexual acts are to be found in these so-called "holy books". Incredible! Just listen to this extract from the Jewish and Christian holy books ...' He read enthusiastically from a tattered piece of paper.

How fair and how pleasant art thou, O love, for delights!
This thy stature is like to a palm-tree, And thy breasts to its clusters.

115

I said, I will climb up into the palm-tree, I will take hold of the branches thereof: Let thy breasts be as clusters of the vine, And the smell of thy breath like apples, (ASV Bible, Song of Songs 7:6-8)

'A brazen, shameless, and shockingly explicit public description of his intended sexual acts! Immodesty like this would be impossible in a virtuous Islamic world.' He shook his head theatrically. 'Shocking, shameless, brazen … Words fail me. But even this is as nothing when you read the story of the two nymphomaniac sisters called Oholah and Oholibah. The "holy books" of the Jews and Christians contain luridly explicit descriptions of their sexual exploits with Egyptians, Assyrians, Babylonians, Chaldeans, and others (Bible, Ezekiel, chapter 23). There is even a graphic and lewd description of Oholibah's fond memories of her dissolute youth.' His eyes flashed as he read again, loudly and with great gusto, from his piece of paper.

There she lusted after her lovers, whose genitals were like those of donkeys and whose emission was like that of horses. So you longed for the lewdness of your youth, when in Egypt your bosom was caressed and your young breasts fondled. (NIV Bible, Ezekiel 23:20-21)

The young speaker paused for effect. 'My brothers, these are but some of the filthy and pornographic contents of the so-called "holy books" of the Jews and the Christians. Terms such as filthy and pornographic are totally inadequate to describe the unbelievable shamelessness of Jews and Christians. Of course, all these abominations come as no surprise to chaste followers of Islam, for God has told us that "most of them are perverse transgressors" (YA Koran 3:110). Even worse, their own holy books tell these degraded slaves of delinquent religions, that these very same "holy books" were corrupted by the scribes penning the words of their prophets!'

How can you say, "We are wise, for we have the law of the Lord," when actually the lying pen of the scribes has handled it falsely? (NIV Bible, Jeremiah 8:8)

The listeners cheered as the speaker read this passage. Flecks of spittle and foam flew from his mouth, speckling his beard white as he concluded, 'My brothers in Islam, these Jews and these Christians are abhorrent and degenerate creatures. They know the filthy and corrupt nature of their holy books, yet they are proud of every one of these loathsome abominations, singing their praises as they gladly wallow in the mire of their sordid perversions! As followers of the one true and uncorrupted religion, we know Jews and Christians to be willingly misguided followers of lewd and fraudulent "holy books". We know them to be truly "people of the fire", for that is their fate in the glorious afterlife – eternal torment in the blazing furnaces of hell! Oh my brothers, the rule of Holy Islamic Law cannot come soon enough to cleanse the world of all such pathetic and degenerate whoremongering pornographers! Let their bellies seethe and burn with the fruit of the Zaqqum tree as they undergo the torment of boiling water in the hell reserved for such sinners (Koran 45:43-48)! Pray that the light of Islam will one day illuminate the whole world! Pray this happens soon!' At these words the group of listeners went berserk, jumping up and down, waving their fists and chanting in unison, 'Allah! Allah! Sharia! Sharia! Sharia!'

'Fascinating stuff Ben,' said Thomas, 'but a gross travesty of Biblical reality. That citation from Jeremiah was ripped totally out of its original context.'

'You're right there Thomas, but it made breathtakingly good rhetoric. That fellow really is a talented rabble-rouser. As I said earlier, I enjoy seeing a real expert at work. Shall we go and get a beer at one of the café's along the New Rhine Canal? The sun is shining and it's still warm.'

'Sounds like a wonderful idea to me.'

Ben and Thomas mounted their bicycles and departed just as the call to prayer sounded from the Mare Mosque, '*Allahu Akbar Allah, Allahu Akbar Allah, Allahu Akbar Allah, Allahu Akbar Allah ...*'

'Oh no!' moaned Ben. 'This means we won't be able to sit outside. Café's aren't allowed to serve anything on terraces outside for at least an hour during Islamic prayer times. Ah well, a cold beer inside is almost as good ...'

Chapter 5

The blind can see!

The misshapen bundle of rags sitting next to the door of the café rattled some coins in a dirty plastic container. Ben looked carefully. The bundle of rags was a woman of North African origin. Her sallow blotched face was made all the more hideous by unequally bulging and diverging eyes coated with a white film of scar tissue. She was blind. Almost unseen in the fading light, a baby with sunken half-closed eyes, wrapped in a thick and greying threadbare quilt, lay listlessly in her other arm. Dried snot crusted the baby's upper lip, and a fresh supply of the same green-yellow slime oozed slowly out of one nostril. A pungent smell of unwashed human combined with urine wafted in Ben's direction as the woman rattled her coins ever more insistently.

Ben threw a few coins into the container as he and Thomas walked into the café. The beggar glared balefully, and spat a particularly juicy grey-yellow gobbet in their direction, narrowly missing Thomas's shoe as he tore his eyes away from a queasy contemplation of her repulsive visage. Inside, the normally busy café was half-empty. Ben turned towards Thomas, and asked, 'So Thomas, what did you think of the performance of the hideous hag outside?'

'How can you say that?' retorted Thomas. 'The poor woman is obviously blind and destitute.'

'Oh, I don't doubt that for one moment either. But out of all the places on this busy street, she chose to sit next to the door of this particular café. Strange isn't it? I've also read in the local newspaper that the café owners in this part of town are engaged in a fairly bitter competition with each other. Knowing this, I ask myself how much this woman is being paid to sit next to the door of this particular café. Paying a filthy beggar with a gaggle of snotty, sickly children to sit next to the entrance of a café is a well-known trick to discourage customers (Personal Note). Look, this café is almost half-empty at a time it would normally be full.'

'You can't be serious Ben? Who would stoop to tricks as low that?'

'Enemies and competitors are the only ones who would be interested enough. Who else?' Ben continued, 'However, the fact the woman is a beggar, and evidently a follower of Islam does raise two interesting points: the noble Islamic concept of Zakat, and the fact she refused to speak to us. In fact her only communication with us was to rattle her money and spit.'

'She certainly did appear ungrateful – and the way she glared at us ...'

'Ah, the poor woman isn't helped by her repellent appearance. Even so, she still manages to earn a living just because of it. Moreover, as a follower of Islam she feels free to offend all customers of the café who pass her. After all, they are all people intending to consume alcohol, which is forbidden by the Koran (Koran 5:91), as is associating with Jews, Christians such as you, and unbelieving dogs such as me.'

> *O ye who believe! Take not the Jews and Christians for friends. They are friends one to another. He among you who taketh them for friends is (one) of them. Lo! Allah guideth not wrongdoing folk. (Koran 5:51)*

'So a devout follower of Islam may trade with peoples who do not follow Islam, live in countries ruled by people following other religions, but is forbidden to have any further relations with them. Effectively this means that devout followers of Islam really want nothing to do with the people of the Jewish or Christian lands in which they live, even though they may derive considerable material benefits from being there. That's prejudice Thomas.'

'Oh Ben, I've heard that one before,' laughed Thomas. 'I've read the Bible too. Just look at the laws of Moses. They're very similar. These ancient laws of Moses forbid Jews forging friendships or deeper relations with non-Jews. Nothing new there.'

> *When Jehovah thy God shall bring thee into the land whither thou goest to possess it, and shall cast out many nations before thee, the Hittite, and the Girgashite, and the Amorite, and the*

Canaanite, and the Perizzite, and the Hivite, and the Jebusite,
seven nations greater and mightier than thou; and when Jehovah
thy God shall deliver them up before thee, and thou shalt smite
them; then thou shalt utterly destroy them: thou shalt make no
covenant with them, nor show mercy unto them; neither shalt
thou make marriages with them; thy daughter thou shalt not give
unto his son, nor his daughter shalt thou take unto thy son. (ASV
Bible, Deuteronomy 7:1-3)

'Well Thomas, if we're going on like this, then Christians are just as bad. All the early church leaders discouraged association with people of religions other than Christianity. It's all so depressingly similar.'

Whosoever goeth onward and abideth not in the teaching of
Christ, hath not God: he that abideth in the teaching, the same
hath both the Father and the Son. If any one cometh unto you,
and bringeth not this teaching, receive him not into your house,
and give him no greeting: for he that giveth him greeting
partaketh in his evil works. (ASV Bible, 2 John 1:9-11)

Ben sighed, 'What you hear in these passages is a manifestation of behavioural control unconsciously designed to keep people under the control of a particular religion or sect. A summary of the basic principles reads like this: don't associate with non-believers in your religion, insult them and say they are inferior, demonize their leaders and their prophets, say they all will go to hell, while at the same time idolize your leaders and prophets. These are all common elements in the sad passages above. The cantankerous crone outside is but a small manifestation of these attitudes.'

'Heeey ...' was Thomas's surprised reaction. 'This is the first time I've heard you being anything else other than cynical. Are you taking medication, or have you undergone some sort of epiphany?'

'None of those. The sight of extreme manifestations of belief further distorting and handicapping the lives of those already crippled by disease, as with the harridan outside, is something unspeakably sad. But Thomas, we're in a café, and we haven't even ordered a beer yet! Barman – two beers!'

Ben and Thomas sighed contentedly as they sat at a table, glasses of foaming amber fluid before them. Ben drank deeply, emptying half his glass, wiped foam from his mouth, 'Just what I needed. Now we can return to a discussion of one of the nobler aspects of Islam – Zakat.'

Thomas looked surprised. 'What do mean by Zakat? And noble? I thought you didn't like Islam.'

'You might be surprised. I've told you before, Islam is a religion which has done much to ennoble and empower its followers, just as Judaism and Christianity have ennobled and empowered their followers. However, a major problem with these three religions, is that extremely literal interpretations of the holy texts of these religions can stifle free thought, encourage bigotry, and result in behaviour degrading and demeaning to all that is noble and worthy of praise in the followers of these religions.' Ben paused, 'But I'm digressing as usual. In Islam, as in some other religions, earthly material possessions are considered to be temporarily given to their owner to be used while alive. Those privileged to enjoy excess are therefore expected to share this excess with others less fortunate. Zakat is the obligatory levy imposed by Islam on this excess, and indeed the payment of Zakat is one of the five pillars of Islam. These five pillars are actually very reasonable, and well worth knowing. As for Zakat, there are also several passages in the Koran enjoining believers to pay Zakat.'

> *But those of them who are firm in knowledge and the believers believe in that which is revealed unto thee, and that which was revealed before thee, especially the diligent in prayer and those who pay the poor due [Zakat], the believers in Allah and the Last Day. Upon these We shall bestow immense reward. (Koran 4:162)*

'But don't confuse Zakat with charity. Charity is something you give voluntarily in excess of the Zakat. Curiously, there is no control exercised on collection of the Zakat. Payment of Zakat is entirely voluntary, and made directly to the recipients. These are generally orphans, poor travellers, beggars, people in debt because of the necessity to feed their families, slaves who want to buy their freedom, and works intended to propagate Islam. Nowadays Zakat is a religious underpinning of social welfare programs in Islamic lands.'

'Fascinating Ben, but how much Zakat are followers of Islam expected to pay?'

'Even that has been determined. Zakat is payable on income and property surplus to the requirements of the family, and is presently fixed at 2.5% for money, and about 10% for agricultural produce (Wikipedia).'

'Sounds a lot like Christian tithing to me ...'

'Actually, tithing is not a Christian practice at all! Nowhere in the New Testament is there anything about the Christian Church requiring a tithe. Tithing is actually a custom taken over from ancient Judaism. After escaping from serfdom in Egypt under the leadership of Moses, the tribes of Israel wandered the deserts of the Middle-East for many years before finally arriving in Canaan, the land promised them by God. God distributed territories within Canaan to only eleven of the twelve tribes of Israel, granting no territory to the tribe of Levi, because their divinely appointed task was to function as clergy serving God. But possessing no lands of their own meant the Levites had no source of income, so God levied a taxation of one tenth, or a tithe, upon the agricultural produce of the other eleven tribes of Israel to support the Levites in their divinely appointed role as intermediaries between God and the peoples of Israel. This is the origin of the custom of tithing (see also Bible, Deuteronomy 14:22-27).'

And unto the children of Levi, behold, I have given all the tithe in Israel for an inheritance, in return for their service which they serve, even the service of the tent of meeting. And henceforth the children of Israel shall not come nigh the tent of meeting, lest they bear sin, and die. But the Levites shall do the service of the tent of meeting, and they shall bear their iniquity: it shall be a statute for ever throughout your generations; and among the children of Israel they shall have no inheritance. For the tithe of the children of Israel, which they offer as a heave-offering unto Jehovah, I have given to the Levites for an inheritance: therefore I have said unto them, among the children of Israel they shall have no inheritance. (ASV Bible, Numbers 18:21-24)

Thomas sat, hand wrapped around his beer glass, 'I'm sure Jesus intended people to tithe to help the needy, and not just because it was required by law at the time. There is even good evidence for his concern for the poor. For example, when a rich young man asked him how he could attain eternal life in heaven, he told him to sell all he had, and give the proceeds to the poor.'

Jesus said unto him, If thou wouldest be perfect, go, sell that which thou hast, and give to the poor, and thou shalt have treasure in heaven: and come, follow me. (ASV Bible, Matthew 19:21)

'Thomas, I'm not so sure Jesus was all that concerned about the needy. He was actually a bit of an egoist. Once when he was staying at the house of Simon the leper, a woman came and anointed his head with costly ointment. The apostles were affronted, saying the ointment could have been sold and the proceeds used to help the poor. The reaction of Jesus was startlingly blunt.'

But Jesus perceiving it said unto them, Why trouble ye the woman? for she hath wrought a good work upon me. For ye have the poor always with you; but me ye have not always. (ASV Bible, Matthew 26:10-11)

Thomas looked startled, recomposed himself and retorted. 'I'm quite sure Jesus didn't mean what you seem to understand in this passage. He simply meant that incidental costly gestures can also serve a holy function.'

'As you wish Thomas, but the context is such you can interpret it either way. Furthermore, I know Jesus was a somewhat intolerant egoist. So in my opinion, my interpretation is the correct one. He was just saying, "Enjoy my presence, and pamper me while you can. Don't worry about the poor, they will always be there." However, let's get back to the five pillars of Islam which I said are not only well worth knowing, but are also of some considerable interest in their own right. I'll list these five pillars of Islam for you.'

• To acknowledge that there is but one God, and Mohammed is his last and final messenger.

- To pray to God five times each day.
- To give Zakat.
- To fast during the holy month of Ramadan.
- To go on a pilgrimage to Mecca at least once during life.

Ben looked at Thomas. 'When you look at these five pillars of Islam, they are really very reasonable, as well as fascinating in their unstated implications.'

'That's your opinion,' retorted Thomas. 'I don't know what you mean by fascinating unstated implications. Very well, these five pillars do acknowledge belief in a single God, although I doubt whether Mohammed was the last and final messenger of God. For the rest they are no more than a bare statement of duties. These five pillars don't mention core Christian principles such as the mercy of God, and the forgiveness of sins committed on earth, both of which are central aspects of Christian belief expressed in all versions of the Apostles' Creed – the fundamental creed of the Christian church.'

I believe in God the Father, Almighty, Maker of heaven and earth:

And in Jesus Christ, his only begotten Son, our Lord:

Who was conceived by the Holy Ghost, born of the Virgin Mary:

Suffered under Pontius Pilate; was crucified, dead and buried: He descended into hell:

The third day he rose again from the dead:

He ascended into heaven, and sits at the right hand of God the Father Almighty:

From thence he shall come to judge the quick and the dead: I believe in the Holy Ghost:

I believe in the holy Catholic Church: the communion of saints:

The forgiveness of sins:

The resurrection of the body:

And the life everlasting. Amen.

Ben chuckled, 'Oh, oh, oh Thomas, that really is selective blindness.

That wonderful Apostles' Creed you praise so much also includes the passage: "He shall come to judge the quick [the living] and the dead." Great rhetoric, but it sounds very punitive indeed. Is judgment consistent with the forgiveness of sins? After all, if God is determined to judge, and presumably to punish those deserving of punishment, where is this much vaunted Christian forgiveness of sins mentioned a bit later in the same creed? According to me, this glaring inconsistency indicates that people usually rattle the words of this creed off without even thinking whether this creed is internally consistent.'

Thomas was silent for a moment, drank some beer, and slowly crunched a potato crisp. 'Interesting argument ... This looks like another fascinating problem for my tutors. I'm beginning to get a reputation for iconoclastic views verging on the heretical with these problems of yours.'

'I wouldn't worry about that. At least they'll remember you, which is more than you can say about some other students whose opinions and beliefs only echo those of their tutors. But let's get back to the five pillars of Islam again. You don't have to worry about internal inconsistencies in these five pillars of Islam, because they are just a statement of faith and a list of several different obligatory duties. Interestingly enough, you do detect a cult of Arabian adulation in these five pillars.'

'Really Ben, you never cease to amaze me with your totally negative views on religion. You manage to find the worst possible interpretation for just about every aspect of religion. How do you do it?'

Ben grinned, 'Talent, pure talent, and a desire for logic and consistency. As for the cult of Arabian adulation, it's not difficult to come to that conclusion at all. To begin with, all followers of Islam must go on pilgrimage to Mecca at least once during life. This is an incredible boost to the local economy of Mecca, providing the keepers and controllers of the holy places, as well as the local businesses, with enormous riches from the pilgrim trade. Furthermore, the very fact that these holy places are within Arabia, and that the Arabic peoples were chosen above all others to receive the revelations of the Koran – these things all indicate the holy and God-chosen nature of the Arabic peoples, as well as their way of life. This idea is also found in the Koran where it is explicitly stated that the Arabic people "are the best of the nations raised up for (the benefit of) men" (MHS Koran 3:110). As if this were not enough, the examples provided by the speech and deeds of Mohammed in the Sunnah are also considered to be an exemplary form of life for all followers of Islam, even though this was the way life was lived, and the way people thought in the seventh century. The way Mohammed lived, and the ways he thought while living as a prophet in the small seventh century Arabian towns of Medina and Mecca, were never directly applicable to life in other countries, even during his lifetime. And now, more than thirteen hundred years later, his way of thinking, and his way of living are even less applicable. This brings us to another aspect of Arabic adulation – the Arabic language of the revelations to Mohammed.'

'What do you mean?'

'Many followers of Islam say the true message of the Koran can only be understood in the language in which it was revealed. This was the Arabic dialect spoken by Mohammed, and is now considered to be the purest form of Arabic. Each copy of the Koran since the time it was first committed to paper has been carefully scrutinized to ensure that not one letter, not one dot or accent differs from the original. Islamic purists insist the Koran can only be understood in terms of the archaic dialect in which it was first written, even though they claim it to be a message from God containing a truly universal message applicable to all peoples and all ages. This archaic dialect undoubtedly contains assumptions and words not easily understood, even to modern Arabs, simply because language use, the way of living, and the ways of thinking have changed dramatically since the time of Mohammed. I would argue that if the Koran really is a book handed down by God to mankind with a truly universal message applicable to all peoples and all ages, then translation into other languages should not affect the fundamental truths contained within.'

'Interesting ...'

'This is why many other religions such as Judaism and Christianity are quite happy to have their books translated into other languages. Followers of these religions realize it is impractical to learn the many ancient languages such as Chaldean, Sumerian, Aramaic, Greek, Latin, as well as the many local and equally ancient dialects in which these books were first revealed. So their experts make translations in modern spoken languages using the earliest sources of these texts they can find, believing the fundamental truths contained within will withstand the ravages of translation. The holiest religious authorities of Islam, including the Custodian of the Two Holy Mosques, also realize this same principle, and have authorized the translation and the printing of the Koran in a multitude of modern languages. They too realize that the word of God as revealed in Islam should be spread in the languages of those to whom the message is brought (Koran 14:4). However, the voice of theocratic fundamentalism seems to prevail in popular opinion: still claiming the primacy of the archaic Arabic dialect in which the Koran was written. This also leads to a form of Arabic adulation, because not all people can read or fully understand this archaic Arabic dialect. All such people can do is adore the language of the Koran, saying this is the best and most holy language in which to read it, because this is the language in which God revealed his message to Mohammed, and then slavishly rely upon the authority of sometimes corrupt and self-seeking persons claiming to be able to fully understand all that is written. In this latter situation, you are obviously much better off with a competent, properly authorised translation in your own language.'

'I never looked at it that way before Ben. So that's why the woman outside spat at us, she was just expressing her disgust and loathing of people foolish enough not to believe in, and obey the message of the Koran.'

'Thomas, you've got a lot to learn,' sighed Ben. 'I think she just hates everyone because she is so horribly deformed. However, her attitude does raise an interesting point. As a severely handicapped person in a modern Western country she almost certainly receives a form of government financial support in the form of unemployment benefits, a handicapped pension, or some other form of social welfare income. So she is not entirely destitute. Furthermore, she also earns a bit of extra money by begging and discouraging people from entering café's. The money for government social welfare payments is derived from taxation levied on all earnings and financial transactions. Accordingly, this money is partly derived from taxation levied upon the sale of cigarettes, taxation levied on the sale of alcoholic beverages, taxation paid by prostitutes, taxation paid by criminals, and taxation paid on profits earned by usury, (which is interest paid on loans). This simple analysis of the sources of moneys raised by government taxation has far-reaching consequences for devout followers of Islam.

It means that any follower of Islam accepting government financial support in a modern Western country is actually accepting money derived from activities forbidden by God (see also Koran 2:219, 2:275, 3:130, 5:90-91, 30:39, Bukhari 34:297, 34:439, 58:159, 59:590, 89:284).'

> *Narrated Aun bin Abu Juhaifa: I saw my father buying a slave whose profession was cupping, and ordered that his instruments (of cupping) be broken. I asked him the reason for doing so. He replied, "Allah's Apostle prohibited taking money for blood, the price of a dog, and the earnings of a slave-girl by prostitution; he cursed her who tattoos and her who gets tattooed, the eater of Riba (usury), and the maker of pictures." (Bukhari 34:440)*

Thomas emptied his glass, grinned, 'Oh, are you saying that followers of Islam are actually sinning, and compromising the position of their immortal souls in the Islamic afterlife by accepting government financial assistance in modern Western countries?'

'Yes indeed. Their souls are certainly in jeopardy because they knowingly accept the fruits of usury (see also Bukhari 58:159).'

> *Those who devour usury will not stand except as stand one whom the Evil one by his touch hath driven to madness. That is because they say: "Trade is like usury," but Allah hath permitted trade and forbidden usury. Those who after receiving direction from their Lord, desist, shall be pardoned for the past; their case is for Allah (to judge); but those who repeat (The offence) are companions of the Fire: They will abide therein (for ever). (YA Koran 2:275)*

'So there you have it Thomas – to knowingly accept the fruits of usury, prostitution, soothsaying, and alcohol, is to disobey the injunctions of God in the Koran (Koran 3:76-78). There is only one reward for such transgressors – an eternity in the fires of hell! This is the only logical conclusion you can draw from these holy texts of Islam, together with the origin of the moneys used to pay government financial assistance in modern Western countries. Excuses from these people that they did not know government financial assistance is derived from usury, alcohol, and prostitution, are of no avail. After all, as followers of Islam living in modern Western countries, they know these countries glorify drinking alcohol, have a love of the most depraved forms of immorality and prostitution, as well as the fact that all manner of forms of usury such as mortgages and loans, are common methods of earning money. So they cannot but know deep in their hearts that they are accepting the fruits of alcohol, prostitution, and usury – all of which are clearly prohibited by God (Koran 2:275, Bukhari 58:159). You can develop this idea even further. Foreign aid, freely donated by modern Western countries to some needy Islamic countries, is also derived from the same vile and corrupt sources. Accordingly, needy Islamic countries are committing a collective sin by accepting aid from Western countries – a sin dooming their leaders and peoples to eternal torment in hell. This idea begs the question of whether people in some Islamic countries might even consider aid from non-Islamic Western countries to be a devious ploy – a devious ploy devised by the degraded spiritual heirs of murderous medieval Crusader thugs infesting these countries to drag the pure and holy followers of Islam into hell with them. Ah well, these are just a few interesting random thoughts arising in my mind as I think upon these matters. Now, let's continue with our own sinful perversions. Barman – two packets of salty crisps, and another two beers please!'

They drank in a mutual silence – a silence now and then enlivened by a desultory crunching of crisps until Ben's face lit up with a new, and possibly even more devilishly irreverent thought. 'Ah Thomas, a fascinating thought just occurred to me as I was musing on the matter of usury and the doleful fate of those followers of Islam in the afterlife who accept government social welfare assistance in Western countries.'

'Oh no! Not again!' was the demonstrative reaction delivered with an almost imperceptible grin. 'And what new sacrilegious sophistries have bubbled up in your devious brain?'

'Just think Thomas, if you carefully read the Koran, you realize that this holy book actually provides devout followers of Islam with two methods of sanctifying the proceeds of usury. If properly applied, these two methods would save those followers of Islam unfortunate enough to receive money from modern Western countries the hideous torments of hell.'

'I'm all ears Ben! Do tell. I would imagine that any such explanation could justly be termed the mother of all sophistries!'

'Actually the explanation is as simple as it is surprising. Consider, the Koran states very clearly that trade is not forbidden (Koran 2:275). However, nowhere in the Koran or the Sunnah is there any statement to the effect that trading with unbelievers is forbidden. In fact, even Mohammed himself once even bought a sheep from a man who did not follow Islam (Bukhari 34:419). Moreover, the sources of the moneys gained from an unbeliever by trade are not questioned anywhere. The principle is evident – moneys and goods obtained from unbelievers by means of trade are acceptable. So followers of Islam in Western countries who receive government social welfare could sanctify these moneys by performing some form of trade in exchange for these moneys. Of course, the goods or services offered in exchange should be of equivalent value, otherwise the exchange is usury or cheating, but not trade (Bukhari, Book 34).'

'An interesting system of thought ...' responded Thomas reflectively. 'What is your second method of sanctifying government social welfare payments?'

'It's an effective and time-honoured method. The Koran often mentions the concept of plunder, or booty gained by conquest (see also Koran 8:1, 8:41, 48:15).'

> *And much booty that they will capture. Allah is ever Mighty, Wise. Allah promiseth you much booty that ye will capture, and hath given you this in advance, and hath withheld men's hands from you, that it may be a token for the believers, and that He may guide you on a right path. (Koran 48:19-20)*

'Furthermore the Koran states that one fifth of all such booty must be given to Mohammed and his representatives as their right, as well as to aid less fortunate followers of Islam (Koran 8:41). This concept of booty clearly implies that if you conquer people by force of arms, their persons, goods, and money are yours. Yet many of these conquered people are not followers of Islam, and their wealth and chattels may very well be the fruits of usury, prostitution, sorcery, the sale of dogs or alcohol, or many of the other activities forbidden to followers of Islam. Take the case of the Jews conquered by the followers of Islam during the lifetime of Mohammed.'

> *And He brought those of the People of the Scripture [Jews] who supported them down from their strongholds, and cast panic into their hearts. Some ye slew, and ye made captive some.*
> *And He caused you to inherit their land and their houses and their wealth, and land ye have not trodden. Allah is ever Able to do all things. (Koran 33:26-27)*

'There it is Thomas – usury was very definitely one of the commercial activities engaged in by Jews at the time of their conquest by Mohammed (Koran 4:160-161). Yet Mohammed and his followers did not spurn the wealth of these conquered Jews, in spite of the fact it was acquired by usury and other forbidden activities. Instead they happily took over the responsibility of ownership of Jewish money, chattels, and land. Furthermore, they very gladly seized and enriched themselves with the wealth, possessions, and persons of others who were likewise not followers of Islam. In fact the Koran explicitly states that the possessions of the vile and degraded enemies of Islam are actually predestined as booty and reward for the conquering followers of Islam (Koran 48:19-20). The message is clear, although not explicitly stated – conquest and plunder of hell-destined unbelievers by the holy followers of Islam wondrously transforms their unholy and impure wealth, chattels, and lands into a pure state suitable for use by devout believers in Islam! Moreover, payment of moneys to followers of Islam as rightful tribute gained by prior conquest, miraculously transforms these moneys into a new state holy and pure enough for use by true believers, regardless of whether these moneys were gained by activities forbidden by God (Koran 9:29, Bukhari 59:363, 76:433)! '

'Congratulations Ben!' laughed Thomas. 'You've excelled yourself! That really is the mother of all sophistries! I can't think of any other explanation for these curious passages in the Koran. Luckily the merciful God of Christianity doesn't sanction plunder, so divinely sanctioned plunder is a uniquely Islamic phenomenon.'

'Don't you believe it!' was the almost instant retort. 'The ancient God of Israel sanctioned, and even ordered, the conquest, killing, enslavement and plundering of the designated enemies of God (Bible, Deuteronomy 3:1-7, 20:10-16, Joshua 6:24, 11:7-15). Accordingly, the God of the Jews sanctions plunder, implying that the plundered wealth, chattels, and lands are the just rewards of the conquerors.'

'But that's just the Old Testament,' said Thomas in a heated tone. 'Jesus preached a message of love and peace.'

'Oh? I always thought the God of the Old Testament was the same as the one in the New Testament. In fact, if you think deeply, you realize that Jesus and the founding fathers of the Christian Church also sanctioned conquest and plunder, so continuing this ancient tradition of divinely sanctioned conquest and plundering of God's enemies. I can even prove it.'

'Don't be ridiculous!'

'I'm not being ridiculous. I'm serious,' replied Ben. 'Saint Paul, one of the founding fathers of the Christian Church, tells us that our earthly rulers are placed above us by God, and that we therefore must obey them as we obey God (Bible, Romans 13:1-7). Accordingly to disobey a lawful government is to disobey a representative of God on Earth, which means that to disobey our governments is to commit heresy! This concept means that if our rulers tell us to conquer, torture, rape, kill and plunder, we must conquer, torture, rape, kill and plunder, because this is obviously what God wants us to do. What is more, this statement of Saint Paul implies that that governments are also free to randomly imprison, torture and kill people at will, extort incredible taxes, or cancel all government social welfare payments, because if this is government policy, then these actions are evidently also the will of God. Jesus even indirectly referred to this obedience to our earthly rulers (Bible, Matthew 22:17-22). So as you see, God does indeed approve of conquering, plundering, and mistreating the designated enemies of God.'

Thomas was silent for a moment as he digested this new concept, and drank some beer. He looked at Ben, 'I'll have to get used to this idea that all governments have a God-given right to commit the most heinous atrocities. Unbelievable ...' And he fell silent.

Both sat in silence, occasionally sipping beer, now and then munching a crisp. After a while they looked around. The café remained half empty and quiet. The horrid harridan outside was definitely worth the money paid her by the enemies of the owner of this particular café. Ben began, 'You noticed how our "lady friend" outside narrowly missed your feet with her spit, even though she is quite obviously blind.'

'I was wondering about that,' replied Thomas. 'How could she be so accurate? It reminds me of a newspaper article I read about the fact that blind people sometimes have near-death experiences where they can accurately see and later describe events happening around them during their experiences. Tell me, how could this happen if people don't have a form of sight like a third eye, or a soul?'

'Oh Thomas, you really do want to believe in the paranormal, don't you? Ah well, I guess it must be difficult for you to believe in purely physical explanations if you also believe in supernatural entities such as God, angels, and the human soul.'

'Then you tell me how it is possible for this woman to be so accurate with her spitting, as well as how blind people can see things happening around them during near-death experiences.'

Ben was silent for a moment as he collected his thoughts. 'Consider the basic structure of the human eye (figure 3.1). Total failure of any one or more parts of both eyes means failure of vision, otherwise known as blindness. However, being blind does not mean you possess no other senses, and being blind does not always mean you see absolutely nothing at all. So Thomas, did you carefully look at the eyes of the woman outside? If you did, then you would have seen they were covered by a white film of scar tissue.'

'Now you mention it, I saw they were covered by a white film. So that white film was scar tissue?'

'Yes indeed. It was probably caused by a very nasty eye infection. Light entering her eyes must pass through this thick white film covering the corneas of both her eyes, and if no other parts of her visual system are damaged or destroyed, then this white film on her corneas will have the same effect you would experience if you tried looking at the world through a sheet of white paper. You can see the difference between light and dark, you could probably see some vague colours, maybe some movement, but no shapes, and nothing else. That is most likely all the vision this woman has. So if we stood close enough to her, she would have seen us as a darkness in front of her, as well as hearing where we were. This would have given her more than enough information to spit accurately in our direction.'

Thomas nodded, 'That sounds very reasonable, and is probably quite correct. However, it doesn't explain how blind people can clearly see everything happening around them during near-death experiences. Look, I bought this book called *Mindsight* with me (Ring 1999). It was written by two serious researchers called Kenneth Ring and Sharon Cooper, and is all about the visual aspects of near-death experiences in blind people. It's fascinating reading, and is proof that you don't need eyes to see. In my opinion, it's also proof of the human soul.'

'Oh, I know the book. It's actually quite a good book, describing a reasonably good study of the visual experiences of blind people during near-death experiences. Unfortunately, many people read it uncritically, and draw totally different conclusions from the study reported in this book than do the authors themselves. Even worse, people hear second-, third-, and fourth-hand accounts of blind people being able to see things during near-death experiences, never check the sources, and uncritically accept garbled versions of these stories. So let's examine your so-called proof of the reality of the soul using the experiences studied in this book.' With these words, Ben emptied half his glass and gave Thomas a challenging look, as if daring him to think differently.

'I don't know why I try arguing with you,' sighed Thomas. 'You've already made your mind up on the matter. So come on, tell me why you think the study in this book fails to prove the existence of the human soul.'

'I'll start with a simple testable example of the senses available to blind people. You can make yourself blind by blindfolding yourself so efficiently that not a single glimmer of light enters your eyes. But being blind does not mean you have no senses, nor that you have no idea of what goes on about you. When you are blindfolded in this manner, you can sense whether you are in an open space or a room by feeling gusts of air over your body, the smells of fresh air, of the street, or of open country-side. You can visualize the position of your body clearly, the relationship of the clothes you wear to your body, the relationships of your limbs to your body. You can sense people approaching and walking away from you. Their footsteps tell you whether they are man or woman, young or old, infirm or healthy. The sounds of their breathing, and the smell of their breath tell you about their health and their diet. Odours emanating from their bodies tell you things about their sex, their race, their diet, their health, and how often they wash. Their speech tells you about their sex, where they were brought up, their educational level, as well as revealing information about their health. You feel the ground tremors, and gusts of air from their movements. You integrate all these perceptions consciously and unconsciously to derive a picture within your mind – your mind's eye – of the situation in which your blindfolded body is present. With a bit of training you could become quite adept in building up mental imagery of all that is happening about you. This would only be a temporary exercise for you, but this is the permanent reality of a blind person. To function, to be able to get any measure of enjoyment out of life, a blind person must learn all these skills. And most of them do succeed, so managing to live reasonably full lives. This is how people can learn to "see" without actually seeing with their eyes. The spitting harpy outside has very evidently acquired these very same skills. She detected our presence, was accurate in her assessment of what types of people we are, which is why she knew she had a good chance of getting some money, and was reasonably accurate with her spitting.'

'Okay, I agree, I never looked at blindness quite like that before. But your example of a blindfold is only valid for people who could once see, and then became blind. What about people blind from birth? Their situation would be quite different, as they would never have prior knowledge of how the world was while sighted. *Mindsight* deals with these people too, and tells that there were some people blind from birth who clearly saw what was happening around them during near-death experiences. Explain that!' Now it was the turn of Thomas to look at Ben, as if challenging him to answer with an explanation based upon simple body function and common sense.

'Glad to ... Let's first look at the basics of near-death experiences. Many reports of near-death experiences contain reports of what happened in the vicinity of the people who underwent these experiences. These reports are sometimes quite accurate observations of actual events occurring during a period that they laid apparently dead, or at the very least, apparently unconscious. I say apparently, because people undergoing near-death experiences are very definitely undergoing conscious experiences, because they experience them during a form of consciousness (Blacher 1980). Yet even though people are conscious during near-death experiences, the functioning of their conscious brains is affected by the disorders causing them to undergo these near-death experiences. This is proven by the very fact they cannot arouse their bodies to speak or to move during these near-death experiences, even though some of them do try (Woerlee 2003, chapters 10,11,12). Furthermore, people never tell what they are undergoing during near-death experiences, so they must remember observations made during these experiences in order to report them sometime later when the functioning of their bodies has recovered sufficiently for them to be able to speak. And because these are memories of things occurring during periods of abnormal brain function (Woerlee 2003, chapters 16 and 18), their reports of what they observed during near-death experiences are always memories coloured by the abnormal functioning of their brains during these experiences, as well as being memories coloured by their personal interpretations of their perceptions. Are you following me so far?'

'Yes, yes ... But what about those who are blind from birth? You still haven't said anything about them yet.'

'Okay then ... To begin with, those areas of the brain concerned with vision never really develop normally in people blind from birth. Furthermore, they have no concept of colour, except as told them by sighted people, and have no concept of sight as experienced by sighted people. So the ways they perceive their surroundings are different in many regards to the way sighted people perceive their surroundings, which as you correctly said, means they are most definitely not in the same situation as a blindfolded person. However, all these things do not mean that blind people generate no mental imagery, because regardless of whether people are blind from birth or became blind at a later age, all blind people do build mental images of the world about them based upon information derived from the senses they do possess, so that they can move with some precision through open spaces, or through rooms and corridors (Afonso 2005, Arditi 1988, Baldwin 2005). Those who become blind after having been able to see do have visual dreams (Bertolo 2005, Hurovitz 1999), while those blind from birth generally have dreams without actual visual content, but which do contain mental maps and imagery from the senses they use in their daily lives (Bertolo 2003, Bertolo 2005, Hurovitz 1999). People blind from birth can even draw accurate pictures of things they dream about (Bertolo 2003), as well as being able to draw pictures of things they learn about through the medium of their other senses (Kennedy 1997). These drawings are correct in all proportions, which means that even those blind from birth have a very good idea of spatial relations in the world about them. As for colours – those who become blind at a later date know all about colours, and use their memories of colour to construct mental imagery of the world around them, while those blind from birth use the descriptions of colours to provide some sort of colouring in their mental imagery of the world about them. All these things mean that those who are blind from birth, as well as all other blind people, are capable of generating quite accurate mental images of the world around them using information derived from the senses they do possess.'

Ben paused to slowly wet his throat with beer, taking just a little more time than necessary so as to be irritating. 'Now this brings us to the fascinating accounts of blind people who report having been able to see clearly, as if possessing normal sight, during near-death experiences. Many people refer repeatedly to such apparently veridical reports made by these blind people, claiming these prove the blind can see in much the same way as sighted people during near-death experiences, claiming these veridical reports could only occur as a result of paranormal causes. *Mindsight* is a study by Kenneth Ring and Sharon Cooper of these veridical reports made by blind people of visual perceptions made during near-death experiences (Ring 1999). But a study of this book reveals it does not claim that the blind can see in the same way as sighted people during near-death experiences. Instead this book reveals nuances and differences between different types of blind people.'

'Are we talking about the same book?' responded Thomas. 'This book provided clear proof that blind people can see clearly during near-death experiences. So what did you read in this book?'

'The difference is that you read the book quite differently to the way I read the same book. I'll explain. For example, most stories in this book are reports made by people who had become blind after having possessed the ability to see. Such blind people reported seeing clearly during near-death experiences, seeing actual colours, and seeing their surroundings. Yet these were people who were either partially sighted such as the case of Debbie and Carla (Ring 1999, pages 80-91), or people who became blind after previously having had normal sight such as the case of Marilyn (Ring 1999, pages 91-96). Visual near-death experiences in which the individuals concerned perceive colours are quite understandable in such persons, because they know what colour is, they know the experience of sight, and the parts of their brains necessary for these things are developed, although now little used since they became blind. Moreover, just as all other blind persons, these people are quite capable of building an image in their minds of events they sense – an image in the mind's eye as it were. This is the most likely mechanism by which they underwent a visual near-death experience. Even so, there are interesting aspects to these reports, such as that of the report of a man called Frank (Ring 1999, pages 105-107). This was a man who had become totally blind after having been sighted for at least 40 years. Accordingly he knew the nature of colour and patterns. We are informed in this book that this totally blind man saw the pattern and colours on a new tie during an out-of-body experience, even though everyone denied having ever described it to him. Yet is this entirely true? After all, someone could have later commented to him, "Nice tie ....Great colours, and strong pattern," and then described the tie, a description he later used when telling of his out-of-body experience. However his report was never corroborated, because the one person who could corroborate it, could not remember the exact events on the day this incident occurred, being only able to confirm that Frank was a sensible and down to earth man who was unlikely to lie. So who knows how he learned the exact nature of the pattern, or whether he actually learned of it at the time itself? So while this story of Frank sounds superficially accurate, it falls apart because of lack of corroboration and lack of confirmation of the incident itself. Alternative explanations and doubts are always possible with such uncorroborated stories.'

'But Ben, what about those people who were blind from birth? The parts of the brains of these people concerned with sight, and visual seeing, would never have developed in these people. They would never have developed an understanding of the sense of colour and sight. So the development of those parts of their brains concerned with vision would also be abnormal, making it less likely that they would have visions of what happens around them during a near-death experience.'

'I agree. The parts of the brains concerned with processing and interpreting visual signals never developed normally in those people blind from birth. However, when you examine the veridical reports in *Mindsight*, you see they are often unqualified reports just stating that these people were blind from birth. In the report of Helen, who was supposedly blind from birth, there is a passage where she states, "And then I thought, oh, did I get my sight back?" (Ring 1999, pages 78-79). So was Helen actually blind from birth, or did she become blind at some later date? I do not know from this book. Indeed, there are many such curious inconsistencies in *Mindsight*. Furthermore, many of those blind from birth were not totally blind, but could distinguish dark and light, and could distinguish colour, which means the parts of their brains concerned with vision did function, albeit in a limited manner. Furthermore, all these people had years of experience perceiving the world around them with their remaining senses, which means they too would have developed their own mental imagery of what happened about them, and to them during their near-death experiences. So while some of the reports in the book seem surprising, these reports of veridical visual near-death, and out-of-body experiences require no paranormal causes for their explanation. In fact, the functioning of the human body during adversity and disease explains all such observations made during near-death experiences and out-of-body experiences (Woerlee 2003).'

Ben paused a moment, looked around at the still half empty café, drank some more beer, and continued. 'The conclusion of *Mindsight* is actually a tribute to the scientific impartiality of the authors. They state that blind people do not perceive things during their near-death experiences and out-of-body experiences in the same way a sighted person perceives things, instead they say that blind people perceive them as images in their minds, only in the same terms as they experience their world, yet with greater awareness and accuracy of perception (Ring 1999, pages 185-187). That is why they called this type of mental imagery mindsight, because it is a perceived image built up in the minds of people – an image in the mind's eye. So stories of blind people being able to see in the same way as sighted people during near-death experiences and out-of-body experiences, are no more than wishful, and very literal misinterpretations of an otherwise quite careful study of these wondrous experiences in the blind – wishful and wondrous misinterpretations made by people who often have not carefully examined the book *Mindsight*, or even read it at all. What is left is the fascinating, even wondrous fact, that people can make quite accurate perceptions of their surroundings while apparently unconscious during out-of-body experiences or near-death experiences. But such veridical observations made during these experiences are not proof of anything spiritual or paranormal. The mechanisms by which these visual observations can be made were stated years ago by a near-death experience researcher called Susan Blackmore.'

> *The answers include prior knowledge, fantasy and lucky guesses and the remaining operating senses of hearing and touch. Add to this the way memory works to recall accurate items and forget the wrong ones, and we have the basis for an alternative account of why people are able to see what is going on (Blackmore 1993, page 115).*

'As yet, no-one has managed to provide any real evidence to the contrary. So while these case studies in the book *Mindsight* are interesting, they are no more than that. They provide no evidence for a third eye, or an invisible immaterial soul which can separate from the body to observe all that happens around the body. I guess that answers your questions about this book and the unsightly harpy outside. However, your illusions about what you read in the book of *Mindsight* do raise fundamental questions regarding the sensory capabilities of the supposedly disembodied consciousness during out-of-body experiences.'

'Oh?' grunted Thomas in a questioning, yet somewhat crestfallen tone.

'Yes indeed,' continued a totally unperturbed Ben. 'The phenomenon of blind people supposedly being able to see normally during these experiences raises an important question. Can the disembodied consciousness, or soul, see and hear things directly: or is what the supposedly disembodied consciousness sees and hears, only mental imagery generated from information derived from the senses of the body?'

Thomas looked surprised. 'Huh! I thought you didn't believe in the reality of a disembodied consciousness.'

'I don't,' was the firm response. 'Not for one moment. But this is a theoretical question. I'm asking your opinion on the matter, because I have a suspicion you still believe in the reality of a separable immaterial consciousness, despite all we have discussed before.'

'Hmm ... Okay,' said Thomas. 'If we are talking theoretically, I would say that the soul, or disembodied consciousness, sees and hears things directly.'

'I just knew you'd say that!' was the almost triumphant response from Ben. 'Okay, let's begin with the sense of sight first. Now tell me Thomas, consider an extremely nearsighted person who needs powerful spectacles to see anything clearly. Would the soul, or disembodied consciousness of such a person, need spectacles, contact lenses, or other visual aids to see clearly during an out-of-body experience?'

'Now you're being ridiculous!'

'No ... Not at all Thomas. So tell me, would the soul of an extremely nearsighted person need spectacles, contact lenses, or other visual aids to see clearly during an out-of-body experience?'

'Of course not! After all, if blind people can see clearly during out-of-body experiences, this means that the sense organs of the soul, or separable consciousness, function perfectly without any of the deficiencies manifested by the physical body.'

'Aha! By saying that, you imply that when the soul is confined within the body it must use the sense organs of the body, presumably because the physical substance of the body blocks light from directly affecting the perfectly functioning sense organs of the soul. This is the only logical explanation for this belief, because if the soul was able to see clearly while within the body, no one would be blind, nearsighted, or have other visual handicaps.'

'Sounds logical,' was the cautious response from Thomas. 'It certainly would explain why people with visual defects, or those who are blind, report seeing things clearly during out-of-body experiences.'

'Now Thomas, would you agree with me that light entering the eyes of the physical body interacts with special nerve cells of the retina to generate nerve signals entering the brain, and these nerve signals are somehow perceived by the consciousness housed within the body?'

'Yes … That's true, because the physical eyes of our material bodies do work in that way.' was another cautious response.

'Without this interaction between light, and light-sensitive nerve cells, no nerve signals would be generated by light impinging upon the body, and nothing would be seen. Would you agree with that?'

'Yes …' came even more cautiously from the mouth of Thomas.

'Now Thomas, you claim that the soul, or separable consciousness, can see clearly when separated from the body. This means that the soul also has some sort of interaction with light: otherwise the soul would not see anything by means of light, such as colours, textures, shapes, people, animals, or objects. This interaction must happen: otherwise light would simply pass through the soul without any interaction whatsoever. And if light simply passed through the soul without any interaction with the soul whatsoever, it could not affect the sense organs of the soul, and could not arouse images of the surroundings supposedly seen by the soul. This latter would mean the soul would not only be truly invisible, but would also be blind.'

'But Ben, you know the soul is invisible! Even so, I agree with you, the soul must somehow interact with light: otherwise the soul could not see what is happening in its surroundings during out-of-body experiences.'

'Very well, just for the sake of argument, let's look at the ways it is possible for anything to interact with light. Only four methods of interaction are possible. I'll list them and their consequences for you.'

- Reflection of light. If the sense organs of the soul reflected light, the soul would appear as a shiny reflecting "something".
- Emission of light. If the sense organs of the soul emitted light in response to ambient light impinging upon them, then the sense organs of the soul would appear as something emitting light, or as a vague glow.
- Absorption of light. If the sense organs of the soul absorb light, then the sense organs of the soul would appear as a vague darkness.
- Change the properties of light. If the sense organs of the soul changed the properties of light passing through the soul, or the sense organs of the soul, the light impinging upon the soul would change in colour or intensity.

'Now tell me Thomas, can you imagine any other ways in which light could interact with the soul, or for that matter with anything else?'

'Er … No.'

'Correct – there aren't any other forms of interaction with light. The human soul, or separable consciousness, is supposedly in the vicinity of the body when the body is dying, sleeping, or undergoing an out-of-body experience. Yet throughout many millennia of known history, no one has ever consistently seen or photographed anything absorbing, transforming, reflecting, or emitting light anywhere near the bodies of dying or sleeping people, or near the bodies of people undergoing out-of-body experiences. The conclusion is evident – the soul, or separable consciousness of the body, has no interaction with light, and accordingly does not see anything by means of light. This means that all these observations made during out-of-body experiences by so-called blind people, were consciously or unconsciously perceived using the physical senses of the body.'

Thomas looked disappointed. He stared silently in the distance.

But Ben was not yet finished. 'There is even more reason to believe in the truth of all these things. I've already discussed that the immaterial consciousness or soul does not interact with visible light, which is why it cannot be seen, and cannot be photographed. Now light is but one part of the spectrum of electromagnetic radiation, which ranges from very long electromagnetic waves, to radio waves, to microwaves, to infrared, to visible light, ultraviolet, x-rays, and gamma-rays. And the soul cannot be detected with detectors tuned to any of these frequencies of electromagnetic radiation. What is more, the soul is also able to pass through the dense electromagnetic bonds, molecules and atoms forming solid substances such as the body, walls, doors, windows and roofs without any interaction with these solid substances whatsoever. This is proof that the soul neither interacts with the powerful electromagnetic forces binding the atoms and molecules forming solid matter, nor with the atoms and molecules forming solid matter. All these things mean that the separated soul cannot directly hear or see anything, because hearing requires an interaction with pressure waves in the tenuous physical matter of air molecules, while seeing requires an interaction with the weak electromagnetic forces of which light is composed.'

'Oh,' was the disappointed response from Thomas. 'So how can the soul see or hear anything around the body at all?'

Ben was silent for a moment before continuing, 'The very fact that the soul is supposed to be immaterial, and appears not to interact with material objects or forces, raises the question of how the immaterial substance of the soul could possibly interact with the material substance of the body at all. One possible answer would be to say that the interaction of the unique sum total of the parts of the living human body generates some sort of wondrous portal, enabling transmission of information from the material substance of the body to the immaterial substance of the soul, as well as from the soul to the body. However, this idea still means that the only way the soul could hear or see anything during out-of-body experiences would be through the senses of the body. So during an out-of-body experience, the soul would use information from the senses of the body to hear and see, as well as to construct a mental image consistent with the presumed position of the displaced soul. But this renders fantastical constructs such as wondrous portals and an immaterial soul capable of separating from the body very improbable, because the functioning of the conscious mind in the material body during out-of-body experiences explains everything.'

'Hmm ...' said Thomas. 'I do believe you have a point there. It's disappointing, but when you explain it in this way, there is absolutely no way the separated consciousness of a person can directly hear or see during out-of-body experiences.' Here was yet another possibly paranormal phenomenon explained by simple body function. He looked despondent for a moment as he reflected on these matters, looked at his and Ben's empty beer glasses, and suddenly became more cheerful, 'Our glasses are empty. Let's go and drink some Belgian beer in another café near here.'

'That sounds like a wonderful idea,' was the enthusiastic response. 'Let's go.'

It was dark outside. The beggar had departed some time before with her uriniferous progeny. A gust of wind blew loose newspaper pages over the street, one of which clung to one of Ben's legs. While removing it he saw the headlines, 'Newly elected Jerusalem Purification Party demands expulsion of all non-Jews from Jerusalem!' Ben read further. It appeared that the rabidly fundamentalist Jerusalem Purification Party, which had recently been elected to power in Israel, was proposing a vote in the Israeli parliament to only permit followers of Judaism in the city of Jerusalem. According to the Jerusalem Purification Party, Jerusalem was the holy city of the Jews, a city given to the Jewish nation by God, and was by divine decree only intended for habitation and visitation by Jews. Accordingly, along with forbidding all non-Jews to enter Jerusalem, they demanded a mass expulsion of non-Jewish inhabitants, proposing that compensation be paid to these people for the loss of their property in instalments over a period of twenty years. Ben showed the article to Thomas.

'Explosive ...' said Thomas after reading the article. 'I can't understand how they could do this. This will cause an enormous amount of trouble in the Middle-East. It's simply ridiculous to think of a city in which only people of one faith are permitted to enter. It can't be done.'

'Oh I wouldn't be too sure about that,' was the dry response from Ben. 'Just think of the Islamic holy cities of Mecca and Medina. People who are not followers of Islam have not been permitted to enter either city since the time of Mohammed. Yet almost no one ever says a word about this. Everyone accepts this fact, but they get angry when the Jews in Israel propose the same for Jerusalem and the Jews. Strange isn't it?'

'Put that way – yes. But I would imagine that the Jews do have some historical claim to Jerusalem. After all, they have lived there for thousands of years.'

'That may be true, but they certainly haven't ruled it for thousands of years. The situation in Jerusalem is a bit similar to that of the Jewish community in Rome. There has been a Jewish community living in the city of Rome since about 50 BCE (Jews in Rome), so you might say they also have a historical right to the city of Rome because they have lived there for so long. But do you hear the Jewish community in Rome demanding to rule that city?'

'Er, no ...'

'That's right, they don't. Yet they do demand to rule Jerusalem.'

'Ah, but that's because they ruled it at one stage, which is certainly not the case with the Jews in Rome.'

'That is certainly true, but let's look at their claim more carefully,' said Ben as they slowly walked in the direction of the Saint Peter's Church. 'There is evidence that the town or city of Jerusalem was in existence sometime before 1600 BCE, a time long before the Jewish tribes fled from

Egypt and settled in the area of Israel somewhere around 1250 BCE (Wikipedia). Between 1250 to 1030 BCE, the tribes of Israel were engaged in a divinely sanctioned, but cruel war of dispossession, attrition, and extermination, to cleanse the land of Israel of the pestilential original inhabitants. After all, God had given had given them this land, so the original inhabitants either had to leave or die. It was a period of Jewish history punctuated by orgies of pitiless cruelty and slaughter.'

> *And they found Adoni-bezek in Bezek; and they fought against him, and they smote the Canaanites and the Perizzites. But Adoni-bezek fled; and they pursued after him, and caught him, and cut off his thumbs and his great toes. And Adoni-bezek said, Threescore and ten kings, having their thumbs and their great toes cut off, gathered their food under my table: as I have done, so God hath requited me. And they brought him to Jerusalem, and he died there. And the children of Judah fought against Jerusalem, and took it, and smote it with the edge of the sword, and set the city on fire. (ASV Bible, Judges 1:5-8)*

'What this means is that the Jews conquered the city of Jerusalem, but did not want to settle in the city at that time. Instead they were content with merely carrying out the holy work of killing as many of the original Jebusite (Canaanite) inhabitants as they could find, plundering all that was of any value, and departing, leaving a smouldering, corpse strewn pile of rubble behind. God was indeed good to the chosen people of Israel.'

'But what about the dreadful mutilation of King Adoni-Bezek? Cutting of his thumbs and big toes was not only mutilation, but would have severely crippled him. Quite revolting ... '

'I agree Thomas, but such nastiness, such cruel mutilations, seem to have been quite common during that period of history. After all, King Adoni-Bezek had done the same to seventy others, which is why he very philosophically accepted his own mutilation at the hand of his Jewish conquerors as his just reward. However, throughout history, dreadful mutilations of the conquered seem to have been quite common. Christian holy texts do not prescribe mutilations, although Christians almost certainly mutilated unbelievers. However, more recently, mutilations were prescribed in the Koran for those who fight against the followers of Islam.'

The only reward of those who make war upon Allah and His messenger and strive after corruption in the land will be that they will be killed or crucified, or have their hands and feet on alternate sides cut off, or will be expelled out of the land. Such will be their degradation in the world, and in the Hereafter theirs will be an awful doom; (Koran 5:33)

'So those who struggle against Islam are not only punished dreadfully on this world, but are also treated to eternal torment in hell in the afterlife as well. This is yet another depressing manifestation of the inhumanity of members of the human species to their fellows. Ah well, at least the punishments are horrifically, as well as painfully thorough. But this is a small diversion from the subject of Jerusalem. In fact, members of the tribes of Israel did not settle in Jerusalem until the city was conquered by the great Jewish King David, who ruled the united tribes of Israel from about 1010 to 970 BCE. His armies conquered Jerusalem from the Jebusites somewhere between 1010 and 1000 BCE.'

And the king and his men went to Jerusalem against the Jebusites, the inhabitants of the land, who spake unto David, saying, Except thou take away the blind and the lame, thou shalt not come in hither; thinking, David cannot come in hither.

Nevertheless David took the stronghold of Zion; the same is the city of David. And David said on that day, Whosoever smiteth the Jebusites, let him get up to the watercourse, and smite the lame and the blind, that are hated of David's soul. Wherefore they say, There are the blind and the lame; he cannot come into the house.

And David dwelt in the stronghold, and called it the city of David. And David built round about from Millo and inward. And David waxed greater and greater; for Jehovah, the God of hosts, was with him. (ASV Bible, 2 Samuel 5:6-10)

'See,' said Thomas, 'as you say the Jews ruled Jerusalem from that time onwards until now, a period of more than 3000 years.'

'Not at all,' retorted Ben. 'They inhabited and ruled Jerusalem from its conquest by David until about 135 CE, at which time the second Jewish rebellion against the Roman Empire was crushed. After crushing the rebellion, the ruling Roman authorities drove the Jews out of Israel and made a law forbidding Jews to live in Jerusalem. It was only after about 438 CE that Jews were again permitted to live in Jerusalem (History of Jerusalem), and there has been a Jewish community living there ever since, although the Jewish community there was always under the rule of some other non-Jewish power until the state of Israel gained independence in 1948 CE. You can summarize all this by saying that Jews actually only lived in, and ruled Jerusalem for 1135 years after its conquest by King David. After this, they did not even live in the city for 300 years, and certainly did not rule Jerusalem from 135 CE to 1948 CE. So Jews had absolutely no control over the city for about 1813 years, which is a period nearly twice as long as the period they ruled Jerusalem after usurping it from the Jebusites, and before being expelled by the Romans. So if they carry out the plan of the Jerusalem Purification Party, then this has nothing to do with divine right, it is no more than conquest of the remaining parts of the city not yet directly inhabited or controlled by Jews. After all, if you use the argument of historical right, then the descendants of the Jebusites, (if you can find them), have just as much right to the city as do the Jews, or the followers of Islam who ruled the city for more than a thousand years too. So this nonsense of historical, or even divine right, is absolute drivel!'

'Hmmmn ... I hate to admit it Ben, but I do believe you've raised an interesting point. However, somehow I don't think fundamentalist fanatics such as members of the Jerusalem Purification Party are interested in listening to historical fact, any more than they are willing to listen to reason.'

'I'm just as sure of that as you are. But now for more important things, we've arrived at the café. Now it's time to pour delicious Belgian beer down our throats.'

Chapter 6

Return flight to Paris

'I had a dream …' declaimed Thomas loudly, and promptly emptied his glass. It was evident that the third glass of cheap Merlot within an hour was beginning to exert a detrimental effect upon his ability to express himself normally.

'So … and …' grumbled Ben, glaring enquiringly at his empty glass, and continued, 'Martin Luther King actually said, "I have a dream …", but okay, artistic license is permissible. This so-called wine does seem to taste better after a glass or two, but it really is quite dreadful. Brrrr … Ah well, at least there's some alcohol in it. It really would be fascinating to learn more about the truly wondrous chemical processes required to produce wine as appalling as this. So tell me, what did you dream?' At this, Ben looked quizzically at Thomas, as he leaned back in his chair.

It was late in the afternoon of a yet another warm summer day. Thomas and Ben had met each other at the terrace of one of the café's on the New Rhine Canal. They basked in the warm sun, discussed local politics and many other subjects. They both had begun feeling pleasantly warm from the wine, their thoughts and discussion becoming ever more free ranging, until this sudden random declamation of Thomas.

'It was a strange dream,' replied Thomas, 'Last night, while I was sleeping, I dreamt I was actually flying. I could clearly see the countryside underneath me as I flew. But I had no idea where I was, until I suddenly found myself flying above Paris. I knew it was Paris, because I was floating above the Sacre Coeur Cathedral, only now I believe it's now called the Hamidallah Mosque. Even though it was night in my dream, there was still a dense crowd of visitors at the mosque. And then I suddenly awoke. That's all I remember. Stranger yet, this morning in a newspaper article about the current Ramadan celebrations, I saw a photo of the crowds outside the Hamidallah Mosque, and it was exactly the same scene as I saw in my dream.'

'So how would you explain your dream?' was the guarded response from Ben.

Thomas was immediately alert. He recognized the tone. Ben was testing him, drawing him out to make some statement or say something, so he could demonstrate some new fact or destroy some belief. But Ben knew what he had seen in his dream, knew that what he had seen in his dream exactly matched the picture in the paper, and just knew this could only be explained with some form of separation of his consciousness from his body. He began, 'The picture in the newspaper corresponded exactly with what I saw in my dream. I believe this experience of flying out of my body, or this out-of-body experience, can only be explained by a real separation of my soul, the immaterial vehicle of my consciousness, actually flying to Paris. No other explanation makes sense. Try and find some materialistic explanation for that!'

'Oh, oh, oh, Thomas, your desire to find absolute proof for the reality of the soul and the paranormal is always a predictable source of enjoyment to me, even though it is disappointing. Think critically. We've already discussed and demolished the belief that the soul, or separated conscious-ness of a person can see or sense anything directly (Chapter 5). This means your vision was no more than a dream. Then we have other factors, such as the fact that the recent conversion of the Sacre Coeur Cathedral into a mosque was extensively covered in all national and international newspa-pers and television programs. Pictures and films of the Sacre Coeur, now called the Hamidallah Mosque, taken at every imaginable angle were shown in all these media. So if you dream of flying above this building, you could very easily be remembering one of these images in your dream. Furthermore, it's Ramadan, so of course you will see thousands of worshipers milling around the building at night, just as you describe. So when you see a night photograph of this mosque made during Ramadan, and taken from the same vantage point, you quite understandably will say it is identical to what you dreamed. As for the landscapes you flew over before reaching Paris, you didn't recognize them, so they could have been anywhere. This explains the imagery in your dream quite well, without resorting to any paranormal explanations.'

'Even so, how could have been just a dream? The experience was so vivid, the sensations so real, and what I saw felt so real, that it couldn't have just been a dream. Somehow my consciousness separated from my body, flew to Paris in France, and returned back to my sleeping body. It simply isn't possible to explain this experience in any other way.'

Ben wore a nauseatingly smug grin as he replied, 'Oh, I wouldn't be too sure about that. You're not the only person to have had such a vivid flying dream ...'

'Really Ben, do you have to grin like that? Each time I come with what I believe to be proof of the paranormal, you wear a smile like that, and proceed to demolish the proof, or provide an alternative explanation. You really are an incorrigible sceptic.'

'Sorry, but your reaction was so very predictable. You say your dream cannot be anything else other than proof of an invisible and immaterial soul which is also the vehicle of your consciousness. Actually this is a very old idea. An ancient Roman philosopher and statesman called Marcus Tullius Cicero (106-43 BCE) also expressed this same idea in his book *De Senectute*. He claimed that sleep freed the immaterial and immortal soul from the chains of the physical body.'

And even when man is dissolved by death it is evident to the sight whither each bodily element departs; for the corporeal returns to the visible constituents from which it came, but the soul alone remains unseen, both when it is present and when it departs. Again, you really see nothing resembling death so much as sleep; and yet it is when the body sleeps that the soul most clearly manifests its divine nature; for when it is unfettered and free it sees many things that are to come. Hence we know what the soul's future state will be when it has been wholly released from the shackles of the flesh. (Cicero, page 93)

'And Thomas, you've got to consider that this idea was ancient, even when Cicero wrote it, because he was quoting the opinions of other philosophers.'

'Ah, so my beliefs aren't unjustified after all!' was the almost triumphant reaction.

'Oh I wouldn't go as far as saying that. All this means is that the same type of experience as you told me has been known since ancient times, and that the explanation has always been the same since ancient times – that these experiences are memories of the activity of an invisible and immaterial soul.'

'So? And what's wrong with this explanation if it has stood the test of time for so long? It explains and corresponds perfectly with everything you sense and feel. You can't ask for better confirmation than that.'

'That's just it – sensing and feeling. Let's look at some other common sensations you have when you sleep. I'll begin with a sensation nearly all people have experienced at some in their life. Sometimes just as you are falling asleep, you feel yourself floating above the bed, and then, suddenly you feel like you fall onto the bed and awaken with a jerk. Have you ever had that happen to you?'

'Yes, a number of times.'

'Now this is an experience nearly all humans have undergone since time immemorial. Yet does anyone sharing the same bed with a person undergoing such an experience ever describe seeing that person floating above the bed before that person suddenly falls and awakens with a jerk? No-one throughout all known history has ever described seeing anything like this occurring. All they describe is a person who suddenly awakens with a jerk. The same is also revealed by careful laboratory studies of people as they undergo these experiences (Oswald 1959). So this experience is actually a sensation of floating followed by a sensation of falling, and terminated by a jerking of limbs. The really fascinating aspect of this experience is how the body can generate such sensations.'

'Well Ben, there is an explanation that covers it very well, and which explains all these sensations and observations. The sensation of floating is caused by separation of the soul from the body, while the sensation of falling is due to the soul reuniting roughly and suddenly with the physical body, so causing the body of the person undergoing this experience to jerk (Muldoon 1989, pages 86-97). You cannot see the soul because it is invisible, so all you see is a jerk as the soul roughly reunites with the body.'

'Interesting … Have you any proof for this explanation?'

'No, but it is self-evident when you consider the fact of separation of the soul from the body.'

'Ohhhh ... Thomas ... ,' groaned Ben as he shook his head. 'I think I need more of this revolting wine to deaden the pain of your belief.' He signed to one of the waiters, 'Another two glasses of wine please!' And he continued, 'I suppose it would be a very acceptable explanation, if your basic premise of the reality of the soul were correct. But according to me, these experiences are no more than sensations generated by the functioning of the body. Let's look at another common dream sensation. Sometimes you have a horrible dream where you, or a loved one, is in some sort of danger. In your dream you try to run, but find your legs feel enormously heavy, or it feels like you are trying to run through liquid mud. Sometimes you even feel yourself rooted to one spot, unable to move at all. You try to yell to warn the person, or you try to scream, but little or no sound at all, issues from your lips. The overall sensation is of darkness, paralysis, and helpless fear. Have you ever had a dream like that?'

'Several. They really are unpleasant.'

'So how would you explain such dreams? After all, you believe in the reality of the soul. If dreams are a product of the continued activity of the soul as a the body sleeps, then something really awful is happening to the soul in such a dream, or the dream is a very imperfect memory of events undergone by the soul in some unseen immaterial universe while you sleep.'

Thomas sipped his wine, and answered confidently, 'I'm surprised you haven't thought of the explanation yourself. It's so clear and so evident. The physical body is a prison for the soul. The soul only inhabits this body so as to undergo spiritual development in preparation for the true life – the eternal life after death. This is what Saint Paul clearly implied in a passage in his first letter to the Corinthians where he condemned suicide.'

Know ye not that ye are a temple of God, and that the Spirit of God dwelleth in you? If any man destroyeth the temple of God, him shall God destroy; for the temple of God is holy, and such are ye. (ASV Bible, 1 Corinthians 3:16-17)

'Now, as Cicero said, the soul is imprisoned in the body, and dreaming is actually a full or partial memory of the continued activity of the soul while the body sleeps. So when for some reason the soul is unable to depart from a body immobilised by sleep, the dreamer experiences sensations of helplessness and fear which are later remembered as a nightmare. I would say this explains these unpleasant dreams very well.'

Ben sipped his wine calmly as he listened to this explanation. 'You certainly provide solidly logical explanations for these sensations. But these explanations are totally dependent upon one absolutely basic and essential premise – the reality of the invisible and immaterial soul which is the vehicle of human consciousness. However, in my opinion the reality of such an invisible and immaterial soul is very disputable indeed. No one has ever managed to find concrete proofs for the existence of the human soul. Up till now I've demonstrated that all the direct and indirect proofs of the soul can be explained with natural laws and the functioning of the body. Even if each person does possess a soul, then this immaterial soul must use the functioning of the mechanisms of the material body to express itself in terms able to be understood and expressed by the body as mental images, memories, speech, and actions. After all, if the necessary bodily mechanisms cease to function, no images will arise in the mind, no memories will be generated, the person cannot speak, and no actions will occur.'

'But that's no explanation! These are real experiences, not mere physical sensations!' retorted Thomas. 'The concept of, and the reality of the soul explains them all perfectly.'

Ben groaned theatrically, 'I need wine!' and emptied his glass in an equally theatrical manner, while at the same time calling for more. 'I see this is going to be an uphill task. As I said before, the clue to any explanation of these experiences lies in the mechanisms of sensations, and how the mechanisms of the brain makes the conscious mind aware of these sensations and experiences. To begin with, a person must be conscious in order to have any sort of conscious sensation or conscious experience such as a dream, an out-of-body experience, a near-death experience, or any other sort of conscious experience.'

'Just a minute, someone who is sleeping is not conscious,' spluttered Thomas.

'Then how can a sleeping person dream? A dream is an experience undergone during a form of consciousness, otherwise how can a dreaming person undergo the experience of a dream and remember it? Indeed, proof of this is revealed by studies showing that the electroencephalograms of people who are dreaming are almost the same as those of awake and conscious people (Schwarz 2002). Accordingly, although dreaming people appear unconscious to an observer, they are nonetheless conscious, albeit in an altered state of consciousness. This example demonstrates that consciousness is something quite wondrous, difficult to define, and not always apparent.'

Thomas stared broodingly at his beer. 'After hearing what you just told me about sleep, then I ask myself how you can know when a person is conscious or unconscious. Moreover, you tell me there are different states of consciousness. Now I really don't quite know what to think about the phenomenon of consciousness. I'm puzzled.'

'I agree Thomas, consciousness is a difficult subject. However, you can look at it simply by saying that consciousness is any state of mind where a person has a conscious experience, and this may even be in a state where a person appears unconscious to an external observer. Fortunately, there are millennia of experience with the phenomena of consciousness, so we usually know when a person is conscious or unconscious.'

'Give me some examples Ben, I still really don't understand how an apparently unconscious person, such as someone who is sleeping and dreaming, can have a conscious experience. What is consciousness? I'm still puzzled.'

'Hmm ... I agree Thomas, consciousness is strange, and just like you, I don't understand what consciousness is either. All I know is when it is present or not. So let's use a simple thought experiment to demonstrate the difference between consciousness, unconsciousness, and conscious experiences undergone while apparently unconscious. Thomas, you look like you're conscious. You drink wine, you eat, you move, now and then you speak to protest at what I say. You appear very conscious to me. Would you say you are conscious?'

'Er ... Yes ...' was the cautious response.

'Very well now, if I seize a very large baseball bat, and use it to hit your head with some considerable force, you will collapse onto the floor, still breathing, still with a heartbeat, but unmoving, unresponsive to my speech, unresponsive to pain, and unresponsive to all other stimuli. If you were in such a condition, I do believe I would be correct if I said you were unconscious. Would you agree with me?'

'Don't be silly! Of course I would be unconscious. What a ridiculous example!'

'Not really. It illustrates a very evident change of state from consciousness to unconsciousness. Now Thomas, tell me, do you think you would remember anything happening to you as you lay unconscious on the floor after my hypothetical blow on your head with the baseball bat?'

'Of course not!' retorted Thomas. 'What a stupid question! I would be lying unconscious on the floor. All I would know afterwards is the memory of the look of evil delight on your face as you swung the bat towards my head, after which the next thing I would know about is my aching head as I woke up.'

'In other words you do agree that an unconscious person can have no conscious experiences,' responded Ben. 'This means you do understand that conscious experiences can only be undergone by conscious people.'

'Well, yes … I guess you do have a point there,' replied Thomas.

'So in other words, you now understand that a dreaming person is actually having a conscious experience, because the dreamer consciously undergoes an experience which is remembered, perhaps to be related at another time. However, dreaming is a curious state of consciousness where the critical faculties seem to be suspended, most likely because of reduced activity in the prefrontal lobes of the brain during dreaming (Schwarz 2002).'

'I guess so when you look at it like that.'

'I'll illustrate this further. We've already talked about those horrible dreams where you sensed danger to yourself or another person, during which you try to run, but each movement requires incredible effort, as if you were trying to run through liquid mud or treacle, and sometimes you are unable to move at all. But Thomas, did you also know that as you dream, all your muscles are paralyzed so that you don't act out your dreams (Schwarz 2002). In fact, if you were not paralyzed as you dreamed, you would injure yourself and others as you tried to act out your dreams (Alves 1999, Olson 2000, Schenck 1987). Now the conscious sensations of partial muscle paralysis are actually quite unpleasant. The partially paralyzed person feels that every movement requires incredible mental effort and that their limbs are heavier than normal (Gandevia 1977, Gandevia 1977a, Gandevia 1982, Smith 1947), speech is difficult, also requiring intense mental effort for little result (Smith 1947). Total paralysis of speech muscles, means speech and making sounds is impossible, and paralysis of all other muscles means that even intense efforts fail to produce movement (Buzzi 2000, Smith 1947). These are the same sensations people describe during nightmarish dreams. Accordingly, what people are sensing during such dreams are the conscious unpleasant sensations of partial or complete paralysis that they convert into a dream of terror and fear. So you see Thomas, regardless of whether they are pleasant or unpleasant, dreams are actually conscious experiences undergone when a person appears unconscious during sleep.'

'Wow,' was the only response.

'Now let's go a bit further with more illustrations of situations where people appear unconscious, but are actually conscious. Another good example is given by the effects of the drug Curare. Curare is known as the deadly arrow poison of the Amazonian Indians. There are many fables about its use, but actually its effects on the body are extremely well known, because it has been used in anaesthesia since 1942 CE to make surgery easier and possible in many different parts of the body. However, even though it is used in anaesthesia, Curare is not an anaesthetic drug, because it has absolutely no effect on the brain, it has no pain-killing effects, and causes no loss of consciousness. Instead, when it is administered at the doses used during modern anaesthesia, Curare paralyses all the muscles of the body, except for the muscles of the heart, the muscles of the urinary bladder, and the anal sphincter. People to whom Curare has been administered are conscious, but all their muscles are paralyzed: they cannot breathe, they cannot move, and they cannot speak, no matter how hard they try to do these things. They are conscious, they feel everything happening to their bodies, they hear what is happening about them, they smell the odours of their surroundings, they taste whatever is on their tongues – yet they are unmoving, trapped within totally paralyzed and unmoving bodies (Smith 1947). They appear unconscious, yet are most definitely conscious. So Thomas, would you say a person administered Curare was conscious or unconscious?'

'That's horrible. Actually I would say that such a person was very dead, because their breathing ceases.'

'People given curare in such doses are always attached to a machine which takes over the function of breathing. So a person administered a large dose of curare is conscious, but totally paralyzed and cannot breathe, yet remains alive because of the machine which takes over their breathing. More than 50 years of experience with Curare confirms and proves these things (Smith 1947). Is such a person conscious or unconscious according to you?'

'I guess such a person is conscious, although to be paralyzed and fully conscious like that sounds awful. You're trapped in your body. Your body is truly a prison in this situation. If people inflict pain, you cannot react, but you will feel the pain, as well as all other sensations. Horrible.'

'Indeed, a person paralyzed with Curare is very conscious, and can see, hear, smell, and sense everything (Smith 1947). But you cannot know what a person totally paralyzed with Curare experiences until after they recover the ability to communicate. This is a similar situation to people paralyzed by the effects of sleep, it is a similar situation to people undergoing out-of-body experiences while apparently unconscious, and it is a similar situation to people undergoing near-death experiences while apparently unconscious. Now let's go even further, and look at an example of consciousness in a situation where people very definitely appear unconscious, and are even what is called clinically dead.'

'Oh, but that's impossible. If you're clinically dead, then you're dead.'

'Not necessarily. Let's look at the situation of cardiac arrest. You won't get a situation much closer to death than that. Cardiac arrest is when the heart suddenly stops beating due to diseases such as a myocardial infarct or other heart diseases, when an electronic heart pacemaker is turned off, or when the heart stops beating as a result of being shot or stabbed in the heart. When the heart suddenly stops beating, no more blood is pumped into the brain, which means the brain rapidly begins to fail as a result of oxygen starvation, the first evident manifestation of which is loss of consciousness within five to twenty seconds after the heart stops beating (Aminoff 1988, Gastaut 1957, Rossen 1943). Are you still following me Thomas?'

'Yes, but get to the point Ben. You're taking an awful long time here,' was the somewhat surly reaction.

'What an impatient young fellow you are. First the groundwork and then the superstructure. In 1943 CE, a group of researchers in the USA simulated the effects of sudden cardiac arrest on the brains of themselves and 126 volunteer prison inmates. They placed a specially designed inflatable tourniquet around the necks of all participants, and suddenly inflated this tourniquet to a pressure high enough to stop all flow of blood to the heads of these people for a period long enough to cause loss of consciousness as determined by the experimenters (Rossen 1943). This subjected the heads of all these brave experimental subjects to sudden, increasingly severe, and potentially lethal oxygen starvation. All participants were instructed to follow the left-right movements of a pendulum with their eyes until they lost consciousness. All participants had a finger on a switch with which they could immediately deflate the cuff around their necks should they so desire. All experimental subjects noticed that eye movements were paralyzed just before they lost consciousness. In addition, those few subjects who did try pressing the switch to deflate the cuffs around their necks, also discovered they were paralyzed and totally unable to press the switch just before losing consciousness. So this amazing experiment demonstrated very convincingly that a person can be totally paralyzed and fully conscious at a certain level of brain oxygen starvation, yet appear unconscious to observers because of paralysis of all their muscles induced by oxygen starvation of the brain. This is yet another example of apparent unconsciousness. This is also the situation in which some people undergoing resuscitation for cardiac arrest find themselves – cardiac massage may restore a sufficient flow of oxygen enriched blood to their brains to sustain consciousness, but insufficient to remove the paralysis caused by oxygen starvation. Are you following me?'

'I'm beginning to follow you. It really is surprising stuff you're telling me. Incredible even. But Ben, is this apparent unconsciousness really due to oxygen starvation?'

'It certainly is. A good example of the paralysis induced by oxygen starvation is given by the experiences of early balloonists who ascended to high altitudes with insufficient knowledge of the effects of oxygen starvation.'

In severe hypoxia, an ascending type of paralysis is produced. The

legs first lose their power, so that the subject is unable to stand; as
the paralysis ascends, the arm muscles soon become affected; the
neck muscles are the last of all to be involved. That hypoxia
produces an ascending type of paralysis was dramatically illus-
trated by Coxwell when he made his famous balloon ascent with
Glashier. Coxwell's muscles, except those of his neck, were, for the
most part, paralyzed; he could still move his head and so was able
to grasp the rope valves with his teeth. By so doing, he saved his
life and that of his companion.

Another dramatic instance of muscular paralysis due to oxygen
want is the experience of Tissandier, sole survivor of the three-
man ascent in the balloon "Zenith." At great heights he realized
that he needed oxygen but could not husband the strength to raise
the mouthpiece of the oxygen container to his lips. (Liere 1963,
page 300)

'Dramatic stuff indeed Thomas, and all illustrating the effects of
oxygen starvation on the ability to move. But as you may realize, the
bodily mechanisms by which sleep or curare cause paralysis with the
resulting apparent unconsciousness are of course very different.'

'Okay, I realize now that people can be conscious, even though they
appear unconscious. Nonetheless, all these explanations still don't explain
the phenomenon of consciousness itself. In my opinion, consciousness is
still a wondrous phenomenon generated by the soul.'

'Oh Thomas, you are persistent,' sighed Ben. 'However, it doesn't
really matter whether the soul generates consciousness or not, it still must
use the mechanisms of the brain to generate consciousness in the physical
body. The part of the brain absolutely essential for generating consciousness in the body is located just above the brainstem inside the thalamus,
and is called the centromedian nucleus of the thalamus (Alkire 2000, Bogen
1995, Fiset 1999, Zeman 2001, & figure 6.1). Destruction of the centromedian nucleus of the thalamus by disease or injury causes immediate loss of
consciousness which never returns again, regardless of whether there is an
eternally conscious soul or not (Bogen 1995, Zeman 2001). This is the so-
called thalamic-switch for consciousness (Alkire 2000). Reduction of
activity in this area of the brain by injury, disease, sleep inducing drugs, or

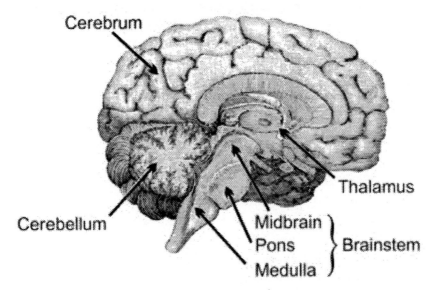

Figure 6.1 A cross-section of the brain showing the Thalamus and the component parts of the brainstem.

general anaesthetic drugs always causes loss of consciousness (Alkire 2000, Bogen 1995). The thalamus is relatively inactive during non-dreaming sleep, but is curiously almost normally active during dreaming, as well as during that phase of sleep just between sleep and awakening (Braun 1997, Kajimura 1999), indicating that some form of consciousness is present during these phases of sleep, but not during dreamless deep sleep. In other words Thomas – people possess a form of consciousness during the transition between awakening and sleep, as well as during dreaming. What do you think of that?'

'Wow ... is the only reaction I can think of again,' replied Thomas as he took a deep sip of wine. 'So what you are actually saying is that a person can actually be conscious, even though they may appear unconscious – such as during muscle paralysis, during severe oxygen starvation, during the phase between awakening and sleep, during dreaming sleep, and so on. A tricky concept – it means you can never be sure when a person is actually conscious.'

'Correct, except in very obvious situations, such as the baseball bat, or unconsciousness due to anaesthesia, and so on. And one last thing about consciousness: if there is such a thing as a soul, then the soul must use the mechanisms of the body to generate consciousness, because without a normally functioning centromedian nucleus of the thalamus, the soul cannot generate consciousness.' On these words, Ben looked around him, looked at Thomas, and said suddenly 'I'm hungry, but there's a lot more to discuss about the fascinating phenomenon of out-of-body experiences. Let's order some food. I'll pay.'

'Sounds like an exceptionally good idea,' replied Thomas enthusiastically, adding, 'especially since you're paying!'

The kitchen in this café-restaurant was fast, and after a few pleasurable minutes spent engulfing part of a meal of French fries and shashlik washed down with more wine, Ben paused, leant back with a contented look on his face, 'So, that's partly taken care of the inner man. I feel a lot better now. How about you Thomas?'

'I agree. Good French fries.'

'Yes, they usually get them just right here – a golden colour, not soggy, not much fat, and really good mayonnaise to go with them. So let's go on with our talk about the way the body can generate sensations of flying, floating, and of heaviness and paralysis. These are the essential components of experiences such as out-of-body experiences and nightmarish dreams, which you seem to think are paranormal experiences. To begin with, you now realize that people may appear unconscious, yet still possess some form of consciousness?'

'Yes, you've made that abundantly clear. You're just repeating yourself.'

'I know, but I'm just checking whether what I told you has remained firmly fixed in your mind. As I also said earlier, your brain is where you think and where your consciousness resides.'

'Just a minute Ben. According to me, mental activity occurs in the soul – the brain is merely the portal through which the mental activity of the brain can manifest in the body. At least that's what I've always been taught.'

'Even so, the soul still requires the mechanisms of the brain to manifest any consciousness or thoughts in the physical body. So where mental activity actually originates is irrelevant. Furthermore, the brain is enclosed within the hard bones of the skull. The brain itself has no sense organs, which is why surgeons can operate on the brain itself without any anaesthesia whatsoever, just using local anaesthesia to open the skin and skull covering the parts of the brain they want to operate upon (Penfield 1937). In fact the only way the brain and the soul can ever learn what is happening in the world around the body is through the nerve signals generated by the sense organs of the body, and transmitted along sensory nerves into the skull, into the brain, where these sensory nerve signals are interpreted. The effect of local anaesthesia proves this conclusively.'

'Oh, how can you say that?'

'Easily ... If you go to a dentist or a doctor you may receive an injection of local anaesthetic so that the dentist can operate on a tooth, or the doctor can perform a small operation. Once the local anaesthetic works, do you feel the pain of the operation in your body, or do you feel the pain of the operation in your soul?'

'Er ... Neither.'

'Precisely. Your soul is supposedly immaterial and unaffected by things affecting your physical body, such as local anaesthetics. So if some sort of wondrous sense organ of your soul sensed the operation, you would feel pain despite the local anaesthetic. But you don't feel anything, which means the soul, or your consciousness, also gains its information from the physical senses.'

'Aha! But what about the phantom limbs of amputees? You cannot see these phantom limbs, yet people who have a phantom limb can definitely sense the presence, the position, and other sensations such as pain in the phantom limb. And because these phantom limbs are invisible and immaterial, they must be a manifestation of the continued presence of the soul in the space occupied by the missing limb.'

'Thomas, you're doing it again, you're still attempting to find proof for the spiritual and immaterial. I'll start with the phenomenon of the pain people feel in phantom limbs. Phantom limb pain is very common, and up to 70% of amputees may develop pain in their phantom limbs (Nikolajsen 2001). You say that phantom limbs are a manifestation of the soul, yet this phantom limb pain can be temporarily removed by injecting local anaesthetic around the nerves going to and from an amputated stump (Birbaumer 1997). Now you always tell me that the immaterial soul is not affected by things affecting the material body. So tell me, how can pain in a manifestation of the soul be temporarily alleviated by something as physical as local anaesthesia?'

'Oh that's an easy question to answer. Phantom limb pain is quite evidently pain due to a multitude of causes in the physical body. The reason is easily understood: the soul feels no pain or discomfort, and the immaterial soul cannot be affected by things affecting the material body. So phantom limb pain must be due to something in the physical body that causes pain.'

'Well you wormed your way out of that one quite nicely. But now tell me the explanation for a curious but well known phenomenon in the medical world. Some people undergo operations upon their arms or legs under local anaesthesia. The effect of this local anaesthesia is sometimes really strange – these people feel that their anesthetized limbs are in very different positions to their real and physical limbs (Gentili 2002, Isaacson 2000, Paqueron 2003). In other words, these people have suddenly acquired phantom limbs which are in very different positions to their real limbs. How would you explain this very real and commonly observed phenomenon Thomas?'

Thomas looked disappointed, and after some thought, replied reluctantly, 'I can't, so this means phantom limbs are actually products of nerve signals transmitted along sensory nerves sending information to the brain from the limbs and other parts of the body.'

Ben looked unhappily at his empty plate. 'I enjoyed that. Good food. Shame it's finished. Ah well, at least now I can concentrate on the rest of my wine and the uphill battle I seem to be having explaining sensations to you. Finally, you've come to realize that the sensation of phantom limbs is a consequence of the functioning of the sensory nerves of the body. I'll give another example of how sensory nerves can generate powerful illusions. But first, I see you've also finished. I want a dessert. Do you also want dessert?'

'Is the Pope a Catholic, was Moses a Jew, was Mohammed an Arab, does a bear shit in the woods? Yes! Of course I want dessert! I was wondering when you'd ask. What have they got?'

'Not much, so I'm going to have a Tartufo, one of those balls of Italian chocolate ice-cream. It's the best looking dessert on the menu.'

'Sounds good to me. I'll have the same.'

The order given, Ben leaned back, 'As a small digression related to your statement about bears ... Did you know God is extremely irritable and conceited? God and the prophets of God cannot endure being teased by children, which is why on one occasion God killed some children for teasing a prophet of God!'

'Come now Ben, don't be ridiculous. God guards over the world and loves everyone, especially little children. Jesus, the Son of God told us this.'

And they were bringing unto him little children, that he should touch them: and the disciples rebuked them. But when Jesus saw it, he was moved with indignation, and said unto them, Suffer the little children to come unto me; forbid them not: for to such belongeth the kingdom of God. (ASV Bible, Mark 10:13-14)

'Nice try Thomas, but you seem to have forgotten that the God of the Jews, the Christians, and of Islam, is not only a God of the gaps, but also a God of inconsistencies. As I remember, we talked about these things the first time we met, as well as on other occasions. Furthermore, this God is in no way a God of mercy. This is a God of blood, of fire, and of violent death!'

'Ben, are you feeling well, have you been drinking too much, or have you been taking strange hallucinogenic pills? There is absolutely no proof of this in the Bible.'

'Oh no? I'll first give a general example. God carefully defined the borders of the land promised to the tribes of Israel when they left Egypt under the leadership of Moses (Bible, Numbers 34:1-12). But this land was already inhabited by tribes such as the Canaanites, Jebusites, Perizzites, Amorites, Girgashites, etc (Bible, Genesis 15:18-21). Predestination is a philosophy believed in by all followers of Judaism (Bible, Jeremiah 1:5), Christianity (Bible, John 6:64-67, Ephesians 1:3-6), and Islam (Koran 14:4, 28:56, 22:18). Now we are not speaking about some trivial, minor, local god here. The followers of these three great religions all believe God to be an eternal, all-pervading, all-knowing, all-powerful God who created and predestined all that was, is now, and will be in the whole universe. So God

165

knew the original inhabitants of the lands promised to the tribes of Israel had to be displaced to make room for the Israelites. Nonetheless, this all-knowing and all-powerful God did not elegantly arrange for these people to spontaneously migrate to another part of the world before the coming of the Israelites, nor did this God leave this part of the world unpopulated. Instead, this "loving and merciful" God told the tribes of Israel to apply a definitive "final solution" to these peoples, telling them to kill all the original inhabitants of the Promised Land: all men, all women, all children, and all animals (Bible, Deuteronomy 20:16). So it is that the Bible treats us to a nauseating chronicle of horrific orgies of destruction and carnage, describing how God's Chosen People reduced thriving cities such as Jericho, Ai, Makkedah, Libnah, Lachish, Eglon, Hebron, Debir, Hazor, and many others (Bible, Joshua 6,8,10,11,12) to scorched charnels heaped with decomposing corpses. All these "good and holy deeds" were carried out by the tribes of Israel on the divine orders of a "loving and merciful" God. Jesus, the Son of God was not one whit better than his father, because he also told his followers that his teachings were likely to precipitate violence and conflict!'

Think not that I came to send peace on the earth: I came not to send peace, but a sword. (ASV Bible, Matthew 10:34)

'Jesus expected violent reactions to his teachings, which was probably why he later exhorted his followers to buy a sword, if they did not already have one.'

And he said unto them, But now, he that hath a purse, let him take it, and likewise a wallet; and he that hath none, let him sell his cloak, and buy a sword. (ASV Bible, Luke 22:36)

'Were these swords intended for offence or self-defence? Is this a statement from a peace-loving prophet? So Thomas, as you can see, Jesus took after his father in his acceptance, and even his advocacy of violence! Is this a merciful God, a God of love, a God who cares for all his creations?'

Thomas looked somewhat depressed upon hearing this impassioned tirade, but brightened upon seeing the dessert arrive. 'I'll have to think about what you just said. It makes sense in a perverted sort of way. But I'm sure you must be wrong. I'm going to check the passages you've cited to see if you haven't just ripped them out of their proper context. As I've told you earlier, you seem to have a talent for finding passages in the Bible putting God and Jesus in the worst possible light. But look, our dessert has arrived, and my Tartufo is speaking clearly to me in a language I fully understand. It's saying, "Eat me, eat me, please eat me ... please ...""

The two men commenced eating, carefully, slowly, almost reverently spooning small amounts of chocolate ice-cream into their mouths. Expressions of delight and pleasure were evident on their faces. All too soon, nothing was left. Thomas sighed, 'I enjoyed that. But now for something serious, you were talking about God killing children with bears.'

'Oh yes,' responded Ben. 'I'd almost forgotten. Elisha was a prophet spreading the word of God. He was apparently also very bald. When he visited the city of Bethel, a crowd of children teased him about his baldness, upon which he was enraged and cursed them.'

And he went up from thence unto Beth-el; and as he was going up by the way, there came forth young lads out of the city, and mocked him, and said unto him, Go up, thou baldhead; go up, thou baldhead. And he looked behind him and saw them, and cursed them in the name of Jehovah. And there came forth two she-bears out of the wood, and tare forty and two lads of them. (ASV Bible, 2 Kings 2:23-24)

'So Thomas, your merciful, children-loving God sent two she-bears to tear 42 of these children to pieces for making fun of the baldness of one of God's prophets. This is true mercy. This is a manifestation of a divine love of children. Is this the true nature of God: irritable, conceited, and bloodthirsty, killing all who offend him, much as you or I would swat a fly?'

'I've never quite understood the reason for this passage either, except that God expects prophets of God to be treated with great respect regardless of their appearance.' Thomas looked rather withdrawn, adding quickly with an evasive and uncomfortable look in his eyes, 'But dessert is finished, and I think we've spent enough time digressing from the subject of how the body can generate sensations of flying and of weight.'

'You're right. I get carried away sometimes. Hmmn … Now where was I? Oh yes … we had disposed of the idea of phantom limbs being a manifestation of the soul. But now on the subject of sensation … For people such as me who do not believe in the existence of the soul, it is the functioning of the brain that generates consciousness, and the brain is the organ generating all properties of the conscious mind, such as conscious thought and processing of sensations. If you believe in the reality of an immaterial soul as the vehicle of the conscious mind, then you would say the physical brain is merely the interface between the immaterial soul and the material body. However, regardless of which of these two systems of thought you prefer, it still means that nerve impulses generated by sensations from the body, can only be perceived by the conscious mind after entering the brain through the very physical sensory nerves entering the brain. Are you following me?'

'Yes, that's elementary stuff.'

'I know, but many people strangely overlook this very basic principle. This basic principle means that the conscious mind can only learn what is happening to the body, and in the world around the body, through the medium of nerve signals transmitted along sensory nerves entering the skull. In turn, this means that if the brain receives sensory nerve signals indicating that the person is flying, or that the person feels light, or that the person feels extremely heavy, or that the person is falling, then the conscious mind of the person will experience these sensations. Look at a common illusion you can easily induce in yourself. Stand in a narrow doorway, arms straight, and press forcefully with the backs of your hands against the doorframe for about twenty seconds, as if trying to raise your straightened arms to shoulder level. Relax suddenly, let your arms hang next to your body, and you will perceive that your arms feel very light, as if they are floating. You know your arms are hanging next to your body, but your brain informs you they are floating away from your body. This is an illusion anyone can perform for themselves, and is an illusion caused by nerve signals from position sense organs in the arms and shoulders telling the brain that the arms are light and floating.'

'Oh yes, I know the illusion. I used to do it as a child, and sometimes it even felt as if my arms were floating upwards.'

'Yes, some people have that too. But as I said, it is an illusion of floating induced by abnormal nerve signals coming from the arm and shoulder position sensing nerves. This and many other illusions of movement, of weight, and of floating or flying, are all products of a particular type of muscle cell called a muscle spindle (figure 6.2). Muscle spindles are a special type of muscle cell that also happen to be the most important motion, weight, as well as position sensing organs in the body. They are sandwiched in between the normal muscle cells, and there is about one muscle spindle per one thousand normal muscle cells. The illusion of floating arms that I just mentioned, is caused by a continuation of sensory nerve activity generated by muscle spindles embedded between the muscle

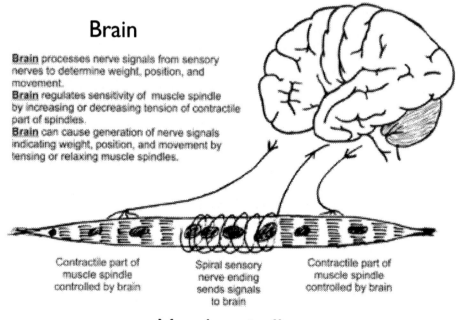

Brain

Brain processes nerve signals from sensory nerves to determine weight, position, and movement.
Brain regulates sensitivity of muscle spindle by increasing or decreasing tension of contractile part of spindles.
Brain can cause generation of nerve signals indicating weight, position, and movement by tensing or relaxing muscle spindles.

Contractile part of muscle spindle controlled by brain

Spiral sensory nerve ending sends signals to brain

Contractile part of muscle spindle controlled by brain

Muscle spindle

Figure 6.2 Muscle spindles are special muscle fibres embedded between the normal muscle fibres. They are actually sense organs signalling sensations of weight, position, and movements to the brain. Furthermore, the brain can also regulate the sensitivity and activity of these sensory organs.

fibres moving the arms away from the body indicating movement of the arms away from the body, even though the surrounding muscle fibres are now relaxed (Hagbarth 1998). Sensations of illusory limb positions and movements can also be aroused by low intensity electrical stimulation of sensory nerves (Gandevia 1985). Vibration of muscle tendons in the frequency range 30-100 Hz selectively stimulates muscle spindles, which then send sensory nerve signals to the brain, also arousing sensations of illusory movements and positions (Cardinale 2003, Goodwin 1972, McCloskey 1978). Indeed, exposure to powerful vibrations selectively stimulates muscle spindle sensory nerves, generating sensations of lightness, and of floating. This is possibly the reason why Harley Davidson motorbikes are so popular. In a world increasingly filled with motorbikes with quiet, almost vibration-free motors, the Harley Davidson stands out with its emphasis on the fact that the riders of these motorbikes want to feel the pounding vibrations of the piston motors powering these almost iconic motorbikes – the real Harley Davidson experience. Indeed, one Harley Davidson owner once confided in me that after an hour or two on his motorbike, he did indeed experience a feeling as if floating over the road, a veritable Harley Davidson epiphany.' Ben paused a moment to wet his throat, only to realize his glass was empty. He gave the empty glass a sour look, and waved his hand at the waiter, 'Two beers please! I saw your glass was also empty, so I assumed you also wanted beer. Much better than that revolting Merlot we were drinking.'

'Yes, you're not wrong there. Thanks.'

'Now you must understand that muscle spindles are active sensory organs – they don't just react passively – the brain also modulates their sensitivity and even the patterns of sensory nerve signals they generate. Put simply, this means that the brain itself can cause these muscle spindles to tense and relax independently of the surrounding muscle fibres between which they are embedded. This, together with small movements of the muscles surrounding muscle spindles, means muscle spindles can generate combinations of sensory nerve signals indicating sensations of illusory movements, such as of flying, or of falling, without any of these events actually occurring (Lanier 1986, Lanier 1994). These sensations can be incorporated into dreams of movements, flying, or falling in people whose consciousness is altered at the same time as their muscle spindle electrical activity is increased, such as occurs during normal dreaming sleep (Askenasy 1990, Hoed 1979), or due to some anaesthetic drugs that activate muscle spindles (Hobbs 1988, O'Sullivan 1988). These dreams of movements, actions, falling, floating and flying, are due the effects of drugs and movements on the functioning of muscle spindles, and trick the mind into feeling the body is flying. Are you still following me Thomas?'

Thomas nodded uncertainly, 'I must admit it is difficult material, but you're the expert.'

'Glad to hear it. But just bear with me a bit Thomas, and hopefully it will all become blindingly clear. Now I've talked about the feelings of lightness, of flight, and movement, but haven't really discussed feelings of heaviness and weight. Not altogether surprisingly, feelings of heaviness and of great weight are also generated by muscle spindles. People sense that a limb or body part feels heavy, or is more difficult to move, when the muscle spindles in that body part are less tense, or more relaxed than the muscle fibres surrounding them (Gandevia 1977, Gandevia 1977a). Now the implications of all these things are truly fascinating!'

'Oh yes ...' was the all but fascinated reaction.

'Now Thomas, this is the really interesting bit. Muscle spindles are the source of sensations of lightness and floating, and of sensations of weight and heaviness, as well as sensations of position. When muscle spindles are more tensed than the muscle fibres between which they are embedded, that part of the body feels lighter than normal, or even that it is floating. And when muscle spindles are less tense than the muscle fibres between which they are embedded, the affected parts of the body feel heavier than normal, or even that they are falling. But muscle spindles are not passive sense organs – they are active sense organs whose activity is also regulated by the brain. This means that conscious and unconscious mental control changes their activity and the sensations they generate. So a person can unconsciously regulate the activity of their muscle spindles such that they are all less tense than the surrounding muscle fibres to generate a sensation of great weight and falling, which sometimes happens just as you are falling asleep. Other people train themselves to uncon- sciously selectively tense the muscle spindles throughout their bodies to generate the sensations of lightness, of flying, and of motion, while at the same time generating visual imagery appropriate to these sensations of flight. This is how people exploit the functioning of the body to generate the out-of-body experiences known as astral travel, where some people claim the ability to voluntarily travel outside the material body with their immaterial consciousness.'

'I don't know about this explanation Ben,' was the pensive response from Thomas. 'It's glib and depressingly plausible, and may even be an explanation for some out-of-body experiences. So you may possibly be correct when you say that some dreams of movements, flying and floating, are due to this type of bodily mechanism. But how common are dreams of flying and floating, and do they reveal anything about whether the body or the soul causes them?'

'Flying and floating dreams are actually not that common, which is probably why most people remember them. Studies of dream reports during normal sleep (Domhoff 2004), as well as during anaesthesia (Huang 2005), reveal that less than 1% of dreams involve sensations of floating or flying.'

As Ben spoke, the beer arrived, and the two thankfully laved their parched throats with the golden elixir. Thomas wiped his mouth, and looked seriously at Ben. 'You've talked a lot about the complex physical mechanisms generating dreams, but you seem to have forgotten the simplest explanation – the same ancient idea of which Cicero wrote, that dreams are messages from the immaterial world of the soul, perhaps even messages from God as is stated in the Bible.'

For God speaketh once, yea twice, though man regardeth it not.
In a dream, in a vision of the night, when deep sleep falleth upon men, in slumberings upon the bed; (ASV Bible, Job 33:14-15)

'Oh Thomas, not that old chestnut again ... Followers of Islam also believe that dreams may be prophetic, or are from God. Much the same as you are claiming for followers of Judaism or Christianity.'

Narrated Abu Huraira: Allah's Apostle said, "The (good) dream of a faithful believer is a part of the forty-six parts of prophetism." (Bukhari 87:117)

'But that's really boring ancient stuff Thomas. We've already discussed that prophecy in dreaming is simply due to chance (Chapter 4). Much more fascinating is how the mechanisms of the body can generate flying dreams. This materialistic approach enables experimental study to increase knowledge of physically provable aspects of dreaming, whereas to regard dreams as manifestations of some sort of paranormal contact with an immaterial spiritual world is to stop all investigation and research, because nothing of these beliefs in the immaterial are amenable to experimental research. So tell me Thomas, what do you think is the yield of knowledge about dreams after thousands of years of belief in their supernatural origin? Don't bother answering. The answer to my question can be summed up in two words. Absolutely nothing! Nothing whatsoever, except the belief that dreams are a form of supernatural contact with an immaterial world. No more than that. A pitiful result for so many thousands of years of profound belief in the paranormal nature of dreams, and after so many thousands of years of human experience and development in all other aspects of human life. Don't you think so too?'

'Er ... I guess so. You try and explain these dreams then.'

'Well, we've discussed the ways the sense organs of the body can trick the mind into thinking the body is flying or floating, but the functioning of the brain can also do the same.' Ben paused for more beer, as he warmed to his subject.

Thomas also drank some beer, leaned back in his chair, and looked with almost exaggerated attention at Ben.

'Why are you looking at me like that Thomas?'

'Oh, I was just thinking of what Saint Paul once said about the types of discussions we've been having. He warned against sophists, philosophers, and others who try to get believers in Christianity to stray from their faith with worldly arguments.'

And my speech and my preaching were not in persuasive words of wisdom, but in demonstration of the Spirit and of power: that your faith should not stand in the wisdom of men, but in the power of God. (ASV Bible, 1 Corinthians 2:4-5)

'I've heard that one before Thomas. It's typical language for many prophets. They all warn their followers against being seduced away from the faith they preach, telling them they should follow a more spiritual path rather than that of this material world. In fact, these words of Saint Paul were mimicked centuries later by a revelation given the prophet Mohammed by God, which some people might say is proof that not all Saint Paul said was Christian propaganda.'

O mankind! Lo! the promise of Allah is true. So let not the life of the world beguile you, and let not the (avowed) beguiler beguile you with regard to Allah. (Koran 35:5)

'Anyway, enough of this; here is some more honeyed atheistic guile and sophistry. Consider Thomas, when you close your eyes and visualize your body, you can precisely sense the positions of your limbs, the appearance of your body, the way your clothing appears, and your position in relation to all things around you. This is the image of your body in your mind. Without this body image in your mind you would be very handicapped, because you use information from this body image to move without hurting yourself or others, to reach and grasp things, and to move in your surroundings. And all this sensory information is derived from sense receptors distributed throughout your body. Would you agree with me?'

'I'm not quite sure. How can you say that this body image is just a product of mental processing of sensations from sense receptors located throughout the body? And what exactly do you mean by sense receptors?'

'By sense receptors, I mean the organs sensing taste, sight, smell, hearing, touch, movement, position, weight, pain, pressure, etc. These are all called sense receptors. There are many types of sense receptors located throughout the body, except within the brain itself. Body image is a product of unconscious integration within the brain of information derived from a multitude of sense receptors, although those receptors sensing weight, movement, and position are the most important (Gandevia 1999, Schwoebel 2001, Spence 2004). We know this is true, because body image becomes distorted and abnormal when sense receptors provide the brain with faulty information, or cease to function altogether due to anaesthesia, injury, or disease (Maravita 2003, Ramachandran 1998a, Vignemont

2005, Zampini 2004). All these things mean there is no intrinsic natural sense of body image within the brain; the brain can only generate and sustain the body image with sensory information derived from sense receptors located throughout the body. Does that answer your question Thomas?'

'Well yes, but only to a certain degree though …'

'Well, what I'm going to tell you now will really knock your socks off. Sensory information from all the sense receptors is processed in certain parts of the brain to generate the body image, such as in the parietal lobes, as well as in the angular gyrus (figure 6.3). Malfunction or injury to these parts of the brain causes abnormalities of the body image (Blanke 2000, Ramachandran 1998a, Zampini 2004). Indeed, detailed electroencephalograph studies, as well as brain scans of living people who report undergoing out-of-body experiences, reveals that abnormal functioning of the angular gyrus can cause people to undergo out-of-body experiences (Blanke 2004). Even more surprisingly, stimulation of the angular gyrus with weak electric currents during brain surgery performed under local anaesthesia, can actually induce out-of-body experiences in some people (Blanke 2002, Blanke 2004, Penfield 1955).'

'That's incredible! Does this mean the angular gyrus is the seat of the soul, or is the angular gyrus the part of the material brain that somehow communicates with the immaterial soul?'

'I don't think you need a soul at all. The angular gyrus is just that part of the brain integrating information from many types of sense receptors to generate a body image in the mind. No more than that. Malfunction of this area of the brain whether it be induced by disease, or by electrical currents, causes this area of the brain to generate a body image whose position and motions no longer correspond with those of the body. Now, you would say that the mechanisms of the angular gyrus do not generate this body image, but that the soul generates this body image. Even so, this soul of yours must use information from the physical senses to do so, and must also use the mechanisms of the angular gyrus to communicate this body image to the body.'

Thomas thought for a short while, and responded, 'Ah, but the soul doesn't need information from the physical senses. So how do you arrive at that idea about the soul needing information from the physical senses?'

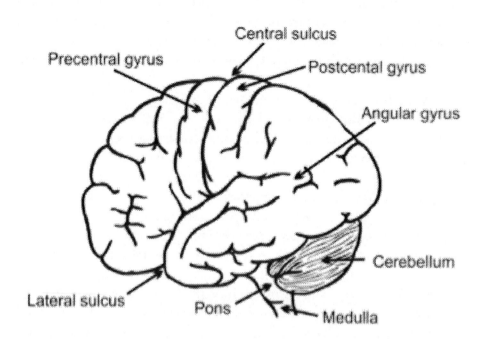

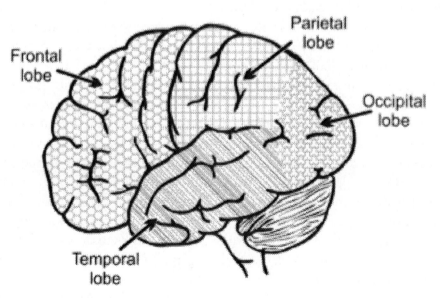

Figure 6.3 Lobes and basic surface anatomy of the human brain.

'Thomas, do you believe the conscious mind with which each of us thinks is actually the consciousness of the soul?'

'Yes ...'

'Then this means that the soul receives and uses information from the physical senses. The reason I can confidently state this as a fact is because injuries, diseases, and local anaesthesia can all profoundly change conscious body image perception (Maravita 2003, Ramachandran 1998a, Vignemont 2005, Zampini 2004). Now if the conscious mind is immaterial, simply communicating with the body through the angular gyrus, and does not use perceptions derived from physical sensations, then changes to physical perceptions should have no effect upon the conscious body image. But changes in body function, injuries, and diseases do alter conscious perception of the body image. These things make only one conclusion possible – if there is a soul, it uses information from the physical senses to generate and utilize the body image.'

Thomas looked dissatisfied. This was not really what he wanted to hear. Suddenly he had a luminous idea. 'You've been talking about illusions and hallucinations induced by changes in body function, but the immaterial soul is unaffected by things affecting the body. So what you have are the perceptions of the immaterial soul, and the perceptions of the material body. The immaterial soul is evidently quite capable of perceiving the material world, a fact proven by the veridical imagery reported by people who undergo out-of-body experiences. In addition to this, the physical brain perceives the world about the body with the physical senses. So the totality of our individual perceptions of the world around us is actually a combination of perceptions derived from the soul and perceptions derived from the body's physical senses!' Thomas looked quite pleased with this idea, and continued enthusiastically, 'Proof of this idea of dual perceptions is actually revealed by these same hallucinations you use to try and explain the soul away. For example, a person experiences illusions and hallucinations due abnormal body function, but realizes the true nature of these perceptions even while experiencing them. You could call this a form of dual consciousness – a consciousness of the physical body and a consciousness of the soul. The reality of such a dual consciousness in people is manifested and proven by situations where the perceptions of the body do not correspond with those of the soul. This explains this dual awareness people sometimes experience.'

'Okay, give me an example of this dual consciousness.'

Thomas thought a moment, 'If you stand up and spin around until you become dizzy, then lie down on the floor and close your eyes, you perceive the world as spinning around, yet you know this is an illusion. This is what I mean by a dual consciousness. Your material brain perceives the information from your physical senses telling you the world is spinning around, yet your immaterial consciousness is unaffected and knows this sensation is an illusion.'

Ben laughed, 'Bravo Thomas. You've excelled yourself with this example. It is nonsense of course, but well reasoned from the perspective of a person who believes in the reality of an immaterial consciousness. However, this concept of a dual consciousness just introduces another complication, making the idea of a soul even less tenable. After all, to accept that the mind is a product of the functioning of the brain, and that the brain generates a mental image of the body from sensations derived from the physical senses, is far less of a leap of faith than what you have just proposed with this idea of a dual consciousness, or dual awareness, or whatever you want to call it. The very idea reminds me of what Saint Augustine, one of the early Christian saints, once said about the nature of faith.'

Faith is to believe in what you cannot see; the reward for this faith is to see what you believe.

Ben paused to wet his throat with more beer. 'I can't prove the presence or absence of an immaterial soul. Instead what I'm trying to do is to show you that all these so-called spiritual phenomena can be explained with physical sensations. To explain these phenomena with physical phenomena gives a way of viewing these phenomena which enables study and experimentation, whereas to believe these phenomena are immaterial and invisible, is to revert to the same system of thought as our ancient forefathers – a system of thought which has not progressed from mere belief for many thousands of years.'

'Well I guess that's one way of looking at these things,' was the grudging reply.

'Furthermore, to believe that the soul and the body may differ in their perceptions, actions, and patterns of thought is to dismiss the concept of a just God altogether.'

'Huh ...! However do you arrive at that conclusion?' was the surprised reaction from Thomas. It was evidently his day to be surprised by all Ben said.

'Just think logically about what you just said about there being a dual consciousness in the human body, whereby the perceptions of the body and of the soul sometimes do not correspond. This implies that the body and the soul are each conscious, each aware, and each can think. But what happens when a soul, determined to behave well so as to attain a just reward in heaven, is imprisoned within a malfunctioning body whose deeds are violent, whose thoughts are depraved and lustful, and prone to commit every sin known to man and God. A soul housed in such a body would have to endure a lifetime of struggle to try and prevent the body sinning. Would death bring any reward in heaven to a soul imprisoned in such a body? Absolutely not! Such a soul would be condemned to hell for the sins of the body, even though the soul tried preventing these sins. Holy books only prescribe eternal torment in hell for sins and crimes committed by the material body. They do not even mention sins committed by the soul, just sins committed by the body. Such a situation would be incredibly unjust, whereas all believers claim God is just. This is a theological reason why a dual consciousness cannot exist in one body.'

'Come on Ben, don't be ridiculous,' spluttered Thomas. 'How could such a thing happen? Body and soul are united, and they never diverge much in character, which is why each soul does indeed receive its just reward in an afterlife.'

'Okay, you pay for the next beer and a kebab later tonight if I can give you two examples proving what I just said. Otherwise I'll pay.'

'I'll be glad to. It's a wager I'm sure to win. I'm sure you can't find any proof for your ridiculous proposition of a soul imprisoned in a body which acts contrary to the wishes of the soul.'

Thomas began to get a sinking feeling in his wallet as Ben began. 'The first example should appeal to you. It was provided by no one less than Jesus of Nazareth himself. You may remember we discussed it earlier (Chapter 1). While still alive in his physical body, Jesus told his disciples to spread his message only among the Jewish people, but not among the Samaritans or non-Jewish peoples (Bible, Matthew 10:5-6). Jesus was more spirit than flesh after his crucifixion and resurrection, and just before ascending to heaven in this form, he instructed his disciples to spread his message among all the peoples of the world (Bible, Matthew 28:18-20). This last command to his disciples was a radical change from his first command to limit his message to the Jewish peoples. So what we have here is a wonderful example of how the functioning of the earthly physical body of Jesus at first distorted the message from his soul. Or don't you think so?'

Thomas groaned. This argument was not going the way he thought it should. He muttered, 'I guess you might have a point there. But I wonder if the manuscript of the book of Matthew isn't corrupt, or has it been modified during the time of writing and now?'

'Thomas, I don't know that. All I know is what is clearly written in the Bible, and this is what I read. However you are quite free to question the veracity of the Bible if you want. But let's get on to the second example I promised you. This is the well-documented story of Phineas Gage, and is a perfect illustration of my proposition. Phineas Gage was a foreman in charge of a group of railway workers preparing the rail bed for a new railway line in the state of Pennsylvania in the United States of America. During the afternoon of 13 September 1848 CE, an accidental explosion drove a large iron staff through his head. The iron staff entered his head just under his left cheekbone, and emerged above his left eye (figure 6.4), and landed about fifteen meters away. He awoke after a short period of unconsciousness, and recovered from this terrible injury after some months. But his personality was dramatically changed by this injury. Before his accident he was an efficient and capable worker. He used no profane speech, and was friendly as well as considerate of his fellows. After his accident, he became erratic and irreverent, at times using the grossest profanity, manifested no deference to his fellows, was impatient of advice and restraint when it conflicted with his desires, and while he made many plans, he was totally unable to remember or carry them out. His friends all stated that he was simply not the same man as before the accident (Damasio 1994, Neylan 1999). Quite a dramatic injury, and a very dramatic effect. Now Thomas, here we have an example of a person who

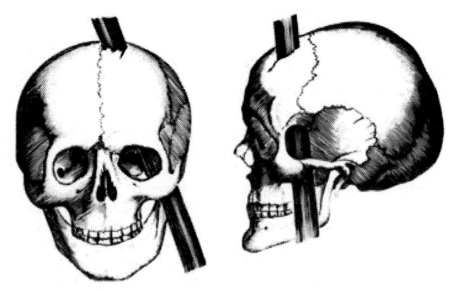

Figure 6.4 The path of the iron staff through the head of Phineas Gage.

changed from being a pleasant God-fearing amiable man, to a profane, potentially violent drunkard as a result of an injury to his physical brain. The physical injury to his brain could not have affected his soul, because the soul cannot be harmed by things harming the body. So his basically good soul was trapped in a profane and drunken body, unable to exert any influence upon this body. Here you have a simply wonderful example of a man whose actions during life merited eternal torment in hell, even though his soul deserved reward in heaven. Now for that beer! I've earned it.'

Thomas looked thoughtful, 'I do believe you have a point there. When you think about the idea of dual consciousness like that, then it doesn't sound so logical after all.' He waved at a waiter, 'Two beers please!'

Ben nodded and continued, 'An example like Phineas Gage makes you realize it is very likely that it is the functioning of the body that generates all the properties of mind. So let's go further, using examples of out-of-body experiences to show how the functioning of the sense organs of the body, or of the angular gyrus, or both together, can generate experiences of flying, of floating, and even of leaving the body. I'll begin with a story of a young man who told me about his out-of-body experience. But first some beer!'

This had just arrived. Ben sighed, 'Ahhh ... that was good. Nothing like some of the amber fluid to lubricate the vocal cords. I was beginning to get thirsty after all that talking. Now, as to the story of the young man.'

The anxious young man, accompanied by his mother, was supposed to undergo a small operation for an ingrown toenail. Local anaesthesia was administered. Shortly afterwards he noticed a strange, but very pronounced taste on his tongue, and started to feel unwell. He told his mother he felt strange, and felt himself losing consciousness. Subsequently he saw his body moving and jerking. He saw all this from a vantage point next to his body, on the side opposite his mother. His mother looked anxious, but he himself felt calm and unconcerned. He also saw his grandmother, (who had recently died), welcoming him with opened outstretched arms. She appeared no different than she appeared in the years before her death. Soon afterwards he awoke back in his body. (A real account told the author by the patient himself).

Thomas looked impressed. 'How could he have seen his deceased grandmother?'

'I'll deal with this man's vision of his deceased grandmother in a moment. The main point of this story is that this young man quite evidently had a generalized epileptic convulsion caused by an accidental overdose of local anaesthetic. The abnormal electrical discharges in his brain due to the generalized epileptic convulsion evidently stimulated structures within the temporal lobes of his brain, so arousing visual memories of his deceased grandmother (Gloor 1982), as well as activating his angular gyrus, to induce an out-of-body experience (Blanke 2002, Penfield 1955). This is an example of an out-of-body experience primarily induced by abnormal nervous activity within the angular gyrus.'

'Fascinating Ben. I'm always impressed the way you manage to wring a flood out of a damp cloth, as with this explanation.'

'I know Thomas, I know. But I can't help myself. So let's look at examples of various vivid flying dreams so we can see common elements. The night journey of Mohammed which is mentioned very briefly in the Koran is a good report to begin with.'

Glory to (Allah) Who did take His servant for a Journey by night from the Sacred Mosque to the farthest Mosque, whose precincts We did bless,- in order that We might show him some of Our Signs: for He is the One Who heareth and seeth (all things). (YA Koran 17:1)

'The Sunnah of Al Bukhari and of Sahih Muslim contain more detailed accounts of this night flight, Islamic scholars have also studied this story in some detail. Sometime during the year 621 CE, the year before persecution in Mecca forced him to flee to Medina in 622 CE, Mohammed slept in the vicinity of, or actually within the Kaaba. This small building in Mecca, the direction in which all followers of Islam pray, was once also the focus of a local religious cult preceding Islam. As he slept, the archangel Gabriel provided Mohammed with a winged creature called Buraq upon which he flew to the furthest mosque, which may have been in Jerusalem or in Medina. There he performed some prayers, and returned to Mecca after also making a short visit to heaven and hell where he met and spoke with Moses, Aaron, Adam, and Allah (Bukhari 93:608). Here is a brief account of the night flight in the Sunnah of Sahih Muslim.'

It is narrated on the authority of Anas b. Malik that the Messenger of Allah (may peace be upon him) said: I was brought al-Buraq Who is an animal white and long, larger than a donkey but smaller than a mule, who would place his hoof a distance equal to the range of vision. I mounted it and came to the Temple (Bait Maqdis in Jerusalem), then tethered it to the ring used by the prophets. I entered the mosque and prayed two rak'ahs in it, and then came out and Gabriel brought me a vessel of wine and a vessel of milk. I chose the milk, and Gabriel said: You have chosen the natural thing. Then he took me to heaven. (Muslim 75:1:309)

'Now Thomas, I won't discuss this experience just now, but compare it with some other experiences. The first interesting experience is the way witches in the Middle-Ages said they were transported to their orgiastic witches' Sabbat celebrations. A typical story of attendance at a Sabbat located far from the witch's home is interesting.'

> *The alternative opinion, which personally I hold most strongly, is that sometimes at any rate Witches are actually conveyed from one place to another by the Devil, who under the bodily form of a goat or some other unclean & monstrous animal himself carries them, & that they are verily and indeed present at their foul midnight Shabbats. This opinion is that generally held by the authoritative Theologians and Master Jurisprudists of Italy and Spain, as also by the Catholic divines and legalists. The majority of writers, indeed, advance this view, for example, Torquemada ... (Summers 1994, page 128)*

'And then you have the more modern variant of this story – abduction by beings from outer space.'

> *When an abduction begins during the night, or, as is common, during the early hours of the morning, the experiencer may at first call what is happening a dream. But careful questioning will reveal that the experiencer had not fallen asleep at all, or that the experience began in a conscious state after awakening. ...*
> *After the initial contact, the abductee is commonly "floated" (the word most commonly used) down the hall, through the wall or windows of the house, or through the roof of the car. They are usually astounded to discover that they are passed through solid objects, experiencing only a slight vibratory sensation. In most cases the beam of light seems to serve as an energy source or "ramp" for transporting the abductee from the place where the abduction starts to a waiting vehicle. (Mack 1994, page 33)*

Ben finished expounding, emptied his beer glass with one gulp, and looked at Thomas with a definitely challenging gaze. 'Now you tell me the similarities in these three accounts.'

Thomas drank some beer to give himself time to think. 'These experiences all seemed to occur during the night, but all similarities cease there. After all, abduction by beings from outer space is quite different to flying with the aid of supernatural animals.'

'Actually, when you examine all these reports carefully, there are more similarities than the miserable single similarity you mentioned. Admittedly it is an important similarity, but there are others you missed. So let's enumerate them systematically.'

'Okay.'

'Firstly, these are experiences where the physical bodies of the persons could never have made the journeys they described during their experiences. They are all journeys made in the minds of the persons concerned. In the case of Mohammed, there is some dispute whether his night journey was to Jerusalem or Medina. Now Jerusalem is about 1200 kilometres, and Medina is 340 kilometres from Mecca. Mohammed could never have gone to either of those places, and returned during the space of one night, because the fastest mode of transport at that time was a horse. The same is also true for the far journeys made by witches – these far journeys were also physically impossible during the Middle-Ages, the time when these stories were current, because horses were still the fastest mode of transport at that time too. Similarly, the modern journeys made to spaceships are also physically impossible. These are not stories of journeys made by the physical bodies of the persons concerned, because those reporting undergoing these journeys are transported as immaterial bodies that could pass through physical walls and roofs. So these three apparently different stories, are stories of transportation of something immaterial, or reports of mental journeys. Secondly, we know that the people undergoing such experiences were sleeping at the time they underwent them. This is clearly stated by Sahih Bukhari in the case of the night journey of Mohammed, who was asleep during his night journey (Bukhari 93:608). The nocturnal journeys of witches in the Middle-Ages to far places also occurred after midnight, and the persons returned to their homes at dawn (Summers 1994, pages 116-118). There are even reports of imprisoned witches under continuous observation in their cells as they slept. Yet upon awakening these witches reported making incredibly wild night journeys to a Sabbat (Summers 1994, pages 129-130). Similarly, the physical bodies of people abducted by extraterrestrial beings also remain in their beds during these abductions, and as with Mohammed and witches in the Middle-Ages, most abductions occur during the night, during the early hours of the morning (Mack 1994, page 33). Now, between midnight and dawn, is just the time period during sleep when most people dream. Furthermore, it has long been known that dreaming occurs during episodes of a particular type of sleep called rapid eye movement sleep, episodes of which occur most often in the early morning. And now we come to the third and final common element in these reports. This is the sensation and actual experience of flight and movement these people reported undergoing, even as their bodies lay sleeping and unmoving.'

Ben paused to wet his throat, pouring a stream of cooling beer past his tonsils. 'Are you following me so far?'

Thomas looked excited, 'Yes, it's quite clear when you explain it like that. I never imagined that such diverse stories from different cultures and ages could actually contain identical elements.'

'As I said, the fundamental elements of these stories are identical, but the imagery is related to the societies and the cultures in which the people reporting them live. What really is fascinating is how the body generates these sensations of movement, motions and flight. Most of the muscles of the body are paralyzed during rapid eye movement sleep, but the electrical activity of muscle spindles is actually increased during rapid eye movement sleep (Askenasy 1990). The activated muscle spindles can generate signals indicating illusory movements of motion and flight to the conscious dreaming brain. And even though the dreaming brain is conscious, this is an altered state of consciousness during which those areas of the brain responsible for critical analysis, such as the prefrontal lobes, are less active than when a person is normally awake (Lövblad 2003, Schwartz 2002). So the dreamer perceives illusory sensations of motions, of actions, or of flight, and uncritically integrates these sensations into imagery containing these sensations. Upon awakening, these memories are further integrated into a coherent story, and may be told to others. This is the genesis of the flying dream. So you see Thomas, the body generates out-of-body experiences as a result of illusions: illusory interpretation of nerve signals from muscle spindles, illusory interpretation of abnormal nerve activity in the angular gyrus, or illusory interpretation of a combination of muscle spindle nerve signals combined with abnormal angular gyrus function. All these illusory interpretations of real sensory nerve signals, together with, or without angular gyrus malfunction, are accepted as real sensations, and as a real interpretation of what is happening by a mind which then uncritically generates the seeming reality of an out-of-body experience.'

'But Ben, what about the imagery? Sometimes people really do accurately report things they could not have seen when they lay motionless during their out-of-body experience. How do you explain that?'

'Easily – we've discussed this before (Chapter 5, "The blind can see"). When a person lies apparently motionless but conscious, they hear things, they smell things, and feel sensations from all that happens about them and to them. If their eyes are open, they can even see things. They hear the voices and conversations of those people about them. Just as blind people do, they sense the size of the room in which they are in. They also have expectations about the appearance of things derived from their life experiences. All these sensations are integrated into a complete picture of their surroundings, and things they expect to see during their out-of-body experiences. These are the things they report to others after returning to a state where they are capable of talking to others. This is the imagery of out-of-body experiences (Ehrsson 2007, Lenggenhager 2007).'

'Even so Ben, it's still a dissatisfying explanation to me, even though I do believe the body may sometimes be able to generate out-of-body experiences by these mechanisms.'

'As I said Thomas, these are the mechanisms by which the body can generate these apparently wonderful experiences. However, this explanation does not exclude any beliefs you still might harbour about the paranormal. Regard it as an alternative explanation. Although I must admit, it does explain everything, and does enable experimentation to be performed to prove it, which is quite different to explanations based on the invisible, immaterial forces and entities you apparently still believe in. Explanations based on such beliefs are a matter of faith. They must simply be believed, because it is impossible to subject them to any sort of experimental proof. But as I say, take your choice of explanation; I'll stick with the provable physical explanation.'

'I'll have to do a lot of thinking on this one,' sighed Thomas, as he stared blankly before him.

'You do that,' said Ben, standing up on somewhat unsteady legs. 'You know something, all this alcohol has lowered my blood sugar to such low levels, all I can think of is a kebab ... Not a good idea to drink so much wine and beer. Come on ... you're paying.'

Thomas stood equally unsteadily, nodded, and the two men slowly made their erratic way to the nearest kebab restaurant.

Chapter 7

Knocking on heaven's door

'Oh dearly beloved,' thundered the preacher from his high pulpit, 'there is not a living being alive that will not die! You will all die, I will eventually die, all followers of Islam will eventually die, and all followers of Judaism will eventually die, as will all followers of other religions. We will all die! This is the certain fate of all who live. This is the punishment suffered by all generations of humankind since the original sin committed by the first woman. It is well to ponder upon how this came to be (Bible, Genesis 2 & 3). Adam was the first man. But he was lonely, so God created him a helpmeet and companion from one of his ribs. This was the first woman, and she was called Eve. God gave them eternal life in the paradise of the Garden of Eden, giving them immortality and freedom to do all they wanted but for one thing – God forbade them to eat the fruit of the apple tree. But Eve, weak as are all women, allowed herself to be seduced by the powers of evil in the form of a serpent, disobeyed God and ate of the fruit, at the same time seducing Adam to follow her in her disobedience of God. She wilfully disobeyed God! She wilfully disobeyed her very creator! She disobeyed her Lord and Master, with whom both she and Adam had such direct contact. She wilfully allowed herself to be seduced to enjoy some brief sensual pleasure, while at the same time dragging Adam with her into the abyss of disobedience to her Creator! And all this for the sake of mere ephemeral earthly gratification! This is ever the way of women! So it was that God punished Eve and Adam, and all subsequent generations of humankind with mortality for this original sin. Oh dearly beloved, my blood boils when I think of her base lust for fleeting sensual enjoyment! The Bible, the true message of God, tells us how God cursed humankind for her sin.'

In the sweat of thy face shalt thou eat bread, till thou return unto the ground; for out of it wast thou taken: for dust thou art, and unto dust shalt thou return. (KJV Bible, Genesis 3:19)

The preacher paused to let the words take effect, and continued, 'It is because of this original sin that we have lost our direct relationship with God! It is because of this original sin that we are condemned by God to grow old and infirm! It is because of this original sin that we are condemned by God to eventually die, to rot away and the substance of our bodies to return to the elements forming them! And all because of this original sin of the first woman! Cursed be Eve! Cursed be Eve the mother of all humankind!'

Ben shifted uncomfortably on the hard pew, eventually finding a position where he could relax somewhat. 'Why did I ever let Thomas talk me into coming with him to an early Sunday service to listen to what he claims is an inspirational preacher? Nothing inspirational here. Half-baked demagogue …' and with these thoughts his head began to nod and he began to doze.

'Tok!' A solid tap of the beadle's cane upon his head returned Ben to full consciousness. He had forgotten about the corpulent, sweaty little beadle, and his cane. Beadles had recently been reintroduced into several churches, especially the more fundamentalist churches. One of their various functions was to patrol churches during services to ensure that people did not sleep. The method used by this particular beadle was to forcefully tap sleeping men on the head with one end of his cane, and with the feathers attached on the other end, to tickle the noses of sleeping women.

The preacher was now in his stride. 'But be of good cheer dearly beloved, death is not the end. We know this short earthly life is but a period of preparation for the true life, the life after death, the life which is eternal, an eternal life in the presence of Jesus and the angels in the Kingdom of God! To die in the grace of our Lord and saviour Jesus is to live forever in the splendour of heaven, there to be united with our forefathers, with the saints, the angels, and God. This is the glory awaiting all true believers. So we must be glad we do not live forever! Our faith, our belief, and our knowledge of this truth burns as a beacon in our hearts, giving us strength and succour in our daily lives. This is the wonder and glory of the message of Jesus, for he told us these very things! Listen to the promise of Jesus!'

> *My sheep hear my voice, and I know them, and they follow me: and I give unto them eternal life; and they shall never perish, and no one shall snatch them out of my hand. My Father, who hath given them unto me, is greater than all; and no one is able to snatch them out of the Father's hand. I and the Father are one. (ASV Bible, John 10:27-30)*

'Rejoice dearly beloved! Rejoice in your faith in Jesus! For life eternal in the Kingdom of Heaven is your reward for your faith. But all those who knowingly repudiate, and refuse to follow the path of Jesus will never receive eternal life. Jesus, the true Son of God, told us this is very clear terms.'

> *He that is not with me is against me, and he that gathereth not with me scattereth. (ASV Bible, Matthew 12:30)*

'The fate of those repudiating the message of Jesus is horrid beyond belief! Their destiny is eternal torment in the fires of hell, in the lake of fire prepared for accursed sinners, apostates, heretics, and all who refuse to follow the way of Jesus the Son of God!'

> *Seeing it is a righteous thing with God to recompense tribulation to them that trouble you;*
> *And to you who are troubled rest with us, when the Lord Jesus shall be revealed from heaven with his mighty angels,*
> *In flaming fire taking vengeance on them that know not God, and that obey not the gospel of our Lord Jesus Christ:*
> *Who shall be punished with everlasting destruction from the presence of the Lord, and from the glory of his power; (KJV Bible, 2 Thessalonians 1:6-9)*

'This is the lot of those refusing to acknowledge and follow the paths of righteousness set out by Jesus, the Son of God. When these loathsome wretches ultimately confront God their maker, as they certainly will, they will be justly condemned for their refusal to follow the true path of our Lord. They will be cast into the lake of fire! They will burn in everlasting fire! Eternal pain! Eternal torment! Horrid and doleful indeed! The very thought of such punishments as these should be sufficient to drive these contemptible dogs into the arms of true Christian belief. Oh dearly beloved, you may well ask why I call such unbelievers vile, loathsome, and contemptible. I do this because the signs of the true belief are all about us. The awesome power and glory of God is manifest in the heavens and in the perfection of the world in which we live. Furthermore, the very truth of the path of righteousness of Christianity is proven by the many miracles performed by Jesus the Son of God, and in particular, the fact that Jesus could raise the dead back to life (Bible, John 5:19-21)! This is conclusively proven by the story of Lazarus (Bible, John 11:1-45), as well as of the raising of the dead ruler's daughter (Bible, Matthew 9:18-26). Only the true Son of God could have power over death such that he could restore life to the dead! Moreover, Jesus himself triumphed over his own death on the cross, returning to life after three days of death (Bible, John 19:41 to 20:17). Truly, such signs are evident to even the most hard-headed of all unbelievers. Yet these obstinate wretches persist in their unbelief, prefer-ring to follow a foolhardy and perverse belief in false religions and false gods, in full knowledge of their ultimate fate. They are truly owners of the fire, and destined to burn forever in the hell they so justly deserve!'

The preacher paused for effect, as well as to wipe the rabid froth from the corners of his mouth. He was evidently in good form. Some members of the congregation used the pause to loudly call, or to mutter, 'Amen.' 'Eternal fire is too good for them!' called one man. 'They deserve continual beatings with iron staves as well as eternal hellfire!'

The preacher drank some water, flashed a quick smile of approval, and launched into his finale, 'But dearly beloved, this does not mean we should feel smug about the certainty of our reward in heaven, or superior to these benighted creatures. Instead we must be sad and have pity upon these wretches who knowingly hurl themselves into hell. However, all that is permitted us is to try and save the souls of those marked as Christians from certain and horrid doom, and this is all. Our leaders in the European Parliament have made laws forbidding the proselytizing of those belonging to other religions, justifying this law with the fallacious argument that all religions are equal, saying that such proselytizing is an affront to other equally noble religions. Personally I find this attitude unbelievable, even unpardonably immoral, when the glories of Christianity are so clear, and so evident. Such laws make it illegal to attempt saving the eternal souls of our Jewish and Islamic fellows by teaching them the errors of their religions, teaching them the promise of Jesus, and converting them to Christianity. However, Jesus whose wisdom is the infinite wisdom of God, instructed us to obey our earthly leaders (Bible, Matthew 22:21). So we can do no more than bow to the superior wisdom of Jesus, for the words of Jesus are part of the inscrutable plan of God for mankind. All we know is that God has placed our earthly leaders above us, to rule us on this physical world, to test our faith, to try us, to see if we are worthy of the Kingdom of Heaven. We know this from the Bible, where we read the words of Saint Paul, confirming and explaining the message of Jesus in language clear to all who can read or hear.'

Let every soul be in subjection to the higher powers: for there is no power but of God; and the powers that be are ordained of God. Therefore he that resisteth the power, withstandeth the ordinance of God: and they that withstand shall receive to themselves judgment. For rulers are not a terror to the good work, but to the evil. And wouldest thou have no fear of the power? Do that which is good, and thou shalt have praise from the same: for he is a minister of God to thee for good. But if thou do that which is evil, be afraid; for he beareth not the sword in vain: for he is a minister of God, an avenger for wrath to him that doeth evil. Wherefore ye must needs be in subjection, not only because of the wrath, but also for conscience' sake. For this cause ye pay tribute also; for they are ministers of God's service, attending continually upon this very thing. Render to all their dues: tribute to whom tribute is due; custom to whom custom; fear to whom fear; honor to whom honor. (ASV Bible, Romans 13:1-7)

'Dearly beloved, obey your rulers. Obey the new laws forbidding the proselytizing of followers of Judaism and Islam. Have pity in your hearts for these pathetic satanically deluded fools who wilfully condemn themselves to eternal hellfire. Rejoice in the knowledge of your own certain reward in heaven, for as believers in the teachings of Jesus, this is your reward and your future. That is my message for today. God be with you, aiding you in your struggle with the forces of evil and all forms of foul demonic temptation.' And with a resounding, 'Amen!' the preacher fell silent, his head bowed in silent prayer.

'Well,' said Thomas enquiringly as they emerged from the church, 'that was really good. That's what I call a really inspiring sermon. What did you think of it?'

'Not much,' was the terse reply.

'Why not? I thought it was very good. Rousing stuff.'

'Thomas, you heard the same things I did. You also have the benefit of having looked critically at some of the basic tenets of Judaism, Christianity, and Islam. What you just heard from this rabid demagogue is actually no more than an obsequious acceptance of future total Islamic dominion over Europe.'

Thomas looked offended, and retorted, 'How do you derive that from his speech? According to me, his sermon was truly inspired by the basic tenets of Christianity and had nothing to do with Islam whatsoever.'

'That's certainly true to a degree, but he also included a very definite Islamic term. At one point he talked about "owners of the fire". Terms such as "people of the fire", and "owners of the fire" are found nowhere in the Bible, yet are repeatedly used throughout the Koran and the Sunnah of Bukhari as terms for heretics and sinners who are destined to go directly into the fires of hell. Here's a good example.'

But they who disbelieve, and deny our revelations, such are rightful owners of the Fire. They will abide therein. (Koran 2:39)

Ben continued, 'When you consider this very definitely Islamic element, and couple it with this preacher's use of the injunction of Saint Paul not to go against the wishes of the ruling government authorities as regards conversion of the followers of Islam to Christianity, then you have a preacher who is something quite different to what he pretends. He is actually a crawling cockroach in the service of Islam, whose true but unsaid purpose, is to sustain the population of Christians to fulfil a disadvantaged role in any future Islamic society. We've already spoken about how Saint Paul did indeed say that our earthly rulers were placed above us by God to rule us (Chapter 5). This indicates that Saint Paul was a clever man, because it made Christianity an ideal religion for slaves, serfs, and conquered peoples – all of whom now heard that their Christian God told them to obey their masters. The rulers of the then ruling Roman Empire must have wriggled with delight upon hearing such a statement. Wonderful! For Saint Paul, it meant that his new cult of Christianity would possibly even propagate with tacit government approval. Subsequent rulers throughout the Christian world have used this same reasoning to justify their rule and subjugate others to it, proudly saying that they ruled by divine right. Just look at the motto on the coat of arms of the sovereigns of England, and of the English government. It says "Dieu et mon droit", which is French for "God and my right", meaning that they rule by divine right! Now this very same Biblical justification is flung in our faces to justify obedience to recent laws forbidding conversion of followers of other religions to Christianity. Not that I care at all for converting followers of other religions to Christianity – all religions are actually equally good. However it is a manifestation of the way the countries of Western Europe are subsiding into a form of de-facto subservience to Islam, because however elegantly this law is worded, its main intent is to forbid the conversion of followers of Islam to Christianity. Furthermore, allowing preachers to rail against the followers of all other religions so as to strengthen the sense of community of Christians, sustains the numbers of non-Islamic peoples living in a form of second-rate citizenry in an Islam dominated region. A consequence of this is also an increased taxation basis, because non-Islamic people will eventually be required to pay the Jizya, or poll tax in some places.'

Fight those who believe not in Allah nor the Last Day, nor hold that forbidden which hath been forbidden by Allah and His Messenger, nor acknowledge the religion of Truth, (even if they are) of the People of the Book, until they pay the Jizya with willing submission, and feel themselves subdued. (YA Koran 9:29)

'That's really paranoid Ben! We aren't subservient to Islam, and we don't pay anything like a Jizya! You're fantasizing!'

'Not really. Why is it that our predominantly Islamic city council has forbidden the sounding church bells at all, while permitting the deafening Islamic call to prayer five times a day, forbids serving alcoholic drinks outside on terraces during Islamic prayer times, as well as the European law forbidding missionary work to convert people to other religions. When you consider these things, then you realize we're well on the way to becoming an Islamic land.' Ben looked sombre for a moment, but suddenly brightened, with a mischievous grin on his face. 'But Thomas, why should we worry about Islamic domination? After all, Islam really is actually a technologically far more advanced religion than Judaism or Christianity. So it must be better. After all, unlike the latter two religions, Islam also acknowledges the reality of intelligent life on other planets!'

Thomas spluttered, 'Really! Don't be ridiculous! This is really too much!'

'I can prove it!' said Ben. 'Just consider the following passage in the Koran.'

And of His portents is the creation of the heaven and the earth, and of whatever beasts He hath dispersed therein. And He is Able to gather them when He will. (Koran 42:29)

Ben looked triumphantly at Thomas, 'You can't get any clearer than that about the reality of extraterrestrial life!'

'I guess you're right when you look at it like that,' was the grudging reaction.

'Ah but Thomas, Islam even tells us why the efforts of America and Russia to develop travel to outer space and other planets have stagnated, and even failed up till now. This passage in the Koran tells us why.'

O company of jinn and men, if ye have power to penetrate (all) regions of the heavens and the earth; then penetrate (them)! Ye will never penetrate them save with (Our) sanction. (Koran 55:33)

'Yes Thomas, it appears from the Koran that only Allah, the name the followers of Islam give to God, can give people permission to travel into outer space. But have the Americans or the Russians ever asked Allah for permission to travel in outer space? Not that I know of! What is more, up till now only Jews, Christians, atheists, agnostics, or others, have been used as astronauts, but no followers of Islam have ever been permitted to travel into outer space. To imagine that space travel could be successful without prior permission from Allah, as well as even thinking that non-Islamic astronauts would be permitted to enter outer space, is not only utter folly and monstrously presumptuous, but is also a heretical negation of the truth of Islam! These are the reasons for the failure of the American and Russian development of space travel up till now!'

Thomas looked bewildered. He examined Ben seriously for a moment to see whether he was serious, before chuckling, 'Okay, okay Ben, you've had your fun, but you still haven't told me exactly why you thought the sermon was rubbish.'

'Very well, I'll continue. The preacher told us that only the followers of Christianity will receive the reward of eternal life in heaven. It's actually no different to the basic tenet of Islam which claims that those who do not follow the injunctions of Islam are doomed to eternal torment in hell – a fate that is absolutely certain for those who ignore the manifestly evident signs of the truth of Islam.'

Aforetime, for a guidance to mankind; and hath revealed the Criterion (of right and wrong). Lo! those who disbelieve the revelations of Allah, theirs will be a heavy doom. Allah is Mighty, Able to Requite (the wrong). (Koran 3:4)

'And,' continued Ben, 'there are countless other passages in the Koran saying exactly the same. Who is right? After all, the followers of each religion claim their religion is the one true belief. So who are the followers of the one true religion: the followers of Judaism, the followers of Islam, or the followers of Christianity? To begin with, I cannot see the souls of the dead. I cannot visit the world of the dead. And I cannot look into heaven to see which the one true religion is. In fact, it's even very disputable whether humans have an invisible and immaterial soul, or whether there is a life after death at all. It's all a matter of faith, of belief. No more than that.'

'Aha,' responded Thomas, 'but there is evidence for all these things. There are the death-bed experiences of the dying, as well as the experiences of those who were clinically dead and returned to life. These experiences are true glimpses of the truth of a life after death, the nature of this promised eternal life after death, and proof of the ultimate truth of Christianity.'

'Oh dear Thomas, I do believe you're talking about the so-called evidence from near-death experiences. This could be a rather long discussion. Let's go and have a cup of coffee somewhere, and discuss these experiences you seem to believe prove the reality of Christianity as the one true faith.'

'I'd be interested in hearing how you're going to try wriggling your way out of the true proofs provided by these experiences. So let's go.'

Soon the two men were seated with steaming mugs of coffee in a neighbourhood café. Ben sipped and sighed happily, 'Ah, that's what I needed. There's nothing like irrigating your throat with fresh black coffee to loosen up the vocal cords. Good coffee! Strong, black …'

'Come on Ben, enough of your delaying tactics. Get on with it,' said Thomas as he also appreciatively drank his coffee. He desperately needed to recover from Ben's comments on the church service, as well as the concept of Islam-sanctioned astronauts.

'Impatience is not a virtue young man. Just enjoying my coffee … But I'll start. A short while ago you were speaking about the proofs of the reality of a life after death provided by those who returned to life after a period of clinical death. I assume you mean those wondrous experiences called near-death experiences?'

'Yes I do. Near-death experiences are a uniform and consistent group of experiences. And the uniformity and the consistency of these experiences prove the reality of a life after death. Why otherwise would these experiences be so similar across so many centuries and so many different peoples?'

'Okay, just checking that we're talking about the same thing. It's true that throughout all human history, stories have been told of the wondrous revival of some people from death, of inexplicable happenings associated with the dead, of the ghosts of the dead visiting the living, of people who visited the realm inhabited by the souls of the dead while they themselves were near to death. Such stories have been told and retold since the dawn of time. Many people are awed by such stories. Many people really do believe them to be proof of the reality of the continuation of some form of life after death of the body. They tell and retell these stories. They clasp them to their bosoms, cherishing them as true proof of a life after death. More recently, a certain Doctor Raymond Moody, and subsequently many others have published books describing these wondrous experiences undergone by the nearly, or apparently dead. These stories are indeed wonderful. They also reveal common patterns and similar elements. Just as you said, the very fact that these near-death experiences contain so many similar elements is proof to many people of the reality of these reports, as well as giving them proof of the reality of a life after death. Moody even constructed an archetypal near-death experience report.'

A man is dying and, as he reaches the point of greatest physical distress, he hears himself pronounced dead by his doctor. He begins to hear an uncomfortable noise, a loud ringing or buzzing, and at the same time feels himself moving very rapidly through a long dark tunnel. After this, he suddenly finds himself outside of his own physical body, but still in the immediate physical environment, and be sees his own body -from a distance, as though he is a spectator. He watches the resuscitation attempt from this unusual vantage point and is in a state of emotional upheaval.

After a while, he collects himself and becomes more accustomed to his odd condition. He notices that he still has a 'body' but one of a very different nature and with very different powers from the physical body he has left behind. Soon other things begin to happen. Others come to meet and to help him. He glimpses the spirits of relatives and friends who have already died, and a loving, warm spirit of a kind he has never encountered before a being of light appears before him. This being asks him a question nonverbally, to make him evaluate his life and helps him along by showing him a panoramic, instantaneous playback of the major events of his life. At some point he finds himself approaching some sort of barrier or border, apparently representing the limit between earthly life and the next life. Yet, he finds that he must go back to the earth, that the time for his death has not yet come. At this point he resists, for by now he is taken up with his experiences in the afterlife and does not want to return. He is overwhelmed by intense feelings of joy, love, and peace. Despite his attitude, though, he somehow reunites with his physical body and lives.

Later he tries to tell others, but he has trouble doing so. In the first place, he can find no human words adequate to describe these unearthly episodes. He also finds that others scoff, so he stops telling other people. Still, the experience affects his life profoundly, especially his views about death and its relationship to life. (Moody 1976, pages 21-23)

'Now Thomas, I agree with you, these experiences are amazing. It's not at all surprising that people change after undergoing such profound and wondrous experiences occurring in conjunction with a life threatening event. Moody actually constructed this archetypal report from the ten elements he found people reported most often (Moody 1976).'

- A feeling of peace and calm.
- The sense that death was imminent or had occurred.
- Hearing a noise or music.
- The experience of entering a tunnel or darkness.
- The experience of leaving one's body.
- Meeting figures, strangers, deities or deceased relatives.
- Meeting a being of light, or entering into a brightness or light.
- A review of the major events of one's life.
- The experience of encountering a border, or limit, the passing of which means certain death.
- The conscious decision to return to the body.

Ben paused to drink a little coffee, and continued, 'Wonderful visions, and wonderful experiences. However, it's debatable whether these features really do define the near-death experience, because this is simply a list of the most common elements reported by those who underwent such an experience. There is also a distinct possibility that many of these common elements might actually be related to the cause of the near-death experience, rather than being components of the near-death experience itself.'

'Sounds like splitting hairs to me,' was the somewhat sour reaction from Thomas. 'Of course these are all component elements of the near-death experience, otherwise why do people report them so frequently?'

'That's a bit too simple for me and other people too. Luckily a Doctor Bruce Greyson once thought the same too, and did a very good statistical analysis of all the various elements of near-death experiences reported by people to determine which experiences were related to one another. His reasoning was that elements of these experiences that are strongly related to one another are components of the near-death experience, while elements unrelated to any of the other component elements of the experience were very likely due to the cause of the near-death experience, rather than being component elements of the near-death experience itself (Greyson 1983) He found there were basically four different clusters of components truly belonging to the near-death experience. He defined these four different clusters as: affective, cognitive, transcendental, and paranormal (Greyson 1985).'

The didactic rigor with which Ben approached this subject began to wear on Thomas. He shifted uncomfortably, and in a half-interested tone asked, 'What do you mean by the terms affective, cognitive, transcendental, and paranormal?' fully knowing this would elicit yet another torrent of meticulous, but tedious analysis. 'Why,' he thought. 'Why me? All I wanted was confirmation of whether near-death experiences were proof of the truth of Christianity ...' He moaned inwardly as he sipped the remainder of his coffee.

But Ben was totally immune to subtlety, and equally immune to disinterest. He was in his stride, continuing enthusiastically, 'I knew you'd be interested. These four basic groups of experiences, or rather the four basic near-death components, are defined as follows:'

- *Cognitive components:* time seems to speed up, thought is very rapid, review of scenes from the past, understanding of the universe, oneself and others.
- *Affective components:* a feeling of relief, peace or pleasantness, a feeling of joy or happiness, a sense of harmony or unity with the

universe, seeing, or being surrounded by bright light.

- *Paranormal components:* senses are more vivid than usual, extrasensory perception, seeing scenes from the future, separation from the body.
- *Transcendental components:* entering a mystical or unearthly world, encountering a mystical being or presence, seeing deceased relatives, friends, or religious figures, coming to a barrier, or point of no return.

Ben began to get really enthusiastic, leaned towards Thomas, and said, 'This may surprise you, but this classification of near-death experience components doesn't include the well known tunnel or darkness experience, which most people think typifies near-death experiences. Bruce Greyson found that even though a "tunnel experience" does occur in about 32% of near-death experiences, it isn't related to any other element. This indicates the experience of being in a "tunnel" is more likely to be a product of the disorders causing near-death experiences, rather than being a component of the experience itself (Greyson 1983). A really surprising conclusion, don't you think?'

Thomas began to rouse and show more interest. 'That is surprising. Go on.'

'Now most near-death experiences contain some, but not all of these elements, which means that near-death experiences can differ between different people. Indeed, this same indefatigable Bruce Greyson found these component groups also defined different types of near-death experiences. He found in another analysis of near-death experience reports, that some people had predominantly affective near-death experiences, although their experiences might also include some paranormal, transcendental, or cognitive components. He also found that some people had predominantly cognitive near-death experiences, while others had predominantly transcendental near-death experiences. However, he found that no-one ever reported undergoing predominantly paranormal near-death experiences (Greyson 1985). This concept of different types of near-death experiences is fascinating. It makes it possible to compare the nature of near-death experiences undergone by different people, different groups of people, as well as between people of differing cultures.'

'Are there any differences?'

'Indeed there are. One surprising observation was that women and men are equally likely to have affective, transcendental, or cognitive near-death experiences (Greyson 1985).'

'So why is that surprising?'

'Because the upbringing of women and men is quite different, their social expectations and roles are also different, and they have a somewhat different biology. All these things mean you might expect women and men to have different chances of undergoing each of the three types of near-death experiences. But what really is surprising from Greyson's studies is that expectations modify the types of near-death experiences people undergo (figure 7.1). People undergoing totally unexpected life-threatening events, are equally likely to undergo a cognitive, an affective, or a

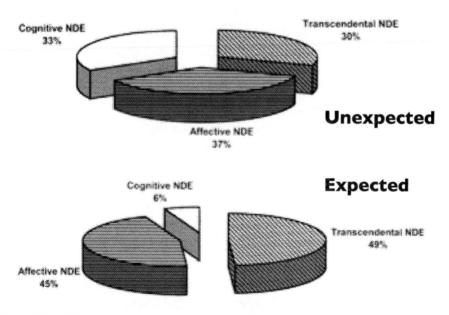

Figure 7.1 The chances of undergoing affective, cognitive, or transcendental near-death experiences (NDE's) are quite different when undergoing a totally unexpected life-threatening event, than when consciously undergoing an event known and perceived to be life-threatening (data from Greyson 1985, p < 0.001).

transcendental near-death experience. However, when people undergo an event they believe to be life-threatening, they either undergo transcendental or affective near-death experiences, but almost never undergo cognitive near-death experiences (Greyson 1985). So people undergoing near-death experiences as a result of expected, or perceived life-threatening events such as serious illness or major operations, often report felling calm, seeing transcendental worlds, or seeing deceased people who act as guides in the world inhabited by the souls of the deceased. Now that's what I call a wonderful demonstration of the way expectations modify a so-called paranormal experience!' finished Ben in an almost triumphant tone.

'I agree,' said Thomas. 'It's not actually what you would expect from an experience proving the reality of a life after death. Strange ... I can't understand it.'

'Well Thomas, it's actually not that strange when you look at it from my point of view. If near-death experiences are a true glimpse of an afterlife, then expectations should not have any effect on the nature of this life after death. But here you have an example of expectations changing the nature of the afterlife experienced by those undergoing near-death experiences. To me this constitutes proof that near-death experiences occur only within the minds of those undergoing these experiences, rather than that they are glimpses of an afterlife.'

'Hmmnn ...' was all a pensive Thomas managed to say.

Ben continued his discourse, 'However, despite the above indication of the true nature of these experiences, the real question is whether near-death experiences truly are products of the functioning of the body during life threatening situations, or are they true revelations of the truth of God, of a human soul, and of a life after death? I approach this problem by studying the functioning of the human body. We know the human body is the same for all people, and has remained the same for thousands of years. So if the ultimate mechanism of death is the same for most people, then the functioning of the body will change in a similar way for all people during the process of dying, so generating similar patterns of sensations and experiences for most dying peoples. This would also explain the many similarities between near-death experiences reported by people in different cultures very well.'

Thomas thought for a short time. 'I can't believe that. There are so many different causes of death. How could this veritable plethora of causes of death result in similar experiences?'

'I really do hate relieving you of yet another of your delusions,' smirked Ben with an expression indicating completely the opposite, 'but when you analyze the worldwide causes of death, you realize that the cause of the terminal, and everlasting loss of consciousness of death in more than 90% of dying people is ultimately due to failure of oxygen supply to their brains (Murray 1997). I won't bore you with the exact details, but because the cause of the terminal loss of consciousness of death is failure of oxygen supply to the brain in more than 90% of all dying people: more than 90% of all dying people will experience the effects of failing oxygen supply to their brains and senses during the period they slide into the eternal unconsciousness of death (Woerlee 2003, chapter 15). Such increasingly severe oxygen starvation of the brain and sensory organs generates a really quite standard set of sensations, emotions, and experiences. This is why many near-death experiences contain similar elements.'

'I find that hard to believe,' was the pensive reaction. 'So what are these similar elements caused by oxygen starvation?'

'A large number of studies have been done to study the effects of oxygen starvation on brain function. All these studies were summarized many years ago, and no one has really added much more of any significance. I'll summarize these changes for you. But first let's have some more coffee. This is thirsty work. Waiter, two black coffees please!'

Soon, fortified with another mug of steaming black coffee, Ben began again. 'You've always got to look at the sensations and experiences generated by oxygen starvation in terms of the organ systems most sensitive to oxygen starvation. The organ systems generating conscious sensations and experiences that are most sensitive to oxygen starvation are the eyes and the brain. So let's look at these changes systematically.'

- Anxiety and the reaction of the human body to severe disease, as well as to severe oxygen starvation, cause the pupils to widen. As you know by now, widened pupils can result in people seeing "bright light that does not hurt the eyes", to "enter the light", as well as all manner of light experiences. Furthermore, widening of the pupils can cause people to see "figures of light", or "beings of light", as well as to see coloured auras of light surrounding people and objects (chapter 3, "Windows of the Soul").

- The retina requires more oxygen than those parts of the brain generating consciousness. This is why increasingly severe oxygen starvation will cause varying degrees of failure of retina function before affecting consciousness, all of which means that vision fails before consciousness is lost due to oxygen starvation. This manifests as greying of vision, as darkness, and as passing through a tunnel (chapter 3, "Windows of the Soul").

- Oxygen starvation induces a relatively consistent pattern of brain dysfunction. One of the first and most consistent effects of brain oxygen starvation is to cause malfunction of the prefrontal lobes of the brain (Gastaut 1957, Gastaut 1961, Aminoff 1988). Malfunction and failure of this part of the brain results in feelings of a generalized lack of concern, calm, serenity, and an indifference to pain or life-threatening situations (Liere 1963, pages 299-322).

- Together with these visual and psychological changes, moderately severe brain oxygen starvation also causes malfunction of other areas of the frontal lobes of the brain (figures 6.3 & 7.2). One of the most evident changes is a sensation of muscle weakness caused by partial dysfunction of the primary motor cortex, whereby the affected person feels that every movement requires intense effort. More severe degrees of oxygen starvation cause failure of extensive areas of the surface of the frontal lobes, (or frontal cortex). Failure of the supplementary motor cortex induces a state whereby the person lies passive and still, initiating no spontaneous movements. In fact, the idea of moving does not even arise in the minds of people with supplementary motor cortex failure. Failure of all functions of the frontal lobe cortex results in a total inability to move any muscle, no matter how hard a person tries to move. For example: failure of Broca's speech area means a person cannot speak even though they may try to do so, failure of the frontal eye fields means the person cannot move their eyes even though they may try to do so, and failure of the primary motor cortex means the affected person

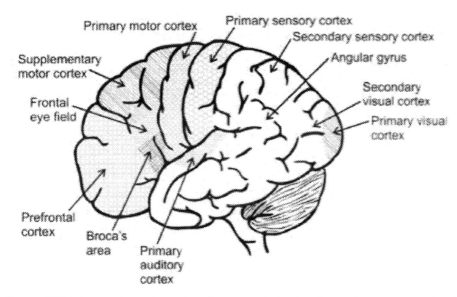

Figure 7.2 The various functional areas of the brain surface, or cerebral cortex.

cannot move any part of their body even though they may try to do so. This is really amazing. It means that people may be conscious, yet appear unconscious during a period of severe oxygen starvation, because they are totally paralyzed, trapped within an unmoving unresponsive body (Rossen 1943, Liere 1963, pages 299-322). This is what I call apparent unconsciousness, and this apparent unconsciousness is the reason why people undergoing near-death experiences cannot move or tell people they are awake and alive, only being able to tell of their experiences after recovering the ability to speak.

- Sudden severe brain oxygen starvation almost always causes generalized epilepsy (Aminoff 1988, Rossen 1943, Gastaut 1961). Generalized epilepsy is like an electrical storm in the brain, causing a generalized malfunction, yet at the same time sometimes arousing other parts of the brain to generate conscious sensations. Such abnormal electrical activity within the brain is similar to stimulating some parts of the brain with electrical currents. When this occurs in the structures of the temporal lobes: sounds, memories of events, memories of people, and memories of music may be aroused (Gloor 1982, Gloor 1990), as well as visions of gods and holy figures (Dewhurst 1970). This is how the malfunctioning body can generate visions of a life review during near-death experiences. This is how the malfunctioning body can generate visions of people living and dead during near-death experiences. And this how the malfunctioning body can generate visions of religious figures during near-death experiences.

• This same generalised epilepsy causes abnormal function and stimulation of those areas of the brain involved with generating the sense of body position, such as the sensory cortex and the angular gyrus, as a result of which oxygen starved people may undergo out-of-body experiences (Chapter 6, "Return flight to Paris").

Ben paused, drank the rest of his coffee, stared reflectively at the dregs in his cup, and continued, 'As you see Thomas, everything, all sensations, and all components of near-death experiences can be explained in terms of the functioning of the body during the life-threatening events arousing these near-death experiences. You don't need to invoke anything divine or spiritual such as an immaterial soul, or a world inhabited by the souls of the dead, to explain these experiences.'

'Hmmm … I agree with you to a degree. You've convinced me that some elements of these near-death experiences are caused by abnormal body function. Even so, you still haven't provided a really satisfyingly convincing explanation for the fact that many people see Christian saints, Jesus, and sometimes even God during their near-death experiences – all of which is proof of the truth of Christianity, and the reality of the glorious life after death in a Christian heaven promised us by Jesus.'

Ben was taken aback – stunned. He thought he had just demonstrated the true biological nature of the near-death experience. And now Thomas refused to believe it, simply saying that to have seen Christian saints, Jesus, or even God during such experiences was proof of the reality of an eternal life after death in an exclusively Christian heaven! This was shocking! This was a regression from reasoned analysis to wilful ignorance and blind faith! This was a repellent and low form of recidivism!

Ben took a deep breath, mentally counted to ten, and firmly said, 'Thomas, I do believe we need lots of beer before I start explaining the visions you call proof. Waiter! Two beers please!'

'I think I needed that,' sighed Ben emptying a half glass of foaming, golden fluid. 'There is nothing like rinsing your parched throat with cold beer to get the vocal cords back in condition, as well as to calm the disappointed brain.'

'I agree,' sighed Thomas in an equally satisfied tone. 'Ben, you seem a little upset by what I said about near-death experiences being proof of a life after death.'

'Quite right – I am. But I guess it's difficult for someone like you to dispense with articles of belief after a short discussion. So I'll explain why I was peeved. To begin with, all the sensations and emotions reported by people who underwent near-death experiences can be explained by changes in the functioning of their bodies during these experiences. Many people say this diminishes, trivializes, or actually demeans these experiences in some way. This is absolutely not true. The fact you can explain these experiences in terms of changes in body function does not mean they are any less profound or wonderful. It simply means the genesis of these experiences is explicable, and rooted in the functioning of the body, as are all our conscious experiences and sensations. Then we get to the matter of the religious figures, saints, holy people, and deities seen by people during their near-death experiences. Examination of the near-death experiences reported by people from different cultures and religions all reveal the same thing – people see the religious figures, and gods of the pantheon of the religion in which they believe, and were brought up with (Osis 1986, Pasricha 1986). So a Christian will see religious figures related to the Christian pantheon, a Hindu will see figures related to the Hindu pantheon, a follower of Islam will see figures related to the Islamic pantheon, a Buddhist will see figures related to the Buddhist pantheon, while a Jew will see figures related to the Jewish pantheon. This is no more than confirmation of an already old observation expressed in the Tibetan Book of the Dead (Evans Wentz 1960, pages 33-34). This is the reality of the religious figures seen during near-death experiences. Accordingly, seeing figures related to the pantheon of a particular religion during a near-death experience is very definitely no proof of the truth of that specific religion.'

Thomas looked crestfallen. He was silent for a while as he stared vacantly at his beer. Suddenly he brightened, 'Aha, so perhaps religious imagery perceived during near-death experiences is no proof of the truth of the truth of Christianity, but people do definitely see their deceased relatives who guide them in their new life after death. I would also definitely consider this to be one of the best proofs of a life after death.'

'I wouldn't be too sure of that either if I was you,' was the immediate reaction, accompanied with a mischievous smile. 'It's true, many people reporting near-death experiences do tell of meeting with deceased relatives and friends during these experiences. But as I already told you, these visions can also be products of memories of these people aroused by abnormal nervous activity in the structures of the temporal lobes (Gloor 1982). So I very much doubt whether these visions of deceased relatives people report seeing during near-death experiences really are the souls of their departed relatives and friends.'

'How can you be so certain of that Ben? After all, the people reporting these things actually positively recognize their relatives as well as the other people they see.'

'Well Thomas, there are two lines of evidence proving that the images these people see during near-death experiences are just hallucinations, or remembered images of the people they say they saw. A large study of the relationships of the people seen during near-death experiences was published by two parapsychologists Karlis Osis and Erlendur Haraldsson (Osis 1986). They compared the relationships of deceased relatives seen during near-death experiences reported by 240 persons living in the USA with those reported by 178 persons living in India, and found them to be very different indeed. People living in the USA mainly reported seeing their deceased spouse or mother during their near-death experiences, while those living in India mainly reported seeing other deceased relatives and strangers during their near-death experiences (figure 7.3). This is a profound difference – so different that the possibility this difference would have occurred by chance is less than one in one thousand (p < 0.001, Chi-square test).'

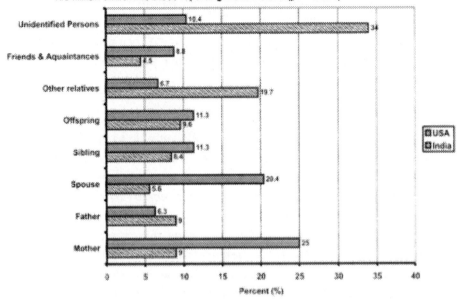

Relationships of people seen in the near death visions of 240 USA citizens and 178 Indian citizens to those reporting these visions (p << 0.001)

Figure 7.3 Graph showing the differing percentage chances of seeing different types of family members, or even strangers during near-death visions of people living in the USA and India (data from Osis 1986). This graph clearly shows the differences between the visionary experiences of those undergoing near-death experiences in the USA and India.

'That is strange,' was all Thomas managed to say.

Ben continued, 'Now the body structure and function of an inhabitant of India is precisely the same as that of an inhabitant of the USA. So if the visionary content of near-death experiences is only determined by the functioning of the body, or by the immutable nature of an eternal afterlife, there should be no differences in the nature of the apparitions seen during near-death experiences undergone by adults living in the USA or in India; they would see each type of deceased relative, acquaintance, or even strangers with equal frequency during near-death visions. But they do not. This fact is proof that the visions of deceased peoples seen during near-death experiences are more likely to be socio-culturally determined hallucinations, rather than being proof of a life after death, or manifestations of the functioning of the body. And this brings us to the most conclusive evidence for the hallucinatory nature of these visions.'

'You can't prove that!' retorted Thomas.

'Oh, but I can. The evidence is well illustrated by a near-death experience report where a person saw her deceased parents in the Christian heaven during her near-death experience.'

The peace that I felt was indescribable, it was something I have never known before and I have never been able to reach again, even in moments of meditation or great beauty. I saw my parents approaching me, they appeared as I always remembered them to be. They seemed not at all surprised to see me, in fact they looked as if they were waiting for me and saying, 'We've been waiting for you.' I know we communicated some things and I believe many things, but I don't remember really what they were. I know that I was in the surroundings of something very beautiful, very spiritual. I can only say that I believe that I was in a state of total cosmic consciousness. I know that I communicated with my parents and with people around me, but it was not in words, it was a form of telepathic communication. (Grey 1986, page 51)

'Tell me Thomas, what do you notice about this report?'

'I would normally say this was an example proving the reality of a life after death, but now I'm not so sure what you want to prove with this experience.'

'Aside from the spiritual and paranormal smokescreen in this story, one thing stands out – this woman saw her parents as she always remembered them to be! She saw them as an older man and woman. Incredible! Why wouldn't her father want to resume his younger appearance in heaven – to appear as he was when he was young, powerful, handsome, and attractive. The same reasoning also applies to her mother. Why wouldn't she want to appear as she was when young, at a time when she was a beautiful and desirable young woman? Yet the report of this woman is very similar to many other near-death experience reports where prior deceased elderly family members appeared to those reporting these near-death experiences as idealized, and healthier versions of how they appeared shortly before they died. There are some improvements to their appearances though, because amputated limbs are miraculously restored in the life after death (Rawlings 1979, page 80)! But such reports are very different to what you read in Christian holy texts, which tell us that the souls of the deceased in heaven are transformed into vital, healthy, strong, and perfect angelic beings (Bible, Luke 20:34-36, 1 Corinthians 15:42-50). The Koran also propagates the same ideas about the youthful and vital appearance of the soul in the life after death. Now Thomas, I'm quite certain that if you had a choice, you would rather spend an eternal afterlife in a young, beautiful and vital form, rather than in an elderly and wrinkled, albeit vital form. So according to me, all this is proof of the hallucinatory nature of visions of deceased people seen during near-death experiences, and not proof of a life after death.'

Thomas was silent for a moment. 'I must admit you have made a few very convincing points. I'm even beginning to seriously doubt whether near-death experiences are proof of a life after death. A pity ... However, there must be some other proof of life after death, because I still have a strong feeling that there is some sort of life after death, even though I can't prove it.'

'There's only one certain way to find out whether there is a life after death, and that is to die. A very radical solution, requiring either a lethal disease which you don't have at the moment, or find someone willing to kill you, or that you commit suicide. After our last discussions I'm not sure you would want to do that, because I do believe you're beginning to doubt the reality of a life after death.'

'You're right there. I wouldn't contemplate suicide for even one moment. I enjoy my life. I even enjoy our discussions. Would you like another beer?'

'Thomas ... Really! You should know better. If you're paying, of course I want another beer! Waiter!'

The two men sat companionably, drinking beer, exchanging small-talk about local politics, events, and the theological study of Thomas. It was a pleasant afternoon. Another beer followed, and another, until Thomas looked at his watch, and realized he was late for an appointment with some of his fellow students for an evening meal. 'Got to go Ben ... See you next week?'

'Okay. I'd enjoy that.'

So it was that an edified, but unsteady Thomas walked off in the direction of the café where he and his fellow students were to meet.

Chapter 8

Killing for God

'Thomas, we are truly privileged men. There are not many countries on this world where you are privileged to enjoy a delight such as this, a delight denied to all but a lucky few! Urinating against a tree or behind bushes is for plebeians. It's ... It's so ordinary, so common. Nothing can equal the satisfaction a man derives from the sound of a healthy stream of urine splashing and tinkling into the still waters of a canal on a quiet and windless evening. Listen! Listen to it splash! Listen to the drops as they fall! Listen to the variation in the sound as you move, and as you change the force of urination. Listen to the echo of the splashing and tinkling along the canal. There's no sound in the world quite like it! Only one thing is missing; the weather is too warm for the maximum auditory delight you experience on evenings with temperatures near freezing point. It is then that water is at its most dense, water movements and waves possess a heavy oleaginous appearance, sounds are sharper, louder, echoing in a most satisfactory manner, and steam rises due to the more extreme temperature differences. Ah well, you can't have everything. "Pluck the day" and all that. In any case, there are few pleasures equalling the bodily and auditory delight of emptying a full bladder into a canal!'

Thomas sighed with the relief known to all those emptying an overly full bladder, and nodded in agreement. This was how men were meant to live! An evening spent talking in a restaurant to the accompaniment of a bottle or two of wine, and now a pause for relief before starting on a bottle of very promising Merlot.

A feeling of pleasurable calm enveloped them as they listened to the pleasurable echoing of their urination, only to be rudely shaken back into full consciousness.

'Are you dogs that you expose your private members and piss in

215

public?' roared a passing bearded jellaba clad man on a bicycle. 'Scandalous! Have you no modesty? Shame, shame on you both!'

'Bugger off Ali!' was Ben's immediate response.

'Oh, do you know him?'

'Of course not!' snapped Ben. 'I just used a common name. I wouldn't even want to know anyone as priggish as that! Furthermore, a Moslem with a beard and wearing a jellaba is not a person who I'd consider well integrated in Dutch society, unless he's one of those "born again Moslems", or just plain fanatical. I think one of the last two explanations is more likely, because he spoke quite good Dutch.'

'Then why do you think he was so offended? After all, he also has to urinate every now and then. Furthermore, there is no-one else around to offend, and we were indulging in a fairly typical, admittedly slightly illegal, but nonetheless socio-culturally tolerated Dutch custom.'

'All to do with cultural ideas of modesty Thomas,' and Ben assumed his lecture giving stance. 'This fellow, along with many of his fellow believers, apparently takes Koranic exhortations regarding modesty rather literally.'

'You mean there are even verses regarding modesty in the Koran?'

'Yes indeed. The Koran really is a complete book in some regards. It even discusses male modesty in some parts where Allah instructed the prophet Mohammed to tell men to cover their private parts ...'

Say to the believing men that they cast down their looks and guard their private parts; that is purer for them; surely Allah is Aware of what they do. (MHS Koran 24:30)

'This is why those professing a belief in Islam frown upon nudity and exposure of the body.'

'Hmmm ... If you interpret those passages as literally as that, then the attitude and reaction of that man to us is very understandable,' responded Thomas in a thoughtful tone. 'But if you say that the Koran is a complete book, does it also explain why people in Islamic countries are persecuted, and sometimes even killed for converting from Islam to Christianity? Really quite appalling. After all, we tolerate and respect the right of believers in Islam to practice their religion here, and even accept the fact that some people spontaneously convert from Christianity to Islam. So why don't they do the same in their countries?'

'Ah Thomas,' replied Ben, as he sat on a nearby park bench. 'You've really got a lot to learn. Of course conversion from Islam to Christianity is a criminal activity! That you would even think otherwise! Unbelievable...'

Thomas looked confused, surprised even, and looked carefully at Ben.

'Don't look so surprised Thomas. Various passages in the Koran definitely condemn all those who convert from the ultimate and perfect religion – Islam – to any other religion. This is a heinous crime known as apostasy, and is clearly condemned in the Koran.'

> *Lo! those who disbelieve after their (profession of) belief, and afterward grow violent in disbelief: their repentance will not be accepted. And such are those who are astray. Lo! those who disbelieve, and die in disbelief, the (whole) earth full of gold would not be accepted from such an one if it were offered as a ransom (for his soul). Theirs will be a painful doom and they will have no helpers (Koran 3:90-91)*

'The Sunnah of Bukhari is even more definite regarding the loathsome transgression of apostasy, and provides clear instructions on how to deal with apostates. Apostates must be killed (see also Bukhari 83:17, 84:58)!'

> *Narrated Abu Musa: A man embraced Islam and then reverted back to Judaism. Mu'adh bin Jabal came and saw the man with Abu Musa. Mu'adh asked, "What is wrong with this (man)?" Abu Musa replied, "He embraced Islam and then reverted back to Judaism." Mu'adh said, "I will not sit down unless you kill him (as it is) the verdict of Allah and His Apostle. (Bukhari 89:271)*

'This is only one of several passages in the Sunnah of Bukhari stating this same thing. Now if apostasy is forbidden and punishable by death, this means conversion from Islam to another religion is equivalent to suicide. Accordingly, Islamic governments are actually serving the best interests of their people by forbidding them to convert to another religion, because they are forbidding them from doing that which is equivalent to suicide.

After all, misguided potential apostates from Islam must be protected from themselves.'

Thomas grinned ever so imperceptibly at this newest cynical sophistry, 'But Christianity and Judaism don't punish apostasy with death; so it's very evident that they are more tolerant and better religions.'

'I wouldn't be too sure of that,' laughed Ben. 'Killing people for apostasy is an ancient Jewish and Christian tradition, strongly encouraged and enjoined upon all true believers by the prophets of these religions long before Mohammed was born. Passages in the holy books of Judaism and Christianity state this very directly at a time more than 600 years before the first revelations of God to Mohammed.'

> *If thy brother, the son of thy mother, or thy son, or thy daughter, or the wife of thy bosom, or thy friend, that is as thine own soul, entice thee secretly, saying, Let us go and serve other gods, which thou hast not known, thou, nor thy fathers; of the gods of the peoples that are round about you, nigh unto thee, or far off from thee, from the one end of the earth even unto the other end of the earth; thou shalt not consent unto him, nor hearken unto him; neither shall thine eye pity him, neither shalt thou spare, neither shalt thou conceal him: but thou shalt surely kill him; thy hand shall be first upon him to put him to death, and afterwards the hand of all the people. And thou shalt stone him to death with stones, because he hath sought to draw thee away from Jehovah thy God, who brought thee out of the land of Egypt, out of the house of bondage. (ASV Bible, Deuteronomy 13:6-10)*

'Here you have a very definite divine law, delivered by none less than God to Moses, and binding upon all true followers of Judaism,' said Ben. 'Very definite language with no room for any alternate interpretation.'

'Ah, but that's the Old Testament. In the New Testament of the Bible we have the message of love preached by Jesus. I know that Jesus would never have required apostates to be punished. He preached a universal message of love and tolerance.'

'Oh dear, here we go again,' sighed Ben. 'After all we've talked about, you still persist in believing the message of Jesus was one of mercy. Very well, then consider this following passage expressive of the message of "love" preached by Jesus.'

> *Every one therefore who shall confess me before men, him will I also confess before my Father who is in heaven. But whosoever shall deny me before men, him will I also deny before my Father who is in heaven. Think not that I came to send peace on the earth: I came not to send peace, but a sword. For I came to set a man at variance against his father, and the daughter against her mother, and the daughter in law against her mother in law: and a man's foes shall be they of his own household. He that loveth father or mother more than me is not worthy of me; and he that loveth son or daughter more than me is not worthy of me. (ASV Bible, Matthew 10:32-37)*

'Oh ...' responded Thomas. 'That does seem fairly definite. But I was always taught that the message of Jesus did away with the bloodthirsty old laws handed down by God to Moses, the major prophet of Judaism. Indeed, Saint Paul told that the coming of Jesus nullified the old laws of Moses.'

> *But now we have been discharged from the law, having died to that wherein we were held; so that we serve in newness of the spirit, and not in oldness of the letter. (ASV Bible, Romans 7:6)*

'Certainly true,' answered Ben. 'But who do you want to believe – Jesus or Saint Paul? Do you prefer to believe in Jesus, the Son of God, who presumably had some sort of direct communication with his father? Or do you want to believe some mortal holy man like Saint Paul, a turncoat Jew who interpreted what Jesus said several decades after his death? I would think the answer is obvious – of course you believe the Son of God. Now Jesus had a very definite opinion on the laws of laws of Moses. He preached that the laws of Moses were valid and should be obeyed (see also Bible, Luke 16:17).'

> *Think not that I came to destroy the law or the prophets: I came*

*not to destroy, but to fulfil. For verily I say unto you, Till heaven
and earth pass away, one jot or one tittle shall in no wise pass
away from the law, till all things be accomplished. (ASV Bible,
Matthew 5:17-18)*

Ben continued, 'Actually this is not very surprising at all. After all, we
are speaking about an eternal God here, so why should this eternal God to
whom one thousand years is as a day, give one set of laws at one time, and
another different set of laws at another time. This is why some long estab-
lished Christian sects state that Old Testament Biblical laws are valid, and
applicable to Christians unless specifically negated, or rather abrogated by
a specific statement in the New Testament. Long before the baby
Mohammed started filling his mother's womb, the followers of Judaism
and of Christianity were having a simply wonderful time persecuting and
killing their fellows for the heinous crimes of heresy and apostasy. The
subsequent Islamic attitude to apostasy is no different, and may even be
derived from these traditions. Who knows?'

'Oh,' was all Thomas managed to say.

'I wouldn't get too upset about it all Thomas. Luckily for everyone in
Western Europe, all these laws are ancient history. Imagine, if they were
actually applied, most people would have to be put to death. In fact, strict
application of Biblical laws would mean that about 70% of the Western
European population would have to die.'

'Wow!'

'If you think that's impressive, then try this wine,' said Ben. 'We've
been sitting here a while without doing anything much except exercising
our tongues. Let's tickle our palates and rinse our tonsils with some of this
really delicious Merlot.' Ben filled and passed Thomas a plastic cup, and
filled another for himself. For a few minutes they sat in silence looking
over the canal as they sipped their wine.

'Nice wine Ben', said an approving Thomas as he took another liberal
sip.

'Nice wine!' retorted Ben. 'Is that all you can say about it? Young
man, I'll have you know that this is a wonderful wine, ambrosia, food of
the gods. This is what wine is all about. Drinking wine is not about
drinking sour, fermented grape juice out of a bottle with a fancy label.

Wine is a total sensuous experience induced by the oral sensations of a truly delicious tasting product of the fermentation of noble grapes grown and harvested with love and care by fanatical wine makers.'

'Okay, okay, okay. I agree I understated it somewhat. It is a very good wine. Next time I'll bring a bottle. As you said, this truly is the way a man should live – wine and stimulating discussion. Now just a moment ago you said about 70% of the Western European population would have to die if Biblical laws were strictly applied. How do you arrive at a figure like that?'

Ben sipped, answering thoughtfully, 'By a quick consideration of the Biblical laws in relation to social reality in most Western European countries. Probably the figure is somewhat inflated, but I don't think by much. The "loving God" of the Jews and Christians actually requires huge numbers of people be killed for infringements of holy laws handed down to the prophets of this same loving God. Killing vile transgressors against God's laws is a holy and just deed, so killing for God is one way true believers can express their love of God!'

'Come on now Ben: isn't that a bit extreme?'

'Absolutely not! Just look at the books of Exodus, Deuteronomy, and Leviticus in the first five books of the Bible. These three books are also part of the Torah, the primary Jewish holy book. They are books full of unspeakable vileness and horrors. They prescribe punishments so dementedly extreme, that most people now alive in most modern Western European countries have deserved the death penalty many times over. If these divine laws were suddenly enforced at this very moment, Western Europe would change immediately into a stinking charnel strewn with rotting corpses! Let's look at a few examples. To begin with, there is the question of filial piety. Did you know that parents can get their disobedient sons stoned to death?'

'Now I think you really are joking.'

Ben took another sip, looked at Thomas with a triumphant glint in his eyes. 'Then consider the following passage (see also Bible, Leviticus 20:9).'

If a man have a stubborn and rebellious son, that will not obey the voice of his father, or the voice of his mother, and, though they chasten him, will not hearken unto them; then shall his father and his mother lay hold on him, and bring him out unto the elders of his city, and unto the gate of his place; and they shall say unto the elders of his city, This our son is stubborn and rebellious, he will not obey our voice; he is a glutton, and a drunkard. And all the men of his city shall stone him to death with stones: so shalt thou put away the evil from the midst of thee; and all Israel shall hear, and fear. (ASV Bible, Deuteronomy 21:18-21)

'Good stuff hey Thomas? That's the way they treated unruly sons in the "good old days".'

'But Ben, that's the Old Testament. Very well, strictly applied, it may still be binding upon Jews, but Jesus did away with the laws of Moses in the New Testament of the Bible. So this type of extreme law is no longer binding upon Christians.'

'Aha, but as I told you earlier, Jesus didn't remove any of the old laws of Moses. In fact he reaffirmed many of them, and certainly reaffirmed the ruling requiring parents to put their disobedient sons to death. Consider this passage from the book of Mark where Jesus criticised a group of Pharisees for hypocrisy.'

Ye leave the commandment of God, and hold fast the tradition of men. And he said unto them, Full well do ye reject the commandment of God, that ye may keep your tradition. For Moses said, Honor thy father and thy mother; and, He that speaketh evil of father or mother, let him die the death: but ye say, If a man shall say to his father or his mother, That wherewith thou mightest have been profited by me is Corban, that is to say, Given to God; ye no longer suffer him to do aught for his father or his mother; making void the word of God by your tradition, which ye have delivered: and many such like things ye do. (ASV Bible, Mark 7:8-13)

'Aside from his criticism of Pharisees for their hypocritical selective application of the laws of Moses, I would say that this was a very definite reaffirmation of this particular ancient Mosaic Law.'

'Indeed ...' was the crestfallen response. 'I'm going to have to speak to my tutors about this one.'

'Your poor tutors must be having a hard time with all the heresies I've been filling your ears with.'

'I don't consider them heresies at all Ben. Some of my tutors do call them heresies, but personally I regard them as a refreshing, albeit iconoclastic look at some tenets of my Christian faith.'

'Glad to hear you think like that. But this is a digression. Let's have a look at the Islamic viewpoint regarding filial respect and obedience. In fact, Islam enjoins filial respect and piety in exactly the same way as Christianity and Judaism, although no similar strict punishments are mentioned.'

Thy Lord hath decreed, that ye worship none save Him, and (that ye show) kindness to parents. If one of them or both of them to attain old age with thee, say not "Fie" unto them nor repulse them, but speak unto them a gracious word. (Koran 17:23)

'In Islam, the punishment of those who fail in their filial duties and respect to their parents is eternal torment in a life after death, and not in this physical life.'

Narrated Jubair bin Mut'im: That he heard the Prophet saying, "The person who severs the bond of kinship will not enter Paradise." (Bukhari 73:13)

'Hmmm. So Ben, you mean that if you live in a society where people apply these wonderful "God-given laws" very literally, you're much safer and better off being an unruly rebellious teenager in an Islamic society, than in a Christian or a Jewish society.'

'Quite correct Thomas. That's certainly a practical way of looking at these matters. However we're not finished with Biblical laws yet. There are a lot more laws requiring the death penalty.'

'You're not going to quote Leviticus again are you?'

'I certainly am. It's a wonderfully bloodthirsty book. Just look at some of the "God-given" laws demanding the death penalty.'

And the man that lieth with his father's wife hath uncovered his father's nakedness: both of them shall surely be put to death; their blood shall be upon them. (ASV Bible, Leviticus 20:11)

'And another.'

And if a man lie with his daughter-in-law, both of them shall surely be put to death: they have wrought confusion; their blood shall be upon them. (ASV Bible, Leviticus 20:12)

'It goes on and on.'

And if a man take a wife and her mother, it is wickedness: they shall be burnt with fire, both he and they; that there be no wickedness among you. (ASV Bible, Leviticus 20:14)

And if a man lie with a beast, he shall surely be put to death: and ye shall slay the beast. And if a woman approach unto any beast, and lie down thereto, thou shalt kill the woman, and the beast: they shall surely be put to death; their blood shall be upon them. (ASV Bible, Leviticus 20:15-16)

And if a man shall take his sister, his father's daughter, or his mother's daughter, and see her nakedness, and she see his nakedness; it is a shameful thing; and they shall be cut off in the sight of the children of their people: he hath uncovered his sister's nakedness; he shall bear his iniquity. (ASV Bible, Leviticus 20:17)

'And to illustrate the similarities between the Judeo-Christian traditions and Islam, the Koran also contains similar regulations.'

And marry not those women whom your fathers married, except what hath already happened (of that nature) in the past. Lo! it was ever lewdness and abomination, and an evil way. Forbidden unto you are your mothers, and your daughters, and your sisters, and your father's sisters, and your mother's sisters, and your brother's daughters and your sister's daughters, and your foster

mothers, and your foster sisters, and your mothers-in-law, and
your stepdaughters who are under your protection (born) of your
women unto whom ye have gone in but if ye have not gone in
unto them, then it is no sin for you (to marry their daughters) and
the wives of your sons who (spring) from your own loins. And (it
is forbidden unto you) that ye should have two sisters together,
except what hath already happened (of that nature) in the past.
Lo! Allah is ever Forgiving, Merciful. (Koran 4:22-23)

Ben began warming up to this subject, which was clearly providing him with a good deal of irreverent amusement. 'The Old Testament also enforces the tradition of Levirate marriage. If a man dies without any male children to ensure survival of his line, his oldest surviving brother has a duty to impregnate his widowed wife. A son resulting from such a relationship would then be raised as the son of the deceased brother. Levirate marriage was not voluntary, but a binding law in ancient Jewish society. The penalty for non-compliance by an unwilling brother-in-law was public humiliation, where the widow would rip a sandal off his foot and spit in his face, after which he suffered permanent disgrace for his crime (Bible, Deuteronomy 25:5-10). However, the fate of Onan indicates that God considered public humiliation insufficient punishment for this scandalous crime.'

And Judah said unto Onan, Go in unto thy brother's wife, and
perform the duty of a husband's brother unto her, and raise up
seed to thy brother. And Onan knew that the seed would not be
his; and it came to pass, when he went in unto his brother's wife,
that he spilled it on the ground, lest he should give seed to his
brother. And the thing which he did was evil in the sight of
Jehovah: and he slew him also. (ASV Bible, Genesis 38:8-10)

'According to this passage, Onan had sexual intercourse with his sister-in-law, and having had his fun, practiced coitus interruptus so she would not get pregnant, and the resulting child be raised as his deceased brother's. God evidently thought this was such incredibly mean-spirited misuse of a sister-in-law, as well as being a shameless waste of semen intended by law for making a baby, that God immediately struck Onan dead. That's the official interpretation. But there is another way of looking at this incident. I think it's more likely that Onan was a kindly man, forced by law to have sex with his widowed sister-in-law, but practiced coitus interruptus because he ultimately refused to defile her body with his unclean Jewish semen.'

Thomas's mouth hung open, surprise and amazement writ large on his face. 'Huhhh ...' was all he managed to say as he turned to look at Ben. Flabbergasted, was a term woefully inadequate to describe the surprise and amazement displayed upon his face.

'Don't look so surprised Thomas. We know this is true from this very passage (Bible, Genesis 38:8-10). This passage states very clearly "that he spilled it on the ground", which clearly indicates he made very sure his semen made no contact with the body or clothing of his sister-in-law, so preventing her being defiled. After all, the five holy books of Judaism called the Torah, the very same five books dictated by God to Moses, and the first five books of the Bible tell us that ejaculated semen is a foul and unclean fluid.'

> *And if any man's seed of copulation go out from him, then he shall bathe all his flesh in water, and be unclean until the even. And every garment, and every skin, whereon is the seed of copulation, shall be washed with water, and be unclean until the even. The woman also with whom a man shall lie with seed of copulation, they shall both bathe themselves in water, and be unclean until the even. (ASV Bible, Leviticus 15:16-18)*

'In other words, any contact with ejaculated semen renders a person unclean, which means that semen is an impure and filthy slime roiling in the testicles of all fertile men. Now the ancient Jews knew that sexual intercourse was a necessary, albeit unclean duty, because God had told them long before to have children.'

> *And God created man in his own image, in the image of God created he him; male and female created he them. And God blessed them: and God said unto them, Be fruitful, and multiply,*

and replenish the earth, ... (ASV Bible, Genesis 1:27-28)

Ben smiled as he completed his chain of reasoning. 'So when ancient Jewish men such as Onan, managed to force themselves to engage in the onerous task of sexual intercourse with women, they gained inner strength, steeling themselves and their generative organs for this foul and unclean deed, by thinking of the happy little children to come as they performed God's dirty work, defiling themselves and their women with their unclean semen. From all this we can only conclude that Onan was not a criminal, but merely misguided in the performance of his legal obligation to his deceased brother. He foolishly forgot God's requirement for children, and thought only of not defiling the purity of the body of his brother's wife. And God punished him cruelly for his short-sightedness.' Ben nodded his head, adding in an unspeakably fake tone of compassion, 'I think you would agree with me Thomas that this is a very sad story.'

Thomas began to smile, even to laugh, 'You had me wondering what was going on for a moment, but I see you're toying with biblical texts. I once thought your explanation of the ways followers of Islam could purify social welfare payments received from Western European governments was the "mother of all sophistries" (Chapter 5). But I was wrong. This explanation of why God killed Onan deserves that title!'

'Ah Thomas, I thought you might enjoy this explanation of the death of Onan. However, the treatment of Onan by God does raise an important question. It begs the question of which of the God-given laws of Moses are binding, and which are not. After his second sojourn on Mount Sinai, Moses told the Jewish people the laws of God as to how they should organise their lives (Bible, Deuteronomy 10:10-13). Yet, just as among the followers of other Abrahamic religions, you also see multiple forms of cafeteria religion among the more fanatical followers of Judaism. Some bind copies of the laws of Moses to their heads and arms as was literally instructed by Moses (Bible, Deuteronomy 11:18), they rigidly follow the dietary, clothing and Sabbath laws, yet they do not carry out other equally binding laws such as killing adulterers, disobedient sons, or homosexuals (Bible, Leviticus & Deuteronomy). Don't misunderstand me Thomas, I'm very happy they don't kill people for these so-called crimes, but even so it does mean their application of the laws of Moses is very selective. This criticism is nothing new. Mohammed also criticised followers of Judaism for not stoning adulterers as prescribed in the Torah, which was a direct criticism of their selective application of the laws of Moses as listed in the Torah (Bukhari 82:825). In other words, nearly all followers of Judaism also practice a form of cafeteria religion. Now, returning to the subject of Onan, the laws relating to Levirate marriage were very clear laws given by God (Bible, Deuteronomy 25:5-10). So why did God kill Onan instead of having him publically disgraced as God's own Law demanded?'

'But the laws given by God to Moses were given many years after the time Onan lived,' objected Thomas.

'Strange, I always thought that a thousand years were as a day to an eternal God. The laws of God are unchanging. They are for eternity. God does not give one law on one day, and change it the next day. So according to the eternal laws of God, Onan should not have been killed, but should have received the treatment prescribed in the laws given by this same eternal God to Moses. The sad story of Onan is one of random injustice – not divine justice. Is this the true nature of God?'

'It certainly is a fascinating argument Ben. Even so, the ways of God are inscrutable to mere mortals such as you and me. But I'm certainly going to ask the opinions of my tutors about this explanation of God's treatment of Onan, as well as its implications. It might be amusing to see their reactions. However, to continue our digressions, what about other bizarre laws of Moses. For example, verse 23:2 in the book of Deuteronomy of the Bible has always puzzled me. This is a very strict injunction about bastards, clearly stating that bastards – also termed the misbegotten – which are defined as children conceived as a product of forbidden sexual relations between related men and women (Bible, Leviticus 18: 6-18), or under certain circumstances out of wedlock (Bible, Deuteronomy 22: 23-25), are not permitted to enter a synagogue or temple, nor are their children permitted to enter a synagogue or temple for ten generations.'

A bastard shall not enter into the assembly of Jehovah; even to the tenth generation shall none of his enter into the assembly of Jehovah. (ASV Bible, Deuteronomy 23:2)

'Ohhhh ...' responded Ben with a delighted glint in his eyes, while at the same time thinking how Thomas was now beginning to reveal a sense of humour. 'Wonderful! You've just raised another interesting point. Jesus the Son of God regularly visited synagogues, as well as the temple in Jerusalem. His mother Mary was married to Joseph the carpenter. But Joseph was not the father of Jesus, because his mother Mary was impregnated by God before her marriage to Joseph, and at a time when she was officially betrothed to Joseph (Bible, Luke 1:26-38). Jewish law current at the time of Joseph and Mary, unequivocally states that a free woman and man who have consensual sexual relations while the woman is betrothed to another man, should both be put to death (Bible, Deuteronomy 22: 23-25). Joseph undoubtedly realized that stoning God to death together with Mary was a mind-bogglingly ambitious task, even if it were possible. So Joseph seriously thought about divorcing, or breaking his betrothal with Mary in secret in order to avoid public shame and scandal, yet was ultimately convinced by an angel of God to marry Mary (Bible, Matthew 1:18-19). Accordingly, Jesus can be defined as God's bastard Son! As a first generation bastard, it was certainly illegal for Jesus to enter a synagogue or the temple in Jerusalem, yet he did just that on many occasions, even though as the Son of God, and as a person knowledgeable in the laws of Moses enjoining strict adherence to these same laws (Bible, Matthew 5:17-19), he most definitely knew of this law! Does this mean Jesus was a hypocritical lying bastard? Does this mean he was exempted from this law, because he was the Son of God? Or does this mean this particular law of Moses is nonsense, which again raises the fascinating question of which laws of Moses are then valid?'

Thomas was stunned into silence for a moment as he digested this new irreverence, but after a few seconds his face brightened, and he responded in a mischievous tone, 'I think I'm going to talk to my tutors about that question, because I know they particularly enjoy discussing this type of problem.' He looked seriously at Ben and continued, 'But now, let's stop these fascinating digressions, and return to the subject of Levirate marriage.'

'Okay, okay, I get carried away every now and then. There is actually not too much more to say about the subject except that Levirate marriage can sometimes get really unpleasant. If the oldest surviving brother fails to get his deceased brother's wife pregnant, then the other surviving brothers must take over this task, raising the spectre of true Bible-sanctioned gang rape if the woman is unwilling. After all, the obligation to have a descendant is as binding on the widow as on the surviving brothers.'

'But that's only in the primitive times of the Old Testament!'

'Not at all! Jesus never rescinded the laws regarding Levirate marriage. He even had theological arguments about the very subject, indirectly reaffirming the principle of Levirate marriage (Bible, Matthew 22:23-34, Mark 12:18-27, Luke 20:27-40). Furthermore, no one else in the New Testament rescinded the laws regarding Levirate marriage. So the law still remains, just as the laws requiring the death penalty for homosexuals and lesbians remain.'

By now, Thomas had a somewhat harried expression. This evening's conversation was one arousing an incredible assortment of emotions in his previously dogma dominated mind. He took another sip of wine, and looked enquiringly at Ben.

'Yes Thomas, as you know, the Old Testament is very definite on the matter of homosexuality. Homosexuals must die!'

And if a man lie with mankind, as with womankind, both of them have committed abomination: they shall surely be put to death; their blood shall be upon them. (ASV Bible, Leviticus 20:13)

Thomas had learnt his lesson. He no longer protested. He remained silent, and only squirmed uncomfortably as Ben continued with his discourse. 'Some people may say that Jesus abrogated this law in the New Testament, but Jesus actually said nothing about homosexuality at all. Fortunately for all those who hate homosexuals, Saint Paul rectified this deficiency, reaffirming the Law of Moses that homosexuals should be put to death, as well as adding that lesbians also deserved the same fate.'

For this cause God gave them up unto vile passions: for their women changed the natural use into that which is against nature: and likewise also the men, leaving the natural use of the woman, burned in their lust one toward another, men with men working unseemliness, and receiving in themselves that recompense of their error which was due. And even as they refused to have God in their knowledge, God gave them up unto a reprobate mind, to do those things which are not fitting; being filled with all unrighteousness, wickedness, covetousness, maliciousness; full of envy, murder, strife, deceit, malignity; whisperers, backbiters, hateful to God, insolent, haughty, boastful, inventors of evil things, disobedient to parents, without understanding, covenant-breakers, without natural affection, unmerciful: who, knowing the ordinance of God, that they that practise such things are worthy of death, not only do the same, but also consent with them that practise them. (ASV Bible, Romans 1:26-32)

'This is the reason homosexuality was frowned upon and quite savagely punished throughout many centuries. In fact, homosexuality has only relatively recently been decriminalized in Western European countries. Islamic countries also face the same problems. After all, about one in twenty persons is homosexual by nature, so it is not surprising that the Koran also has a very definite opinion on homosexuality.'

And as for the two of you [men] who are guilty thereof, punish them both. And if they repent and improve, then let them be. Lo! Allah is Relenting, Merciful. (Koran 4:16)

'Unfortunately,' continued Ben, 'we don't know what punishment Allah told Mohammed to apply to homosexuals, although this passage very clearly implies it was not death. However, Islamic jurists solved this problem very elegantly by using the story of the fate of the ancient city of Sodom (see also Koran 11:77-82, 15:59-74).'

And Lo! (Remember) when he said unto his folk: Will ye commit abomination such as no creature ever did before you?

Lo! ye come with lust unto men instead of women. Nay, but ye, are wanton folk.

And the answer of his people was only that they said (one to another): Turn them out of your township. They are folk, forsooth, who keep pure.

And We rescued him and his household, save his wife, who was of those who stayed behind.

And We rained a rain upon them. See now the nature of the consequence for evil doers! (Koran 7:80-84)

'So God sent his angels to warn his faithful prophet Lut [the Biblical Lot] to escape before destroying Sodom and its inhabitants by turning it upside down, as well as raining stones and stones of baked clay upon the city (Koran 11:82, 15:74). Except for Lut and his two daughters, all the inhabitants of Sodom were killed by falling walls, falling from buildings, or directly by the rain of stones. This is the basis for the official Islamic punishment of homosexuality by means of stoning, by collapsing stone walls upon them, hurling them from high buildings, or any combination of these penalties. When you consider these things, you realize that strict followers of Judaism, Christianity, and Islam have identical attitudes towards homosexuals. It's their holy duty to kill them all.'

They sat in silence, looking at the calm waters of the canal, now and then sipping their wine.

Thomas finally broke the silence. 'How depressing. Almost unbelievable that people could actually wish such cruelties upon themselves and their fellows. It's even more surprising that Jesus and the New Testament saints weren't exempt from wishing these same cruelties upon their fellows. Horrible, horrible ...'

'Well Thomas, all these things are just scratching the surface of the insane cruelties fanatical believers of these faiths are prepared to inflict upon their fellows in the name of God. Let's have a look at the ages old crime of adultery. Nowadays, most people in Western European countries cannot conceive that adultery would merit the death penalty, yet this was normal in many ancient societies, and even now in some strict Islamic societies. Let's start with what the Bible says about adultery.'

'I know,' said Thomas. 'It's in Leviticus. Adulterers must die.'

'Quite correct,' responded Ben.

And the man that committeth adultery with another man's wife, even he that committeth adultery with his neighbor's wife, the adulterer and the adulteress shall surely be put to death. (ASV

Bible, Leviticus 20:10)

Thomas gave a triumphant, 'Aha! Now I know that Jesus definitely abrogated this cruel law in the New Testament. There is the story of the woman accused of adultery to prove this.'

> *And the scribes and Pharisees brought unto him a woman taken in adultery; and when they had set her in the midst,*
> *They say unto him, Master, this woman was taken in adultery, in the very act.*
> *Now Moses in the law commanded us, that such should be stoned: but what sayest thou?*
> *This they said, tempting him, that they might have to accuse him. But Jesus stooped down, and with his finger wrote on the ground, as though he heard them not.*
> *So when they continued asking him, he lifted up himself, and said unto them, He that is without sin among you, let him first cast a stone at her.*
> *And again he stooped down, and wrote on the ground.*
> *And they which heard it, being convicted by their own conscience, went out one by one, beginning at the eldest, even unto the last: and Jesus was left alone, and the woman standing in the midst.*
> *When Jesus had lifted up himself, and saw none but the woman, he said unto her, Woman, where are those thine accusers? Hath no man condemned thee?*
> *She said, No man, Lord. And Jesus said unto her, Neither do I condemn thee: go, and sin no more. (KJV Bible, John 8:3-11)*

Thomas continued, 'This story is a well known one illustrating the mercy and kindness of Jesus. The way he diverted the execution of her sentence clearly reveals that he abrogated this harsh law.'

Ben gave a cynical laugh. 'That's the official interpretation told by the Christian Church. But this official explanation is absolute drivel! Look at the story carefully. The whole thing was a conspiracy by the Pharisees to trap Jesus on a point of theological orthodoxy. To begin with, the accused woman was actually "taken in adultery". In other words, they caught her in the act. So where was the man with whom she committed adultery? He is conspicuously absent in this story. In fact the man with whom she committed adultery is not even mentioned. The story does not mention that he ran off before they could catch him, or that they let him go, or that he disappeared in a puff of smoke, or anything else for that matter. You only notice a deafening silence in these passages regarding the man with whom she was "taken in adultery". Yet, according to the laws of Moses, both the adulterer and the adulteress must be stoned to death. These scribes and Pharisees were profoundly knowledgeable regarding the laws of Moses, but they only wanted to stone the woman. This fact alone rendered the accusation extremely dubious, and execution of the punishment a gross miscarriage of justice. Jesus also had a profound knowledge of the laws of Moses, and realized that to give judgment upon this woman was no more than the purest form of entrapment instigated by his enemies – these same scribes and fanatical Pharisees. It was no more than a ploy intended to trick him into uttering flagrantly heretical statements, for which he could possibly be arrested for sacrilegious rabble-rousing, as well as knowingly abetting a criminal miscarriage of justice. Fascinating isn't it Thomas?'

'Certainly is when you look at it like that.'

'It gets even better. Jesus never at any moment in this story questioned the justness of the sentence. For him it was an obvious crime with a standard punishment. So there was no question that he abrogated the sentence at all. What he did do, was to implicitly question whether the persons accusing this woman, and wanting to stone her, were doing so according to the law and their consciences. Both were found deficient. The man was not present to be stoned along with the woman. So it was glaringly evident that their application of the law was deficient, criminal even, as a result of which their consciences were certainly not clear. Accordingly, all the accusers departed, even though they initially claimed to have caught the woman in the act. The woman was not stoned, and Jesus sent her away with the admonition to sin no more. Jesus had defeated the Pharisees at their own game! He realized they wanted to entrap him by getting him to apply the law incorrectly. This is a more correct interpretation of this story, which also clearly demonstrates that that Jesus in no way abrogated this Law of Moses regarding adultery. So this law is still applicable to Christians.'

'I guess that's true when you look at it in the way you do. It's certainly a radical departure from the traditional interpretation of this passage.'

'According to me, the facts of this story support my interpretation better, which is why fanatical Christians and Jews alike should still be stoning adulterers. But luckily we don't stone adulterers any more, another mercy for which I am very grateful. However, this is not the case in Islam. Islamic law is very definite on the matter of adultery. The initial revelations to Mohammed stated that the accused woman should only be confined.'

As for those of your women who are guilty of lewdness, call to witness four of you against them. And if they testify (to the truth of the allegation) then confine them to the houses until death take them or (until) Allah appoint for them a way (through new legislation). (Koran 4:15)

'Okay,' replied Thomas. 'Most people have heard about this curious requirement for four witnesses being needed to accuse someone of adultery in Islam. I couldn't even conceive of someone committing adultery in full view of four witnesses, let alone even one witness. So I guess it would be almost impossible to get a conviction for adultery in Islamic countries. Furthermore, I always thought that the punishment for adultery in Islam was stoning to death, but here the Koran simply says that woman must be locked up. How do you explain that?'

'As regards the number of people required to witness against an adulterer, a subsequent verse makes it clear that really only one witness is needed, provided the witness satisfies the requirements.'

As for those who accuse their wives but have no witnesses except themselves; let the testimony of one of them be four testimonies, (swearing) by Allah that he is of those who speak the truth; (Koran 24:6)

'So you actually only need just one witness who testifies four times, which nicely gets around the almost impossible requirement for four witnesses. Then we come to the matter of the punishment required for adultery. The revelation in the verse stipulating that the woman be confined to her home until she dies was abrogated by a subsequent revelation of Allah to Mohammed.'

> *The adulterer and the adulteress, scourge ye each one of them (with) a hundred stripes. And let not pity for the twain withhold you from obedience to Allah, if ye believe in Allah and the Last Day. And let a party of believers witness their punishment. (Koran 24:2)*

'But what about the modern practice of stoning?' asked Thomas.

'Patience young man,' said Ben. 'The Sunnah of Bukhari is a collection of the sayings and deeds of Mohammed compiled after his death. Here we read that Mohammed very definitely condemned adulterers, both male and female to death. The usual punishment was lapidation, better known as stoning to death (see also Bukhari 38:508, 82:824-825, 89:280, 92:432, 93:633).'

> *Narrated Jabir: A man from the tribe of Bani Aslam came to the Prophet while he was in the mosque and said, "I have committed illegal sexual intercourse." The Prophet turned his face to the other side. The man turned towards the side towards which the Prophet had turned his face, and gave four witnesses against himself. On that the Prophet called him and said, "Are you insane?" (He added), "Are you married?" The man said, 'Yes." On that the Prophet ordered him to be stoned to the death in the Musalla (a praying place). When the stones hit him with their sharp edges and he fled, but he was caught at Al-Harra and then killed. (Bukhari 63:195)*

'So that's where the stoning to death for adultery in Islam comes from. It's not in the Koran at all!'

'Indeed ... You must consider that about 85% of all followers of Islam belong to the Sunni sect, a sect that reveres the Sunnah of Bukhari as being almost equivalent in authority to the Koran itself. So it is quite understandable that they stone adulterers. There is an interesting procedural refinement resulting from the events described in the last verse. Some of the more cowardly adulterers try to run away while being stoned for their crime, so modern Islamic penal practice is to bury condemned adulterers up to their waists to prevent them from running away. This is a major improvement in lapidation efficiency. No one can claim there is any lack of development and improvement in Islamic penal procedures!'

Thomas looked rather uncomfortable upon hearing this. A silence developed between the two men. They sipped the last of their wine and looked at the canal. It was now very late.

Ben stood, stretched, took a deep breath, and said, 'Thomas, I realize I haven't fully explained why Biblical laws would require the deaths of about 70% of people in Western Europe, but the wine is finished, and it's getting late. So I'm going home. Tomorrow will be another warm day, and it will be really beautiful here in the park next to the canal. Let's meet here tomorrow afternoon, and we'll continue our discussion of the nastiness, and the mind boggling holocaust that would result in Western Europe if the laws contained in the Bible, or the other holy books of the Abrahamic religions were strictly applied.'

Thomas yawned, 'Good idea. I'll bring the wine. Five o'clock?'

'Sounds good to me.'

Chapter 9

Holy misogyny!

Ben stretched slowly and luxuriously in the warm afternoon sun. It was another wonderful, almost magical summer day. The sky was blue, the sun pleasantly warm. Before him, couples, groups and individuals sat on the grass enjoying the warmth of the sun. Brightly dressed people walked past the old Kamerlingh Onnes laboratory on the other side of the canal. This was summer at its best. Eyes half closed, he sat soaking up the sunlight, mind empty, except for the occasional fleeting random thought. This was paradise.

Full awareness returned as Thomas sat next to him. 'Hi Ben! It looks quite different here now compared with last night. I always enjoy the view along the Rapenburg from this end. A wonderful spot, and ohhh ... sun ... after a morning spent in a dimly lit room with my tutor.'

'Ah, so you had a talk with one of your tutors? How did he react to your heretical questions?'

'Well, the tutor I spoke with this morning did look rather unhappy when he heard your alternative version of the story of Jesus and the woman accused of adultery. All he did was grunt, and say that it was an alternative view, not the correct view, but an alternative view. He then proceeded to tell me the official view on this passage, and absolutely refused to discuss the matter of Saint Paul's re-affirmation of the death penalty for homosexuals, and his extension of this penalty to lesbians.'

'What a shame. In any case you probably gave him something else to think about.'

'I think so too. I've been doing some further browsing in the Old Testament. I mainly read the New Testament, and never examined the Old Testament in such detail before. Now I begin to realize what an evil and horrifying book it is.'

'Oh, and what brought you to this startling conclusion?'

'The things we discussed last night, as well as reading other parts of the Old Testament. For example, everyone knows the story about how the Israelites marched around the walls of the city of Jericho, blowing their trumpets until the walls collapsed. This was a wonder wrought by the power of God! Hallelujah, God is great! But no one ever emphasizes what happened afterwards. Except for the prostitute Rahab and her family, everyone, the total population of Jericho: men, women, and children were slaughtered at the behest of God. Rahab and her family were allowed to live, because Rahab had helped the Israelite spies. After the slaughter and plundering by God's chosen people was complete, the remains of the city were set on fire, reducing the once thriving city of Jericho to a burning, stinking charnel (Bible, Joshua 6:20-24)! To think, this was but one of a seemingly endless chain of conquests, mass killings, and plunder. In fact, the books of Numbers and Joshua in the Bible are little more than a paean to the extermination of whole populations by the tribes of Israel to create living space for God's Chosen People. They weren't content with just killing most of the people and driving the rest away. No, they killed every single man, woman, child, and animal in the cities and towns they conquered, leaving nothing but smouldering piles of rubble strewn with rotting corpses in their wake, as they cleared the land of its original inhabitants (Bible, Deuteronomy 20:10-16). Just look at this dreary series of repetitious verses, each a short report of unspeakable horrors perpetrated by these paragons of nastiness.' Thomas pulled a Bible out of his bag.

> *And Joshua took Makkedah on that day, and smote it with the edge of the sword, and the king thereof: he utterly destroyed them and all the souls that were therein; he left none remaining; and he did to the king of Makkedah as he had done unto the king of Jericho.*
>
> *And Joshua passed from Makkedah, and all Israel with him, unto Libnah, and fought against Libnah: and Jehovah delivered it also, and the king thereof, into the hand of Israel; and he smote it with the edge of the sword, and all the souls that were therein; he left none remaining in it; and he did unto the king thereof as he had done unto the king of Jericho.*

And Joshua passed from Libnah, and all Israel with him, unto Lachish, and encamped against it, and fought against it: and Jehovah delivered Lachish into the hand of Israel; and he took it on the second day, and smote it with the edge of the sword, and all the souls that were therein, according to all that he had done to Libnah.

Then Horam king of Gezer came up to help Lachish; and Joshua smote him and his people, until he had left him none remaining.

And Joshua passed from Lachish, and all Israel with him, unto Eglon; and they encamped

against it, and fought against it; and they took it on that day, and smote it with the edge of the sword; and all the souls that were therein he utterly destroyed that day, according to all that he had done to Lachish.

And Joshua went up from Eglon, and all Israel with him, unto Hebron; and they fought against it: and they took it, and smote it with the edge of the sword, and the king thereof, and all the cities thereof, and all the souls that were therein; he left none remaining, according to all that he had done to Eglon; but he utterly destroyed it, and all the souls that were therein.

And Joshua returned, and all Israel with him, to Debir, and fought against it: and he took it, and the king thereof, and all the cities thereof; and they smote them with the edge of the sword, and utterly destroyed all the souls that were therein; he left none remaining: as he had done to Hebron, so he did to Debir, and to the king thereof; as he had done also to Libnah, and to the king thereof.

So Joshua smote all the land, the hill-country, and the South, and the lowland, and the slopes, and all their kings: he left none remaining, but he utterly destroyed all that breathed, as Jehovah, the God of Israel, commanded. (ASV Bible, Joshua 10:28-40)

'Well I guess this extermination campaign must have been holy and good if God ordered it,' said Ben with a mischievous glint in his eyes.

Thomas was really very upset by what he had read, and not at all amused by Ben's facetious remark. He glared at Ben, 'It gets even worse. In one passage you read how some Jewish kings treated women in conquered cities.'

'You mean the usual rape and enslavement?'

'That's bad enough, but I mean truly unspeakable cruelties. Look at this passage describing atrocities sanctioned, and even demanded by God,' retorted Thomas in a vehement tone, shoving his Bible under Ben's nose.

> *Samaria shall bear her guilt; for she hath rebelled against her God: they shall fall by the sword; their infants shall be dashed in pieces, and their women with child shall be ripped up. (ASV Bible, Hosea 13:16)*

'That's grim stuff indeed Thomas,' sighed Ben sadly. 'Women always seem to get the worst treatment in just about all such situations. But before we get on to the sad treatment of women, you also have to realize that the Islamic attitude to non-believers in Islam is much the same as that of God to the Samaritans. After all, Allah revealed to his prophet Mohammed that conquered unbelievers must either convert to Islam, pay tribute, or die (see also Koran 9:73, 5:33).'

> *Then, when the sacred months have passed, slay the idolaters wherever ye find them, and take them (captive), and besiege them, and prepare for them each ambush. But if they repent and establish worship and pay the poor due, then leave their way free. Lo! Allah is Forgiving, Merciful. (Koran 9:5)*

Thomas also sighed and looked equally unhappy. 'I guess that the horrors visited upon unbelievers by both the ancient Jews and the followers of Islam are about the same. Luckily the followers of Christianity never committed abominations like those perpetrated by the Jews or Moslems.'

'Don't you believe it! Jesus was just as hateful to those who rejected the religion he preached as were all the others.'

'But I still believe Jesus preached a philosophy of love and tolerance.'

'Oh yes? Then look at this passage where Jesus instructed his apostles to spread his teachings, telling them what would happen to those who refused to listen to the word of God as interpreted by Jesus.'

And into whatsoever city or village ye shall enter, search out who in it is worthy; and there abide till ye go forth. And as ye enter into the house, salute it. And if the house be worthy, let your peace come upon it: but if it be not worthy, let your peace return to you. And whosoever shall not receive you, nor hear your words, as ye go forth out of that house or that city, shake off the dust of your feet. Verily I say unto you, It shall be more tolerable for the land of Sodom and Gomorrah in the day of judgment, than for that city. (ASV Bible, Matthew 10:11-15)

'In this archaic language, Jesus told his apostles that God would punish the loathsome inhabitants of cities refusing to listen to his teachings in a manner even more horrific than the punishments visited upon the inhabitants of Sodom and Gomorrah. This is tolerance! This is a message of love to his fellow man! And the history of Christian intolerance from ancient times until the end of the Middle-Ages is as equally bloody and appalling as that of ancient Judaism and Islam.'

'Okay, okay. I take your point. Ben, you certainly seem to have a gift for finding Bible passages bringing out the worst side of Jesus!'

'I know,' said Ben with a loathsomely smug expression.

'Another matter Ben, last night you told me that if we rigidly applied Biblical laws, about 70% of people in Western Europe would have to be put to death. I was thinking about the so-called crimes meriting the death penalty you discussed with me last night. But I came to the conclusion that the proportion of the Western European population that is adulterous, incestuous, homosexual, commits bestiality, is heretical, or abusive of their parents just isn't anywhere near enough to make up 70% of the total population. So how do you arrive at that figure?'

'Oh that's not so difficult. There is a part of the book of Deuteronomy in the Old Testament of the Bible that explicitly states that a free woman found not to be a virgin on her wedding-night must be stoned to death in front of her father's house.'

But if this thing be true, that the tokens of virginity were not found in the damsel; then they shall bring out the damsel to the door of her father's house, and the men of her city shall stone her to death with stones, because she hath wrought folly in Israel, to play the harlot in her father's house: so shalt thou put away the evil from the midst of thee. (ASV Bible, Deuteronomy 22:20-21)

'But that's a really vicious law! It was almost certainly abrogated in the New Testament,' exclaimed Thomas.

'Not at all. Just as with adulterers, homosexuals etc, there is not a single passage in the New Testament abrogating or mitigating this law in any way. So it is officially still applicable to Christians even today. When you add the fact of the almost total absence of virgin marriages in Western Europe to the list of crimes deserving death, a figure of about 70% of Western Europeans who deserve to die according to Old Testament laws is probably an underestimate.'

'Oh,' was all Thomas managed to say, adding on a more cheerful note, 'That would certainly solve the problem of unbelievers for all fanatical followers of Islam.'

'It certainly would. But now it's time for wine, and I do believe you were bringing the bottle. So what did you bring?'

'It's a warm and sunny day, so I got something totally conventional – a bottle of rosé. It's chilled. I even brought some proper glasses. Actually they're tumblers, but who uses long-stemmed wine glasses on a park bench anyway? Much too unstable.'

'Sounds good to me,' was the cheery response. 'I see you even brought a bottle with a screw cap. Good idea. Come on, let's have some. I'm thirsty after all that talking.'

Two glasses were filled in almost no time at all, and shortly after, a simultaneous sigh of pleasure was heard from the two.

'Well Thomas, I had my doubts about your possible choice of wine, and I was right. This is truly appalling. Okay, it's drinkable, but no more than that. Fortunately it's cold and loaded with alcohol, which more than makes up for all its many other deficiencies.'

'One of my worldlier, actually alcoholic, tutors recommended it. Now and then we share a glass of wine while discussing things, and I always thought he had a good taste for cheap, but reasonably good wine.

He recommended this one.'

'You mean he knows you're coming to speak with me?'

'Certainly. He is actually a bit of a rebel in the theology department. But they can't get rid of him because of a really good contract, plus the fact that the theology department would be seriously undermanned without him.'

'Well I hope he knows more about theology than he knows about wine,' said Ben sipping with a somewhat sour expression. 'Returning to our discussion – have you noticed something special about all the Judaic, Biblical, and Koranic laws we've been discussing?'

'Apart from their almost demented cruelty – not really.'

Ben took another sip, looked in front at the view of people enjoying the warmth of this wonderful day, 'Most of these laws are actually directed against women. Just consider the composition of the 70% of Western Europeans deserving of death according to Biblical laws. Most of the persons deserving to die are women.'

'Hmmm ... Thinking ... You're actually quite right! It really is quite awful when you think about it, but women seem to bear the brunt of most of these punishments and atrocities.'

'Yes indeed. Judaism, Christianity, and Islam regard women in general as friendly little creatures, necessary for fun, cooking, and children, but treat them as being less valuable than men, as well as being very sinful and ungrateful. Indeed, the sinful nature of women was confirmed by Mohammed who told his followers that the majority of the inhabitants of hell were women (see also Bukhari: 62:124-126).'

> Narrated Ibn 'Abbas: The Prophet said: "I was shown the Hell-fire and that the majority of its dwellers were women who were ungrateful." It was asked, "Do they disbelieve in Allah?" (or are they ungrateful to Allah?) He replied, "They are ungrateful to their husbands and are ungrateful for the favors and the good (charitable deeds) done to them. If you have always been good (benevolent) to one of them and then she sees something in you (not of her liking), she will say, 'I have never received any good from you.'" (Bukhari 2:28)

Ben continued, 'If you think this passage illustrates a low opinion of women, then think again. This is only a mild and trivial illustration. There are many, many incredibly evil passages in the holy books of all Abrahamic religions. One illustration is given by the behaviour of Lot.'

'You mean the holy man Lot who lived in Sodom.'

'The very same Lot. Lot, his wife and two daughters lived in the incredibly sinful city of Sodom. God finally decided to destroy the city of Sodom because of the sinfulness of its inhabitants. So God sent two angels in the form of men to Sodom to warn Lot and his family of the impending destruction of Sodom. The men of Sodom saw the beauty of the angels and wanted to sodomize them. A group of them went to the door of the house of Lot where these angels were staying, hammered on the door, and demanded he send the two angels outside. As a host, Lot was obliged to protect his guests, and accordingly could not turn them over to the mob outside. So he offered them his daughters instead ...'

And Lot went out unto them to the door, and shut the door after him. And he said, I pray you, my brethren, do not so wickedly. Behold now, I have two daughters that have not known man; let me, I pray you, bring them out unto you, and do ye to them as is good in your eyes: only unto these men do nothing, forasmuch as they are come under the shadow of my roof. (ASV Bible, Genesis 19:6-8)

'In other words, Lot offered his two young virgin daughters to be gang-raped by a mob of violent Sodomites, as long as they left his guests alone! Luckily for these two girls, God intervened to save them from the mob. But did God and the angels think any less of Lot after this? Not at all! Lot was still regarded as a holy man, beloved of God. Unbelievable! Incredible! This is a horrid illustration of the low regard for women in Judaism and Christianity.'

'I agree. It truly is appalling. But perhaps God used this as a test of the faith of Lot, in much the same way as God tested the faith of Abraham, founder of the Israelite nation, by asking him to sacrifice his only son Isaac. Just as Abraham was about to plunge the sacrificial knife into his son, he heard God telling him to stop, heard that God was well pleased with his faith, and heard that God had provided a lamb in a nearby bush for sacrifice instead (Bible, Genesis 22:1-19).'

'Nice idea, and a nice try Thomas. Unfortunately it doesn't correspond with the facts. A similar incident is reported in another part of the Old Testament, only this time without any divine intervention whatsoever. This part of the Bible tells of a man from the Levite tribe of Israel, who together with his concubine stayed overnight in the city of Gibeah. As they were being entertained by their host, a group of men came to the door and demanded he send the Levite man outside for their pleasure ...'

> *As they were making their hearts merry, behold, the men of the city, certain base fellows, beset the house round about, beating at the door; and they spake to the master of the house, the old man, saying, Bring forth the man that came into thy house, that we may know him. And the man, the master of the house, went out unto them, and said unto them, Nay, my brethren, I pray you, do not so wickedly; seeing that this man is come into my house, do not this folly. Behold, here is my daughter a virgin, and his concubine; them I will bring out now, and humble ye them, and do with them what seemeth good unto you: but unto this man do not any such folly.*
>
> *But the men would not hearken to him: so the man laid hold on his concubine, and brought her forth unto them; and they knew her, and abused her all the night until the morning: and when the day began to spring, they let her go. Then came the woman in the dawning of the day, and fell down at the door of the man's house where her lord was, till it was light.*
>
> *And her lord rose up in the morning, and opened the doors of the house, and went out to go his way; and, behold, the woman his concubine was fallen down at the door of the house, with her hands upon the threshold.*
>
> *And he said unto her, Up, and let us be going; but none answered: then he took her up upon the ass; and the man rose up, and gat him unto his place. And when he was come into his house, he took a knife, and laid hold on his concubine, and divided her, limb by limb, into twelve pieces, and sent her throughout all the borders of Israel. (ASV Bible, Judges 19:22-29)*

Ben paused to allow Thomas to fully digest the meaning of the passage. 'Passages like this turn the Bible into a stomach-churning book of horrors. Just consider this passage. The host of the Levite offered this aggressive group of homosexual rapists his virgin daughter, but they didn't want her. Then the Levite throws his concubine outside, and this group of homosexual thugs gang-rapes and abuses her all night while this Levite has a good sleep. They finally stop raping and abusing her at daybreak. This unfortunate and severely injured woman crawls to the house where her master is sleeping, collapses, and dies with her hands reaching out for the front door. Her master wakes up after a refreshing sleep, sees her lying at the front door after an invigorating all-night gang-bang, and simply says, "It's time to go!" Mere words are totally inadequate to express revulsion at such behaviour.'

Thomas took a deep sip of wine. 'I agree, it is an almost unbelievable story by today's standards. But perhaps this was quite normal behaviour with concubines and slaves at this time.'

'Yes, that might be true, but what about the virgin daughter? God certainly didn't intervene to save her from the rapists outside, as God did in the case of the daughters of Lot.'

Thomas thought a bit, and suggested with impish glint in his eye, 'Perhaps she was so desperately ugly that they didn't want her – not even in the dark.'

'Ah Thomas ... I do believe I detect a spark of humour, and so facetious too ... Actually, it is very possible the gang didn't want the virgin daughter, because raping her would have brought shame on the house of her father. The rapists were far from being anonymous, because they were known to be the sons of Belial. So after abusing and raping the daughter, there would have been enormous problems with the inevitable subsequent demand for revenge and financial compensation (Bible, Deuteronomy, chapter 22). Nonetheless, if this was the reason, then why did her father offer her to them at all? The most likely explanation is the low value placed upon women and daughters at this time. The concubine was not the wife of the Levite, only his plaything, which meant she was definitely of inferior social status. Furthermore, another important consideration was that she was a stranger in the city, which meant no one would avenge any injury done to her. So she was the most logical person to throw out to the mob.

The end of this story is as strange as it is horrid. The Levite finally realizes she is dead, loads her corpse onto his donkey, and simply goes home. Once home he cuts her body into twelve pieces, and sends these pieces to the leaders of the twelve tribes of Israel. These tribal leaders didn't say, "This Levite is totally deranged, and richly deserves to die along with the sons of Belial!" Instead they formed an army from the united tribes of Israel, and slaughtered nearly every man, woman, and child within the city of Gibeah! Only a few men managed to escape the massacre. The follow-up to the escape of those men was equally strange, but that's something you can read yourself.'

'I agree Ben. It is an appalling story. But how can you say people of the tribes of Israel regarded women as inferior beings? These stories are incidents. True, they are atrocious incidents, but I've always understood that the ancient followers of Judaism, Christianity, and Islam had an exceptionally high regard for women.'

'I can't understand where you get that idea. Read the Bible, the Koran, and the Sunnah of Bukhari. Having read these books you only come to one inescapable conclusion – the ancient followers of Judaism, Christianity, and Islam regarded women as no more than inferior chattels.'

'But that's contrary to most of what I've been taught.'

'I know,' sighed Ben. 'However, when interpreted literally, the holy texts of all these three religions are actually perverted instruments for enforcing the vilest forms of female oppression.'

'Oh?'

Ben took another sip, 'I'll begin with the fact that God orders women to obey men. In the first book of the Bible, Eve the first woman, seduces Adam the first man to sin against the laws of God. God is really angry and curses both Adam and Eve. But God especially curses Eve, telling her and all women to come, that childbirth would in future be a painful reminder of their original sin, as well as the fact that they were henceforth to be subject to the rule of their husbands.'

Unto the woman he said, I will greatly multiply thy pain and thy conception; in pain thou shalt bring forth children; and thy desire shall be to thy husband, and he shall rule over thee. (ASV Bible, Genesis 3:16)

Ben took another sip, 'Surprising how much better this wine tastes after a glass or two.' He continued, 'Before you start saying that Jesus and the New Testament prophets abrogated this Old Testament law, I'll just say that the New Testament prophets reaffirmed the divine right of men to rule women (see also Bible, 1 Corinthians 11:3, 1 Timothy 2:11-12, 1 Peter 3:1).'

Wives, be in subjection unto your own husbands, as unto the Lord. For the husband is the head of the wife, and Christ also is the head of the church, being himself the saviour of the body. But as the church is subject to Christ, so let the wives also be to their husbands in everything. (ASV Bible, Ephesians 5:22-24)

'Hmmm ... It does seem as if you're right here. But Ben, what about Islam? I've always heard that women in Islam have the same rights as men, and don't have to obey them as demanded by the Judaic or Christian tradition.'

'Oh Thomas, you already know that Islam is just as bad as Judaism and Christianity. As you told me some time ago, Islam also requires women to subject themselves to men (see also Chapter 2).'

Men are in charge of women, because Allah hath men the one of them to excel the other, and because they spend of their property (for the support of women). So good women are the obedient, guarding in secret that which Allah hath guarded. As for those from whom ye fear rebellion, admonish them and banish them to beds apart, and scourge them. Then if they obey you, seek not a way against them. Lo! Allah is ever High Exalted, Great. (Koran 4:34)

'Thomas, there is only one possible reaction to this short verse – amazement at how these few simple words can exert such a profound socio-cultural influence! In this single terse verse, God reveals to Mohammed that women must be obedient to men, and tells men to admonish their women if they even suspect they may be planning any ill-conduct or disloyalty. It even stipulates the exact nature and level of admonishment! Admonishment of potentially, and actually wayward wives can vary in severity from a verbal reprimand, to refusing sexual relations, and ultimately to scourging. However, even though the Koran instructs believers to scourge their wives if necessary, these women were to be treated kindly, and with consideration after a well-earned scourging. This is proven by the fact that Mohammed stipulated that a husband should not engage in sexual intercourse with his wife on the same day as he flogged her.'

Narrated Abdullah bin Zam'a: The Prophet said, "None of you should flog his wife as he flogs a slave and then have sexual intercourse with her in the last part of the day." (Bukhari 62:132)

Thomas looked decidedly uncomfortable on hearing this, but Ben continued, apparently unconcerned by the effect of his words. 'I suppose Mohammed had some very practical reasons for making such a statement. After all, I imagine very few women would be interested in sexual intercourse with their husbands after being severely flogged by these very same "loving" husbands, and that is aside from the fact that lying on their backs would be decidedly painful after such a flogging ...'

Ben paused to drink more wine. 'And to think Thomas, all this cruelty is amply justified by the fact that women are supposedly inherently inferior to men because God created them from the rib of the first man. If you think these are the only examples of "holy" rulings detrimental to the condition of women, then think again, because there are many more laws and customs discriminating against women in Judaism, Christianity, and Islam.'

Thomas unhappily gulped a mouthful of wine, 'Continue – I'm all ears.'

'We know from the Torah, Bible, Koran, and Sunnah that women are not only ungrateful, but they are also inherently unclean, sinful and vile, dragging men with them into the horrid and filthy pit of hell. Fortunately the early Christian prophets found a way for men to save themselves from the defiling toils of women, a way enabling some especially fortunate men to become chosen companions of Jesus. However, it was a rigorous and harsh regime, suitable only for a select few.'

And I heard a voice from heaven, as the voice of many waters,

and as the voice of a great thunder: and the voice which I heard
was as the voice of harpers harping with their harps: and they sing
as it were a new song before the throne, and before the four living
creatures and the elders: and no man could learn the song save the
hundred and forty and four thousand, even they that had been
purchased out of the earth. These are they that were not defiled
with women; for they are virgins. These are they that follow the
Lamb whithersoever he goeth. These were purchased from
among men, to be the firstfruits unto God and unto the Lamb.
And in their mouth was found no lie: they are without blemish.
(ASV Bible, Revelations 14:2-5)

Ben really started warm up to his chain of thought, 'So do not defile your body or your soul by having anything to do with women. Stay a virgin, and you too can become one of the chosen 144,000. Ah Thomas, all these things lead you to only one conclusion – Judaism, Christianity and Islam actually consider women to be sinful, and rather unclean little creatures, especially menstruating women.'

And if a woman have an issue, and her issue in her flesh be
blood, she shall be in her impurity seven days: and whosoever
toucheth her shall be unclean until the even.
And everything that she lieth upon in her impurity shall be
unclean: everything also that she sitteth upon shall be unclean.
And whosoever toucheth her bed shall wash his clothes, and
bathe himself in water, and be unclean until the even.
And whosoever toucheth anything that she sitteth upon shall
wash his clothes, and bathe himself in water, and be unclean until
the even.
And if it be on the bed, or on anything whereon she sitteth,
when he toucheth it, he shall be unclean until the even.
And if any man lie with her, and her impurity be upon him, he
shall be unclean seven days; and every bed whereon he lieth shall
be unclean. (ASV Bible, Leviticus 15:19-24)

'Menstruating women are unclean for seven days! Other books in the

Old Testament reaffirmed this belief, and the New Testament of the Christians never abrogated this ruling. The natural, but sometimes messy act of childbirth also requires women to purify themselves. Furthermore, according to Judaism, giving birth to female babies is inherently much filthier than giving birth to male babies, because a woman must purify herself twice as long after giving birth to a female baby!'

> *Speak unto the children of Israel, saying, If a woman conceive seed, and bear a man-child, then she shall be unclean seven days; as in the days of the impurity of her sickness shall she be unclean. And in the eighth day the flesh of his foreskin shall be circumcised. And she shall continue in the blood of her purifying three and thirty days; she shall touch no hallowed thing, nor come into the sanctuary, until the days of her purifying be fulfilled.*
>
> *But if she bear a maid-child, then she shall be unclean two weeks, as in her impurity; and she shall continue in the blood of her purifying threescore and six days. (ASV Bible, Leviticus 12:2-5)*

'This ruling was also never abrogated in the New Testament. And if you think that only followers of the Judaism and Christianity had ideas like this, then think again. The followers of Islam have much the same attitude. They also regard menstruating women as unclean.'

> *They question thee (O Muhammad) concerning menstruation. Say: It is an illness, so let women alone at such time and go not in unto them till they are cleansed. And when they have purified themselves, then go in unto them as Allah hath enjoined upon you. Truly Allah loveth those who turn unto Him, and loveth those who have a care for cleanness. (Koran 2:222)*

'This inferiority of women is manifest in regulations regarding the taking of oaths in Judaism, and in Christianity too, because these regulations were not abrogated in the New Testament. So when a Jewish or Christian man makes a vow, he is always obligated to carry out the vow. However, when a woman makes a vow, her father, or her husband can nullify that vow at the moment it is made. (Bible, Numbers 30:6-15). Presumably this is because women in the Judeo-Christian tradition are not free agents, but always property controlled by fathers or husbands. This is quite different to the Islamic tradition where both men and women were expected to perform that which they agreed upon under oath (Koran 5:89).'

'Laws regarding the ability of women to testify in legal matters differ somewhat as well. For example, in Islam, the testimony of a woman is only worth half that of a man.'

> *And call to witness, from among your men, two witnesses. And if two men be not (at hand) then a man and two women, of such as ye approve as witnesses, so that if the one erreth (through forgetfulness) the other will remember. And the witnesses must not refuse when they are summoned. (Koran 2:282)*

'I think that's all fairly clear Thomas,' stated Ben in a definite tone.

'Yes it is indeed,' was the reply. 'But is this all you have to say about women?'

'Not at all! I've only just begun to scratch the surface of this problem. More wine?'

'Yes please! I'm glad I bought a litre bottle.'

'You're right there. This wine really only begins to taste tolerable after a few glasses.'

They sat in silence looking at the colourful flow of people passing through the park and on the Rapenburg. Now and then, they sipped their wine. Finally, Thomas spoke, 'What about the other evidences of female inferiority and discrimination?'

'A human lifespan is too short to list all the indignities fanatically religious men require women to endure. However, for your delectation, here are another few. One interesting law is about wearing clothing of the opposite sex. The followers of Islam report that Mohammed was revolted by men who wore women's clothing, and behaved as if they were women. Similarly, he cursed women who wore men's clothing, and acted as if they were men.'

> *Narrated Ibn 'Abbas: Allah's Apostle cursed those men who are*

in the similitude (assume the manners) of women and those women who are in the similitude (assume the manners) of men. (Bukhari 72:773)

'But as you see, this was merely mild revulsion, because they didn't require these people to be flogged, beaten, killed, or thrown out of the tribe. Jewish and Christian tradition also forbids the wearing of clothing of the opposite sex.'

A woman shall not wear that which pertaineth unto a man, neither shall a man put on a woman's garment; for whosoever doeth these things is an abomination unto Jehovah thy God. (ASV Bible, Deuteronomy 22:5)

'This is really fascinating. Wearing the clothing of the opposite sex is an abomination to the God of the Jews! The New Testament prophets never explicitly abrogated this statement, and Saint Paul, the major New Testament interpreter of the philosophy of Jesus actually indirectly reaffirmed this belief (Bible, Romans 1:26-31). So wearing the clothing of the opposite sex remains an abomination to all good Jews and Christians.'

'So? And?' was the enquiring response.

'You might think this is a trivial ruling, but it sometimes had profound consequences for women who wore men's clothing in the Middle-Ages. For example, consider the French heroine, Joan of Arc. Joan of Arc was born in France in 1412 CE and died in 1431 CE. During her short life she heard voices of God and the Saints. She was inspired by these things, and somehow, for a short time, she came to command the armies of the king of France during the wars to drive the English armies out of France. She was a charismatic and inspirational leader, who together with the armies she led, succeeded in driving the English armies out of many cities, her most famous victory being the lifting of the siege of Orleans. Ultimately, she was betrayed, captured, and handed over to the English, who then allowed the Bishop of Rouen to conduct a farcical trial. The main charges were of heresy, because of the voices she heard, and curiously enough, the wearing of men's clothing. This last charge was an important charge, because it was evident and provable, whereas charges of spiritual heresy were more difficult to prove. Not only was the wearing of men's clothing an abomination in the sight of God as is incontrovertibly stated in the Bible, but she also committed the heinous heresy of saying God required her to wear this clothing. This latter really was heresy, because how could she know the will of God? Even worse, she persisted in her heresy by continuing to wear men's clothing during her imprisonment. This was one of the charges with which her accusers ultimately succeeded in sentencing her to death, and she was burnt alive at the stake in Rouen on May 30, 1431 CE (Gower 1893, chapter 6). So you see, the New Testament had not abrogated this ruling at all. Amazing isn't it.'

'Wow ...' was the only reaction of Thomas. 'I never realized that some of these more trivial Old Testament laws were actually applied so literally by Christians. But if Joan of Arc knew of the seriousness of the charge, why did she continue wearing men's clothing in prison? She could have renounced it, and asked for women's clothing.'

'Her accusers actually allowed her to select men or women's clothing to wear in prison, yet she persisted in wearing men's clothing while imprisoned. Her reasons were undoubtedly very practical. She was chained to the bed in her dungeon in the company of three jailers selected more for their depravity than any other qualities they may have possessed. So she was almost certainly assaulted, or worse, raped repeatedly by her jailers. Her trial report even mentions that on occasions she looked as if she had been struggling. The use of repeated abuse by her jailers was almost certainly a tactic employed by the Bishop of Rouen to break her spirit and achieve a conviction. Wearing men's clothing was her only way of making rape more difficult – skirts versus pants. The story of her captivity and trial is desperately sad and horrid. Her sufferings in captivity were apparently so terrible, that she ultimately chose death in preference to continued imprisonment (Gower 1893, chapter 6). This little known aspect to the short existence of Joan of Arc brings us to the loathsome matter of rape, or at the very least, forced sex, sanctioned by the God of Judaism, Christianity, and Islam.'

Thomas took a deep gulp of rosé, 'Come on now Ben. Now you really are making a mockery of these religions.'

'Not at all Thomas. Not at all ... Let's look at the oldest passages in Genesis, the oldest book of Judaism and Christianity. Here we can read of the exploits of Jacob, son of Isaac, and father of the twelve sons who each founded one of the twelve tribes of Israel. Jacob was married to two sisters, Leah and Rachel. Leah had born several sons to Jacob, but Rachel whom he loved more than Leah, had never born him any children. Rachel was really jealous of Leah. Jacob said it wasn't his fault that she had no children. So Rachel came up with a solution which incidentally provided Jacob with a good deal of pleasure ...'

> *And when Rachel saw that she bare Jacob no children, Rachel envied her sister; and she said unto Jacob, Give me children, or else I die.*
>
> *And Jacob's anger was kindled against Rachel: and he said, Am I in God's stead, who hath withheld from thee the fruit of the womb?*
>
> *And she said, Behold, my maid Bilhah, go in unto her; that she may bear upon my knees, and I also may obtain children by her.*
>
> *And she gave him Bilhah her handmaid to wife: and Jacob went in unto her. And Bilhah conceived, and bare Jacob a son. (ASV Bible, Genesis 30:1-5)*

'Now,' continued Ben, 'there is absolutely no talk of Bilhah's consent being required, just that Jacob had sexual intercourse with her, and she had a child. Presumably maidservants had little to say in this matter as was illustrated elsewhere in the Bible (Bible, Genesis 16:1-4). Presumably concubines, maidservants, bondservants, and slaves were not even considered real people; they were similar to real people of course, but not quite the same. This viewpoint is nicely illustrated by a law in the book of Leviticus of the Bible.'

> *And whosoever lieth carnally with a woman, that is a bondmaid, betrothed to a husband, and not at all redeemed, nor freedom given her; they shall be punished; they shall not be put to death, because she was not free. And he shall bring his trespass-offering unto Jehovah, unto the door of the tent of meeting, even a ram for a trespass-offering. (ASV Bible, Leviticus 19:20-21)*

Ben shook his head, took a sip of his wine. 'Now, if a man had consensual sex with the betrothed virgin daughter of a free man, both he and she would be stoned to death. Furthermore, if a man had consensual sex with an unbetrothed virgin daughter of a free man, he would have to pay a fine of fifty shekels of silver to her father as compensation, and also have to marry her (Bible, Deuteronomy 22:23-29). But in the passage we just saw, you have a situation of consensual sex with a betrothed bondmaid, and a bondmaid clearly does not have the same status as a free woman. This is why the bondmaid is punished by just being scourged, while the man must pay a fine for illegal use of another person's property – in this case, the bondmaid. Just imagine Thomas: this is a holy law given by God to the prophet Moses! Presumably the all-knowing, all-powerful, eternal God of Moses, creator of the universe, and all within this universe, approves of slavery and bonded labour. More than one thousand and seven hundred years of human development later, Mohammed, the final prophet of this same God, expressed exactly the same ruling regarding consensual sex between slave women and men other than their owners (see also Bukhari 34:363, 34:436, 46:731, 82:822).'

Narrated Abu Huraira: The Prophet said, "If a slave-girl commits illegal sexual intercourse and it is proved beyond doubt, then her owner should lash her and should not blame her after the legal punishment. And then if she repeats the illegal sexual intercourse he should lash her again and should not blame her after the legal punishment, and if she commits it a third time, then he should sell her even for a hair rope." (Bukhari 34:362)

'Presumably a promiscuous slave-girl was considered a worthless reprobate harlot after repeated sex with men other than her owner, which was why the owners of such a slut were advised to get rid of her for even a worthless give-away price. Now you should consider that the punishment for adultery in Islam is exactly the same as in Judaism and Christianity, so what this ruling illustrates is another example of divine sanction for the institution of slavery, and the inferior position occupied by slaves, especially women.'

Thomas had listened attentively to all these things. He managed to say, 'This is really quite appalling. But how can you say that God sanctioned slavery?'

'Quite easily. God is the all-knowing, all-powerful, all-pervading, creator of the universe, and all within the universe. Now if God did not sanction the institution of slavery, God would have ensured that it never occurred, or would have expressed his disapproval of slavery to all the prophets of Judaism, of Christianity, and to Mohammed. But nowhere do we find any disapproval of the institution of slavery in the holy texts of Judaism, of Christianity, or of Islam – only acceptance of the reality of slavery, and regulations governing the treatment of slaves. Even Jesus, the Son of God, and the Christian prophets who succeeded him never disapproved of slavery. They simply told slaves to obey their masters in the same way as they would obey God (see also Bible, Ephesians 6:5-8, Titus 2:9-10)'

Slaves, obey your masters in everything; and do it not only when their eye is upon you and to win their favour, but with sincerity of heart and reverence for the Lord. (NIV Bible, Colossians 3:22)

'For female slaves, obeying their masters in everything certainly also included satisfying the sexual demands of their masters. Just think, neither Mohammed, nor any of the many prophets of Judaism or Christianity, or even Jesus the Son of God were inspired by God to express disapproval of slavery. They simply accepted slavery and all its consequences, forcing us to the inescapable conclusion that slavery is approved by the merciful and loving God of Judaism, Christianity, and Islam.'

Thomas was silent. He looked unhappily at the brightly clad, well-fed, free men and women, walking, chattering and laughing in the bright sunlight before him. What he had heard opened a vision of the gaping maw of the black and filthy pit of dogmatic literal interpretation of holy texts. This was a system of thought so dark and so oppressive, that his world suddenly seemed dark and chill. He shivered.

Ben noticed this, looked at Thomas, and said, 'Thomas, if you think this is appalling, then realize that the full truth is even worse. The all-knowing God of Judaism provided the Israelite nation with extensive laws, among which regulations governing whom to kill, and which women and children they were permitted to let live after conquering a city.'

When thou drawest nigh unto a city to fight against it, then proclaim peace unto it. And it shall be, if it make thee answer of peace, and open unto thee, then it shall be, that all the people that are found therein shall become tributary unto thee, and shall serve thee.

And if it will make no peace with thee, but will make war against thee, then thou shalt besiege it: and when Jehovah thy God delivereth it into thy hand, thou shalt smite every male thereof with the edge of the sword: but the women, and the little ones, and the cattle, and all that is in the city, even all the spoil thereof, shalt thou take for a prey unto thyself; and thou shalt eat the spoil of thine enemies, which Jehovah thy God hath given thee.

Thus shalt thou do unto all the cities which are very far off from thee, which are not of the cities of these nations.

But of the cities of these peoples, that Jehovah thy God giveth thee for an inheritance, thou shalt save alive nothing that breatheth; (ASV Bible, Deuteronomy 20:10-16)

'In other words, if the Israelites waged war against a city, and that city surrendered, then these people would pay tribute in all its forms. If they refused to surrender, and God gave the Israelites victory, they were instructed to kill all the men, and take the women, children, and everything else portable as God-given spoils of war with which they could do as they wished. However, there was a distinction – if the city was one in a territory given them by God for habitation by the Israelite nation, they were instructed to kill everything that breathed! This merciful and loving God of all peoples was a good God, especially to the Israelites.'

Ben moistened his throat with a sip of wine and continued, 'Accordingly, God appears to sanction conquest and genocide. Furthermore, God did not want his chosen people, the Israelites, to expend too much energy making difficult decisions. So this loving and merciful God gave them detailed instructions as to when they could rape their female captives in a manner expressive of the sensitivity due to young women who had just seen their families slaughtered before their eyes.'

When thou goest forth to battle against thine enemies, and

Jehovah thy God delivereth them into thy hands, and thou carriest them away captive, and seest among the captives a beautiful woman, and thou hast a desire unto her, and wouldest take her to thee to wife; then thou shalt bring her home to thy house; and she shall shave her head, and pare her nails; and she shall put the raiment of her captivity from off her, and shall remain in thy house, and bewail her father and her mother a full month: and after that thou shalt go in unto her, and be her husband, and she shall be thy wife.

And it shall be, if thou have no delight in her, then thou shalt let her go whither she will; but thou shalt not sell her at all for money, thou shalt not deal with her as a slave, because thou hast humbled her. (ASV Bible, Deuteronomy 21:10-14)

Thomas' mouth hung open, a stunned expression on his face ...

'I agree Thomas; this is truly sensitive treatment of young women held captive by the very same people who brutally slaughtered their families. Moreover, it is treatment sanctioned by God, so it must be good. Translated into modern English, this simply means that if you like one of the captive women: give her a month to mourn her father and mother before raping her. This passage has profound implications. It means such a woman was actually a young unmarried virgin, because it specifically does not mention children, husbands, married sisters, or brothers – just the mother and father of this woman. Presumably the Israelites treated conquered cities in the same way as Moses treated the Midianites: kill all men, kill all married women, kill all male children, and leave only the unmarried virgin girls alive (Bible, Numbers 31:1-18). Paring the nails of a captive girl was a sensible precaution to prevent being severely scratched while exercising the just and God-given rights of a captor. Similarly, waiting for a menstrual period was very practical, because a captive girl might be pregnant due to one of their dead enemies, which would mean she was certainly no virgin, and had to be killed anyway. Practical experience had taught the Israelites that isolated, dispossessed, and terrified young girls whose family members had been slaughtered before their eyes, subsequently enslaved, forced to work hard while subjected to the sexual demands of their new masters, and therefore regularly pregnant, seldom rebelled or sought revenge. So after a month of mourning, which was evidently deemed sufficient to mourn the savage murder of family and friends, God rewarded the new owner of the captive woman for performing God's work of killing her parents, by permitting him to rape her and call her his wife. God even said that if the man didn't like the woman after performing this holy deed, he could always throw her out, but could not sell her because he had "humbled" or "dishonoured" her, which is a nicer term for raping her. Ah Thomas, the tears flow down your cheeks when you think of the sensitivity shown these poor young orphaned girls by God's chosen people ...'

Thomas was revolted by what he heard, but understood Ben's facetiousness was his way of dealing with such divinely sanctioned abominations. He no longer even asked whether the ruling had been changed in the New Testament of the Bible. He just looked at the happy, brightly clad girls, women, and children walking to and from the city centre in the bright sunshine of this glorious afternoon. And he was glad he did not live in ancient times. He asked, 'What about the followers of Christianity and Islam?'

'Christianity is rather vague on the matter. The pronouncements of Jesus and all other New Testament prophets were often contradictory in some aspects regarding treatment of other people, and no passage in the New Testament deals specifically with the acquisition and division of the spoils of war. So you cannot really say anything specific about Christians in this regard. However, Islam has always been very specific about the spoils of war. Indeed, during the lifetime of Mohammed between 570 to 632 CE, which is about 600 years after the death of Jesus, and more than one thousand seven hundred years after the laws given by God to the Israelite nation, God still revealed an abiding and healthy interest in the acquisition and division of the spoils of war (Koran, Sura 8, *The Booty*). Only now, God told the Arabic followers of Islam that they were a superior race who would be rewarded with much booty (see also Koran 3:110).'

Allah was well pleased with the believers when they swore allegiance unto thee beneath the tree, and He knew what was in their hearts, and He sent down peace of reassurance on them, and hath rewarded them with a near victory; And much booty that they will capture. Allah is ever Mighty, Wise. (Koran 48:18-19)

'Female and male captives were also classified as booty, or spoils of war. They had a definite commercial value, either for ransom, for use as personal slaves, or for sale as slaves. So it was that this merciful, all-knowing, and all-powerful God sanctioned the sexual exploitation of female slaves taken as spoils of war. God revealed this specifically to Mohammed as well as granting Mohammed special personal privileges.'

O Prophet! Lo! We have made lawful unto thee thy wives unto whom thou hast paid their dowries, and those whom thy right hand possesseth of those whom Allah hath given thee as spoils of war, and the daughters of thine uncle on the father's side and the daughters of thine aunts on the father's side, and the daughters of thine uncles on the mother's side emigrated with thee, and a believing woman if she give herself unto the Prophet and the Prophet desire to ask her in marriage, a privilege for thee only, not for the (rest of) believers. We are aware of that which We enjoined upon them concerning their wives and those whom their right hands possess that thou mayst be free from blame, for Allah is Forgiving, Merciful. (Koran 33:50)

'Not only did God sanction sexual intercourse with captured women for Mohammed and his followers, but also explicitly permitted them to engage in sexual intercourse with their married female captives. This latter means the victors were permitted to indulge in sexual intercourse with their female captives while their husbands were still alive, presumably being held for ransom, or to be sold as slaves.'

And all married women are forbidden unto you save those (captives) whom your right hands possess. (Koran 4:24)

'God is indeed good to true believers! What a relief for these warriors of Islam, these brave emissaries of God. In contrast to the ancient Israelites, they no longer had to distinguish between married and unmar-

ried captive women, nor did they have to bother searching for virgins! As
if these improvements in religion were not enough, nowhere in the Koran,
or in the Sunnah of Bukhari, is there any regulation determining when they
could commence raping their female captives. So they could begin at once.
No more frustrating waiting for one month! Who says religions never
evolve and improve? These were very definite improvements in the laws
regarding the treatment of captive women. God is indeed all-knowing and
merciful! But even so, the fervently religious followers of Mohammed
were troubled by a pressing theological problem regarding these captured
women. Fortunately, Mohammed always had a ready answer to most
problems – answers which were presumably revealed to him by God.'

> *Narrated Abu Said Al-Khudri: that while he was sitting with
> Allah's Apostle he said, "O Allah's Apostle! We get female
> captives as our share of booty, and we are interested in their
> prices, what is your opinion about coitus interruptus?" The
> Prophet said, "Do you really do that? It is better for you not to do
> it. No soul that which Allah has destined to exist, but will surely
> come into existence. (Bukhari 34:432)*

'These brave God-fearing warriors of Islam wanted to rape their
female captives and sell them afterwards, but pregnant slaves evidently
fetched lower prices than non-pregnant slaves. So they asked the last and
most important prophet of God for guidance to help them solve this difficult, but nonetheless pressing theological problem, and they received it.
The advice of Mohammed was as brutal, unfeeling, clear and simple, as it
was fatalistic. No coitus interruptus. No contraception whatsoever. Not a
single word of disapproval of raping female captives. If God wishes a child
to exist, it will be born. This concept raises the fascinating possibility that
the rape and resulting pregnancies of these women were predestined by
God. Accordingly, these women as well as their rapists were merely
instruments of the will of God, acting out their small roles in God's grand
plan for the universe. So instead of committing an ugly deed of rape, these
Islamic conquerors were actually performing a holy deed for which these
"fortunate" women were presumably very grateful.'

Ben paused, drank the last of his wine, and threw the cup into a nearby rubbish bin. 'So Thomas, to sum matters up, all these things illustrate the profound low regard of the followers of Judaism, Christianity, and Islam for women. It's not an attitude you would term inspirational, nor is it an attitude of which these Abrahamic religions can be proud.'

'Ben, words such as vile, abominable, repulsive, and loathsome arise in my mind, but actually words are totally inadequate to describe all the horrors perpetrated against women in the name of God! Dreadful ... Dreadful ... I don't think I'll ever be able to look at the relation between religion and women in quite the same way again.'

As he finished, they heard the call to evening prayer from the Mare Mosque, '*Allahu Akbar Allah, Allahu Akbar Allah, Allahu Akbar Allah, Allahu Akbar Allah ...*'

The sound was enough to decide Ben. His response was typically abrupt and short. 'Well Thomas, it sounds like it's time to go. The bottle is empty too. Let's meet again sometime this week. Give me a call when you've got a spare moment.'

'Okay.'

Chapter 10

Terrors of anaethesia

Ben peered at the wine in his glass, swirled, inhaled, and approved of what he saw and smelled. He looked at Thomas who was engaged in the more mundane task of leaning back in his chair and inspecting condensation droplets running down his glass, 'I'm looking forward to tasting this wine Thomas. We don't get much New Zealand wine here. Wonderful aroma.' He sipped, tasted carefully and gave a satisfied sigh, 'Ahhh ... ambrosia ...'

Thomas said nothing, but did take a sip. 'Indeed. A very decent white. You wouldn't expect a place as cool as New Zealand to produce wine as good as this.'

'An understatement young man. Very well, perhaps it's not a great wine, but it's still a very good wine for the price. A lot of flavour. This wine, together with the very decent meal we've just enjoyed makes this evening just that more perfect. How are you bearing up? After all, this is our third bottle tonight.'

'Well Ben,' was the slightly slurred response, 'just now I think I'm in some sort of preliminary stage of anaesthesia. Riding my bicycle back home at this moment would be a decidedly hazardous activity. So what about a cup or two of really strong coffee? While we're drinking that, you can tell me something about anaesthesia. As a layman and theology student, anaesthesia appears to me to be a strange and fearful condition. After all, how is it possible for a person to be asleep, and yet not to feel, or even respond in some way to the horrific pain of a surgeon cutting into their flesh, severing body parts, or tugging at raw wounds. The horror and the pain of an operation are almost unthinkable, which is why I think anaesthesia must be a condition similar to death to make it possible for people to endure such pain. In fact, aren't sleep and death a bit similar? I remember a passage I once read in one of my study books called *De*

265

Senectute, written by an ancient Roman philosopher called Cicero.'

Again, you really see nothing resembling death so much as sleep;
(Cicero, paragraph 81)

'Statements like these make you think,' said Thomas. 'Other ancient philosophers also had similar thoughts. Another ancient Christian theologian called Tertullian also once said something about the relationship between the soul, sleep, and death in his book *A Treatise on the Soul.*'

Meanwhile the soul is circumstanced in such a manner as to seem to be elsewhere active, learning to bear future absence by a dissembling of its [the soul] presence for the moment [during sleep]. We shall soon know the case of Hermotimus. But yet it dreams in the interval. Whence then its dreams? The fact is, it cannot rest or be idle altogether, nor does it confine to the still hours of sleep the nature of its immortality. It proves itself to possess a constant motion; it travels over land and sea, it trades, it is excited, it labours, it plays, it grieves, it rejoices, it follows pursuits lawful and unlawful; it shows what very great power it has even without the body, how well equipped it is with members of its own, although betraying at the same time the need it has of impressing on some body its activity again. Accordingly, when the body shakes off its slumber, it asserts before your eye the resurrection of the dead by its own resumption of its natural functions. Such, therefore, must be both the natural reason and the reasonable nature of sleep. If you only regard it as the image of death, you initiate faith, you nourish hope, you learn both how to die and how to live, you learn watchfulness, even while you sleep. (Tertullian, Chapter XLIV.)

'In other words,' continued Thomas, 'Cicero and Tertullian, as well as many other ancient philosophers taught that awakening from sleep is a bit like a resurrection of the body from death!'

'It certainly sounds like you've been given a reasonable grounding in the ancient classics, so I'll respond in kind,' said Ben. 'Actually, what you're illustrating with these hoary old quotes and popular beliefs about sleep, is an almost universal belief found in nearly all cultures of the world. Good examples of the same thoughts about the nature of sleep are also found in the writings of living religions such as Islam, where one passage in the Koran tells us (see also Koran 6:60):'

Allah receiveth (men's) souls at the time of their death, and that (soul) which dieth not (yet) in its sleep. He keepeth that (soul) for which He hath ordained death and dismisseth the rest till an appointed term. Lo herein verily are portents for people who take thought. (Koran 39:42)

'Wow!' was all Thomas said. 'If you put that on a wall of an operating theatre, you won't find a single patient willing to undergo an operation under general anaesthesia any more.'

'Now if you think that was fascinating, then the beliefs of some other cultures are even more to the point about the relationship between sleep, death, and separation of the soul from the body.' Ben gazed outside across the square in front of the restaurant. 'Do you know an old book called *The Golden Bough*, written by a certain J.G. Frazer (1854-1941 CE) towards the end of the nineteenth century?'

'Yes I do. According to my lecturers it's full of lies, half-truths, a few fantasies, and occasionally some insights and truths. But I haven't read it.'

'Shame about that, because it really is a wonderful book. Frazer collected and collated legends from all over the world and integrated them in a book whose grand design revealed the fundamental similarities of all human beliefs, and how the human condition often results in similar solutions to common problems, regardless of where one is in the world.' Ben paused, looked at Thomas to see whether he was still alert, and continued. 'For instance not only do many cultures believe the soul departs from the body during sleep, but also that the return of the soul can be prevented by altering the appearance of the body. Frazer gives a beautiful description of one of these beliefs.'

Still more dangerous is it in the opinion of primitive man to move a sleeper or alter his appearance, for if this were done the soul on its return might not be able to find or recognise its body, and so the person would die. The Minangkabauers deem it highly improper to blacken or dirty the face of a sleeper, lest the absent soul should shrink from re-entering a body thus disfigured. Patani Malays fancy that if a person's face be painted while he sleeps, the soul which has gone out of him will not recognise him, and he will sleep on till his face is washed. In Bombay it is thought equivalent to murder to change the aspect of a sleeper, as by painting his face in fantastic colours or giving moustaches to a sleeping woman. For when the soul returns it will not know its own body, and the person will die. (Frazer 1922, chapter 18, part 2 – Absence and Recall of the Soul)

'But this idea is quite different to what many people report during out-of-body experiences,' Ben continued, 'because most people report that they recognize their bodies during these experiences, no matter how their body appears, or is covered. However, enough mutual display of our fascination with long-dead authors, and the fascinating insights they give regarding ages-old human attitudes – you want to hear something about anaesthesia.'

'Er … yes,' said Thomas, as he sniffed a cup of syrupy black coffee, 'that's what I was hoping to hear something about.'

'Well, to begin with I'll only talk about general anaesthesia. General anaesthesia is a condition where people are rendered unconscious and insensible to the pain of surgery by administration of drugs. This is the condition most people talk about and fear most of all. You seldom hear the same things being said about regional anaesthesia, which is a situation where local anaesthetic drugs are used to render part of the body insensible to the pain of surgery, while the person being operated remains conscious. I emphasize this difference between regional and general anaesthesia, because some people talk about both of these conditions interchangeably when talking about anaesthesia, even though they are totally different. Okay?'

'Yes, yes … Get on with it,' was the impatient response of Thomas. 'Good coffee here, even the aroma gets your brain cells tingling with anticipation.'

Ben looked at the younger man appraisingly, 'Thomas, I sometimes wonder what your teachers think of your changed way of thinking, and your theological explorations with someone like me ... Ah well, back to the subject of anaesthesia ... General anaesthesia has somehow acquired very bad publicity in many modern Western countries. In my personal experience this may even be expressed in the rather extreme attitude: "It's permissible to die as a result of an operation, but it's not permissible to die as a result of the anaesthesia needed to make the operation possible!" Many people seem to forget that most operations are simply not possible without anaesthesia. Furthermore, they also seem to forget, or simply do not realize, that some operations are only possible under general anaesthesia, either because of the technical requirements of the operation, or simply because of the mental or physical condition of the person who is to undergo the proposed operation. A certain Professor Meursing once summarized this attitude to anaesthesia in a pithy little sentence: "The surgeon gets the flowers, and the anaesthesiologist gets sued."'

Thomas's eyes had a pawkish glint as he responded to Ben's enumeration of some of the frustrations occupying the minds of anaesthesiologists: 'It sounds like anaesthesiologists have a real attitude problem.'

'Yes, the lot of an anaesthesiologist is not a happy one,' sighed Ben. 'Many people seem to have the idea that anaesthesia is only administered by nurses, or even the hospital porter. They think an anaesthesiologist is only a sort of surgical appendage, doing only what the surgeon wants, and when the surgeon wants it. And like you said, many people believe general anaesthesia to be a state akin to death, considering it to be a dangerous condition indeed.'

'You certainly make anaesthesiology sound like a thankless medical specialty.'

Ben glanced at Thomas to see whether this was more than light-hearted banter, 'Indeed it is. Let's begin with the qualifications of an anaesthesiologist. An anaesthesiologist is a person who has studied medicine, and is qualified as a medical practitioner. For all manner of reasons, some of these newly qualified doctors decide to specialize in the field of anaesthesiology, just as other newly qualified doctors decide to become surgeons, internists, venereologists, etc. The duration of the specialization in anaesthesiology varies from one country to another, usually lasting from three to five years, during which the aspiring anaesthesiologist must complete several difficult examinations in all aspects of the field of anaesthesiology ...' said Ben before being distracted by Thomas, who was now waving both arms to attract the attention of a waiter.

'So,' said Thomas, 'I guess that's a load off your chest. You must feel a lot better now after having said all that.' Just at that moment he finally managed to attract the attention of a waiter and order some brandy for both of them. He turned to Ben and asked, 'But what about the well-known fact that general anaesthesia is dangerous? After all, if you read the newspapers, you read that general anaesthesia is quite dangerous.'

'It's all a public perception without any basis in fact,' growled Ben in an irritated voice.

'Even so,' replied Thomas, 'it is something you do read a lot about, and which most people are afraid of.'

Ben sighed, looked unhappy, but cheered up on the arrival of the waiter with two glasses of brandy. He took a sip, and began to look rather more cheerful. 'Yes, it's true, the thought of undergoing general anaesthesia often strikes terror in the hearts of many people. I regularly speak with persons whose main fear is not the operation, nor the prospect of pain after the operation, nor the prospect of crippling mutilations, complications, infections, or death after the operation, but an unreasoned fear of the general anaesthesia needed to make the operation possible. They tell me they hear general anaesthesia is dangerous, and that there is a very real chance of never awakening. So I try to reason with them, and to comfort them with statistics of the mortalities of various events with which they are familiar. It's always illuminating to look at the mortalities of reasonably common planned operations, such as an operation to remove the womb (uterus), or an operation to remove a gallbladder, and compare them with the mortalities of anaesthesia and pregnancy. When you look at the statistics you get the following:'

- Pregnancy is a common life-event for nearly all women. Yet pregnancy and delivery of a baby can cause death. The chance of dying as a result of pregnancy in the USA or Western Europe is small, but is still about 5 to10 deaths per 100,000 live births (Hill 2001).

- The chance of dying as a result of general anaesthesia is somewhat less than 11 to 16 deaths per 100,000 operations (Arbous 2001).
- The chance of dying due to complications resulting from an operation to remove the womb is about 120 deaths per 100,000 operations (Bachmann 1990), while the chance of dying from an operation to remove the gallbladder is about 160 to 290 deaths per 100,000 operations (Shea 1996).

'So,' responded Thomas, 'that's what I would call a clear illustration of relative mortalities and relative perceptions.'

'Indeed it is. It's a wonderful illustration of how public opinion, socio-cultural factors, and rumour determine perceptions. Most people about to undergo an operation on their womb or gallbladder are not at all afraid of the operation, yet they are scared out of their wits by the thought of general anaesthesia, which is the least deadly of these events! Many people are ecstatically happy when they hear that they themselves, their wives, their sisters, or their daughters are pregnant: a condition whose mortality is comparable to that of general anaesthesia. They are happy with pregnancy, but afraid of anaesthesia. Curious indeed .... I explain these things to these people, hoping to comfort them, while explaining at the same time that statistics and emotions are two different things. However, I never tell them the mortality of the surgery they are about to undergo. That's the responsibility of the surgeon.'

'So why doesn't the surgeon inform these women about the potential mortality of the operations they're about to perform. In my opinion it's scandalously immoral not to do so,' was the heated reaction.

'There is actually a very practical reason not to tell about every possible complication resulting from an operation. Some people may refuse surgery upon learning these things, even though the complications of their diseases eventually have a higher mortality than the operation they must undergo. Not informing them of all the possible risks of an operation means they are more likely to accept the necessity for surgery, and accordingly have a better chance of recovery.'

'Okay, I'm with you there, although it does go against my personal belief that people should be informed so as to make better, informed choices.' Thomas paused, took a sip of his brandy, and smeared a particularly redolent piece of goat cheese on a cracker which he proceeded to eat with manifest relish. He paused, bits of reeking cheese and cracker between his teeth. Ben wrinkled his nose, curled his lips and toes, groaned inwardly, and looked outside as he determinedly sipped his brandy. Thomas continued, 'Ah well, so much for informing patients ... But what about the stories and television programs about people who were awake during operations under general anaesthesia? Some of these people were not only awake, but also felt the excruciating pains of surgery while unable to do or say anything. Terrifying experiences. How are such experiences possible in people who are unconscious under general anaesthesia?'

Ben made a mental note never to eat in this restaurant with Thomas again. The smell of goat cheese, together with the unappetizing manner, and very evident gusto with which Thomas gobbled it, induced improbable intestinal gymnastics within his sensitive body. He took another fortifying sip of brandy: 'Ah hah, but that is where most people who are not anaesthesiologists make a mistake. These people were just awake. Indeed, many studies reveal that somewhere between zero to five percent of people undergoing modern general anaesthesia report experiencing episodes of partial or full awareness during anaesthesia (Abouleish 1976, Breckenridge 1983, Kerssens 2003, Mainzer 1979, Munte 2002, Schwender 1998).'

'Oh, but how is that possible?'

'To understand this, you first have to know a bit more about general anaesthesia. General anaesthesia consists of three separate components: unconsciousness, analgesia (relief from pain), and muscle relaxation (paralysis or weakness). In the past, anaesthesiologists used high concentrations of anaesthetic gases such as ether or chloroform to provide these three components of anaesthesia. But these high anaesthetic gas concentrations had disadvantages. So modern anaesthesiologists use three separate categories of drugs to provide this triad of general anaesthesia.'

- Sleep-inducing drugs are used to keep people asleep and remove all memory of events occurring during the operation. Lower concentrations of these drugs in the blood also suppress breathing to some degree, while at higher concentrations they cause breathing to stop altogether.

- Muscle-paralyzing drugs are administered to paralyze all the muscles of the body. This is necessary because the pain of surgery causes the muscles surrounding the areas being operated upon to go into spasm, or the person to move and thrash about, making many forms of surgery on bones and inside the abdomen impossible. Muscle-paralyzing drugs are nearly all similar to curare, the deadly arrow poison of the Amazonian Indians. All muscles are paralyzed, so a paralyzed person cannot move, cannot speak, and cannot breathe. This latter is the reason why people receiving these drugs are attached to a machine called a respirator or ventilator, which takes over the function of breathing. These muscle-paralyzing drugs do not cause paralysis of heart muscles, otherwise everyone would die while under general anaesthesia. These muscle-paralyzing drugs also do not cause paralysis of the bladder or bowel muscles, which is why people under general anaesthesia are not incontinent of urine or faeces. These muscle-paralyzing drugs only paralyze the muscles of the body, and do not affect the functioning of the brain, which is why a person can be totally paralyzed by these drugs, but remain fully awake (Smith et al 1947).
- Powerful morphine-like drugs are administered to remove the pain of operations. These drugs administered at higher doses may cause the muscles of the body to become stiff, they always cause people to feel calm and indifferent, but not to lose consciousness, and in higher doses they also cause people to forget to breathe.

'Interesting ...' said Thomas, 'but what you are actually saying is that a person under general anaesthesia with this more modern combination of drugs is unconscious, feels no pain, and does not breathe. In other words, general anaesthesia is a condition which really is near to death.'

Ben sighed patiently. 'Absolutely untrue! I've already told you before what death is. Death is the irreversible failure of the basic thalamic and brainstem functions required to generate and sustain consciousness and breathing. This is quite different from general anaesthesia. The functioning of the thalamus and brainstem are only temporarily suspended – not irreversibly terminated – but temporarily suspended by general anaesthetic drugs. Furthermore, the bodies of people under general anaesthesia still possess basic vital functions: their breathing is supported by machines if needed, their hearts pump blood, all their organs and tissues are alive, and when the effects of the anaesthetic drugs cease, these people are conscious and breathe again. All that is suspended during modern general anaesthesia are breathing and consciousness – not life. People under modern general anaesthesia are far from being nearly dead. Indeed, some desperately sick patients are in better condition under modern general anaesthesia than when awake and not under anaesthesia. Their vital functions, such as blood pressure, the amount of blood pumped by their hearts, etc, are actually improved by the anaesthetic drugs, extra medicines, fluids, blood, and oxygen administered by the anaesthesiologist.'

'Okay, I understand what you mean. Even so, how can people undergo some of the experiences described in newspapers, magazines, or television?' asked Thomas.

'Well Thomas, I talked about the three different groups of drugs needed to provide the triad of general anaesthesia. The effects of combinations of these three groups of drugs explain all these sometimes alarming reports. So I'll list these experiences and their causes (Editorial 1979, Mainzer 1979, Schwender 1998). Are you ready?'

'As I'll ever be Ben.'

'Okay here it comes.'

- *The person was awake during surgery, was able to move, but felt no pain.* These people have adequate concentrations of painkilling drugs in their body, but insufficient concentrations of muscle-paralyzing or sleep-inducing drugs in their bodies to prevent movements or keep them unconscious.

- *The person was awake during surgery, was unable to move, but felt no pain.* These people have concentrations of painkilling drugs in their bodies sufficient to keep them pain free, as well as sufficient concentrations of muscle-paralyzing drugs in their bodies to prevent them moving, speaking, or breathing, but are awake because of insufficient concentrations of sleep-inducing drugs.

- *The person was awake during surgery, was able to move, and felt the pain from the operation.* These people have inadequate concentrations of all three groups of drugs in their bodies, so they are conscious, can move, and can feel the pain of the operation.

- *The person was awake during surgery, felt the pain of the operation, but was unable move, speak, or do anything.* Inadequate concentrations of sleep-inducing and painkilling drugs mean that the person was conscious and could feel the pain of the operation. However, the person was totally unable to move, speak, or breathe because of paralysis due to muscle-paralyzing drugs. It is a terrible situation not unlike the torments of hell visited upon the living. This is a disaster, a situation dreaded by anaesthesiologists and patients alike. Usually this situation is immediately recognized and appropriately dealt with, but some people react so minimally to the pain of their operations that the situation is sometimes not recognized. This is profoundly upsetting to anaesthesiologists, as well as being unspeakably horrible for those undergoing the experience.

'Well that certainly explains a lot of the different experiences people report during anaesthesia,' said Thomas. 'However, I still don't quite understand out-of-body experiences occurring during general anaesthesia. You once told me all about how the body can generate out-of-body experiences, but that explanation doesn't explain how they can occur during general anaesthesia, because people are unconscious during general anaesthesia. This is quite a different situation to what you described occurs when people undergo out-of-body experiences during other situations. So if unconscious people under general anaesthesia can undergo out-of-body experiences, then this is surely proof of the supernatural nature of such experiences?'

'Oh Thomas,' groaned Ben demonstratively, 'what have I been telling you all the time? People reporting undergoing conscious experiences with verifiable elements while apparently unconscious, were certainly conscious at the time of undergoing the experience (Blacher 1980). The same is also true of general anaesthesia. Some people do indeed awaken during anaesthesia as we discussed above, but the effects of anaesthetic drugs in their bodies means their brain and body function are abnormal, and this, combined with the effects of the other anaesthetic drugs can generate wondrous experiences such as out-of-body experiences (see chapters 6 & 11, as well as Mainzer 1979). Out-of-body experiences occurring during general anaesthesia are no proof of the reality of anything supernatural.'

'Oh … Okay, but I still don't quite understand how out-of-body experiences can occur in people supposedly unconscious due to general anaesthetic drugs.'

'Well Thomas, this looks like it's going to be a long session. They're closing up here, so let's go to a café over there along the canal for a cup of coffee, or something more fortifying, and talk some more. It's a beautiful evening for sitting outside.'

A few short minutes later, Ben sighed contentedly as he leaned back in the soft green cushions filling his chair while licking a fleck of beer foam from his lips. Thomas wore a similar contented expression: one hand wrapped around his beer glass as he sat slumped comfortably in his chair. This café alongside the New Rhine Canal had opened recently, and was notable for outstanding service, good beer and wine, as well as the comfortable padded cane armchairs made all the more luxurious with cushions covered with various shades of green silk. Not surprisingly, it was busy, a bustle of students and other people filled the café, drinking and chatting animatedly.

Ben wriggled deeper in the cushions on his chair, 'Ah Thomas, we're privileged men. We live in a paradise. Here we are, sitting alongside this canal in a form of decadent luxury the like of which our ancestors could only dream of, drinking delicious cold beer on a beautiful balmy evening in Leiden. This is the way we were meant to live, to enjoy ourselves, to engage in fruitful dispute and discussion.'

'No argument there Ben. But you were going to tell me about out-of-body experiences during general anaesthesia.'

Ben sipped his beer, and sighed, 'Ah … Nectar … What a serious young man you are. However, you're quite correct; I was going to tell you how out-of-body experiences during general anaesthesia are possible. First the basics. We've already discussed the fact that out-of-body experiences are conscious experiences (Chapter 6). So a person who has a conscious experience such as an out-of-body experience, even an experience during general anaesthesia, was conscious at the time of the experience.'

'Er, yes ...' responded Thomas cautiously, 'that's true, although I'm not quite sure where you're going.'

'Very well, I've already described a number of situations where people are quite conscious during inadequate general anaesthesia. And you must always remember that even though these people are awake, the combined effects of general anaesthetic drugs still present in their bodies, means their brain function is often abnormal. Alright so far?'

'Yes ...'

'During an operation, a patient is touched and manipulated by the surgeon, who also does things like cutting them with a knife, sawing, drilling, or chiselling their bones, pulling at bits and pieces of their organs and tissues, as well as burning bleeding blood vessels. The body senses all these things, and some of these things also activate muscle spindles. The combination of all these things is enough to arouse consciousness in some people, a bit like shaking someone awake, or doing something painful to a sleeping person to arouse them (Lanier et al 1986, Lanier et al 1994, Smith et al 1986). But because of abnormal brain function due to the effects of anaesthetic drugs still present in the body, a person so awakened may interpret the sensations of movement from their body position sensors as the movements of displacement out of their body, of flying, or of floating, and so build up a hallucination of displacement out of the body. In other words, they may undergo an out-of-body experience.'

'I understand,' responded Thomas, 'but if these people are awake, why don't they tell everyone at the time they are having an out-of-body experience?'

'Oh ... Thomas, Thomas, Thomas ...' groaned Ben theatrically, and continued, 'I can tell you everything, but it seems I cannot give you understanding. Perhaps it's because the effects of anaesthesia are so far removed from your daily world that some of the curious effects of general anaesthetic drugs on people are inconceivable to you. People who awaken during general anaesthesia do not speak at that moment simply because they are unable to do so due to the effects of the anaesthetic drugs. So these people can only tell of their out-of-body experiences after recovering from the effects of the anaesthetic drugs, and after returning to a state where they are able to speak. This is why out-of-body experiences during general anaesthesia are always remembered experiences. Moreover, these remembered experiences are also modified by the effects of anaesthetic drugs, which is why memories of these experiences may be disjointed, incomplete, inaccurate, or even fantastical. This is the mechanism by which out-of-body experiences can occur during general anaesthesia.'

'Okay, I agree it is a logical extension of what you previously told me about out-of-body experiences (Chapters 5 & 6). You're probably right. There is nothing supernatural about out-of-body experiences occurring during general anaesthesia. But what about people who say they "fell into a black pit" at the beginning of general anaesthesia? I have an aunt who recently underwent a number of operations under general anaesthesia. She says that each time, just as she falls asleep, she feels terrified, feels burning pain, and then falls into a black pit. She clearly sees the black pit into which she falls, and loses consciousness as she falls into the total blackness of the pit. I like my aunt a lot, but I know she led a shamelessly sinful life when she was young: parties, alcohol, and lots of boyfriends. I also know she even lived with one of her boyfriends without marrying. Is this the dark pit of death spoken of in the Bible – a taste of what she must endure after she passes away? As I said, I like my aunt, and even though the scriptures tell me she richly deserves eternal torment in hell, I wouldn't want that to happen to her. How would you explain this experience?' Thomas pulled a small Bible out of a pocket, opened it, and said, 'I can't explain it any other way when you look at this passage in the Bible …'

> *He is chastened also with pain upon his bed, And with continual strife in his bones; So that his life abhorreth bread, And his soul dainty food.*
>
> *His flesh is consumed away, that it cannot be seen; And his bones that were not seen stick out.*
>
> *Yea, his soul draweth near unto the pit, And his life to the destroyers.*
>
> *If there be with him an angel, An interpreter, one among a thousand, To show unto man what is right for him; Then God is gracious unto him, and saith, Deliver him from going down to the pit, I have found a ransom. (ASV Bible, Job 33:19-24)*

'So,' continued Thomas, 'when you read this Bible passage, you realize that general anaesthesia may be a form of death after all.' He looked enquiringly at Ben.

'I guess that's one way of looking at it!' sighed Ben in a depressed tone, as he sipped his beer. 'I understand from this question of yours that you still have some very strange ideas about anaesthesia and the supernatural.'

'Not at all,' said a man's voice near to Ben. 'I've been listening to your fascinating discussion. Your companion is quite right. His aunt is doomed.'

Ben and Thomas turned towards the voice. 'Who might you be?' asked Ben of the young man of evident North African descent sitting at an adjacent table with a blond haired woman. He looked at the woman. She was strikingly beautiful, with incredibly large blue eyes. As he drank in her beauty, passages in the Koran describing the qualities of the multiple female companions allotted to faithful Islamic men attaining the reward of paradise flashed through his mind.

> Wherein (are found) the good and beautiful. Which is it, of the favours of your Lord, that ye deny?
> Fair ones, close guarded in pavilions. Which is it, of the favours of your Lord, that ye deny?
> Whom neither man nor jinn will have touched before them. Which is it, of the favours of your Lord, that ye deny?
> Reclining on green cushions and fair carpets. Which is it, of the favours of your Lord, that ye deny? (Koran 55:70-77)

Another passage also passed through Ben's momentarily entranced mind.

> And (there are) fair ones with wide, lovely eyes, Like unto hidden pearls, (Koran 56:22-23)

And another, as he noticed her firm breasts straining against her tight shirt...

> Surely for the godfearing awaits a place of security, gardens and

vineyards and maidens with swelling breasts, like of age, and a cup overflowing. (AJA Koran 78:31-34)

He awoke to reality upon hearing, 'My name is Mehmet, and this is my girlfriend Bridget. I couldn't help hearing what you were talking about. Even the Koran supports his fears about his aunt. I'll show you.' With these words, he pulled a copy of the Koran out of a pocket, opened it, laid it on the table between Ben and Thomas, and pointed to a passage.

The Calamity! What is the Calamity? Ah, what will convey unto thee what the calamity is! A day wherein mankind will be as thickly scattered moths. And the mountains will become as carded wool. Then, as for him whose scales are heavy (with good works), He will live a pleasant life. But as for him whose scales are light, The Bereft and Hungry One will be his mother. Ah, what will convey unto thee what she is! Raging fire. (Koran 101:1-11)

'How is it that you carry a copy of the Koran in your pocket?' was the surprised reaction of Thomas. 'I study theology, so that's my excuse for carrying a copy of the Bible. But what about you Mehmet? Are you an Islamic Studies student, or something like that?'

'No,' replied Mehmet, 'But I did attend very strict Islamic primary and secondary schools in Rotterdam. Like your Catholic Priests say, "Give me a boy until he is seven, and I will give you a Catholic for life." So Islam is embedded in me, and is an essential part of my being, which is why I always carry a copy of the Koran. The Koran answers all my questions, and gives guidance and certainty in my life. As I said, I was sitting here enjoying the evening, and overheard your fascinating discussion. I'm fascinated. I'd love to hear how the experiences of your aunt could be explained otherwise than by the proof contained within these passages.'

A sound akin to soft music emanated from the lips of Bridget, 'I don't agree Mehmet, conscious human experiences like these are usually just epiphenomena of body function, so I don't believe the experiences of this woman are any sort of supernatural eschatological insight.'

'Huhh ... ?' was heard from three lips at the same time as three pairs of eyes simultaneously gazed in surprise at her. Mehmet glared irately at

Bridget, who continued in a hesitant tone, 'Just an opinion ... a few points to consider ... er, I study philosophy ...' and fell silent, fidgeting with a ring.

Ben recovered his composure, 'Actually Bridget is quite right, the experiences of Thomas's aunt are readily explained by the functioning of her body.' He continued, 'A while ago I talked about the components of general anaesthesia. Well, at the start of all general modern anaesthetics, a dose of a sleeping drug is injected into a vein. The drug most commonly used these days is called Propofol, and most adults fall asleep 20 to 30 seconds after a sufficient dose is injected into a vein. Unfortunately Propofol is very irritating and causes a burning pain in the arms of many people when injected. This is the burning pain described by your aunt. Furthermore, it is a common observation of many anaesthesiologists that anxious people often become even more anxious or restless just before falling asleep. This is the terrified feeling described by your aunt.'

'Okay, okay ...' responded Thomas. 'But what about falling into the dark pit?'

'Yes, what about the pit?' asked Mehmet, as he took a sip from the whisky glass in front of him.

Ben irrigated his parched throat with beer, 'Ah ... needed that,' and continued. 'Surprisingly enough, that bit is also easily explained. Propofol is injected into a vein over a period of about 10 to 20 seconds. It mixes with the blood flowing in the veins, and is transported in blood pumped by the heart into the head, where it diffuses out of the blood capillaries into the tissues of the head. This is not an instantaneous process. It takes about 20 to 30 seconds for a person to fall asleep after Propofol, or other similar drugs, are injected into a vein. Now the most important parts of the head as regards conscious sensation are the brain, ears, and eyes. Are you all following me so far?'

Thomas and Bridget nodded, while Mehmet stared at his whisky glass. It was nearly empty.

Ben continued. 'Not all sense organs, and not all parts of the brain are affected equally or at the same time by sleep inducing drugs such as Propofol. Those parts of the brain generating consciousness are less sensitive to Propofol than are the eyes and the rest of the brain. So just before falling asleep, a person first experiences the effects of Propofol on those more sensitive parts of the brain and sense organs. To begin with, diffusion of Propofol into those parts of the brain controlling muscle tension causes all muscles and muscle spindles to suddenly relax, and affected people suddenly feel themselves falling. This is the same mechanism generating the sensation of falling that people sometimes experience in the stage between consciousness and sleep (Derry 2006, Gandevia 1977, Gandevia 1977a). Everyone following me so far?'

'Yes, I follow your reasoning, but you still haven't explained the black pit!' said Mehmet. 'And until you explain that, I remain unconvinced.'

Bridget interjected, 'But he's getting there. This is fascinating! This is extra proof of my personal belief that all conscious experiences really are epiphenomena of body function!' The three men looked at her again, Ben and Thomas seeing her in a new light, while Mehmet was visibly annoyed. She added nervously, 'I'd ... I'd love to hear the rest of your explanation.'

Mehmet hissed angrily at her, 'Then be quiet sharmuta, and listen!' and muttered an inaudible string of expletives.

The colour drained from Bridget's face, her eyes narrowed, and she began thumbing through the Koran lying on the table as Ben continued. 'At the same time as all the above is occurring, blood containing Propofol flows into the blood vessels of the eyes. The light sensitive part of the eye is called the retina, which is a thin membrane packed full of cells reacting to light coating the back of each eye. All these nerves and light sensitive cells need blood to provide them with oxygen and nutrients, as well as to remove waste products of cell function. Now the flow of blood to the retina is maximal at the fovea in the centre of the retina, and declines rapidly towards the edge of the retina (Alm 1973 & figure 3.3). So as the Propofol enters the blood vessels of the eye, the highest Propofol concentrations are initially in the tissues of the central region of the retina, which means that the central region of the retina is the first part of the retina to malfunction, followed soon afterwards by the whole retina. So a person receiving Propofol, or other similar drugs, will first notice a central dark spot, followed a few seconds later by total darkness. This is the darkness of the opening of the pit seen by your aunt; and this is the total darkness of the pit into which your aunt fell! As her vision failed, the concentration of Propofol in those parts of her brain generating consciousness finally became high enough to cause her to lose consciousness. Your aunt remembered all these sensations and emotions upon awakening from general anaesthesia, and combined them into a coherent total experience of a terrified falling into a black and burning pit. No supernatural explanations are needed to explain this experience, just some knowledge about the functioning of the body.'

'Wow!' said Thomas, 'That explains it! It's possibly even a partial explanation for other biblical passages about the darkness of the pit of death. It also means my aunt was almost certainly not given a glimpse of hell before losing consciousness.'

Mehmet looked calm, and said, 'I admit it's certainly one way of looking at the experiences of his aunt, although I'm sure it's the wrong way, because it contravenes the irrefutable evidence given us by the Koran.'

'That's your arrogant opinion Mehmet,' responded Bridget vehemently, adding, 'but I certainly enjoyed your explanation Ben. It's given me further confirmation of my belief about epiphenomena resulting from the functioning of the human body.' She looked at Mehmet, her eyes flashing as they filled with tears, and a voice filled with impassioned detestation, 'You really are a smug swine! You insult and disregard me, and just a moment ago, you did it again in public, and this last time was once too often! So I browsed through your wonderful Koran to see if I could find a reason here for your attitude here and in private, and I found it. You're just a self-centred, supercilious slime-bag! You just think I'm there to be used! Well if that's all you think of me Mehmet, I'm dumping you! You don't care about me! You don't love me! You don't think much of me at all! You just want sex! You don't even think I'm intelligent. But I can think, and I do very well with my philosophy study! Whatever you imagined we had with each other is finished, and I'm off!' She threw the Koran on the table, opened at the last page she read, and stormed off. Mehmet looked calmly at her going, and ordered another glass of whisky for himself. Thomas looked at the Koran on the table, read the opened pages and was struck by the following passage.

Your women are a tilth for you (to cultivate) go to your tilth as ye will, and send (good deeds) before you for your souls, and fear Allah, and know that ye will (one day) meet Him. Give glad tidings to believers, (O Muhammad). (Koran 2:223)

'Hey Mehmet,' said Thomas, 'that's a really rotten way to treat a woman as intelligent and beautiful as Bridget. Why don't you go after her and try to make it up with her, or at the very least apologize?'

'So what if the bitch decides to leave,' replied Mehmet indifferently. 'There are a lot more women, and this one was getting boring as well as demanding. I'll find another one.'

Thomas was somewhat taken aback by this attitude. 'What an egotistical toad!' he thought. 'I'll see if I can't upset him with his own Koran and his own Islam!' He continued aloud, 'Aren't you worried about eternal punishment in hell for extramarital sex and drinking alcohol? After all, the Koran forbids both of these things.'

'Nonsense,' responded Mehmet. 'The Koran actually supports me in all I do.'

'Then how would you consider this passage?' Without any further ado, Thomas opened the Koran. 'Look at what the Koran says about alcohol.'

Satan seeketh only to cast among you enmity and hatred by means of strong drink and games of chance, and to turn you from remembrance of Allah and from (His) worship. Will ye then have done? (Koran 5:91)

Mehmet shrugged his shoulders indifferently. 'So what?' was his lukewarm reaction. 'This passage doesn't actually forbid alcohol. It only warns that drunkenness is a ploy of Satan to distract people from the path of religion (Koran 5:90). In fact the revelations of God in the Koran indicate that God tolerates the use of alcohol, but condemns drunkenness (Koran 2:219, 4:43).'

'That's possibly true,' replied Thomas hesitantly, adding in a firmer voice, 'but even so, Mohammed himself forbade the use of alcohol entirely, banning it totally. I remember this from a passage in the Sunnah of Bukhari we were once taught.'

Narrated by Abi Burda That Abu Musa Al-Ash'ari said that the

Prophet had sent him to Yemen and he asked the Prophet about certain (alcoholic) drink which used to be prepared there. The Prophet said, 'What are they?' Abu Musa said, 'Al-Bit' and Al-Mizr?' He said, 'Al-Bit is an alcoholic drink made from honey; and Al-Mizr is an alcoholic drink made from barley.' The Prophet said, 'All intoxicants are prohibited.' (Bukhari 59:631)

'Yes, but that doesn't really apply here,' was Mehmet's calm reaction as he took another sip of whisky. 'Furthermore, other later passages in the Sunnah of Bukhari clearly contradict this ruling. They show that Mohammed accepted and tolerated drinking alcohol.'

Narrated As-Sa'ib bin Yazid: We used to strike the drunks with our hands, shoes, clothes (by twisting it into the shape of lashes) during the lifetime of the Prophet, Abu Bakr and the early part of Umar's caliphate. But during the last period of Umar's caliphate, he used to give the drunk forty lashes; and when drunks became mischievous and disobedient, he used to scourge them eighty lashes. (Bukhari 81:770)

'This and other similar passages in Bukhari clearly indicate that while drinking alcohol was tolerated, public drunkenness was condemned. So to say I'll go to hell for drinking is ridiculous. Your way of looking at the subject of alcohol is amusingly simple. But do continue. I'm interested in hearing what you have to say about the wonderful sex I had with that ungrateful bitch.'

'Hmm ... Really Mehmet ... No wonder Bridget up and left you. The Koran gives strict injunctions about which women a devout believer in Islam is permitted to have sex. It clearly states that men are only permitted to have sex with their own wives, captives, and slaves (Koran 4:19-24). Furthermore,' continued Thomas, 'the Koran also states that it is better not to have sex with women who do not follow Islam.'

Wed not idolatresses till they believe; for lo! a believing bondwoman is better than an idolatress though she please you; and give not your daughters in marriage to idolaters till they believe, for lo! a believing slave is better than an idolater though he please you. These invite unto the Fire, and Allah inviteth unto the Garden, and unto forgiveness by His grace, and expoundeth thus His revelations to mankind that haply they may remember. (Koran 2:221)

'Now, you aren't married with Bridget, and she was neither slave nor captive. Even worse, she wasn't even a follower of Islam. In other words, according to the logic of Islam you are doomed to go to hell. A clear argument,' was the final summation by Thomas.

Ben leaned back in his chair with a slight smile upon his lips. Every now and then he took a sip of beer. He listened with a feeling of tranquil amusement. Thomas was beginning to learn the art of specious theological argument. 'Ah, the joys of seeing one's training bear fruit,' he thought.

Mehmet was unimpressed. He took a sip, emptying his glass. 'All very well, but you forgot to mention some basic and very fundamental facts. Women are inherently inferior to men (Koran 2:228, 2:282, 4:11, 4:34), and they exist for the pleasure of men (Koran 2:223). Furthermore, God revealed to us in the Koran that those who do not believe in the tenets of Islam are made of baser matter than believers, never rising above the inferior animal nature of their foul unbelief.'

Now what is the matter with the Unbelievers that they rush madly before thee – From the right and from the left, in crowds? Does every man of them long to enter the Garden of Bliss? By no means! For We have created them out of the (base matter) they know! (YA Koran 70:36-39)

'This is clear proof that we believers in the one true God of Islam are superior to all infidel vermin such as you. That ungrateful bitch was actually honoured by her association with me. After all, during sex, the base and inferior substance of her infidel body made intimate contact with the superior and refined substance of my body. And as if this were not enough proof of the innate superiority of the followers of Islam, another irrefutable revelation of God in the Koran clearly demonstrates the superiority of the followers of Islam – God revealed to Mohammed that the followers of Islam are the chosen of God, and far more evolved than lowly Jews and Christians.'

> *Ye are the best of peoples, evolved for mankind, enjoining what is right, forbidding what is wrong, and believing in Allah. If only then People of the Book had faith, it were best for them: among them are some who have faith, but most of them are perverted transgressors. (YA Koran 3:110)*

'Moreover,' continued Mehmet, 'aside from your inherent inferiority, this land is not ruled by an Islamic government. Accordingly, all you unbelievers enjoy no protection from Islamic law, which means I can do what I like here. This is also quite clearly stated by the message of God to Mohammed. Look here,'

> *Fight against such of those who have been given the Scripture as believe not in Allah nor the Last Day, and forbid not that which Allah hath forbidden by His messenger, and follow not the religion of truth, until they pay the tribute readily, being brought low. (Koran 9:29)*

Thomas was taken aback. No debate was possible with such conviction. He had met his match. Mehmet was evidently even more skilled than he in the art of specious argumentation, an accomplished sophist, a man for whom truth was unimportant as long as he and other followers of Islam believed his arguments.

Mehmet gathered up his pocket Koran, stood up, and said, 'Well unbelieving dogs, I'm off. Enjoy your theology. One day, as I recline on my couch in the gardens of Paradise, I'll cheer and jeer as I watch you both undergoing your richly deserved torments in the scorching fires of hell (Koran 7:44-50)!' And with these encouraging words he departed.

Ben looked at Thomas, and Thomas looked at Ben. 'So,' said Ben, 'that was an interesting lesson in Islamic superiority. The attitude of Mehmet and other similar-minded believers is truly fascinating. It raises all manner of fascinating questions about the possibility of supernatural atomic and molecular transmutation of human flesh. After all, if a person converts to Islam, the evidently inferior atomic, and molecular structure of their previously unbelieving body, will suddenly and miraculously transmute into the superior atomic and molecular structure appropriate to the body of a believer in Islam. Such a wondrous atomic and molecular transmutation also permits the new believer in Islam to treat unbelievers in an unbelievably brutish and abominable manner, yet be rewarded for this behaviour with a place in paradise after death. Fascinating, wondrous even ...'

'I agree ...' began Thomas, but had no chance to finish his sentence as Ben unheedingly continued.

'But I didn't have the heart to tell Mehmet that he, and all his fellow believers in Islam actually had gotten it all wrong. Poor fellow, he didn't realize that God had told Christians that they can also do whatever they want.'

'Ohhh ...'

'Yes, it's true,' replied Ben confidently. 'Just look in your Bible at what Jesus says in the book of Matthew.'

'I don't believe you. You can't be serious!' replied Thomas, as he thumbed through his pocket Bible.

'Believe me. Would I lie to you? It's a wonderful statement, and one made by no less a person than Jesus, the Son of God.'

Therefore I say unto you, Every sin and blasphemy shall be forgiven unto men; but the blasphemy against the Spirit [God] shall not be forgiven. (ASV Bible, Matthew 12:31)

'Now if you were a very simple fundamentalist Christian, who thought that every word of the Bible was literally true, and looked very selectively at the verses of the Bible, then you would believe that you can do everything you want: behave abominably, commit unspeakable crimes, and you would still be forgiven by God! A fearful and wonderful concept!' and Ben continued. 'In other words, as a Christian you have a license to do as you will. As a Christian you have biblical proof that God will forgive you for your most vile, evil, and perverse thoughts and deeds. According to this passage, God will forgive you for all these things. This is a horrifically amoral passage, and one reinforced by the holy Saint Paul himself.'

Who shall lay anything to the charge of God's elect? It is God that justifieth; (ASV Bible, Romans 8:33)

'Hmm ...' mumbled Ben. 'This is not as clear as more modern translations that clearly state that God's elect, which means Christians, are always forgiven by God!'

Who will accuse God's chosen people? God himself declares them not guilty! (GNB Bible, Romans 8:33)

'Now these statements were all written within a hundred years after the death of Jesus. This was at the time when persecution of Christians by the authorities of the ruling Roman Empire had begun.'

'So ...' responded Thomas. 'But these statements are no more than the promise of God to all believers that sin does not automatically mean condemnation to eternal punishment in hell.'

'That's the way you interpret it.' Said Ben, and continued. 'And think of this, the same eternal, all-pervading and all-knowing God made the very same promises to the followers of Islam 600 years later! Amazing isn't it! It begs the question of whose religion is the true religion. Anyway, returning to the subject, if I were a member of the ruling authorities, and I heard of a religious sect espousing and actually believing in such things, then I would look with a good deal of disapproval at that sect.'

'Huh? Why? This passage is very clear.'

'Exactly! And if interpreted literally by fanatical dim-wits, it turns into a passage meaning you can do what you want, disobey who you want, murder whom you want, rape whom you please, steal and plunder as much as you desire: but because you believe, all these sins will be forgiven you by a loving God. In the minds of people in authority in an authoritarian empire, such as the Roman empire 2000 years ago, such a belief was license to commit civil disobedience. Such a belief meant the end of civil authority, and potentially the end of empire. It was nothing less than an insidious form of sedition in the guise of religion! Those espousing such beliefs were considered a cancer in the empire, and richly deserved suppression and extirpation from the body of the empire! This was undoubtedly one of the many reasons for Christian persecution during the period of the Roman Empire.'

'Hmmm ...' was the thoughtful reaction of Thomas. 'I'll have to think seriously about that one. Certainly a matter for more discussion ... I'll ask one of my theology lecturers about this idea. Ah well, in any case, tonight I also learned how the functioning of the body causes the strange sensations many people report during general anaesthesia. I enjoyed this evening, but I'm going home. I've got some early lectures tomorrow.'

'I enjoyed this evening too,' replied Ben, 'and I guess it's also time for me to go home.' Without further ado, they rose, mounted their bicycles, and cycled unsteadily in the directions of their homes.

Chapter 11

She was dead!

It was another warm sun-drenched afternoon. Smiling, chattering, brightly dressed people were everywhere to be seen. The whole city seemed suffused with a bright and sunny mood. A cheerfully humming Thomas sauntered along the canals and through the winding streets of Leiden on his way to meet Ben at the terrace of a café situated on one of the more beautiful canals at the edge of the old city. Suddenly he stopped. His humming ceased as he read the graffiti on an alley wall where someone had written in fluorescent, almost poisonously green paint, "God hates everyone!"

Thomas stopped for a moment, frowned thoughtfully as he considered the text, and continued further on his way to meet Ben. 'Is this piece of ugly graffiti more than it appears?' he mused. 'Is it an expression of some vague dissatisfaction? Is it a howl of despair? It was arrant nonsense of course! After all, God certainly loves Christians. God also loves the followers of Judaism and Islam, and even loves the followers of other religions. Even so, it was a curious piece of graffiti ... Strange ...'

Musing on the implications of this graffiti he arrived at the café and sat himself on a chair next to Ben on the sunny terrace. 'Ah ...' Thomas sighed contentedly as he sat, 'Nice ... What a magical day!'

'I agree. It's a shame they don't happen more often. But I guess we wouldn't appreciate them as much if they were so common. What do you want to drink? I was thinking of some cold rosé. Perfect weather for it.'

'Sounds good to me.'

Service was good, and soon they were sipping a delicious cool rosé. It was a perfect accompaniment to the day.

Thomas told of the graffiti he had seen on his way to the café, and how it had struck him as a wail of despair. 'It's nonsense of course. Have you any idea why anyone would feel so alienated from God that he would write something like that?'

Ben sipped his rosé as he thought. 'Actually it's quite an understandable opinion. If you look carefully at the texts of the Jewish, Christian, and Islamic holy books, you quickly come to the conclusion, that God does indeed hate everyone, and may even just be toying with humanity, so that they can later be tormented for eternity in hell.'

'Rubbish!' laughed Thomas. 'The Torah, the Bible, and the Koran are full of expressions of God's love for humanity. So how could this misguided and evidently unhappy graffiti writer, or you for that matter, come upon the dementedly insane idea that God hates everyone?'

'Because the texts of these holy books tell us that God hates everyone. I'll prove it with the very texts that you say prove that God loves everyone. According to me God loves no-one, is intolerant of everyone regardless of religion, and even stoops to deceiving people so they can be tortured for all eternity in hell!'

'Absolute drivel!' retorted Thomas. 'This is awful! You're really going to have to squirm and wriggle to prove all these things. I'm going to enjoy this, because it's impossible to prove, even for a hard line atheistic sophist like you.' He leaned back in his chair, took a sip of wine, and looked expectantly, even challengingly at Ben.

'Hmmnn …' mused Ben, as he contemplated the fact that Thomas did not rant and scream at such evident heresy. 'This really is a change of attitude. He's actually challenging me instead of resorting to dogma. Is he becoming a critical theologian, or has some weird and wonderful epiphany converted him into a closet humanist?' He sipped his rosé as he ordered his thoughts. 'I don't know who wrote the words of the graffiti you saw, but they are so redolent of despair that they cannot be anything but a desolate howl of impotent rage. Why desolation and rage? Because the statement reeks of a despair derived from an ultimate understanding of the true meaning of predestination, of an understanding of the intolerance of Judaism, Christianity and Islam for each other, even though they worship the same God, as well as an understanding of the horrid deceit openly admitted by an all-powerful God to condemn more souls to the unspeakable eternal torments of hell. So tell me Thomas, do you believe Judaism, Christianity, or Islam truly encourage free and critical thought?'

'Such passion and such rhetoric Ben! It is a tricky question though. I do know Christianity encourages free thought, but I don't know about Judaism or Islam.'

'Then I'll disillusion you about all these religions. Judaism certainly doesn't encourage free and critical thought. After all, the Jewish holy books state that fear of God is the beginning of wisdom (see also Bible, Job 28:28, Proverbs 1:7 & 9:10).'

The fear of Jehovah is the beginning of wisdom; A good under-standing have all they that do his commandments: His praise endureth for ever. (ASV Bible, Psalms 111:10)

'And,' continued Ben, 'as if that were not enough, those who are not terrified enough to slavishly carry out every law, wish, and whim of this same so-called loving and merciful God must be killed (see also Bible, Deuteronomy 13:6-10, 30:16-19).'

And they entered into the covenant to seek Jehovah, the God of their fathers, with all their heart and with all their soul; and that whosoever would not seek Jehovah, the God of Israel, should be put to death, whether small or great, whether man or woman. And they sware unto Jehovah with a loud voice, and with shouting, and with trumpets, and with cornets. And all Judah rejoiced at the oath; for they had sworn with all their heart, and sought him with their whole desire; and he was found of them: and Jehovah gave them rest round about. (ASV Bible, 2 Chronicles 15:12-15)

'The logical conclusion of this chain of thought is that killing apostates and unbelievers is a good and holy deed, because then God can begin torturing them in hell sooner than if they were allowed to die of old age.' Ben paused to drink more wine. 'And now we come to the matter of deceit on the part of God.'

'God would never deceive,' protested Thomas, 'and certainly not the Jews who were originally the chosen of God.'

'Unfortunately you're wrong there. God does admit to deceiving individual Jews and non-Jews alike, even to deceiving whole populations of Jews and non-Jewish peoples (see also Bible, Isaiah 6:9-10, Jeremiah 4:10, 15:18, 20:7, Ezekiel 14:9).'

> *O Jehovah, why dost thou make us to err from thy ways, and hardenest our heart from thy fear? Return for thy servants' sake, the tribes of thine inheritance. (ASV Bible, Isaiah 63:17)*

'Then this same deceitful and so-called merciful God of the Jews tells of punishing those he deceives, Jews and non-Jews alike! This doesn't seem to me like the way a loving God treats his chosen people, and is certainly a very unpleasant God for those who are not Jewish. So much for the loving nature of the God of the Jews,' Ben paused to drink more wine. He looked at Thomas, but Thomas remained silent. 'Now we come to the God of Christianity, which also happens to be the same God as that of the Jews, but with the one true and improved message of God – at least according to the Christians. Yet when you look at the mercy displayed by this God, you find absolutely no difference to that displayed by the God of the Jews.'

'Really Ben, this is too much! How can you say that?' spluttered Thomas.

'Well, to begin with, it would actually be quite surprising if there were any difference. After all, the God of the Jews is the same eternal, all-powerful, all-knowing, and all-pervading God of the Christians. So you would not expect to find any significant differences in the behaviour of this God between these two religions. You can read the proof of this in the New Testament. To begin with, Jesus and the prophets of Christianity all profess the reality of predestination (Chapter 1, see also Bible, Acts 13:45, Romans 8:29-30, 9:11-22, Ephesians 1:4-5). Then they go on to threaten dire punishments for heinous crimes such as intellectual freedom, freedom of thought, and criticism: all of which were predestined by God anyway!'

> *For though we walk in the flesh, we do not war according to the flesh (for the weapons of our warfare are not of the flesh, but mighty before God to the casting down of strongholds), casting*

down imaginations, and every high thing that is exalted against the knowledge of God, and bringing every thought into captivity to the obedience of Christ; and being in readiness to avenge all disobedience, when your obedience shall be made full. (ASV Bible, 2 Corinthians 10:3-6)

'In other words, because all these things were predestined, God was the originator of the very sins and disobedience that God avenges! So as you can appreciate Thomas, the founders of Christianity were not one whit better than the founders of Judaism. They both preach the same thing. There is one difference though, people who strayed from the true religion of Christianity, or whom were not Christian at all were never punished on earth. Instead, God and Jesus promise everlasting vengeance and torment in the fires of hell during an eternal life after death.'

He that believeth and is baptized shall be saved; but he that disbelieveth shall be condemned. (ASV Bible, Mark 16:16)

'Good rousing stuff Thomas. It all means that if you're not a baptized Christian you're doomed to go to the eternal fires of hell. In other words, both the followers of Judaism and the followers of Christianity say the same about sinners and the followers of other religions. To make matters worse, the Christian God also deceives the wicked, deluding them to make sure they stay wicked, so that they may be punished with eternal torment in hell (see also Bible, John 12:40, Acts 28:25-27)!'

And then shall that Wicked be revealed, whom the Lord shall consume with the spirit of his mouth, and shall destroy with the brightness of his coming:
Even him, whose coming is after the working of Satan with all power and signs and lying wonders,
And with all deceivableness of unrighteousness in them that perish; because they received not the love of the truth, that they might be saved.
And for this cause God shall send them strong delusion, that they should believe a lie: That they all might be damned who

believed not the truth, but had pleasure in unrighteousness. (KJV Bible, 2 Thessalonians 2:8-12)

'Yes Thomas, well may you gape. That's really the only reaction possible to insanity like this. If this was a God of mercy and love, why doesn't this God try to save the evil and the sinners from themselves? Instead, this God apparently spares no effort to ensure their eternal damnation by sending them delusions to make sure they continue their evil ways! God's arrogance and lust for earthly glory and power is revealed by another passage where God tells the prophets that it is God who determines what happens to the souls of people after death – telling us in no uncertain terms that it does not matter how people think, how they speak, or how they act – God determines their fate in a life after death.'

Nay but, O man, who art thou that repliest against God? Shall the thing formed say to him that formed it, Why didst thou make me thus?

Or hath not the potter a right over the clay, from the same lump to make one part a vessel unto honor, and another unto dishonor?

What if God, willing to show his wrath, and to make his power known, endured with much longsuffering vessels of wrath fitted unto destruction: and that he might make known the riches of his glory upon vessels of mercy, which he afore prepared unto glory, ... (ASV Bible, Romans 9:20-23)

Thomas began to look increasingly unhappy as Ben continued. 'So not only does God ensure the eternal damnation of many people, but God also actually creates people whose function is to live lives of sinful wickedness and evil, and who are automatically doomed to eternal torment in a life after death so they can function as examples revealing the "glory of God"! When you read passages like this you realize that this eternal, all-powerful, all-knowing and all-pervading God has some decidedly strange and even human traits: such as a lust for human recognition of the power of God, a refusal to accept other points of view, and a very malignant lust for vengeance and torture. Depressing isn't it?'

'Incredibly,' was the terse response of Thomas, as he drained his glass. 'This brings us to the situation of Islam. Allah, or God, is the same eternal, all-pervading, all-powerful, and all-knowing God as is worshipped by the Jews and the Christians. The followers of Islam claim the revelations of God through the prophet Mohammed are the final and true revelations of God, even though this same claim was also made by the Jews and the Christians many centuries before the birth of Mohammed. Who knows which of these three religions is correct? I don't. In any case, Islam also propounds the philosophy of predestination, and as I have said earlier, Islam also requires the death of apostates, and says that all who are not believers in Islam are destined to suffer the horrors of everlasting torment in hell (Chapter 1). In other words, Islam is as fundamentally intolerant of other religions as are Judaism and Christianity. No real difference there at all. Furthermore, just as in Judaism and Christianity, the God of Islam also leads people astray so that they can later undergo ghastly torments in hell for all eternity (see also Koran 7:178, 7:186).'

And We never sent a messenger save with the language of his folk, that he might make (the message) clear for them. Then Allah sendeth whom He will astray, and guideth whom He will. He is the Mighty, the Wise. (Koran 14:4)

Ben paused, drained his glass with a satisfied, 'Delicious,' and paused to order more rosé. 'God also revealed to Mohammed that it does not matter what individuals think, want, or do, it is God who ultimately decides the fate of each individual during their mortal life, as well as in a life after death (see also Koran 2:142, 7:178, 14:4, 22:18, 81:29).'

Lo! thou (O Muhammad) guidest not whom thou lovest, but Allah guideth whom He will. And He is best aware of those who walk aright. (Koran 28:56)

'Now Thomas you may think it merely reveals a dogma similar to that of Judaism and Christianity. But it is actually more than that. It is a startling passage with far-reaching implications. Consider the various collections of the deeds and sayings of Mohammed called the Sunnah.

These have almost as much authority as the Koran itself, and their use is even justified by a revelation in the Koran.'

Verily in the messenger of Allah ye have a good example for him who looketh unto Allah and the last Day, and remembereth Allah much. (Koran 33:21)

Ben paused to drink more rosé, and continued, 'This verse is the Koranic justification for the use of the Sunnah. Yet while the Koran is believed to be a product of direct revelations of God to the prophet Mohammed, and therefore infallible, the Sunnah is merely a compilation of the sayings and deeds of Mohammed as he lived, preached, and worked. The prophet Mohammed may have led an exemplary life as the passage above suggests, but he was still a man, so not all his words and deeds during his daily life were directly controlled by God.'

'Just a moment,' interrupted Thomas. 'As a Christian student of theology, I don't believe in the sacred nature of Mohammed's revelations from God for one moment. However, just for the sake of argument, let's just assume that Mohammed truly was inspired by God, so what do you mean by saying that not all his words and deeds during his daily life were controlled by God?'

'Just this, the followers of Islam say Mohammed was a prophet inspired by God, hence all his words and deeds were divinely inspired. But Mohammed was also a man. So tell me, were his urination and defecation under divine control? Were his eating, going to the market for food, and his haggling over the price of food under divine control? He was married with many wives. Were his sexual activities and settling of personal marital problems divinely inspired? Other followers of Islam, and even godless unbelieving-dog heathens, perform these same activities without any evident divine control by the God of Islam. At these times, his deeds and his words were almost certainly his own, because I cannot imagine that the urination, defecation, eating, buying food in the market, or the sexual activities of Mohammed were divinely controlled by God. This means that Mohammed was certainly not receiving revelations from God all the time. Unfortunately, the Sunnah does not differentiate which of the words and deeds of Mohammed were from Mohammed himself, and which originated from divine revelation. This is an important weakness of the Sunnah which no-one has ever completely explained to me. There is another, even more important weakness in the Sunnah. The revelations of God in the Koran are considered to be true revelations from God. But in this very same Koran, even though God said that Mohammed is a good example to follow (Koran 33:21), God also revealed that regardless of what Mohammed desired, did, or said, it is God who ultimately determines what happens (Koran 28:56). Accordingly, these mutually inconsistent passages also undermine the authority of the Sunnah, by undermining the use of the sayings and deeds of Mohammed as a supplement to the Koran. After all, the Sunnah tells only us what Mohammed desired, did, and said, but does not tell us if God ultimately approved of it. And we cannot know what God really wants, because God is unknowable. I suppose that all you can do to get out of this quandary, is to compare the deeds and speech of Mohammed as reported in the Sunnah with the Koran, accepting only those things that agree with the text of the Koran. This is actually really fascinating material Thomas.'

'Certainly is Ben. There is nothing like a good, rousing theological argument. But I do believe you're digressing. So how do you conclude from all this that God hates everyone?'

'Sorry about that. Digression is a bit of a habit of mine as you will have noticed already. Oh it's easily explained, but first one last thing.' Ben was evidently in his stride. 'The holy texts of Judaism, Christianity, and Islam, all propound a form of predestination where God has determined the exact lifespan and fate of each individual long before their birth.'

My frame was not hidden from thee, When I was made in secret, And curiously wrought in the lowest parts of the earth.

Thine eyes did see mine unformed substance; And in thy book they were all written, Even the days that were ordained for me, When as yet there was none of them. (ASV Bible, Psalms 139:15-16)

'And Thomas, this is just an example from the Bible, and is from the Old Testament, which is both a Jewish and Christian holy text. But the Koran of the followers of Islam says exactly the same (Koran 11:6). These texts have far reaching implications. They mean that God is not only a God of deceit, but is also a God who has planned the deaths of all humans long before they were born: by miscarriage, abortion, murder, accident, and disease! Accordingly, it might even be considered sacrilege to prevent miscarriages, abortions, murders, lethal accidents, and lethal diseases, because after all, they are all the will of God. This means that the God of Abraham, and now the same God worshipped by Jews, Christians, and followers of Islam alike, is not only a God of inconceivable malevolence, but is also a God of an unholy trinity of deceit, disease, and death! But I suppose we shouldn't be too surprised by all this, because God is unknowable as well as all-powerful, and as mere mortals we cannot even begin to understand the purpose of God in all these things. What do you think of that Thomas?'

'That you're quite a demagogue ... However, I suppose there is a sort of perverted logic in your arguments, although I'm sure it's no more than a form of delusional sophistry,' retorted Thomas. 'But get on with your main argument – explain why you think God hates us.'

Ben paused to sip some wine, and continued, 'Very well, here it comes. Followers of Judaism, Christianity, and Islam all profess to worship the same God. Yet each of these three religions sets its followers against the followers of the other two religions, as well as forbidding conversion from one to another of these three religions on pain of death or eternal damnation in hell. God also punishes followers of each of these religions for not being followers of the other of these three religions, while at the same time deceiving and deluding the followers of each of these religions into believing they are following the correct religion. The end result is the same – the followers of these three religions are all punished on earth, as well as undergoing eternal torment in hell for believing in the wrong religion. The conclusion is as obvious as it is horrid – you will undergo everlasting torment in hell regardless of whether you do believe in Judaism, Christianity, or Islam, and you will certainly undergo everlasting torment in hell if you don't believe in any of these three religions. When you consider these texts, you realize God is actually trying to get the souls of as many people as possible into hell so they can be subjected to hideous sufferings for all eternity! Followers of all religions have deluded themselves for millennia by seeking comfort and succour from a horrifically malignant God of inconceivable mendacity! But why is God so unspeakably cruel and sadistic? Only two conclusions are possible – God is a God of lies, and God really does hate everyone! This is the despairing cry you read in the graffiti you saw.'

'I must admit, you've presented an interesting argument,' said Thomas reflectively. 'However, last night I was watching television and saw a program about near-death experiences. This program presented the story of a woman called Pam Reynolds. She underwent a dangerous brain operation with a revolutionary operation technique where her body was cooled to 15 degrees Celsius, the blood drained out of her head, and her heart and breathing stopped for the period of the operation. During this period of clinical death, she had a near-death experience during which she departed from her body, heard and saw things in the operating theatre she couldn't possibly have heard or seen while in her body, and after passing through a dark vortex, she met with her relatives in a wonderful world inhabited by the souls of the dead. This story was verified by her doctors, and indicates there must be more to this universe than just this physical material existence. But it doesn't correspond at all with your speciously reasoned belief in a future ghastly eternity of torment inflicted upon us by a monstrously sadistic, hateful, and lying God.'

'Of course this near-death experience doesn't correspond to the reality presented by these holy books,' said Ben. 'What I've been talking about is what we learn about the hateful nature of God from the holy texts of Judaism, Christianity, and Islam. However, as a result of my extensive studies of religion and the paranormal, I don't believe in a conscious life after death for one single moment, and certainly not in a God as horrendously malignant as is revealed by the texts of these holy books. If there is anything like a God, then such an entity would not concern itself with individuals, or small tribal groups on one of the undoubtedly countless billions of planets in this universe on which sentient life exists (Koran 42:29). Notwithstanding the fact that an afterlife is no more than a wishful fantasy, there are still many people who believe they will go to some sort of paradise after death. However, this belief is only supported by some very disputable texts in their holy books, and their faith in what is expounded by these texts. So these believers welcome near-death experiences such as that of Pam Reynolds with open arms and cries of joy, because such near-death experiences buttress their belief in an eternal afterlife in some sort of paradise. The apparent confirmation provided by these wondrous stories makes people feel all is well, and makes them feel there is a real chance of going to heaven. It gives them a warm and gooey feeling that there truly is a wondrous reward for the faithful at the end of a hard life. But this belief is nonsense, and even though the story of Pam Reynolds truly is wondrous, it is no proof of an afterlife.'

'That sounds really arrogant Ben. How can you say there's no after-life? After all, for many thousands of years people of all races and creeds have always believed in some form of life after death, which means there must at least be some truth in this belief. Otherwise how could such a belief have arisen and continue unabated for thousands of years? Pam Reynolds' story truly is proof of some sort of afterlife, because even doctors cannot explain her experience except with the reality of an afterlife of some sort: and you arrogantly say it's not proof of an afterlife! Okay, it's wonderful weather, we're sitting in a beautiful place, and I'm in a good mood today. So prove it to me, and I'll pay for the next bottle of wine,' upon which he looked contentiously at Ben as he settled in his chair.

'Done! Order a bottle now! I'm not going to miss this opportunity,' agreed Ben with almost indecent alacrity.

'I've got a suspicious feeling this is going to be an expensive after-noon,' groaned Thomas theatrically as he ordered a bottle of the same rosé they had been drinking. 'But do continue ... At least you can earn your wine.'

Ben emptied a half glass of rosé with evident pleasure. 'Ahhh ... Wonderful. Warm afternoon sunshine, a beautiful view, and wine paid for by someone else. This is the true meaning of paradise. Now the fact that people have believed in some form of afterlife for many millennia is no proof of the reality of an afterlife. I can't see this afterlife. I can't experience this afterlife. I can't detect this afterlife with any device. This either means I'm just an unbelieving dog, or it means the supposed reality of an afterlife is merely a product of fervent hope and faith, because as I said already, the story of Pam Reynolds in no way proves the reality of an afterlife. I can say this with some confidence because it just so happens I know a lot about this particular near-death experience, and can explain every detail of Pam Reynolds' story.'

'Ohhh ...' groaned Thomas again. 'I should have known better than to challenge you. Okay, get on with it.'

'The report of Pam Reynolds' story was first published in a book called *Light & Death* written by an American cardiologist, Doctor Michael Sabom (Sabom 1998, pages 37-51). This is actually a quite accurate account, and contains more than enough information with which to explain this quite astonishing story. Furthermore, being the first report of this story, it also has the advantage of being free of the inaccuracies, contaminations, and outright fantasies now circulating as a result of the telling and retelling of this story.'

'So you claim this story has become wilder and more inaccurate with the retelling?'

'I certainly do. Pam Reynolds' story as you tell it is wondrous, astounding even, but does not correspond at all with the original accurate report of this story presented in the book *Light and Death*. In fact the story you told me is a gross misrepresentation of the story, which would certainly lead people to believe they have a consciousness or soul that can temporarily depart their bodies during sleep or death – precisely is as stated in the Koran (see also Koran 39:42).'

It is He who doth take your souls by night, and hath knowledge of all that ye have done by day: by day doth He raise you up again; that a term appointed be fulfilled; In the end unto Him will be your return; then will He show you the truth of all that ye did. (YA Koran 6:60)

'Yes, Thomas this, and similar other texts sound like a miraculous confirmation of her story. But her story doesn't confirm this text at all. Let's examine her story as told in the book *Life & Death*. The woman whose pseudonym was Pam Reynolds was 35 years old in 1991 CE when she underwent an operation to remove a giant swelling (an aneurysm) of one of the most vital blood vessels supplying her brain with blood (the Basilar artery). The operation was necessary because the wall of the aneurysm was so thin and weak it could burst at any moment, depriving the most vital parts of her brainstem of blood, and result in her death. The size and position of the aneurysm were such that a special surgical technique was required to remove it. Her neurosurgeon decided on a technique where he would surgically expose the aneurysm, while at the same time cardiac bypass tubing would be connected to the large blood vessels in her groin. When he was ready to remove the aneurysm, her body would be cooled by the cardiac bypass apparatus to 15 degrees Celsius, her heart and breathing would be stopped, and the blood drained from her head to make removal of the aneurysm safe and very much easier. After the aneurysm was removed, her body would be warmed up again to her normal body temperature of 37 degrees Celsius, her heartbeat would be restored, and she would receive artificial respiration until she awoke again.'

'But she would have been dead if this was done!' said Thomas. 'How could she survive a period of no heartbeat and no breathing, as well as draining the blood from her head?'

'Well Thomas, the principle is the same as keeping meat fresh in the refrigerator. Cold meat decays more slowly that warm meat. The same is true of the living tissues of the body. The cooler the tissues, the lower the rate of metabolism, and the longer the tissue can survive without any circulation at all. For example, it's known that increasing degrees of brain damage begin to occur after the flow of blood to the head stops for more than 3 minutes at the normal body temperature of 37 degrees Celsius, but when the body is cooled to 10 to 15 degrees Celsius, about 45 to 60 minutes can elapse before any brain damage begins to occur. This is why profound cooling of the body has been a technique used to provide ideal surgical conditions for some types of brain and heart operations since the 1950's. During these operations, the bodies of the patients are cooled to about 8.4 to 15 degrees Celsius, and their breathing and heartbeat stopped for up to 45 to 60 minutes during which the surgeon can operate upon their hearts (Dobell 1997, Gordon 1962), or their brains (Koch 1991, Williams 1991). So as you see, the technique employed by the neurosurgeon of Pam Reynolds was nothing new or revolutionary. It was a known, albeit infrequently used method for enabling these difficult operations. Anyway, that's the background to the technique used for the operation on Pam Reynolds.'

'I see ...' said Thomas. 'But you still haven't got to the specific case of Pam Reynolds.'

'Patience young man, patience.' Ben sipped some wine, and paused for an irritatingly long period. 'The best way to look at the story of Pam Reynolds is to examine the timeline of her operation in relation to the experiences she reported. If you carefully examine the excellent account of her experience in *Life & Death* (Sabom 1998, pages 37-51) you can construct just such a timeline. Now, as chance would have it, I also saw exactly the same television program on which this garbled version of her story was presented. I just knew you would want to talk about it, which is why I wrote down the timeline of the main events of her operation.' Ben took a piece of paper from his pocket and laid it before them.

07:15-08:40 hours.
- Pam Reynolds arrived in the operating theatre.
- An intravenous line was inserted.
- General anaesthesia was started. Pam Reynolds was now unconscious under general anaesthesia.
- Invasive monitors of vital body functions were inserted. This is often done after starting general anaesthesia because it consists of some painful or uncomfortable procedures.
- Electroencephalogram electrodes were attached to monitor her brain electrical activity.
- Closely fitting earplugs, with speakers were inserted into both her ears so as to administer clicking sounds for measuring her brainstem response to clicking sounds (Vestibular Evoked Potentials – VEP's).
- Her head was fastened firmly to the operating table with a three-point head fixation clamp. This clamp prevents small movements of the head that would otherwise make using an operating microscope impossible.
- Her head was shaved, and her body draped for operation.
- Pam Reynolds' body temperature and heartbeat were normal throughout this period, and she received artificial respiration with a machine.

08:40-10:50 hours.
- The neurosurgeon began the operation. A scalp incision was made, and the skin covering her skull retracted.

- A pneumatic bone saw was used to remove a piece of bone from her skull in order to give access to the brain and the aneurysm within.
- The cardiothoracic surgeon exposed the Femoral artery and vein in her right groin, only to find these blood vessels were too small for the cardiac bypass tubing. She told this to the neurosurgeon.
- The cardiothoracic surgeon then proceeded to operate on Pam's left groin to expose the Femoral artery and vein there.
- In the meantime the neurosurgeon also continued operating to expose the giant aneurysm. The last step of this part of the operation was to gently move the tissues of the brain aside to reveal the expected giant Basilar artery aneurysm.
- Pam Reynolds' body temperature and heartbeat were normal throughout this period, and she received artificial respiration with a machine.

10:50-11:00 hours.
- The neurosurgeon found, as was expected, that the aneurysm was too large to operate safely without profound body cooling and cardiac arrest.
- The cardiothoracic team inserted cardiac bypass tubing into the already exposed left Femoral artery and vein.
- The cardiac bypass machine was switched on, and started to lower Pam Reynolds body temperature by pumping her blood through the heat exchanger of the cardiac bypass machine.
- Even though Pam Reynolds body temperature was lowered at the end of this time period, her heartbeat was normal throughout this period, and she received artificial respiration with a machine.

11:00-11:25 hours.
- Pam Reynolds body temperature was now 22.8 degrees Celsius, at which time she was definitely unconscious (Fay 1941, Stocks 2004).

- Even though Pam Reynolds body temperature was low, her heartbeat was normal, and she received artificial respiration with a machine.

11:25-12:00 hours.
- Pam Reynolds body temperature was now 15.5 degrees Celsius.
- At this point no more electroencephalogram or VEP's could be detected.
- Potassium chloride was administered to totally stop the heartbeat and the irregular heart rhythm resulting from her low body temperature.
- Artificial respiration from the respirator was turned off.
- The body of Pam was tilted head-up to drain the blood from her head.
- The neurosurgeon clipped the aneurysm at its neck and excised it.

12:00-12:32 hours.
- After successful removal of the aneurysm, the cardiac bypass pump was turned on again to start re-warming Pam Reynolds' body.
- Artificial respiration was resumed.
- As her body warmed up, the VEP's returned.
- Pam developed an abnormal and lethal heart rhythm called ventricular fibrillation – a rhythm where the heart just twitches in an uncoordinated manner without pumping blood.
- Normal heart rhythm was restored with a 50-Joule electrical shock.
- Even though Pam Reynolds body temperature was low, her heartbeat was now normal.

12:32-14:10 hours.
- Cardiac bypass was stopped at a body temperature of 32 degrees Celsius.

- The various wounds in her head and groin were closed to the accompaniment of music, among which a tune called 'Hotel California' composed and sung by a group called 'the Eagles'.
- Pam Reynolds body temperature and heartbeat were normal throughout this period, and she received artificial respiration with a machine.

14:10 hours.
- Pam Reynolds body temperature was now a normal 37 degrees Celsius.
- Pam was brought into the ICU while still under general anaesthesia.
- Pam Reynolds body temperature and heartbeat were normal throughout this period, and she received artificial respiration with a machine.

Sometime later that day.
- Later in the day she awoke again.
- When she was able to breathe normally again without assistance, the respirator was turned off, and the respirator tube (endotracheal tube) was removed from her windpipe and larynx.
- Only after she awoke, only after she was able to breathe normally for herself again, and only after the respirator tubing had been removed, was she able to talk and tell of her experience.

'So Thomas, this is a clear timeline of the events occurring during Pam Reynolds operation.'

'Okay,' said Thomas. 'It's clear what happened during her operation, but how does this explain her experience? After all, no-one else saw what she saw, or experienced what she underwent.'

'I know, but no-one sees things exactly as you see them, or experiences what you experience inside your head either, and the same was true for Pam Reynolds too. So let's examine her experiences in a step by step manner. The first thing she remembered after losing consciousness due to general anaesthesia, was awakening to the sound of a "natural D" and leaving her body.'

The next thing I recall was the sound: It was a natural D. As I listened to the sound, I felt it was pulling me out of the top of my head. The further out of my body I got, the more clear the tone became. I had the impression it was like a road, a frequency that you go on .... I remember seeing several things in the operating room when I was looking down. It was the most aware that I think that I have ever been in my entire life.... I was metaphorically sitting on Dr. Spetzler's [the neurosurgeon] shoulder. It was not like normal vision. It was brighter and more focused and clearer than normal vision. . . . There was so much in the operating room that I didn't recognize, and so many people. (Sabom 1998, page 41)

'This all occurred during the period that the neurosurgeon used a pneumatic bone saw to open her skull. At this time her body temperature was perfectly normal, her heartbeat was normal, and her breathing was taken over by a machine because of muscle paralyzing drugs and high doses of opiates administered as part of the anaesthetic technique. So normal amounts of oxygen-rich blood flowed through her brain, and she was unconscious under general anaesthesia until the bone saw was used to open her skull. The powerful vibrations of the bones of her skull were also transmitted to other bones in her body, vibrating and activating her muscle spindles (Burke 1976), causing them to transmit sensory nerve signals to her brain, so arousing her to consciousness (Lanier-1994). These same powerful vibrations and sounds of the bone saw were also transmitted through the bones of her skull to her ears. Sounds transmitted through the bones of the skull are heard, even if the ear canals are totally occluded and admit no sound at all. This was the sound of the natural D she reported hearing. While so awakened, but rendered serene, uncritical, pain-free, paralyzed and unmoving by anaesthetic drugs, the changes in body position signalled by sensory nerve signals from her activated muscle spindles informed her mind that she was displaced outside her physical body. Her mind accordingly generated an image of a view from outside her body consistent with the information from these sensory nerve signals (Chapter 6). This was her out-of-body experience.'

'I won't dispute this matter of arousal by the pneumatic saw, but Ben, how could the vibrations of the bone saw have informed her brain she was displaced outside her body?'

'Hmmm … How can I explain it to you?' said a pensive Ben as he drank more rosé. He thought a moment. 'We've discussed how sensory signals from muscle spindles can generate out-of-body experiences before (Chapter 6). So there is nothing new there. Powerful vibration of muscles caused by the bone saw activated the sensory nerves going to her brain from her muscle spindles to induce awareness (Lanier 1986, Lanier 1994), and generate the illusion of displacement out of her body in the mind of Pam Reynolds (Goodwin 1972, McCloskey 1978, Vignemont 2005). This is how the powerful vibrations of the bone saw aroused an out-of-body experience in the supposedly unconscious Pam Reynolds. She filled in the imagery of the operation theatre in her mind, so completing the imagery of being out of her body and observing the operation.'

'But she was unconscious under anaesthesia.'

'Not at all. She was conscious. She didn't say she was having an out-of-body experience at the time, because the effects of anaesthetic drugs meant she was calm and did not even think of speaking. Moreover, had she even tried to speak, speech would have been impossible anyway, because of muscle paralyzing drugs and the tube from the respirator through her larynx. Nonetheless she was awake, because an out-of-body experience is a conscious experience. After all, we've discussed before about how people can be awake during anaesthesia even though they appear unconscious (Chapter 10).'

'Okay,' Thomas grudgingly conceded. 'I begin to understand how the out-of-body experience could have been generated by vibrations of the bone saw, but how could she have described the shape and size of the bone saw so well? That must have been due to some form of sight or paranormal perception.'

'Not at all,' was the confident reply. 'If Pam Reynolds was 35 years old in 1991 CE, then she must have been born in 1956 CE. As a child raised in the USA during the years subsequent to her birth, she would have regularly visited a dentist where she undoubtedly saw, heard and felt the drill of the dentist. Pneumatic and electrical dental drills in use since about 1950 CE have much the same shape, and make much the same sounds as the bone saw used to open her skull. So it is not surprising she associated the two, and could make a reasonably accurate description of the neuro-surgical bone saw. And remember, her description of the whole event was a memory formed within a brain influenced by anaesthetic drugs and the effects of surgery: a memory she was only able to recount many hours later in the intensive care after the sedation had been stopped and the respirator tube removed from her larynx.'

Thomas thought a bit as he drank a little more wine. He looked dissatisfied. 'Okay,' he grumbled, 'you seem to have explained her out-of-body experience. Nonetheless, how could she have heard the cardiothoracic surgeon say her blood vessels were too small?'

Someone said something about my veins and arteries being very small. I believe it was a female voice and that it was Dr. Murray, but I'm not sure. She was the cardiologist. I remember thinking that I should have told her about that ... (Sabom 1998, page 42)

'She heard the exact words of what Doctor Murray said. But she was wearing closely fitting soundproof earphones to measure her vestibular evoked responses, so she couldn't possibly have heard what the cardiothoracic surgeon said with normal hearing. This means her disembodied consciousness, or soul, must have heard these words.'

Ben laughed, 'Oh, oh, Thomas. Look around you, and you see young people all around you wearing tightly fitting earplugs attached to electronic music players. Try these earplugs for yourself, and you realize they fit tightly and allow little sound to enter the ears. Yet these young people also carry on conversations while wearing these earplugs and listening to music, which clearly indicates that being able to hear while wearing earplugs or earphones is really nothing special.'

'But those earphones she wore were really sound proof according to the television program.'

'That's what they say, but Pam Reynolds still heard the sound with her ears. We know this for several reasons. We know she heard the cardiothoracic surgeon speaking by means of air conduction of the sound, because the cardiothoracic surgeon was not attached in some miraculous way to the bones of her skull, which would have enabled her to hear the surgeon by means of bone conduction. Did the supposedly separated consciousness of Pam Reynolds hear the voice of the cardiothoracic surgeon by means of telepathy? I don't think so; otherwise she would have heard the thoughts of the cardiothoracic surgeon instead of just the verified spoken words of the surgeon. Furthermore, if the separated consciousness of Pam had telepathic powers, why didn't she hear the thoughts of others in the room? As you know yourself, your personal thoughts go further than what you express in words: you think about what you are going to eat for lunch, you might want to go to the toilet, your clothing is uncomfortable, you are annoyed with someone in the room, you are happy about something, etc, etc. But Pam Reynolds mentioned none of these things. She only stated what the cardiothoracic surgeon said in words: no more, and no less. Could her separated consciousness have heard the sound waves of the spoken words of the cardiothoracic surgeon? This is very unlikely, because it would mean that the immaterial separated consciousness of Pam Reynolds responded to the material sound waves forming the sounds of the cardiothoracic surgeon's words (Chapter 5). We know her immaterial separated consciousness supposedly separated from her body by passing through the solid material substance of her body, as well as through the solid material drapes covering her body. So if her supposedly immaterial consciousness failed to interact with these solid and material things, how much more likely is it that her immaterial conscious-ness could interact with the very much more tenuous variations of air pressure that form sound waves? As if this were not enough, we know from millennia of experience with deaf people that a person can only hear when the physical mechanisms of the body needed for hearing function, because when the physical mechanisms of the body needed for hearing do not function, the person is deaf. The many millions of deaf people now living on this world are living proof that the supposedly immaterial consciousness associated with the body can only hear sounds by means of the functioning of the physical mechanisms of the body needed for hearing. No living person hears with their immaterial consciousness, otherwise no-one would be deaf. So Pam Reynolds heard the words of the cardiothoracic surgeon with her ears.'

'Aha, but Pam Reynolds was clinically dead, with no heartbeat or breathing when she heard the cardiothoracic surgeon speaking. This means she must have heard the surgeon with her disembodied consciousness in spite of all you say.'

'Ridiculous! Twaddle! Absolute nonsense!' snorted Ben. 'Just look at the timeline of the operation. Pam Reynolds was very much alive at the time the surgeon made this statement. The surgeon had just found that the blood vessels in Pam's right groin were too small for the cardiac bypass tubing. So she was very evidently not yet on cardiac bypass, which meant her body temperature was normal at the time, that she had a normal heartbeat, and that she was receiving artificial respiration from the anaesthetic machine. Pam Reynolds was very much alive at the time, and she was also conscious because she clearly heard the surgeon saying the blood vessels in her right groin were too small for the cardiac bypass tubing. Her words even indicated that her brain function at the time was abnormal, because she also said something very strange, "I remember thinking that I should have told her about that ..." Tell me Thomas do you know the sizes of the veins and arteries in your right groin?'

'Er ... No.'

'Nor do I, and nor does anyone else for that matter either. The very fact Pam Reynolds actually thought at the time that she knew the sizes of the blood vessels in her right groin, and that she should have told the cardiothoracic surgeon about them being too small for cardiac bypass tubing beforehand, certainly indicates her brain function was rendered abnormal by the effects of anaesthetic drugs. And we definitely know these anaesthetic drugs must have affected her brain, because even though she was conscious, she felt no pain from the operation, proving that the powerful painkilling drugs used for anaesthesia were working, removing pain, which means they very definitely had altered her brain function. She was simply awake, even though she appeared to be unconscious under anaesthesia. We've talked before about people who are awake, even though they appear unconscious under general anaesthesia (Chapter 10). This is the explanation of her ability to hear the words of the cardiothoracic surgeon.' Ben looked at Thomas with a smug mile, as if to say, 'I dare you to contradict that!'

'Hmm ...' sighed Thomas. He lapsed into a short silence, digesting what he had just heard, and drinking more rosé before Ben got the chance to empty most of the bottle. 'But what about the experience she had while clinically dead during her period of profoundly low body temperature, at which time her heartbeat was stopped, and the blood was drained from her head?'

'Oh you mean her experience of passing through a dark vortex into a place of light where she had contact with her grandmother, grandfather, as well as various aunts and uncles, all of whom were bathed in light, communicated telepathically with her, and fed her in some way before finally bringing her back to her body.'

'Yes. How do you explain that? She must have seen them, during the period the blood was drained out of her head and she was clinically dead.'

'Not necessarily Thomas. This part of her experience is reasonably easy to explain. Her experience of falling into a dark vortex was very likely due to rapid onset of profound muscle relaxation as she descended into unconsciousness during the period of rapid cooling of her body. This is a sensation very similar to the falling sensation people sometimes experience in the period just between awake and falling asleep. Her near-death experience in this period was an absolutely stereotype experience undergone by a person expecting to undergo a potentially lethal event (Chapter 7 & figure 7.1). This is why she had a near-death experience with affective and transcendental components, where she entered a transcendental world to meet other deceased people who acted as guides or mentors in this world. Typically, as a person born and raised in the USA, she saw her deceased close family members (figure 7.3), encountered a barrier, and returned to her body. So her experience is exactly what you would expect from a person with her background.'

'But how could she have such an experience while she was clinically dead without any heartbeat, breathing or flow of blood through her brain. She was dead, so if she had an experience like this, then her consciousness was very evidently something separate from her body.'

'Ohh Thomas ...' groaned Ben, as he theatrically rolled and closed his eyes, 'Ohhh Thomas ... What have I been telling you all the time? Experiences like this don't have to last a long time. They sometimes only last seconds, even though the person themselves feel as if they last a long time. This experience evidently occurred during a period of awareness either before, or after she was unconscious due to cooling of her body. People are simply unconscious below a body temperature of 26 degrees Celsius (Fay 1941, Stocks 2004), and while unconscious a person can have no conscious experiences such as a near-death experience, out-of-body experience, or any other type of dream, hallucination, or conscious experience for that matter.'

'But isn't it still possible?'

'No,' was the very definite reply. 'Look at it this way Thomas, if I hit you on your head with a brick so that you drop unconscious to the ground, would you expect to undergo any experience while lying unconscious there on the ground.'

'Er, no, I guess not.'

'Precisely. Your period of unconsciousness would be a black hole during which no conscious experience occurred at all, so why would you expect other people to have some sort of wondrous experience while they are unconscious. Unconsciousness means just that – no conscious experience. The only experience you might have after being hit on your head with a brick is that I might try rifling your pockets for money, so you could pay for all the wine we're drinking today. But you wouldn't notice that, because you would be unconscious at the time.'

'I understand what you mean. But even so, there is a problem with your explanation. The conscious experience of Pam Reynolds was continuous from the moment she departed from her body to the end. She reports being conscious the whole time, from the beginning of the experience, when the piece of bone was sawn from her skull, until she was brought to the intensive care after completion of surgery. How could this be possible unless her consciousness was somehow separated from her physical body?'

'Oh yes, that old argument of a continuous conscious experience,' sighed Ben, and emptied his glass. He looked unhappily at the now empty bottle, and sighed again. 'Waiter, another bottle of the same again please! Now Thomas, this argument of a continuous conscious experience is absolute nonsense! Pam Reynolds could only remember those experiences she had while conscious, because while unconscious she had no conscious experiences at all. Her periods of unconsciousness were simply a blank emptiness. In addition to this, she was simply unable to tell of her experiences as she underwent them: during her periods of consciousness she was sedated with anaesthetic drugs, the respirator tube between her vocal cords made speech physically impossible, and her muscles were paralyzed with a curare-like drug which made it impossible to move or breathe, let alone speak. Furthermore, she was kept in this condition after the operation was finished, as well as during the time she was transported to the intensive care unit where she eventually woke up several hours later at the earliest. Only then, only after she was able to breathe again, and the respirator tube was removed from between her vocal cords, was she finally in a condition where she was able to relate her experiences. All these things mean that the wondrous experience related by Pam Reynolds was a remembered experience. So what she did was to string her periods of consciousness onto a superficially continuous timeline, threading the individual beads of short episodes of consciousness onto a string to form the necklace of a continuous conscious experience. This is why her experience sounds like a continual unbroken period of consciousness, even though this wondrous so-called continuous experience was actually no more than a chain of remembered snippets of consciousness.'

'I understand,' was the reaction of Thomas. 'So you mean that the last part of her experience when they were closing her wound to the accompaniment of the song "Hotel California" was simply a period of awareness while apparently unconscious under anaesthesia.'

'Indeed I do. At the time of her experience they were closing her wounds, so she was disconnected from the cardiac bypass tubing, her body temperature was normal, she had a normal heartbeat, and received artificial respiration from the anaesthetic machine. She was also very much alive at this point, and very evidently aware of what was happening around her. Her description is an absolutely typical experience of awareness during anaesthesia.'

> *When I came back, they were playing 'Hotel California' and the line was 'You can check out anytime you like, but you can never leave.' I mentioned [later] to Dr. Brown that that was incredibly insensitive and he told me that I needed to sleep more. [laughter] When I regained consciousness, I was still on the respirator.'*
> (Sabom 1998, page 47)

'Examine the wording carefully Thomas. Pam Reynolds said the wording of the song was incredibly insensitive. I suppose that if you were Pam Reynolds, then it certainly would appear that way. After all, she was awake and felt no pain, but could neither move nor speak because of muscle paralyzing drugs. In other words, she was locked inside her body, even though she tried to leave the imprisonment of the anaesthetic drugs paralyzing her body. And then she mentions that she lost consciousness yet again, awakening later while still on the respirator. This latter indicates she realized she underwent periods of consciousness and unconsciousness during the whole procedure. So there you have it Thomas, the wondrous story of Pam Reynolds explained.'

'Now Ben, I would tend to agree with you, if it weren't for one thing still bothering me.'

'What's that?'

'Her story is so coherent, so clear, and not at all like the vague and disjointed story told by someone delirious or confused by drugs. This was obviously an experience undergone by a person with a fully functioning consciousness. How would you explain this?'

A short silence fell as both men basked in the sun and sipped wine. Ben took another sip with evident relish, 'It actually seems incredible to most people, but periods of awareness during anaesthesia are often very clear, and people often tell a very coherent story about what they heard and felt during such a period of awareness (Editorial 1979, Mainzer 1979, Schwender 1998). The story of Pam Reynolds is a report of several remembered periods of awareness, and is typically clear, and superficially unaffected by any mental effects of the anaesthetic drugs. I say superficially, because her mental function was definitely affected by anaesthetic drugs. There is evidence for this: she was calm and not at all frightened during her periods of awareness, she seemed to think she knew the sizes of the blood vessels in her groin, and she felt no pain even though she was undergoing an operation. So the functioning of her brain was definitely affected by the anaesthetic drugs. Furthermore, her story is a report of a remembered experience, because it was physically impossible for her to relate her experience until the anaesthetic drugs had worn off, and the ventilator tubing removed from between her vocal cords. All these things mean she could only relate her story while awake in full possession of all her mental faculties, and because she was awake and in full possession of all her mental faculties, she was able to relate a very coherent story.'

'So you're saying that this story is simply a product of anaesthetic drugs and being awake during the operation. Then what about the vestibular evoked potential (VEP) monitoring which indicated she was unconscious?'

'Monitoring of VEP's is never 100% accurate. Furthermore, these potentials are considerably influenced by body temperature, and during 1991 CE, analysis of VEP's was done manually which is never as accurate as computer trend analysis. All these things influenced the interpretation of the vestibular evoked potentials from Pam Reynolds during her operation (Thornton 1998). So even though this apparatus indicated unconsciousness, she was very definitely conscious at times. Her story indicates and proves this was so. All these things explain the wondrous story of Pam Reynolds. The experience of Pam Reynolds was not proof of the reality of an immaterial soul or mind which can exist separately from the body. Instead her experience was a product of anaesthetic drugs, abnormal interpretations of bodily sensations, together with a perception of personal imminent death, all of which caused her body to function in such a way that she underwent a truly wondrous experience. I do not belittle this experience, because it was a truly wondrous experience, even though it was a product of abnormal body function. Her experience possibly confirmed her vision of the world, possibly even gave her a new vision of the world, and possibly even gave her a reason for existence. To Pam Reynolds, and indeed to us all, this experience is significant, for all such stories are powerful and wonderful demonstrations of the functioning of the human body, as well as being demonstrations of the true nature of our being.'

'I guess you're right again Ben,' sighed Thomas. 'It cost me a bottle of wine, but it was worth it. The second bottle you ordered goes on your bill. I didn't order it, you did.'

'Okay, okay,' grumbled Ben. 'Sounds reasonable. What about some food? I'm feeling hungry after all this wine. They serve quite edible shashlik and French fries here. So let's live up to the reputation Jewish priests once gave Jesus!'

The Son of man [Jesus] is come eating and drinking; and ye say,

318

Behold, a gluttonous man, and a winebibber, a friend of publicans and sinners! (ASV Bible, Luke 7:34)

Ben continued, 'This reputation was good enough for Jesus, so it's good enough for me. There's nothing wrong with publicans and sinners, and I also happen to enjoy food, especially after a lot of wine which I enjoy even more! Waiter! More of the same wine and the menu please!'

Chapter 12

They were certainly dead

Thomas entered the smoke filled café, looked around, and found Ben seated at a table in animated discussion with a tall and distinguished man of Middle-Eastern origin. Ben looked up as he approached the table, 'Ah Thomas, good to see you. I'd like you to meet a colleague of mine, Abdulaziz, a visiting cardiologist from England. Abdulaziz, this is Thomas whom I told you about.'

'Pleased to meet you Thomas,' said Abdulaziz in an impeccable English accent, as he rose to shake Thomas' hand with a firm and warm grasp.

The three sat and ordered beer. Abdulaziz told of his experiences in Kulsthan while visiting a cardiologist colleague of his whom he had met in London. He was a good storyteller, regaling them with story after story of various incidents occurring during his stay there. The time passed quickly, as did a succession of glasses of beer. Eventually Abdulaziz talked about the household of his Kulsthan colleague, 'Ah he's really got everything well organized. He has a man who does the garden, and two girls who look after the house, serve food and tea, or whatever, and cook. Much better than what I have in England. And these people don't cost him anything. They just work for their food and keep, and they don't want to leave.'

'Oh?' Ben remarked. 'How did he come by such paragons of homely virtue? You won't find anyone willing to work for nothing, even in countries like Kulsthan.'

'I believe he got them from a cousin in the south,' replied Abdulaziz. 'He told me he sent his cousin a four-wheel drive car, and received the two girls in return. It's a fairly normal custom there.'

'Ah,' said Ben, 'you mean they're slaves. I believe Kulsthan is one of the few remaining places in the world where slavery unofficially still exists.'

'I suppose so,' was the nonchalant reply of Abdulaziz, 'but it's a custom there. True, the government officially condemns slavery, but a lot of the well-to-do there have household slaves. If these people weren't household slaves, they would be unemployed, and very likely starve in the streets or in the desert.'

Thomas looked appalled as he asked, 'But don't you feel a sense of shame at such exploitation of fellow humans?'

'Not at all,' was the prompt reply. 'Subsistence wages paid to so-called free employees is equivalent to providing food and keep, because subsistence wages are just that – sufficient for food and keep. Slaves are actually in a better position than free subsistence workers. Their masters take care they are well fed, and also look after them when they are ill or aged, whereas people paid subsistence wages are simply dumped and left to fend for themselves without any resources whatsoever when ill, aged, or whenever they no longer yield a profit. So you may well ask yourself whether the exploitation of people as slaves is worse than the exploitation of workers paid subsistence wages. Furthermore, why should people feel ashamed about owning slaves, or the institution of slavery? After all, the divine revelations in the Koran tell us that God sanctions the institution of slavery. We know this, because throughout the Koran, just as in your Christian Bible, the institution of slavery is mentioned and accepted without a single word of divine disapproval. As if this were not enough evidence of implicit divine approval of the institution of slavery, Mohammed himself, the final and most perfect messenger of God's will, also owned slaves. On one occasion he even gave some captured girls to his friends as gifts (Bukhari 8:367). And if this were not enough evidence for you, God required one fifth of all booty captured by the warriors directly serving Mohammed be given to Mohammed and the needy (see also Koran 8:1, 8:69).'

And know that whatever ye take as spoils of war, lo! a fifth thereof is for Allah, and for the messenger [Mohammed] and for the kinsmen (who hath need) and orphans and the needy and the wayfarer; if ye believe in Allah and that which We revealed unto Our slave on the Day of Discrimination, the day when the two armies met. And Allah is Able to do all things. (Koran 8:41)

'Captives were also regarded as booty,' continued Abdulaziz, 'to be used or sold as slaves. So slavery is very definitely an institution sanctioned by God as is proven by all the many revelations of God to Mohammed. Who are we to disapprove of an institution sanctioned by God? To do so would be heresy.'

Thomas decided to explore this way of thinking further, 'Aha, but there is a difference. A free subsistence worker can depart at any time and seek other, perhaps better paid employment. But what happens if a slave owned by a follower of Islam wants to leave, or just runs away?'

'To do so would be very ungrateful for all that their masters have done for them. Accordingly an ungrateful slave who runs away should be punished, and the nature of the punishment is at the discretion of the master. But Islam also encourages the manumission of slaves. For example, a slave can ask his master to set a price so that he can buy his freedom.'

And such of your slaves as seek a writing (of emancipation), write it for them if ye are aware of aught of good in them, and bestow upon them of the wealth of Allah which He hath bestowed upon you. (Koran 24:33)

Abdulaziz even began to get enthusiastic about the charity of Islam to slaves. 'Indeed, emancipation of slaves is considered a deed of great merit, and something all true followers of Islam are encouraged to do.'

It is not righteousness that ye turn your faces to the East and the West; but righteous is he who believeth in Allah and the Last Day and the angels and the Scripture and the Prophets; and giveth his wealth, for love of Him, to kinsfolk and to orphans and the needy and the wayfarer and to those who ask, and to set slaves free; (Koran 2:177)

'But followers of Islam still possess slaves ...'

'Oh yes, but slavery is also a tradition among the followers of Judaism as well as Christianity,' said a somewhat nettled Abdulaziz. 'Just look at the abominable history of slavery in the ancient Jewish world, as well as slave-owning Christians. I don't know how they justified owning slaves, but they certainly did have them.'

Ben had been listening quietly, drinking his beer. 'Well Thomas, I'm afraid that Abdulaziz is quite correct. The holy books of Judaism sanction the capture of people in war for later use as slaves. This was a law given by God to Moses, the greatest prophet of Judaism.'

> When thou drawest nigh unto a city to fight against it, then proclaim peace unto it. And it shall be, if it make thee answer of peace, and open unto thee, then it shall be, that all the people that are found therein shall become tributary unto thee, and shall serve thee. And if it will make no peace with thee, but will make war against thee, then thou shalt besiege it: and when Jehovah thy God delivereth it into thy hand, thou shalt smite every male thereof with the edge of the sword: but the women, and the little ones, and the cattle, and all that is in the city, even all the spoil thereof, shalt thou take for a prey unto thyself; and thou shalt eat the spoil of thine enemies, which Jehovah thy God hath given thee. (ASV Bible, Deuteronomy 20:10-14)

'Not only is this bloodthirsty stuff which we've already discussed, but it also explicitly states that captives are to be used as desired – as slaves, serfs, servants, or whatever you want to call them. Furthermore,' continued Ben, 'this God, the very same God worshipped by all Christians, as well as by all followers of Islam, sanctioned the buying and selling of slaves, as well as their transmission as chattels to their heirs.'

> And as for thy bondmen, and thy bondmaids, whom thou shalt have; of the nations that are round about you, of them shall ye buy bondmen and bondmaids. Moreover of the children of the strangers that sojourn among you, of them shall ye buy, and of their families that are with you, which they have begotten in your land: and they shall be your possession. And ye shall make them an inheritance for your children after you, to hold for a possession; of them shall ye take your bondmen for ever: but over your brethren the children of Israel ye shall not rule, one over another, with rigor. (ASV Bible, Leviticus 25:44-46)

'And,' continued Ben, 'this idea of slaves as mere chattels was also applied to the wives and children of slaves.'

> *If thou buy a Hebrew servant, six years he shall serve: and in the seventh he shall go out free for nothing.*
>
> *If he come in by himself, he shall go out by himself: if he be married, then his wife shall go out with him. If his master give him a wife and she bear him sons or daughters; the wife and her children shall be her master's, and he shall go out by himself.*
>
> *But if the servant shall plainly say, I love my master, my wife, and my children; I will not go out free: then his master shall bring him unto God, and shall bring him to the door, or unto the door-post; and his master shall bore his ear through with an awl; and he shall serve him for ever.*
>
> *And if a man sell his daughter to be a maid-servant, she shall not go out as the men-servants do. (ASV Bible, Exodus 21:2-7)*

Abdulaziz nodded, adding with a touch of pious venom, 'This passage is a perfect example of the way Jews regard women and slaves – as chattels and inferior beings with whom you can do as you want. A male Jewish slave can leave after six years servitude, but a Jewish slave-girl is condemned to a life of servitude. Even worse, who asks the Jewish slave-girl's opinion if her master decides to have sex with her (Bible, Genesis 16:1-4, 30:1-5, Deuteronomy 21:10-14), or gives her to another slave as a wife! And in the latter situation, when the male slave eventually leaves, the slave-woman and her children fathered by the male slave, are considered to be mere chattels of the master and must remain (Bible, Exodus 21:4). What a repulsive way to treat fellow humans! Just what you would expect from Jews!'

'And followers of Islam too (Koran 4:24)!' retorted Thomas. He thought a moment, and added, 'Luckily Christianity is a religion disapproving of slavery.'

Abdulaziz gave a cynical snort, while Ben laughed, 'An idle hope Thomas. You should know better. After all, many supposedly Christian nations engaged in slave trading and slave owning for many centuries. In fact neither God nor Jesus ever spoke out against slavery. Not a single word. Furthermore, unlike the holy books of Judaism and Islam which provide many opportunities and situations for emancipation of slaves, Christian holy books do not specify when, or under what circumstances slaves may be emancipated. Christianity only acknowledges the presence and reality of slavery. Accordingly, Christianity seems by implication to consider slavery as a permanent condition from which emancipation never occurs. Jesus even explicitly acknowledges the sanctioning of slavery by God, saying that wilfully disobedient slaves should be punished.'

'Ridiculous!' was all Thomas managed to say.

'It's true!' said Ben. 'Jesus considered punishment of disobedient slaves as something quite normal.'

And that servant, who knew his lord's will, and made not ready, nor did according to his will, shall be beaten with many stripes; but he that knew not, and did things worthy of stripes, shall be beaten with few stripes. And to whomsoever much is given, of him shall much be required: and to whom they commit much, of him will they ask the more. (ASV Bible, Luke 12:47-48)

'Even worse Thomas, the later saints such as Saint Paul, the founder of the Christian church also never disapproved of slavery, even enjoining slaves to obey their masters as if they were representatives of God on earth (see also Bible, Titus 2:9-10, Colossians 3:22)!'

Servants, be obedient unto them that according to the flesh are your masters, with fear and trembling, in singleness of your heart, as unto Christ; not in the way of eyeservice, as men-pleasers; but as servants of Christ, doing the will of God from the heart; with good will doing service, as unto the Lord, and not unto men: knowing that whatsoever good thing each one doeth, the same shall he receive again from the Lord, whether he be bond or free. (ASV Bible, Ephesians 6:5-8)

Thomas looked unhappy, 'That's really depressing Ben. I never really looked at passages like these in that way before. It really does seem that God tolerates, or even approves of slavery. This is really contradictory, strange even, and matters are even worse when you think of what Jesus, the Son of God, tells us.'

> *But I say unto you that hear, Love your enemies, do good to them that hate you, bless them that curse you, pray for them that despitefully use you.*
>
> *To him that smiteth thee on the one cheek offer also the other; and from him that taketh away thy cloak withhold not thy coat also. Give to every one that asketh thee; and of him that taketh away thy goods ask them not again.*
>
> *And as ye would that men should do to you, do ye also to them likewise. (ASV Bible, Luke 6:27-31)*

Thomas continued, 'It's strange, but when you think about these texts, you begin to get the idea that Christianity is a religion suitable only for the weak, the oppressed, and for slaves. This would mean that God really is cruel! How could Jesus, the Son of God, say, "And as ye would that men should do to you, do ye also to them likewise," while at the same time sanction slavery? I don't want to enslave other people, and I certainly don't want to enslaved! This statement made by Jesus certainly contradicts his acceptance of slavery. All I can conclude is that the holy texts of Christianity contain so many contradictions, that we can never really learn the true wishes of God from these texts. I'm confused.'

'Yes, that's true, Christian holy books are full of contradictions. After all, that's why God gave the world the perfection of the Koran (Koran 25:33, 85:21-22),' was the pious rejoinder from Abdulaziz. He added in a more sombre tone, 'But I must admit that I also don't know why God sanctions slavery. Nonetheless slavery is sanctioned by God, and I know for certain there is a God. Not only do I know it from what I feel in my heart and from the Koran, but also because there is hard evidence for the reality of an afterlife from careful studies of people successfully resuscitated from cardiac arrest (Lommel 2001, Parnia 2001). Now, if there is an afterlife, then there is also an eternal, all-pervading, all-powerful and all-knowing God – a God standing so far above us that we cannot conceive or understand the nature of God. Accordingly, even though I cannot understand why, I accept that slavery is sanctioned by God.'

'Yes, I've heard about these cardiac arrest studies, and I'm told they are solid medical proof of the reality of an afterlife,' said Thomas in a thoughtful tone. 'However, is the evidence really that solid?'

'Let's get a bottle of wine and drink that instead of this weak beer. Waiter, a bottle of the house red wine please!' called Ben, continuing in a cheerful voice, 'I do believe I have to exorcise another misconception. Ah Thomas, I do believe the gaps in which God manifests are getting smaller and smaller.'

'I don't know what you mean by the gaps in which God manifests, but I do know one of these studies was extremely well performed,' grumbled Abdulaziz, adding, 'So you'll have to do some very clever arguing to convince me these studies don't prove the existence of an after-life.'

In the meantime the wine had arrived, and the glasses filled. Ben sipped, his lips puckered, and he looked unhappy, 'Brrrr ... Cheap and nasty rubbish. Tonsil-shrivelling vinegar! Ah well, after a few glasses, and we won't notice it any more. Now I happen to know a lot about these studies you mentioned. They revealed that 11% to 18% cardiac arrest survivors reported undergoing near-death experiences, or being partially conscious during cardiac resuscitation (Lommel 2001, Parnia 2001).'

'So what,' remarked Abdulaziz with a sour expression, which became even sourer after sipping some wine. 'Now you know the incidence of near-death experiences among people surviving cardiac arrest. These statistics only mean that some people really did visit heaven and see their relatives during a short period in an afterlife revealed to them during their near-death experiences. So you know there is an afterlife, but you knew this already. These studies only prove the reality of this afterlife, because these near-death experiences occurred under carefully defined conditions. Putting a figure on how often people remember visiting this afterlife doesn't prove anything extra.'

'I wouldn't say that,' replied Ben. 'These statistics make it possible to calculate, or to assess whether the functioning of the body during cardiac resuscitation is such that consciousness is possible. After all, I'm sure you would agree that if the functioning of the body during cardiac resuscitation is sufficient to sustain consciousness in some people, then these near-death experiences reported by people surviving cardiac arrest may well be the result of the functioning of the body and the brain during these periods of consciousness, rather than being a result of the separation of an immaterial consciousness or soul from the body.'

'Don't be ridiculous, you can't calculate that,' spluttered Abdulaziz as he drank more sour wine with an equally sour expression.

'Can that be calculated?' asked Thomas, as he cautiously drank his wine.

'Indeed it can,' responded Ben, as he emptied his glass. 'First the basic principles. What is the basic effect of a cardiac arrest?'

'That really is basic,' said Abdulaziz. 'But if you want to play it that way, here we go. A cardiac arrest occurs when the heart stops beating, or when it functions so abnormally that it no longer pumps blood. In both situations, no blood containing oxygen is pumped around the body, and affected persons lose consciousness within five to twenty seconds due to total brain oxygen starvation (Rossen 1943, Aminoff 1988). Furthermore, increasing degrees of permanent brain damage occur after 5 minutes of absent circulation, and the longest time someone has ever survived without circulation at normal body temperature is about 10 to 20 minutes (Safar 1988).'

'Precisely,' said Ben pouring himself another glass, and taking a cautious sip. 'Hey, this doesn't taste so bad after one glass. Anyway, to return to our subject, cardiac arrest causes rapid failure of body function due to sudden failure of oxygen supplies to the tissues of the body. The first organs and tissues of the body to fail are those consuming most oxygen, which is why the functioning of the brain and the eyes are first affected. Furthermore, the effects of differing degrees of oxygen starvation on the eyes and the brain are similar for each person, because body structure and function are the same for all people. This explains why there are so many similarities in the reports of the experiences undergone by people resuscitated for cardiac arrest.'

'But people undergoing resuscitation for cardiac arrest aren't oxygen starved at all!' interjected Abdulaziz. 'Measurements show that the blood of people undergoing cardiac resuscitation often contains more oxygen than normal (Fillmore 1970, Langhelle 2000, Tucker 1994)! So how can you say people undergoing cardiac resuscitation are oxygen starved? That's nonsense.'

'Not at all. A given volume of blood can only carry so much oxygen, and the maximum amount of oxygen able to be carried by a given volume of blood is about 20 millilitres oxygen per 100 millilitres blood. In the situation of cardiac arrest, blood may contain as much oxygen as it is possible for blood to contain, but because the heart no longer pumps any blood around the body, this oxygen is going nowhere, and therefore does not reach any of the tissues of the body. Cardiac massage generates a pumping action, and accordingly does result in oxygen carrying blood being pumped around the body. However, the amount of blood being pumped around the body during cardiac massage is usually much less than normal, so although the blood is full of oxygen, not enough reaches the tissues needing it, which is why nearly all people are oxygen starved during resuscitation for cardiac arrest. I would say this is a basic fact of resuscitation. Wouldn't you agree Abdulaziz?'

'I guess so when you look at it like that,' he grumbled, as he drank more wine. He had also begun his second glass. 'You're right Ben, this stuff does start tasting better after a glass or two. Even so, it's still outrageously awful wine. However, as to what you just said, you're quite correct. Those are the basic facts of body function. If the heart pumps too little blood, then the tissues of the body will be starved of oxygen, even though the blood contains maximal amounts of oxygen. So you tell me how much pumping action is generated by cardiac massage, and here I mean cardiac massage as is applied by a person rapidly and forcefully compressing the chest of a person. This is called external cardiac massage to distinguish it from internal cardiac massage where the chest is cut open and the heart is rhythmically squeezed to simulate the normal action of the heart.'

Thomas sat quietly and reflectively drank his wine. It was indeed a dire and desperately sour concoction whose only redeeming features were its price and its alcohol content. This fascinating discussion was telling him the answers he wanted to hear on this very same subject. He settled himself to listen further.

'There are actually surprisingly few measurements of the efficiency of external cardiac massage in adults,' said Ben. 'I've only ever managed to find a total of 18 measurements (Christensen 1990, Del Guercio 1963, Del Guercio 1965). It's a shame there are so few measurements, but even these few measurements do provide sufficient information to determine whether people without any heartbeat or breathing can be conscious during cardiac massage.'

This was too much for Abdulaziz. He, an experienced specialist in cardiology was getting a lesson in cardiology from some general practitioner! He spluttered, 'This is nonsense, absolute twaddle! I've never heard of, or seen people being conscious during heart massage. People cannot be conscious during heart massage for cardiac arrest, because they are clinically dead, meaning they have no heartbeat and do not breathe. So near-death experiences during cardiac arrest and resuscitation are due to separation of an immaterial consciousness from the material, clinically dead body.'

Ben calmly drank some wine, and grinned mischievously, 'Hmmm, what an interesting idea ... So you mean that all people without a heartbeat are dead?'

'Yes, very definitely, because their hearts no longer beat.'

'Ah, but what about people with artificial hearts, for example those with implanted artificial hearts awaiting heart transplantation?'

'What do you mean by that?'

Ben now hammered his argument home, 'Precisely this. Some people awaiting heart transplantation have a heart so diseased that they will most likely die before a suitable donor heart becomes available. So in some wealthy, technologically advanced countries, the diseased heart is removed and replaced with an artificial heart. This artificial heart pumps blood around the body, sustaining consciousness and life in the person until a transplant heart becomes available, sometimes months later. People with such an artificial heart can often even lead a nearly normal life (Copeland 2004, Takatani 2002). In other words, you don't need a heart to stay alive and active. You just need something to pump blood around the body. Don't you agree?'

Abdulaziz began to look uncomfortable, 'Er ... Yes ... that is true.'

'In other words my esteemed colleague, this means that absence of heartbeat does not necessarily mean a person is dead at all. Life, consciousness, and the level of physical activity are determined solely by the amount of blood pumped by the heart each minute. So if the amount of blood pumped by the heart decreases sufficiently, the flow of blood through the brain is reduced sufficiently enough to affect brain function (Bornstein 1995, Gruhn 2001, Saha 1993), and when the amount of blood pumped by the heart is very low indeed, unconsciousness and death occur. Absence of breathing is also no definition of death. People who no longer breathe can be kept alive with artificial respiration, and still be fully conscious. Accordingly, under certain circumstances, absence of heartbeat, and absence of breathing do not mean a person is dead. So the real question with people undergoing cardiac massage, is how much blood must the heart pump each minute to sustain some sort of consciousness? Are you still following me?'

'Yes, yes. But you're still only stating known facts again.'

Thomas listened with ever growing amazement as he heard the way Abdulaziz changed his opinions without blinking, blushing, or any sort of manifest embarrassment. He drank more wine. This was entertainment!

'I know Abdulaziz, but as Thomas can testify, I sometimes suffer from episodes of excessive pedantry, and then I start with basic concepts first so I don't have to repeat them. The lowest cardiac output capable of sustaining consciousness in adults was determined quite inadvertently during studies comparing different techniques for measuring the amount of blood the heart pumps each minute. These studies revealed that some adults can be conscious at cardiac output levels as low as 1.7 litres per minute (Hoeper 1999, Yung 2004),' said Ben.

'Hmm ... That's pretty low when you consider the average cardiac output of a resting adult is about four to six litres per minute. But when are you finally going to get to the point of what you are saying?' was the irritable response of Abdulaziz.

'Okay, here it comes. Do you still agree that the function of cardiac massage is to cause a pumping action of the heart?'

'Of course,' said Abdulaziz.

'Well, those measurements of the cardiac output generated by external cardiac massage I told you about reveal that external cardiac massage performed on adults generates a cardiac output of 1.7 l/min, or above, in about 40% of adults (Christensen 1990, Del Guercio 1963, Del Guercio 1965). This means that about 4 in 10 adults undergoing external cardiac massage for cardiac arrest undergo such efficient resuscitation, that they have a cardiac output potentially capable of sustaining consciousness! Of course this doesn't mean that exactly 4 in 10 people will be conscious during external cardiac massage, it only means that up to 4 in 10 people have the potential to be conscious, or partially conscious during external cardiac massage. The actual proportion of people that really is conscious during external cardiac massage is likely to be much smaller, because it takes a while to recover from unconsciousness induced by several minutes of severe brain oxygen starvation (Cantanzaro 2006). However, there is another way of estimating whether people may be conscious during a cardiac arrest, and this may give a more accurate figure.'

'Okay, you've done a form of sleight of hand with a few measurements of the efficiency of external cardiac massage. So do continue,' grumbled a morose sounding Abdulaziz as he poured himself a third glass of wine, gloomily reflecting upon how this upstart was unimpressed by his expertise, as well as mentioning some annoyingly good points.

Thomas had already begun with a third glass too, and settled back in his chair again, preparing himself to watch the next instalment of this debate.

'The other way to calculate whether people can be conscious during external cardiac massage is to calculate backwards from the minimum flow of blood through the brain needed to sustain consciousness,' began Ben.

'Oh, and how does this doctor propose to do that?' was the sarcasm-laden reaction from Abdulaziz.

'It sounds impressive, but the calculation is really quite simple,' said Ben, as he nonchalantly drained his glass.

- The adult human brain weighs at most about 1500 grams.
- Normal flow of blood to the adult brain is about 52 ml/100 grams brain tissue/minute, which means a total flow of blood through a 1500 grams adult brain of about 780 ml/minute.
- Normal brain function is maintained in adults until the flow of blood through the brain decreases below 31.5 ml/100 gm brain tissue per minute (Bandera 2006, Finnerty 1954, Sundt 1981). But this figure of 31.5 ml/100 gm brain tissue per minute is an average value, meaning that when you measure the level of blood flow at which brain function begins to become abnormal, then you measure levels which are both higher and lower, and you get an

average of 31.5 ml/100 gm brain tissue per minute. So this is why measurements show that consciousness can be sustained in some people until the flow of blood through the brain drops below 17.5 ml/100 gm of brain tissue per minute (Finnerty 1954). This means that if the minimum flow of blood through the brain needed to sustain consciousness in some people is about 17.5 ml/100 grams brain tissue per minute, then you can calculate that a total blood flow of about 260 ml/minute through an average 1500 gram adult brain is all that is needed to sustain consciousness in some people. And I mean some people – not all people.

- About 13% of the blood pumped by the heart goes to the brain, the remainder sustains the rest of the body. So if a minimum blood flow through the brain of 260 ml/minute is needed to sustain consciousness, then the heart must pump at least 2000 mls of blood with normal oxygen content per minute to sustain consciousness in some adults. Notice again – I say only some adults, and not all adults.
- Studies of the efficiency of cardiac massage reveals that cardiac massage generates a flow of blood greater than 2000 ml/minute in about 20% of persons undergoing external cardiac massage. This means that as many as 20% of people may be partially, or fully conscious, while undergoing cardiac massage during a cardiac arrest.

'So you see it is potentially possible for about 20% to 40% of all adults to have some form of conscious experience while undergoing resuscitation from cardiac arrest,' concluded Ben.

'Spoken like a true sophist!' grumbled Abdulaziz. 'I must admit it's a nice calculation, and you'll certainly fool a few people with your reasoning. Even so, I classify it as pure sophistry, which means that if it sounds true, and if you believe it, then it is true for you. But I'm not fooled by you. I still don't think it's possible for people to be conscious during external cardiac massage. After all, I have never heard of, or seen patients who were awake during external cardiac massage, and I've resuscitated a lot of people during my career as cardiologist.'

'A good argument,' thought Thomas as he expectantly looked at Ben, who without pausing for a moment began a counter offensive.

'Aha, my dear Abdulaziz,' he said with a smile on his face, 'you've forgotten one thing. Some people may be conscious while undergoing cardiac massage during cardiac resuscitation, yet appear unconscious because they are incapable of moving due to the effects of oxygen starvation on their brains.'

Abdulaziz laughed, 'This wine is really quite dreadful, but as yet I haven't noticed any hallucinogenic effects on myself or Thomas. So where do you get this bizarre, weird, and even fantastical idea that people can remain conscious, yet be paralyzed due to oxygen starvation?'

Ben demonstratively emptied his glass, 'I've discussed this concept of apparent unconsciousness due to oxygen starvation with Thomas before (see Chapter 6).' Thomas nodded as Ben continued, 'However you've apparently never heard of it. Increasingly severe oxygen starvation causes paralysis of all muscles before causing loss of consciousness. This is why people subjected to increasingly severe degrees of oxygen starvation first notice that their limbs appear to weigh more than usual, as if they were made of lead, and each movement requires intense mental effort. Even more severe oxygen starvation results in total paralysis of all voluntary movements: the eyes remain fixed and staring, and even intense mental effort fails to result in any movement or speech (Liere 1963, page 317 & Rossen 1943). People affected by this degree of oxygen starvation appear unconscious, because they cannot move or speak. Yet they are not unconscious, they are only apparently unconscious. Oxygen starvation due to the lower than normal flow of blood through the brains of people undergoing cardiac massage for cardiac arrest can induce just such a condition of paralysis and apparent unconsciousness in some people.'

'Well, I'm still not convinced.'

'You really are a hard man to convince. There are two ways to answer your doubts. One way is to find actual measurements of the flow of blood through the brain generated by external cardiac massage in humans, and the other is to find clinical cases of people who were actually conscious during external cardiac massage.'

'I doubt very much you'll find anything,' was the very definite response.

'Then I'll surprise you,' said Ben brightly. 'There aren't many measurements of the flow of blood through the brain during external cardiac massage. Even so, there are a few published measurements. These measurements show that the flow of blood through the brain generated by external cardiac massage is potentially capable of sustaining consciousness in about one half of the investigated adults (Christensen 1990). So I looked around for reports of people who were actually conscious during cardiac massage performed for cardiac arrest. I found accounts of two people who were very definitely conscious during cardiac massage for proven cardiac arrest published by a cardiologist called Maurice Rawlings (Rawlings 1979, pages 2-3, and pages 14-16). I also spoke with some intensive care nurses, coronary care unit nurses, as well as anaesthetic nurses, because many of them have extensive experience resuscitating patients. They told me of seeing some patients who were definitely awake during external cardiac massage for proven cardiac arrest. One story was particularly interesting.'

Nurse H.A. told a story of an event she witnessed during 1980-1981 when she was training as an intensive care nurse in the Dijkzigt Hospital in Rotterdam. During one of her duty shifts, an approximately 50-year-old woman was admitted into the intensive care. Shortly after admission she developed a heart rhythm called ventricular fibrillation, which is a deadly heart rhythm – deadly because the heart does not pump blood during ventricular fibrillation. Within a few seconds this woman lost consciousness because her brain received no blood. All this was observed by the doctors and nurses present. Within seconds they began external cardiac massage and artificial respiration. Shortly after cardiac massage began, and while still in ventricular fibrillation according to the heart monitor, the woman awoke, tried to sit up and plaintively called, 'Oh doctor, oh doctor ...' All present were amazed and immediately thought that the heart monitor was only showing electrical noise instead of her real rhythm, and stopped with external cardiac massage. But the heart monitor electrodes apparently were attached correctly, and the rhythm shown on the monitor was correct, because the woman collapsed unconscious back onto the bed a few seconds after stopping cardiac massage. External cardiac massage and ventilation were

started again, and the same occurred again. She again awoke,
tried to sit up, and again plaintively called, 'Oh doctor, oh doctor
...' Everyone stopped again, and events were repeated yet again.
She remained in ventricular fibrillation, ultimately developed no
heartbeat at all, and despite insertion of an electrical pacemaker
during a vigorous two-hour long resuscitation, she ultimately
died. Awakening during cardiac arrest in such a dramatic manner
is rare, which is why Nurse H. A. could so vividly remember these
events even 24 years afterwards (Personal communication-2).

Abdulaziz sniffed disdainfully, 'Are these hoary old stories the only
ones you could dredge up?'

'Of course not. I've heard others, but this was the most dramatic. It's
also a wonderful illustration of the speed of unconsciousness due to
oxygen starvation. But stories like these are stories of people who were
resuscitated within seconds of cardiac arrest and onset of unconsciousness.
However, cardiac resuscitation of people who suffer a cardiac arrest
usually only begins after a minute or more has elapsed. The brains of these
people have been exposed to a longer and more severe period of oxygen
starvation, resulting in a longer recovery time even under optimal circumstances. Moreover, the flow of blood and oxygen to the brain generated by
cardiac massage and artificial respiration is often insufficient to restore
consciousness, and when it is, recovery from such severe oxygen starvation
is not instantaneous (Longstreth 1987 & Liere 1963, pages 302-303). This
explains why not everyone is overtly conscious, or able to undergo a near-
death experience during cardiac massage.'

'Even so Ben, how can people have conscious experiences when they
are "flatlined"?' interjected Thomas.

'By "flatlined" I suppose you mean that brain electrical activity as
manifested by the electroencephalogram is absent. It is true that the
electroencephalogram signal, which is a measure of the electrical activity of
the brain, flattens and disappears 30 to 60 seconds after the heart ceases to
pump blood to the brain during a cardiac arrest (Aminoff 1988, Visser
2001).' Ben paused to wet his throat with some more wine. 'However,
there are very few electroencephalogram recordings of people made during
a sudden spontaneous cardiac arrest. It's simply never done routinely,

because it is too time consuming. Nonetheless, there are some cases where people undergoing resuscitation for cardiac arrest were attached to an electroencephalogram machine at the time. These case studies do reveal that cardiac massage combined with artificial respiration does restore electrical brain activity as measured with an electroencephalograph, although not to normal levels (Chakravarthy 2003, Kluger 2001, Szekely 2002). All these things prove that brain activity is present during efficient cardiac resuscitation for cardiac arrest. In other words, no immaterial souls or separable consciousness are required to explain near-death experiences during cardiac arrest.'

Both Thomas and Abdulaziz looked unconvinced.

'Okay, okay,' continued Ben. 'I see I haven't managed to convince you entirely. I'll explain further. Oxygen starvation due to cardiac arrest generates such a standard set of changes in the brain and sensory organs that it is possible to describe a stereotype near-death experience generated by a cardiac arrest. Here it is.'

- The flow of blood to the body stops because the heart stops beating, as a result of which no blood flows to the brain, and the brain is subjected to total oxygen starvation. Rapidly progressive oxygen starvation of the brain commences. Oxygen starvation of the brain first causes failure of prefrontal cortex function, causing affected people to feel serene and indifferent, or even euphoric, as they "fade away". Subsequently, oxygen starvation of the brain causes failure of those parts of the brain called the supplementary motor cortex, the frontal eye fields, Broca's speech cortex, and the primary motor cortex (figure 7.2). Failure of these parts of the brain causes the eyes to stare fixedly straight ahead, people are paralyzed and unable to move or speak, even when they try to do these things. At this time the retina also fails due to oxygen starvation, and people may first notice tunnel vision, followed by total darkness. Yet surprisingly they are able to hear quite well at this time because hearing is one of the last senses to fail.

- People are unconscious within five to twenty seconds, and can neither sense nor experience anything. Their bodies are discovered and resuscitation with heart massage commences. Cardiac massage performed by some people is so efficient that their efforts generate a flow of blood around the body sufficient to sustain life. Sometimes this flow of blood is even sufficiently high enough to restore consciousness, but usually it is just sufficient to restore some degree of consciousness. But this is not normal consciousness, because the brain does not recover very rapidly. Normal consciousness takes longer to return than it takes to restore pumping action of the heart.

- Oxygen starvation of the eyes is somewhat reversed, restoring tunnel vision and subsequently normal vision. At the same time, oxygen starvation, stress, and adrenaline administered as part of the resuscitation medication causes the pupils to widen, and so people see bright light at the end of a tunnel. Furthermore, abnormal interpretation of bodily sensations, together with abnormal muscle spindle function, generates sensations of movement and floating, and so some affected people perceive themselves to be travelling down this tunnel towards the bright light. Restoration of function of the entire retina restores the ability to see light, but does not restore normal pupil size (adrenaline effect). So affected people perceive themselves to be passing out of the tunnel into the light – they are "enveloped by the light".

- At this same time, during a period of partial consciousness, people may undergo wondrous hallucinatory experiences such as life-review, seeing deceased relatives, or seeing gods and other holy figures from their religious pantheons. Such experiences are partly delusory due to misinterpretation of bodily sensations, and sometimes due to abnormal electrical activity caused by oxygen starvation within the structures of the temporal lobes of the brain.

- During eventually successful resuscitations, blood flow through the organs of the body is restored, and consciousness gradually returns to near normal. People being resuscitated may then be sufficiently conscious to be able to hear doctors and nurses speak – hear what they say, what they do, and all other sounds in their vicinity, even though they appear unconscious due to oxygen starvation. Doctors and nurses regularly open the eyelids of people undergoing resuscitation to check pupil reactions to light. And sometimes the eyes remain open during resuscitation. This is how some people can see what is happening around their bodies during their resuscitation. These sensations, combined with abnormal sensory information from muscle spindles, together with abnormal interpretation of muscle spindle sensations can generate a sensation of displacement and movement out of the body. All these things generate out-of-body experiences during which people see and hear everything occurring to their bodies and around their bodies. Failure of prefrontal function means they still feel calm and serene at this time, as well as indifferent to pain.

- Successful resuscitation means that pumping action of the heart is restored and normal consciousness returns. Some people remember these wondrous conscious experiences, and are able to tell others of the experiences they underwent during the period they lay motionless, apparently unconscious and dead, while undergoing resuscitation for cardiac arrest.

'So,' continued Ben, 'supernatural explanations are not needed to explain reports of near-death experiences undergone by people during resuscitation for cardiac arrest. Nor are explanations such as a soul, or a mind which exists separately from the body required. The functioning of the body explains all aspects of near-death experiences occurring during cardiac resuscitation.'

'Yes, that's all very well,' said Abdulaziz, 'but what about the report of Pim van Lommel of a patient who recognized a male nurse present during his cardiac resuscitation. This man was unconscious and being resuscitated at the time this male nurse appeared, and so could not possibly have seen this male nurse. Yet more than a week later, this man not only recognized the male nurse, but also remembered where this nurse placed his dentures while he was unconscious and being resuscitated (Lommel 2001). You can't explain that with plain physiology.'

Thomas nodded slowly, and looked expectantly at Ben.

'Oh,' sighed Ben in a tired voice, 'that story again. Let's first look at the report, then we can analyze it.'

During the pilot phase (of Pim van Lommel's research) in one of the hospitals, a coronary-care-unit nurse reported a veridical out-of-body experience of a resuscitated patient: "During a night shift an ambulance brings in a 44- year-old cyanotic, comatose man into the coronary care unit. He had been found about an hour before in a meadow by passers-by. After admission, he receives artificial respiration without intubation, while heart massage and defibrillation are also applied. When we want to intubate the patient, he turns out to have dentures in his mouth. I remove these upper dentures and put them onto the 'crash car'. Meanwhile, we continue extensive CPR [cardiac resuscitation]. After about an hour and a half the patient has sufficient heart rhythm and blood pressure, but he is still ventilated and intubated, and he is still comatose. He is transferred to the intensive care unit to continue the necessary artificial respiration. Only after more than a week do I meet again with the patient, who is by now back on the cardiac ward. I distribute his medication. The moment he sees me he says: 'Oh, that nurse knows where my dentures are'. I am very surprised. Then he elucidates: 'Yes, you were there when I was brought into hospital and you took my dentures out of my mouth and put them onto that car, it had all these bottles on it and there was this sliding drawer underneath and there you put my teeth.' I was especially amazed because I remembered this happening while the man was in deep coma and in the process of CPR. ..." (Lommel 2001)

'How can you explain this story other than with some sort of paranormal perception?' said Abdulaziz. 'This man was incapable of seeing where his dentures were placed, and incapable of having seen the male nurse.'

'You buy a decent bottle of wine if I can explain this, otherwise I'll buy a bottle. Is that a deal?' asked Ben expectantly.

Abdulaziz looked carefully at Ben's insincerely innocent smile, 'Okay, I'll do it, but only if you can explain it.'

'Very well, here it comes,' began Ben. 'This man was found in a meadow, but was evidently still alive, although unconscious – otherwise he would simply have been brought to the mortuary. Once admitted to the hospital he developed a lethal abnormal heart rhythm called ventricular fibrillation. This necessitated the application of cardiac massage and artificial respiration. During this procedure he was evidently conscious, although unable to indicate the fact, because of oxygen starvation induced muscle paralysis. Part of the normal procedures during cardiac resuscitation is to open the eyelids to assess the size of the pupils, because pupil size is an indication of the severity of brain oxygen starvation (Steen-Hansen 1988). At this time this man would have seen the face of the male nurse he later recognized, as well as the room in which he was being resuscitated. Being conscious, he would have felt the procedures being applied, he would have felt his dentures being removed, and heard the sound of them being placed in a metal drawer of the "crash car", he would have heard the speaking of the people resuscitating him, and the sounds of activity in the room. He may have even heard people confirming that his dentures were placed in the "crash car", because nurses and doctors in Holland always take great care not to lose dentures. He would be able to hear this very well, because hearing is one of the last sensations to disappear, being preserved even when a person is rendered blind and paralyzed by oxygen starvation (Liere 1963, page 306). This man was paralyzed but conscious during these events, so he could only relate his story as a memory after recovering from his cardiac arrest and regaining the ability to speak. This is the background of this superficially remarkable account. So there you have it, no paranormal perceptions or other fantastical immaterial wonders are required to explain the observations of this man. I'm going to enjoy this wine!'

Abdulaziz looked unhappy. This was going to cost him a bottle of good wine – a bottle of wine much more expensive than the cheap and nasty house red wine they had slowly been forcing down their throats. Suddenly, he brightened, as if he had seen a "bright light that does not hurt the eyes". But it was not a light he saw – it was the sound of the Mare Mosque calling the faithful to prayer, 'Allahu Akbar Allah, Allahu Akbar Allah, Allahu Akbar Allah, Allahu Akbar Allah ...' He suddenly stood up, saying, 'I've got to go to the mosque. It's time for my prayers. However, it's improper for a true believer such as me to buy or serve alcohol during prayer times, so I can't buy you another bottle of wine. However, feel free to pollute your infidel bodies with more alcohol during my absence.' And without further ado, he left, walking quickly in the direction of the Mare Mosque.

'An opportunist, and a poor loser,' commented Ben, 'as well as one who is going to prayers after drinking alcohol. Not quite what is generally permitted.'

O ye who believe! Draw not near unto prayer when ye are drunken, till ye know that which ye utter, nor when ye are polluted, save when journeying upon the road, till ye have bathed (Koran 4:43)

'At least he's not drunk,' responded Thomas.

'We won't be getting any wine from him, but what about a reasonable bottle and some food? It's time for dinner, and I'm hungry after all that talking.'

'Sounds like an outstanding idea to me ...'

Chapter 13

Nightfall

'Now that's what I call a decent Shiraz', said Ben as he unabashedly and appreciatively slurped from his wineglass. 'Much better than that red-coloured, tonsil-withering battery acid we just had. Ah well, look at the bright side, at least Abdulaziz also drank some that wretched stuff too.' He looked approvingly at the meal set before him, and sighed happily. 'Good food and wonderful wine. This is paradise. Let's enjoy ourselves.'

Thomas sipped his wine with equal appreciation, but remained silent, wrapped in thought. He picked listlessly at his food.

'Okay Thomas, come on, out with it. For the last few minutes you've been looking like you've lost your last cent. You've got something on your mind. Something is bothering you. What is it?'

'We've been talking and discussing any number of subjects related to religion for several months. I've really enjoyed our discussions, and they have certainly changed the way I regard Christianity, Judaism, and Islam. My way of thinking has become more liberal, and yet more constructively critical. I don't just accept things on faith alone any more. I ask for proof. I look about me at my fellow theology students, at some of my teachers and preachers, and I see only benighted, dogma driven bigotry in many of them. Throughout my life, and despite my changing views on religion, I've always been sustained by a belief in the ultimate reality of God, as well as the reality of an immaterial soul which lives eternally after death of the body. But now, after this last discussion I find it difficult to believe in the reality of God, the soul, or an afterlife. Your logic and explanations of how natural laws, as well as the functioning of the human body provide apparent evidence for my belief in what I once thought were the fundamental truths of religion, have finally almost hammered my last shreds of faith in these beliefs into nothingness. Once I was comforted and strengthened by these beliefs, but now I only have a few shreds of my once strong faith to sustain me. I am even beginning to feel my life is as bleak, empty, and purposeless as expressed in the book of Ecclesiastes in the Bible.'

> *Man's fate is like that of the animals; the same fate awaits them both: As one dies, so dies the other. All have the same breath; man has no advantage over the animal. Everything is meaningless. All go to the same place; all come from dust, and to dust all return. (NIV Bible, Ecclesiastes 3:19-20)*

'I am sorry you look at things that way Thomas. That's an appalling way of looking at life. Admittedly I have emphasized the more negative aspects of the holy texts of Judaism, Christianity, and Islam, but I did this because there is an incredible amount of totally insane evil distributed among the very good messages contained within these texts. By knowing the evil and the insane, you are able to expunge them from your personal philosophy, leaving you with an uplifting humanistic religion – or just humanism if you want to eliminate God altogether – a humanism that really does empower and improve its followers.'

'That sounds encouraging, and is possibly even true,' responded Thomas. 'However, even though your explanations of supposedly paranormal phenomena using natural laws and the functioning of the bodily do explain a lot, and have destroyed many of my beliefs, I still feel there is some basic holy force, some guiding principle in all of our lives, a force many people feel and experience within the core of their being, not just now in the present, but have done for countless millennia. So tell me how you would explain this? I think that to deny this incredibly fundamental core of religion is pretty conceited for an atheistic upstart like you who has lived for only a few decades.'

'Ahh Thomas ... The ancient deep-rooted feeling there must be a God, or at least some organizing force greater than man. The fact that people have had this feeling for thousands and thousands of years means nothing. It's no proof of God; it is simply a desire for a God. There are countless logical reasons why the very idea of God, and the reality of God, is no more than a ridiculous delusion (Dawkins 2006). However, I've only discussed how all the apparent indirect proofs of God as revealed by the paranormal, out-of-body experiences, and near-death experiences, can all be explained by the functioning of the body as well as the laws of nature. I did this, because I know that for you and many other people, logical refutations of God are ultimately meaningless. Yours, and many other people's belief in God, is the result of a profound feeling and emotion that there must be something more than this physical world – a profound feeling that is buttressed by all the apparent supernatural proofs of the reality of an immaterial world revealed by the functioning of your body together with natural phenomena. And why do I say this? I know that after explaining all the logical reasons why God does not, and even cannot exist, someone will always stand up and say, "Your logic may be correct, but it's still a load of twaddle, because last night I had an out-of-body experience which proves I have a soul! This is proof of an immaterial world in which there is a God." Or they might say, "My brother had a near-death experience as a result of a cardiac arrest, during which he saw God, Jesus and the angels in heaven! So God is real in spite of all your logic!" This is why I explained how the functioning of the body and natural laws explain all these apparent indirect and direct proofs of an immaterial world in which God is real. And who can really criticize such beliefs? Explanations of these experiences are not always evident. Moreover, belief in a God is really wonderful; it gives everyone the comforting feeling of being guarded and watched over by a loving but stern parent. Better yet, the reality of a God explains everything: the mystery of existence, of life, all natural and seemingly unnatural phenomena, as well as promising those who have done well in the eyes of God everlasting life in a paradise inhabited by the souls of the dead, and a suitably horrid eternity of torment for the enemies of God. God provides believers with a total explanation for the meaning of life and existence in general. Furthermore, this is not just any explanation; this explanation comes complete with an almost irrefutably rigid, and internally consistent logic. But is this true? A Dutch philosopher called Baruch Spinoza (1632-1677 CE) once defined people and the universe in general as aspects of God, saying that the universe itself is God. There is nothing anthropomorphic about this definition of God. This is not a God with a warm affection for the true followers of God, nor is it a God exacting vengeance upon vile unbelievers, nor is it a God that communicates with prophets – the universe itself is God, so we are all part of God (Spinoza 1677, Part 1 – On God). In my opinion this is not a bad definition of God, because we are all part of the universe, and we are all manifestations of the wonders existing in the awesome vastness and grandeur of the totality of this universe. You almost get poetic and lyrical when you consider God in this way. I can accept this idea of God, because I can neither prove, nor disprove this definition of God. Nonetheless many believers hunger for a more anthropomorphic God: a god who watches over them, a God testing them every now and then with adversity, a God who exacts a satisfyingly horrible punishment on those who disobey God, a God with whom they can have a warm and gooey relationship, a God who loves the long suffering weak and meek.'

Blessed are the meek: for they shall inherit the earth. (KJV Bible, Matthew 5:5)

'So Thomas, how do you want your God: personal, warm and gooey, yet at the same time, stern, just and vengeful, or just plain indifferent?' asked Ben as he drank deeply from his glass, and enthusiastically attacked his meal. 'This is really quite good wine. Drink up Thomas! Enjoy your meal! Be cheerful! What we are doing and talking about is predestined anyway.'

'I guess so,' sighed Thomas as he also started eating, and sipped his wine cautiously. 'You're right, this is good wine,' and drank deeply. 'Even so, despite everything you and others have said, Jews, Christians, and followers of Islam all consider the reality of God to be self evident.'

Ben emptied his glass, refilled it, sipped contentedly, 'Oh that old chestnut again. Saint Paul was once in the city of Lystra, where he also claimed God was clearly manifest everywhere in the reality of this world.'

... and saying, Sirs, why do ye these things? We also are men of like passions with you, and bring you good tidings, that ye should turn from these vain things unto a living God, who made the heaven and the earth and the sea, and all that in them is: who in the generations gone by suffered all the nations to walk in their own ways. And yet He left not himself without witness, in that he

did good and gave you from heaven rains and fruitful seasons, filling your hearts with food and gladness. (ASV Bible, Acts 14:15-17)

'And,' continued Ben, 'the followers of Islam and Judaism say exactly the same. They also claim the wonders we see about us in our world are clear proof of the reality of God. This is the old nonsense of creation versus evolution, and the newer unintelligent pseudoscientific drivel vomited up by those believing in "intelligent design". A few minutes with some books on astrophysics and evolutionary biology teaches you there are perfectly natural explanations for all these things. The universe does not require the existence of some paranormal and wondrous creator. Nonetheless, belief in a God is so inherently and profoundly satisfying to the human mind that it is difficult not to believe in a God. God really does explain everything. God explains adversity, because just as in the case of the prophet Job (Bible, Job 1 & 2), God uses adversity to test the faith of those believing in God. In other words, we must give thanks to God for adversity, instead of blaming our own ineptitude or the actions of others. This really is a truly satisfying way of looking at adversity, but as I said, it's a way of putting the blame on someone else instead of acknowledging your own faults, or the fact that nature is sometimes hard. However, God does not only test believers with adversity, God also rewards and aids the believers, and God always punishes the unbelieving in the afterlife.'

He will come down like rain upon the mown grass, As showers that water the earth.

In his days shall the righteous flourish, And abundance of peace, till the moon be no more.

He shall have dominion also from sea to sea, And from the River unto the ends of the earth.

They that dwell in the wilderness shall bow before him; And his enemies shall lick the dust. (ASV Bible, Psalms 72:6-9)

'Nothing like thoroughly good chastisement of unbelievers to make you feel really happy in the knowledge that God is on your side,' continued Ben.

Thou [God] hast also given me the shield of thy salvation: and thy right hand hath holden me up, and thy gentleness hath made me great.

Thou hast enlarged my steps under me, that my feet did not slip.

I have pursued mine enemies, and overtaken them: neither did I turn again till they were consumed.

I have wounded them that they were not able to rise: they are fallen under my feet.

For thou hast girded me with strength unto the battle: thou hast subdued under me those that rose up against me.

Thou hast also given me the necks of mine enemies; that I might destroy them that hate me. (KJV Bible, Psalms 18:35-40)

Ben paused to wet his throat with more wine, continuing his chain of argument. 'Great stuff! I really enjoy these bloodthirsty songs of praise to a "loving" God! Wonderfully vengeful passages like these abound in the holy books of Judaism, Christianity, and Islam. Such passages show the human mind to be a violent cesspool, revealing that deep in the darkest recesses of the human mind there is nothing quite so intensely satisfying as the humiliation, castigation, and crushing of enemies! As for natural phenomena – we know natural phenomena are just products of natural laws, and not the result of Godly intervention. We know this for certain, because if God influenced natural events and laws of nature such that believers were aided, and unbelievers confounded, then prediction and calculation of natural events and natural laws would no longer be identical for followers of different religions. But we know that the natural laws determining the weather, the paths of the planets, satellites, rockets, stones, arrows, and bullets, are the same for followers of Islam, as for followers of Judaism, as they are for followers of Christianity. This is yet more proof that God does not favour believers in what might be construed as the one true religion. All this proves that either God does not exist, or that God is totally indifferent to what happens on this world, and so we return to Spinoza again.' Ben emptied his glass in one gulp. 'I need more wine!'

Thomas had seen Ben thirstily eyeing the remnant of wine in the bottle as he was declaiming, so he had quickly drained his glass, and emptied what remained in the bottle into his empty glass. He sipped some of this wine, but even so, he did not look happy with this little victory. Instead he stared despondently somewhere in the distance. It was not quite clear to Ben whether Thomas was despondent because his plate was empty, or due to a crisis of belief.

Both men sat in silence, staring at nothing, engulfed by the almost palpable dejection emanating from Thomas. Ben broke the silence. He was thirsty, and Thomas had egoistically grabbed the last remaining wine in the bottle. The seriously withered condition of his tonsils, and the parched state of his throat, which was still recovering from the wine they had drunk earlier, decided him. 'Thomas, instead of us just desperately looking at this empty bottle, let's order another one. The ancient Greek historian Herodotus (484-425 BCE) gave some sound and timeless advice to wine-lovers like us about an ancient Persian custom.'

> It is also their general practice to deliberate upon affairs of weight when they are drunk; and then on the morrow, when they are sober, the decision to which they came the night before is put before them by the master of the house in which it was made; and if it is then approved of, they act on it; if not, they set it aside. Sometimes, however, they are sober at their first deliberation, but in this case they always reconsider the matter under the influence of wine. (Herodotus, Book 1, page 143)

'So let's drink more wine and examine this matter of God further. Waiter, another bottle of the same wine please!'

'I suppose you're right Ben,' sighed Thomas. 'I've still got a lot of questions and problems with this idea of a totally indifferent God or universe, or however you would want to view it.'

The new bottle arrived. Both men sipped appreciatively. Ben put his glass down, looked contentedly at it as he idly ran his finger over the rough stem of the cheap glass. 'Okay, what is your problem with the idea that God does not exist, or is at best totally indifferent? After all, we've talked about the fact that God and other beings, such as angels and Satan, are paranormal immaterial beings. The paranormal doesn't exist, which means these beings don't exist in the way most people and you seem to believe.'

'I know ... I realize you also dismiss the evidence of prophecies, because you say these are no more than manifestations of the paranormal, and the paranormal simply doesn't exist. Even so, despite all the logic you and others bring to bear on this matter, and despite all your wonderful explanations of how the functioning of the human body and natural laws explain all paranormal phenomena, I'm not entirely convinced, because there is still the evidence of the power and reality of God revealed to us by the evidence of miracles – some trivial, others spectacular. These miracles were often witnessed by other people, and their witness is actually quite conclusive proof of the reality and veracity of these miracles. What do you say about them?'

'Oh no ... Here we go again ... The old miracle story again. After all my logic, and after all my explanations of how the functioning of the body and natural laws explain the apparent proofs of the reality of God, you come up with another so-called proof of the reality of God! Now it's miracles! You really are persistent,' groaned Ben theatrically. He fortified himself with more wine, and started again. 'Thomas, belief in the reality of God is based upon faith in the reality of an invisible and immaterial all-powerful, all-knowing, and all-pervading entity. You cannot physically see, touch, or sense God in any way. So in fact, all you have is faith in the reality of God. But the believer who only has faith in the reality of God will soon lose this faith, unless this faith is supported in some way. Faith in God must be sustained by works and actions that are clearly due to God, otherwise faith and belief in God and religion will disappear. Indeed, Jesus also said this very same thing.'

> *And it was the feast of the dedication at Jerusalem: it was winter; and Jesus was walking in the temple in Solomon's porch.*
>
> *The Jews therefore came round about him, and said unto him, How long dost thou hold us in suspense? If thou art the Christ, tell us plainly.*
>
> *Jesus answered them, I told you, and ye believe not: the works that I do in my Father's name, these bear witness of me. But ye believe not, because ye are not of my sheep. (ASV Bible, John 10:22-26)*

'Now the necessity for miracles is something really very strange,' continued Ben, 'Christianity, Judaism, and Islam, all require their followers to believe in invisible, immaterial, and supernatural beings such as God, angels, and Satan. Furthermore, the faith of their followers in the belief they propound is proven to be true by supernatural prophecies, miracles, and wonders. Yet these same religions do not tolerate witchcraft, or the use of paranormal forces and perceptions – condemning the use and belief in these same forces and perceptions as the vilest form of heresy deserving of death (see Chapter 4). In other words, it is good if a supernatural God, or genuine card-carrying God-approved prophets of flesh and blood use these powers, but not if anyone else employs them. This is a real double standard. Wonderful and breathtaking hypocrisy! This is the true face of believers in a good and just God revealed! For example, what if an ordinary person prays to God and this prayer is miraculously granted? Who determines whether this miracle was truly approved by God, or whether it was simply witchcraft, upon which the person should be put to death? What do you think Thomas? Don't you find it incredibly strange the way religions are supported by the very things they condemn?'

'Er, yes ...' gulped Thomas with a mouthful of wine. 'However, regardless of the difficulties associated with this seeming double standard, as I said, these miracles were witnessed by many people who vouched for their reality. So how do you explain these miracles?'

Ben thought for a moment. 'There are actually so many miracles, that it is simply impossible to explain them all in detail, suffice to say that they can all be explained with natural forces, which is hardly surprising because paranormal perceptions or forces are illusions. So I'll just illustrate a few of the most interesting miracles. Let's begin with the story of the revival of the widow's son by the prophet Elijah (Bible, 1 Kings 17:8-24). Elijah was a prophet of God in the country of Judah at a time most Jews had forsaken God for a local god called Baal. Prophets and priests of God were proscribed and killed on sight. So Elijah was a hunted man. Fortunately, a widow who believed in God secretly housed and fed him. This woman had a son who became sick, and eventually died. She bewailed her fate, and blamed God for her son's death. Elijah took the boy upstairs to the room where he was staying, laid the boy on his bed, and prayed to God. Then he did something surprising.'

> *And he cried unto Jehovah, and said, O Jehovah my God, hast*
> *thou also brought evil upon the widow with whom I sojourn, by*
> *slaying her son?*
>
> *And he stretched himself upon the child three times, and cried*
> *unto Jehovah, and said, O Jehovah my God, I pray thee, let this*
> *child's soul come into him again.*
>
> *And Jehovah hearkened unto the voice of Elijah; and the soul*
> *of the child came into him again, and he revived. (ASV Bible, 1*
> *Kings 17:20-22)*

'Just think of it Thomas. The prophet Elijah stretched himself upon the boy three times and then the child revived. This sounds suspiciously like Elijah used mouth to mouth resuscitation to revive the boy, or stimulated him to activity in other ways I prefer not to think about. This boy was clearly not dead at the time, because after a time period longer than 15 to 20 minutes after cardiac arrest at a normal body temperature, cardiac resuscitation just does not work, and people simply remain dead (Safar 1988). The boy was evidently just very weak, rendered paralyzed and unresponsive by his illness, so that he had almost imperceptible respiration, and appeared dead, which is why the ministrations of Elijah were sufficient to break the paralysis and restore consciousness. Nothing paranormal is needed to explain this miracle.'

'I guess not. But what about the miracle of the sun and the moon standing still?'

Ben drank some wine, and laughed, 'Oh that one where the ancient Jewish leader Joshua and his army attacked and totally defeated the army of the Amorites (Bible, Joshua 10:7-15). A quick summary of the facts ... After marching all night, Joshua and his army made a surprise attack on the Amorite army. God helped by raining large hailstones upon the Amorites, killing more Amorites than the Jewish army. Joshua also prayed, or rather he ordered the sun and the moon to stand still, so they had a longer period of daylight in which to kill Amorites.'

> *Then spake Joshua to Jehovah in the day when Jehovah deliv-*
> *ered up the Amorites before the children of Israel; and he said in*
> *the sight of Israel,*

Sun, stand thou still upon Gibeon; and thou, Moon, in the valley of Aijalon. And the sun stood still, and the moon stayed, until the nation had avenged themselves of their enemies.

Is not this written in the book of Jashar? And the sun stayed in the midst of heaven, and hasted not to go down about a whole day. (ASV Bible, Joshua 10:12-14)

'How would you explain that miracle?' asked Thomas.

'No problem. This was simply a record of a battle taking place on the day of the summer solstice, which is always on the 21st of June, the longest day of the year. Again, no supernatural explanation is needed, just Joshua exploiting a known natural phenomenon to prove he was inspired by God. This type of thing works very well with the gullible who really do want to believe.'

'Okay, okay,' said Thomas in a somewhat irritated tone. 'What about the miracle of Jesus raising Lazarus four days after his death? You can't get away with using a common sense explanation here. This man was dead and buried for four days, so he very definitely couldn't be resuscitated, even today with modern medical technology, and certainly not with the primitive level of medicine practiced in Judea at that time. Restoring the dead to life under these circumstances is something only God, or Jesus the Son of God can do. So the miracle of Lazarus is true proof of the reality of the divinity of Jesus and the reality of God, which is what the writer of the Book of John in the Bible also clearly realized.'

Jesus therefore answered and said unto them, Verily, verily, I say unto you, The Son can do nothing of himself, but what he seeth the Father doing: for what things soever he doeth, these the Son also doeth in like manner.

For the Father loveth the Son, and showeth him all things that himself doeth: and greater works than these will he show him, that ye may marvel. For as the Father [God] raiseth the dead and giveth them life, even so the Son [Jesus] also giveth life to whom he will. (ASV Bible, John 5:19-21)

'Oh yes ... that passage,' said Ben. 'Only God can restore life to the dead, or "quicken" them as is elegantly expressed in antique English. This passage can also be considered as a breathtakingly effective ploy to divert attention away from any critical analysis of the facts surrounding the supposed resurrection of Lazarus, or of any other person supposedly resurrected by the prophets for that matter. Now I must admit that the story of Lazarus is one of my favourite miracles, because the Bible reveals such a wealth of information about the circumstances surrounding this apparent miracle that it is very easily explained (Bible, John 11:1-45).'

'I've studied the New Testament of the Bible intensively, yet I've never seen this wealth of information you claim is present.'

'The information is all there, only you have to understand what you're looking at.'

'Okay, then tell me. I'm all ears,' said Thomas sitting straighter in his chair.

'Very well Thomas, you asked for it ... Lazarus was a man, and a friend of Jesus, who lived in the town of Bethany where his sisters Mary and Martha also lived. While Jesus was staying in Jordan to evade the fundamentalist Jews who were trying to kill him (Bible, John 10:22-40), he received a message from these sisters that Lazarus was sick, but even so he decided to stay where he was for two more days before travelling to Bethany. He even told his disciples before leaving for Bethany that Lazarus was already dead (Bible, John 11:14). In Bethany they were greeted by the two mourning sisters, whom Jesus asked to take him to the grave of Lazarus. As usual, the presence of Jesus attracted a crowd of interested spectators and friends who followed them to the grave. On their way to the grave, the apparently grief-stricken Jesus groaned demonstratively.'

Jesus therefore again groaning in himself cometh to the grave. It was a cave, and a stone lay upon it.

Jesus said, Take ye away the stone. Martha, the sister of him that was dead, saith unto him, Lord, by this time he stinketh: for he hath been dead four days.

Jesus saith unto her, Said I not unto thee, that, if thou wouldest believe, thou shouldest see the glory of God?

Then they took away the stone from the place where the dead was laid. And Jesus lifted up his eyes, and said, Father, I thank thee that thou hast heard me.

And I knew that thou hearest me always: but because of the people which stand by I said it, that they may believe that thou hast sent me.

And when he thus had spoken, he cried with a loud voice, Lazarus, come forth.

And he that was dead came forth, bound hand and foot with graveclothes: and his face was bound about with a napkin. Jesus saith unto them, Loose him, and let him go. (KJV Bible, John 11:38-44)

'Now this is fantastic stuff,' continued Ben enthusiastically. 'Careful examination of this, and other passages reveals that Jesus had a very good suspicion that Lazarus was not dead, but had been prematurely buried while still alive. Just examine how Jesus behaved at the tomb. Lazarus had not been buried. Instead his body had been laid to rest on a shelf in a family tomb. It is warm in the middle-east, so Martha was quite right when she said Lazarus would stink after four days. Jesus waved her objections away, and the stone covering the entrance of the tomb was rolled away, but no stench of decay is mentioned. The lack of any overpowering odour of decay indicated to Jesus that his guess that Lazarus was not dead was very likely correct. After all, the speed of decay in the warm climate of the Middle-East is the reason Jewish custom required burial of the dead before sunset on the day of death, or as soon as possible on the next day (Bible, Deuteronomy 21:23). Jesus knew these things, but just in case Lazarus really was dead, he remained outside to avoid defilement by contact with a dead person (Bible, Numbers 19:11-22). Now Jesus was clearly a real showman, which is why he first loudly thanked God so everyone could hear, "Father, I thank thee that thou hast heard me. And I knew that thou hearest me always: but because of the people which stand by I said it, that they may believe that thou hast sent me." Only then; only after thus publicly establishing the miraculous nature of this event, did he call to Lazarus. Then this apparent miracle occurred; Lazarus hobbled out of his tomb, bound and gagged in traditional Jewish grave clothing, and without any evident odour of decay whatsoever. Lazarus did not stink when he hobbled out of his tomb, which he certainly would have done had his body been rotting for four days. The stench of decaying bodies is particularly lingering and penetrating; it would certainly have been mentioned had this stench wafted out from the tomb, or clung to the grave clothing of Lazarus. This means Lazarus was never dead at all, but had been buried alive while in a condition of apparent death. Lazarus had been prematurely buried! Once bound up in traditional Jewish grave clothing, his jaw also bound up, and with a large and heavy stone rolled in front of the tomb, all he could do, if at all capable of moving, was to hop, roll around and make muffled "mm, mmm, mmmm" sounds. He was therefore hardly likely to be heard while closed up in his tomb. This was no resurrection, but the release of a prematurely buried man from a slow and horrible death in the pitch darkness of a tomb!'

'I think that's a really cynical interpretation of these passages. But you do have a point about the stench of decay. Why was that absent? They certainly would have mentioned it if a disgusting odour of decay clung to his living body after four days decomposition in the cave.'

'That's why I said Jesus almost certainly knew what was going on beforehand,' said Ben. 'He even admitted as much to his followers, but corrected himself so they would be awed by this seeming miracle.'

'Don't be ridiculous Ben! This is a serious matter.'

'But Jesus did know what to expect. When he first heard of the illness of Lazarus, he first told his disciples that Lazarus would not die.'

But when Jesus heard it, he said, This sickness is not unto death, but for the glory of God, that the Son of God may be glorified thereby. (ASV Bible, John 11:4)

'This is astounding Thomas! He actually told his disciples that Lazarus wouldn't die, and that his disease was intended to glorify the Son of God. In other words, the sickness of Lazarus was intended to glorify Jesus himself! Now why would he say that if he didn't know Lazarus was only sleeping?' This is why he didn't seem particularly worried about the illness of his friend Lazarus, and stayed where he was for another two days. Finally, after two relaxing days he decided to go to Bethany, and told his disciples he was going to awaken Lazarus (Bible, John 11:11). His disciples thought he meant Lazarus was only sleeping, but Jesus quickly corrected them, saying not only that Lazarus was dead, but that his death was intended as proof of the divinity of Jesus to his disciples.'

Then Jesus therefore said unto them plainly, Lazarus is dead. And I am glad for your sakes that I was not there, to the intent ye may believe; nevertheless let us go unto him. (ASV Bible, John 11:14-15)

'So Thomas, as you now realize, the Bible provides us with a wealth of explicit and implicit insights into this miracle,' continued Ben as he drank more wine. 'It's quite evident Jesus knew from his friendship with Lazarus that Lazarus was subject to episodes of a coma-like condition – most likely catatonia. Catatonia is a condition induced in some susceptible people by emotions such as severe emotional stress, severe illness, schizophrenia, or epilepsy. It causes stiffening of the muscles, in addition to which, severely affected people no longer speak or even react to severe pain, and their body functions such as breathing and heartbeat may be reduced to a minimum (Baxter 2003, Freudenreich 2007, Penland 2006). Severely affected people appear as if in a deep coma, or even dead to the untrained eye. Jesus realized it was possible that Lazarus would be buried while in a catatonic state induced by his illness. So Jesus even counted on Lazarus being alive after his four days of entombment! This is why Jesus quickly corrected himself by saying Lazarus was dead, and that he was glad of this, because then he could give his disciples and others an example of his divine powers, and by so doing, glorify himself as the Son of God. Accordingly, he put on a really good performance at the entrance of the tomb, so arousing wonder and awe in all who observed. Yes, Jesus certainly was a "good friend" of Lazarus. He rewarded the friendship of Lazarus by subjecting him to the unspeakable torment of being bound and entombed in total darkness for four days! Who needs enemies when you've got a friend like Jesus? I can only conclude from these passages that Jesus was a sect leader who ruthlessly exploited the weaknesses of the people who believed in him for his own ends, just as Saint Peter later did with Ananias and Sapphira (see Chapter 3). However I may be wrong. It may well be that the ways of God, and the Son of God, are simply inscrutable to a mere mortal such as I.' At this almost triumphant conclusion, Ben drained his glass and looked at Thomas.

Thomas was silent, amazement written large over his face. His jaw hung. It moved up and down a few times as if he wanted to say something. Eventually he recovered some measure of control. 'Unbelievable, unbelievable ...' was all he managed to mutter, and also drained his glass. He looked pale and withdrawn.

Ben refilled their glasses, and seemingly undisturbed by the effect of his last words, continued, 'Now we come to the matter of Islamic miracles. Curiously, there are very few of these in comparison with the traditions of Judaism and Christianity. According to Islamic tradition, the greatest miracle of Islam is the gift of the Koran by God to humankind to reveal the true nature of God. Even so, there are a few other miracles, but I'll discuss only some of them. The first one I'll mention is the splitting of the moon. Yes Thomas, according to legend Mohammed actually caused the moon to split in two!'

Narrated Ibn Masud: During the lifetime of Allah's Apostle the moon was split into two parts; one part remained over the mountain, and the other part went beyond the mountain. On that, Allah's Apostle said, "Witness this miracle." (Bukhari 60:387)

'Huh!' was the amazed reaction from Thomas, who suddenly revived, colour returning to his cheeks, and an animated expression on his face.

'You're back! It's a miracle!' exclaimed Ben. 'So tell me why you reacted so dramatically.'

'I was staggered by your character assassination of Jesus. At the same time I was stunned by the truth of your analysis of the literal meanings of these Bible passages. Your interpretation of one of the most well known miracles of Jesus, using the same Bible passages as do true believers in Christianity, revealed a profound fundamental truth to me. This apparent miracle is a perfect illustration of using selective interpretation to buttress faith, while ignoring other information which is also clearly present. It was a sudden, personally shocking revelation, and a profoundly depressing one. All my years of belief in the reality of this miracle were proven to be no more than mere delusion! And then you go on with another miracle ...

this miracle of splitting the moon. This is patently ridiculous, totally impossible! I don't know too much about astronomy and astrophysics, but if Mohammed split the moon in two pieces such that the two pieces were displaced as far apart as this Hadith tells us, this would be a dramatic and momentous event. It would have been seen in all places on the earth where the moon was visible at that moment. Furthermore, the gravitational effects of such a temporary splitting of the moon upon the earth and the tides of the sea would have been felt by everyone at the time. Such an astounding event would have been recorded in the writings and legends of all lands where the moon was visible at the time. Yet I have never ever heard of ancient writings and legends telling of the splitting of the moon. In fact, ancient writers and ancient legends are strangely silent about seeing the moon split into two pieces, or related phenomena, during the lifetime of Mohammed (570-632 CE). The first I ever heard of such an event is in this Hadith you just told me. So I can only conclude that this story is a product of mass hallucination or a fable.'

'That's what I want to hear … critical analysis,' said Ben. 'However, most people believe this Hadith is a misinterpretation of a part of the Koran talking about the signs of the end of time (Koran 54:1-8).'

The hour drew nigh and the moon was rent in twain. (Koran 54:1)

'Now we come to another miracle of Mohammed,' continued Ben. 'This is the astonishing miracle of the well.'

Narrated Al-Bara: We were one-thousand-and-four-hundred persons on the day of Al-Hudaibiya (Treaty), and (at) Al-Hudaibiya (there) was a well. We drew out its water not leaving even a single drop. The Prophet sat at the edge of the well and asked for some water with which he rinsed his mouth and then he threw it out into the well. We stayed for a short while and then drew water from the well and quenched our thirst, and even our riding animals drank water to their satisfaction. (Bukhari 56:777)

'Come on now,' said Thomas, 'you surely can't classify this as a miracle. The only astonishing thing about it, is that anyone would even call it a miracle. If you have a shallow well, or a well in a water table that is not very porous, then the rate at which the well fills is limited. This means you have to wait every now and then for the well to fill again after withdrawing some water. There is absolutely nothing miraculous about this so-called miracle at all!'

'That's what I call logic and the use of common sense,' was the response from Ben. 'You're quite correct. Shall we discuss the miracle of the earth vomiting up the corpse of a lying Christian no less than three times (Bukhari 56:814)?'

'Er ... do we have to? Is it worth discussing?'

'Not especially. It is easily explained by postulating that some wags or fanatics secretly dug up the dead Christian more than three times.'

'Thank you for not sparing me the gruesome details.'

'Always glad to help cheering people up. Well Thomas, I'm glad to see you've recovered somewhat from this analysis of miracles. Does this short discussion dispel your faith in miracles and wonders?'

'I suppose if you analyze miracles and wonders in the way you do it, then you can always find an alternative logical, mechanistic, or material explanation for each individual miracle and wonder.' Thomas frowned. He sighed unhappily. 'You've clearly demonstrated that prophecies and miracles are mere misinterpretations, or manifestations of quite natural phenomena. So the reality of God is neither confirmed by prophecies, nor by any of the so-called miracles performed by God, or the prophets of God. Nonetheless I still feel deep within myself that there is a God, even though I only have faith to support this belief. I also understand my equally deep-rooted belief in a life after death is totally unreasonable. Yet these beliefs are so deeply ingrained in my being, and so comforting, that I find them impossible to exorcise. How do you deal with this dichotomy between these deep-rooted instinctive feelings, and the logical explanations of all aspects of religion we've been discussing?'

'Hmm ...' Ben drank more wine. 'The best way of approaching these instinctive matters of faith is to first discuss this instinctive and deep-rooted belief in a life after death. What do you imagine a life after death would be like? What would you do during a life after death?'

'Ben, I suppose it sounds very stereotyped, but I would imagine that my soul when freed from my body would spend eternity worshipping the glory that is God. I would speak with others, with my family and ancestors, with Einstein, Voltaire, Descartes, Confucius, many other holy men and women, and countless other great scientists and philosophers. We've discussed an alternative, logical explanation for near-death experiences, but this view of the nature of life after death is what these experiences reveal, and is all we have as a guide. So I imagine that's how it would be during a life after death.'

'You really have sketched a very stereotyped view there Thomas. Let's look logically at the implications of such an eternal life as you sketch it. But first, let's get another bottle of this very decent wine.' Another bottle was brought to their table, and their glasses charged. Ben sipped slowly and began. 'You speak of meeting and speaking with your family and ancestors, as well as with many great scientists, religious leaders and philosophers. I imagine these famous people will be very busy in a life after death, because everyone seems to want to speak with them. These conversations would undoubtedly be fascinating. But for some curious reason, no one ever seems to want to speak with ordinary people. Think of the fascinating discussions you could have with a chimney-sweeper, an exploited housemaid, a slave, a simple peasant, a prissy housewife, a leper, a stillborn baby, members of a primitive tribe, or raped and murdered citizens of a conquered city. Yet no one seems to want to speak with such people, they only want to speak with famous people. Strange isn't it? Then we come to the subject of spending eternity in the company of your family members. They are probably very charming and nice people. Yet how would you think about them after spending one hundred years in their company, or one thousand years, or even one million years. And then to think, we are not talking here about a paltry one million years in their company, but all eternity until the universe itself dies. You would go mad with boredom after only one hundred years. I know I would. Horrible, horrible.'

'Yes, you certainly have a point there. Strange that no one ever mentions this aspect of eternal life.'

'I know, and it gets even weirder. Just think of this. Eternal life is just that – eternal. Just imagine yourself praying in a Synagogue, a Church, or a Mosque, worshipping the glory of God. Can you imagine yourself continuously worshipping the Glory of God without rest, and with the same fervour, for one hundred years, for one thousand years, for one million years, for eternity? I don't think so. You would get bored very quickly. Heaven would be a nightmare of everlasting boredom, which begs the question of whether heaven is actually another name for a Gehenna of eternal tedium. I imagine you sometimes feel bored on a wet afternoon, so just imagine what an endless life after death would be like. Would you still want a never-ending life after death when you consider these things?'

'Ah, but Ben, what if the soul manifests its true character after death, so that none of these things would ever get boring?'

'Nice try Thomas. However, let's imagine you are so religious that your soul enters some sort of mindless holy trance while worshipping God in this life after death. This means you do would nothing all eternity, except remain in some sort of mindless rapture of everlasting worship. Why would God want this? So tell me Thomas, would you want to spend an eternal life after death toadying to God in some sort of never-ending mindless trance? Sounds like a nightmare to me. There is another aspect to this concept of the soul changing to its true character after death. This concept implies that the behaviour of the living mortal body is not a reflection of the true character of the soul, which would make evil and good irrelevant, because these would be manifestations of the body and not of the immortal soul. Where then is the loudly proclaimed justice of God who punishes the souls of those who have been evil, and rewards the souls of those who have been good during their mortal lives? This would make a total travesty of the fundamental religious dogma of punishment of the evil and reward of the good. Furthermore, you cite the so-called evidence of near-death experiences, but when you examine these experiences carefully, you discover that the personality of the disembodied soul is no different to that of the mortal body while alive. So this concept of the soul revealing its true character after death is invalid. It is totally unsupported by logic, and unsupported by the so-called evidence of near-death experiences. Moreover, as we have discussed time and again, there is absolutely no evidence for the existence of an immaterial human soul. And because there is no soul, there is no afterlife in which the soul continues to live after death. I can only conclude from all these things that because we have no souls, and hence no afterlife, we are spared the horrendous tedium of everlasting life after death. So be glad and welcome your ultimate death! It may not be comfortable or dignified, but at least you won't have to live forever!'

'Fascinating Ben ... After listening to all this, I agree eternal life after death is not something I would ever want. Brrrr ... The very thought of the appalling dreary monotony of an everlasting life after death is enough to exorcise the demon of that belief out of my mind forever! But what about my belief in God? Why do I still persist against all reason in entertaining this belief?'

'Because all people, you and I, search for order in the seeming chaos of the vast universe in which we live. Believing in an all-pervading, all-knowing and all-powerful God, the creator and controller of all this magnificence, provides just such order. This belief tells you God has created the universe, and all beings living in this universe, for some grand purpose known only to God.'

'Aha! So you do believe in God!' said Thomas.

'Well ... Yes and no ...' was the cautious response. 'Explaining the physical reality behind the paranormal, wonders, prophecies, and miracles totally destroys these so-called proofs of the reality of God. This, together with the inconsistencies in the holy texts of Judaism, Christianity, and Islam, reveal the concept of God as proposed by these religions to be nonsense, or at best untenable. However, no amount of logic or physical evidence can prove or disprove the existence of a totally indifferent God who simply created the universe, and then left everything to proceed of its own accord. All believers in God really have to sustain them is just faith, but as we have seen, there is absolutely no evidence to support this faith. In fact, the only refuge for the believer in the reality of God is faith, and the uncertainty expressed as, "but what if we're wrong?" There is no answer to this last question. People sensitive to such uncertainty will always remain willing converts, willing prey of any form of faith-driven belief making them feel good, while purportedly offering answers to everything. True courage is to accept uncertainty, to accept the "what if?", while keeping an open mind ready to accept and critically analyze everything. There is no more than this. This is all you can say about the reality of God.'

'So Ben, you're saying Judaism, Christianity, and Islam are nonsense because they spread false ideas about God and a life after death.'

'Oh dear ... I do believe you're getting a bit dogmatic. What I've done is to show you the logical inconsistencies, and dementedly insane cruelties propagated in the texts of these religions. Yet these three religions are not just about foisting dementedly cruel or idiotic behaviour and dogmas upon their followers, they also propagate uplifting and ennobling philosophies very akin to those of humanism. These philosophies are actually a wonderful form of socio-cultural cement based upon fundamentals of human existence: the basic physical necessities of food, water, air, shelter, and children. All societies implicitly build a framework of cooperation to achieve these aims, so allowing most individuals to survive, and the society to perpetuate itself. Judaism, Christianity, as well as Islam all do just this. But why not openly and explicitly acknowledge these basic facts, instead of hiding these truths behind a smokescreen of the non-existent supernatural? Why grovel in nauseating obsequious sycophancy before an illusory God, hoping as do dogs and little children for gifts and rewards from this God? Belief in a God who rewards believers and punishes sinners is a childish belief in a God with the same characteristics as Santa Claus. Such a religion is a Santa Claus religion, where good children get presents, and naughty children are punished! Grow up! Be realistic. Look at everything we've discussed. It all indicates two possibilities – God is indifferent or just plain dead! Religions have served humanity well in the past, but the time is ripe for a new and mature philosophical paradigm. We are humans! We are sentient and proud of it! We know the true facts and fundamental basics of our existence and immortality. Knowledge of these things is a system of thought, a paradigm enabling individuals and societies to review their situation, to adapt, to be flexible, and to change rapidly according to circumstances, while acknowledging the true nature of our being and the universe in which we live. Such materialism or humanism does not mean the end of ethics, nor does it mean we are animals. Instead, it ennobles and uplifts, giving us a new socio-cultural glue, while at the same time placing a great burden upon us the living to practice good husbandry in maintaining the world for posterity. Indeed, each person, no matter how insignificant their role, plays a part in forming this future. And posterity is but part of our true individual immortality. After all, each of us truly is immortal: we are immortal because of the fact of our existence at a given time and place, we are immortal because of the effects each of us exerts upon our world, and we are immortal in the memories of our existence carried in the minds of the living. These three components form the triad of true individual immortality, for these things are engraved upon the fabric of the universe for all time. This is true immortality, and a true philosophy of life based upon the reality of the universe in which we live!' declaimed Ben excitedly.

Thomas and Ben subsided into silence. They sat, slowly drinking the last of their wine. Ben looked blearily at the empty plates and bottles on the table to see if there was something to eat he might have missed. Suddenly, they were aroused, rudely shaken to full consciousness by a frenzied, 'Clang, clang, clang ...' as all the church bells of Leiden suddenly started pealing.

'Listen,' exclaimed Ben, as the bells continued ringing. 'The night is come!'

Thomas stared fuzzily at Ben, 'But it's been night for some time already. So what's new?'

'Listen ...' said Ben again, and they listened to the pealing of the bells. The bells rang loudly, continuously, almost joyously clamouring to be heard after a long silence. 'Listen ... Until now these church bells were forbidden to ring at all. But this year, for the first time, they may now ring on this one evening of the year. They peal to ring in the eve of Eid ul Adha, the Islamic Feast of Sacrifice. Hear them ... These bells herald the descent of all critical thought into the foul murk of dogma and fanaticism. Hear them ... They are ringing in an unending night of mindless obedience to ancient dark doctrines.'

They sat in silence. They listened to the frenetic clamouring of the bells, two men, pawns at the mercy of blind forces propelling their world into the dark of a night so long that dawn was no more than a dream ...

References

Abouleish, E., Taylor, F.H., (1976), Effect of morphine-diazepam on signs of anesthesia, awareness, and dreams of patients under N2O for cesarean section. *Anesthesia and Analgesia*, 55: 702-705.

Afonso, A., Katz, B.F.G., Blum, A., et al., (2005), A Study of Spatial Cognition in an Immersive Virtual Audio Environment: Comparing Blind and Blindfolded Individuals. *Proceedings of ICAD 05-Eleventh Meeting of the International Conference on Auditory Display, Limerick, Ireland, July 6-9, 2005*, pages 228-235.

Akerl, K., Atzmueller, M., Grammer, K., (2002), The scent of fear. *Neuroendocrinology Letters*, 23: 79-84.

Alcock, J.E., (2003), Give the null hypothesis a chance. Reasons to remain doubtful about the existence of psi. *Journal of Consciousness Research*, 10: 29-50.

Al-Fozan, S.S., (1997), *The Book of Tawheed*, translated by M.R. Murad, published by Darussalam, Riyadh, Saudi Arabia.

Alkire, M.T., Haier, R.J., Fallon, J.H., (2000), Toward a Unified Theory of Narcosis: Brain Imaging Evidence for a Thalamocortical Switch as the Neurophysiologic Basis of Anesthetic-Induced Unconsciousness, *Consciousness and Cognition*, 9: 370-386.

Alm, A., Bill, A., (1973), Ocular and optic nerve blood flow at normal and increased intraocular pressures in monkeys (Macaca irus): A study with radioactively labelled microspheres including flow determinations in brain and other tissues. *Experimental Eye Research*, 15: 15-29.

Alves, R., Aloe, F., Tavares, S., (1999), Sexual Behavior in Sleep, Sleepwalking and Possible REM Behavior Disorder: A Case Report. *Sleep Research Online*, 2: 71-72.

Aminoff, M.J., Scheinman, M.M., Griffin, J.C., et al, (1988), Electrocerebral accompaniments of syncope associated with malignant ventricular arrhythmias. *Annals of Internal Medicine*, 108: 791-796.

Arbous, M.S., et al, (2001), Mortality associated with anesthesia: a quantitative analysis to identify risk factors. *Anaesthesia*, 56: 1141-1153.

Arditi, A., Holtzman, J.D., Kosslyn, S.M., (1988), Mental imagery and sensory experience in congenital blindness. *Neuropsychologia*, 26: 1-12.

Askenasy, J.J.M., Yahr, M.D., (1990), Different laws govern motor activity in sleep than in wakefulness, *Journal of Neural Transmission*, 79: 103-111.

Bachmann, G.A., (1990), Hysterectomy, a critical review. *Journal of Reproductive Medicine*, 35: 839-862.

Baldwin, D.L., (2005), Teaching blind children to navigate. This article was published on the internet at: http://www.wayfinding.net/navigate.htm

Bandera, E., Botteri, M., Minelli, C., et al., (2006), Cerebral Blood Flow Threshold of Ischemic Penumbra and Infarct Core in Acute Ischemic Stroke. A Systematic Review. *Stroke*, 37: 1334-1339

Barrett, W., (1986), *Death-Bed Visions. The Psychical Experiences of the Dying*, first published in 1926, republished by the Aquarian Press, England, ISBN 0-85030-520-9.

Bat Ye'Or, (2005), *Eurabia: The Euro-Arab Axis*, published by Fairleigh Dickinson University Press, USA, ISBN 083864077X.

Baxter, C.L., White, W.D., (2003), Psychogenic coma: case report. *International Journal of Psychiatry in Medicine*, 33: 317-322.

Bertolo, H., Paiva, T., Pessoa, L., et al., (2003), Visual dream content, graphical representation and EEG alpha activity in congenitally blind subjects. *Cognitive Brain Research*, 15: 277-284

Bertolo, H., (2005), Visual imagery without visual perception? *Psicológica*, 26: 173-188.

Bhagavad-Gita As It Is. Complete edition. Translated by A.C. Bhaktivedanta Swami Prabhupada, published by the Bhaktivedanta Book Trust, ISBN 0-89213-268-X.

Bible, American Standard Version, (ASV Bible), a translation correcting many inaccuracies and inconsistencies present in the King James Version of the Bible. Published in 1901 CE.

Bible, Good News Bible, (GNB Bible), a modern translation using the source texts. First published in 1976 CE.

Bible, New International Version, (NIV Bible), a modern translation using the source texts completed in 1978 CE.

Bible, King James Version, (KJV Bible), One of the first good English language translations of the Bible. First published in 1611 CE.

Birbaumer, N., Lutzenberger, W., Montoya, P., et al., (1997), Effects of Regional Anesthesia on Phantom Limb Pain Are Mirrored in Changes in Cortical Reorganization. *Journal of Neuroscience*, 17: 5503–5508.

Blacher, R., (1980), Letter, Journal of the American Medical Association, 244: 30.

Blackmore, S., (1993), *Dying to Live. Near-Death Experiences.* Published by Prometheus Books, USA, ISBN 0-87975-870-8.

Blanke, O., Perrig, S., Thut, G., et al., (2000), Simple and complex vestibular responses induced by electrical cortical stimulation of the parietal cortex in humans. *Journal of Neurology, Neurosurgery and Psychiatry,* 69: 553-556.

Blanke, O., Ortigue, S., Landis, T., et al., (2002), Stimulating illusory own-body perceptions. The part of the brain that can induce out-of-body experiences has been located. *Nature,* 419: 269-270.

Blanke, O., Landis, T., Spinelli, L., et al., (2004), Out-of-body experience and autoscopy of neurological origin. *Brain,* 127: 243-258.

Bogen, J.E., (1995), On the neurophysiology of consciousness: 1. An overview. *Consciousness and Cognition,* 4: 52-62.

Bornstein, R.A., Starling, R.C., Myerowitz, P.D., Haas, G.J., (1995), Neuropsychological function in patients with end-stage heart failure before and after cardiac transplantation. *Acta Neurologica Scandinavica,* 91: 260-265.

Braun, A.R., Balkin, T.J., Wesensten, N.J., et al., (1997), Regional cerebral blood flow throughout the sleep–wake cycle: An H215O PET study. *Brain,* 120: 1173-1197.

Breckenridge, J.L., Aitkenhead, A.R., (1983), Awareness during anaesthesia: a review. *Annals of the Royal College of Surgeons of England,* 65: 93-96.

Brugger, P., Kollias, S.S., Müri, R.M., et al., (2000), Beyond re-membering: Phantom sensations of congenitally absent limbs. *Proceedings of the National Academy of Sciences (USA),* 97: 6167-6172.

Bukhari, (Sunnah of Sahih Al-Bukhari). This is a compilation of the sayings and deeds of the Prophet Mohammed by the scholar Muhammad Ibn Ismail Ibn Ibrahim Ibn al-Mughirah Ibn Bardiziyeh al-Bukhari, (810-870 CE). It is considered one of the most authoritative compilations. This compilation enjoys a status almost equal to the Koran in the Islamic world, and especially so among the Sunni Moslems, a group comprising about 85% of all followers of Islam. This book quotes from the M. Mushin Khan translation published by the University of Southern California, Moslem Students Association, found at the internet site: http://www.usc.edu/dept/MSA/fundamentals/hadithsunnah/bukhari/ The format of the citation is: Bukhari Book Y: Number Z, which is shortened to Bukhari Y:Z.

Burke, D., Hagbarth, K.E., Lofstedt, L., et al., (1976), The responses of human muscle spindle endings to vibration during isometric contraction. *Journal of Physiology,* 261: 695-711.

Buzzi, G., Cirignotta, F., (2000), Isolated Sleep Paralysis: A Web Survey. *Sleep Research Online,* 3: 61-66.

Cantazaro, J.N., Makarus, A.N., Rosman, D., et al., (2006), Emotion-Triggered Cardiac Asystole-Inducing Neurocardiogenic Syncope. *Pacing and Clinical Electrophysiology,* 29: 553-556.

Cardinale, M., Lim, J., (2003), Electromyography Activity of Vastus Lateralis Muscle During Whole-Body Vibrations of Different Frequencies.

Journal of Strength and Conditioning Research, 17: 621-624.

Chakravarthy, M., Patil, T., Jayaprakash, K., et al., (2003), Bispectral Index Is an Indicator of Adequate Cerebral Perfusion During Cardiopulmonary Resuscitation, *Journal of Cardiothoracic and Vascular Anesthesia,* 17: 506-508.

Chen, D., Haviland-Jones, J., (2000), Human olfactory communication of emotion. *Perceptual and Motor Skills,* 91: 771-781.

Chen, D., Katdare, A., Lucas, N., (2006), Chemosignals of fear can enhance cognitive performance in humans. *Chemical Senses,* 31: 415-423.

Christensen, S.F., Stadeager, C., Siemkowicz, E., (1990), Estimation of cerebral blood flow during cardiopulmonary resuscitation in humans. *Resuscitation,* 19: 115-123.

Cicero, M.T., *De Senectute.* This book was written by Marcus Tullius Cicero, (106-43 BCE), Translated by M.A. Falconer, Loeb Classical Library, published by Harvard University Press, England, 1996, ISBN 0-674-99170-2.

Copeland, J.G., Smith, R.G., Arabia, F.A., et al., (2004), Cardiac Replacement with a Total Artificial Heart as a Bridge to Transplantation. *New England Journal of Medicine,* 351: 859-867.

Damasio, H., Grabowski, T., Frank, R., et al., (1994), The Return of Phineas Gage: Clues About the Brain from the Skull of a Famous Patient. *Science,* 264: 1102-1105.

Davis, B., (2006), *Royal Air Force Bomber Command 1939-1945.* see website at: http://www.elsham.pwp.blueyonder.co.uk/raf_bc/

Dawkins, R., (2006), *The God Delusion,* published by Bantam Press, USA, 406 pp., ISBN 9780593055489.

Del Guercio, L.R.M., Coomaraswamy, R.P., State, D., (1963), Cardiac output and other hemodynamic variables during external cardiac massage in man. *New England Journal of Medicine,* 269: 1398-1404.

Del Guercio, L.R.M., Feins, N.R., Cohn, J.D., et al., (1965), Comparison of blood flow during external and internal cardiac massager in man. *Circulation,* 31: 171-180.

Derry, C.P., Duncan, J.S., Berkovic, S.F., (2006), Paroxysmal Motor Disorders of Sleep: The Clinical Spectrum and Differentiation from Epilepsy. *Epilepsia,* 47: 1775-1791.

Dewhurst, K., Beard, A.W., (1970), Sudden Religious Conversions in Temporal Lobe Epilepsy, *British Journal of Psychiatry,* 117: 497-507.

Dobelle, W.H., Mladejovsky, M.G., (1974), Phosphenes produced by electrical stimulation of human occipital cortex, and their application to the development of a prosthesis for the blind. *Journal of Physiology,* 243: 553-576.

Dobell, A.R., Bailey, J.S., (1997), Charles Drew and the origins of deep hypothermic circulatory arrest. *Annals of Thoracic Surgery,* 63: 1193-1199.

Domhoff, G.W., Schneider, A., (2004), *Studying Dream Content Using the*

Search Engine and Dream Archive on Dreambank.net. Paper presented to the meetings of the American Psychological Society, Chicago, May 29, 2004.

Drexler, W., Findl, O., Schmetterer, L., et al., (1998), Eye accommodation in humans: differences between emmetropes and myopes. *Investigative Ophthalmology & Visual Science*, 39: 2140-2147.

Duane, T.D., (1966), Experimental blackout and the visual system. *Transactions of the American Ophthalmological Society*, 64: 488-542.

Edgecomb, K.P., (2002), Chronological Order of Quranic Suras. See the internet at address: http://www.bombaxo.com/chronsurs.html

Editorial (anonymous), (1979), On being aware. *British Journal of Anaesthesia*, 51: 711-712.

Ehrsson, H.H., (2007), The experimental induction of out-of-body experiences. *Science*, 317: 1048.

Encyclopaedia Britannica.

Evans-Wentz, W.Y., (translator), (1960), *The Tibetan Book of the Dead*, published by the Oxford University Press, England.

Fay, T., Smith, G.W., (1941), Observations on reflex responses during prolonged periods of human refrigeration. *Archives of Neurology & Psychiatry (Chicago)*, 45: 215-222.

Fillmore, S.J., Shapiro, M., Killip, T., (1970), Serial blood gas studies during cardiopulmonary resuscitation. *Annals of Internal Medicine*, 72: 465-469.

Finnerty, F.A., Witkin, L., Fazekas, J.F., (1954), Cerebral hemodynamics during cerebral ischemia induced by acute hypotension. *Journal of Clinical Investigation*, 33: 1227-1332.

Fiset, P., Paus, T., Daloze, T., et al., (1999), Brain Mechanisms of Propofol-Induced Loss of Consciousness in Humans: a Positron Emission Tomographic Study, *Journal of Neuroscience*, 19: 5506–5513.

Frazer, J.G., (1922), *The Golden Bough.*

Freudenreich, O., McEnvoy, J.P., Goff, D.C., et al., (2007), Catatonic coma with profound bradycardia. *Psychosomatics*, 48: 74-78.

Gandevia, S.C., (1982), The perception of motor commands or effort during muscular paralysis. *Brain*, 105: 151-159.

Gandevia, S.C., (1985), Illusory movements produced by electrical stimulation of low-threshold muscle afferents from the hand. *Brain*, 108: 965-81.

Gandevia, S.C., McCloskey, D.I., (1977), Sensations of heaviness. *Brain*, 100: 345-354.

Gandevia, S.C., McCloskey, D.I., (1977a), Changes in motor commands, as shown by changes in perceived heaviness, during partial curarization and peripheral anaesthesia in man. *Journal of Physiology*, 273: 673-689.

Gandevia, S.C., Phegan, C.M.L., (1999), Perceptual distortions of the human body image produced by local anaesthesia, pain and cutaneous stimulation.

Journal of Physiology, 514: 609-616.

Gastaut, H., Fischer-Williams, M., (1957), Electroencephalographic study of syncope. Its differentiation from epilepsy. *Lancet*, II: 1018-1025.

Gastaut, H., Fischgold, H., Meyer, J.S., (1961), *Chapter 57, Conclusions of the international colloquium on anoxia and the EEG.* in Gastaut, H., Meyer, J.S., (1961), *Cerebral Anoxia and the Electroencephalogram.* Pub. Charles C. Thomas, USA, 1961.

Geller, U., (1987), *Uri Geller's Fortune Secrets*, Sphere Books, U.K., ISBN 0722138121.

Gentili, M.E., Verton, C., Kinirons, B., et al., (2002), Clinical perception of phantom limb sensation in patients with brachial plexus block. *European Journal of Anaesthesiology*, 19: 105-108.

Gloor, P., Olivier, A., Quesney, E.F., et al., (1982), The Role of the Limbic System in Experiential Phenomena of Temporal Lobe Epilepsy, *Annals of Neurology*, 12: 129-144.

Gloor, P., (1990), Experiential phenomena of temporal lobe epilepsy. Facts and hypotheses. *Brain*, 113: 1673-1694.

Goodwin, G.M., McCloskey, D.I., Matthews, P.B.C., (1972), The contribution of muscle afferents to kinaesthesia shown by vibration induced illusions of movement and by the effects of paralysing joint afferents. *Brain*, 95: 705-748.

Gordon, A.S., (1962), Heat exchangers as hypothermia inducers in heart surgery. *Annual Reviews of Medicine*, 13: 75-86.

Gower, R., (1893), *Joan of Arc,* published J.C. Nimmo, London, England.

Grey, M., (1986), *Return from Death. An exploration of the Near-Death Experience.* Published by Akana, London, England, ISBN 1-85063-019-4.

Greyson, B., (1983), The Near-Death Experience Scale: Construction, reliability, and validity. *Journal of Nervous and Mental Disease*, 171: 369-375.

Greyson, B., (1985), A typology of near-death experiences. *American Journal of Psychiatry*, 142: 967-969.

Gruhn, N., Larsen, F.S., Boesgaard, S., et al., (2001), Cerebral Blood Flow in Patients With Chronic Heart Failure Before and After Heart Transplantation. *Stroke.* 32: 2530-2533.

Hagbarth, K.E., Nordin, M., (1998), Postural after-contractions in man attributed to muscle spindle thixotropy. *Journal of Physiology*, 506: 875-883.

Herodotus, (484-425 BCE), *The Histories.* Translated by G. Rawlinson, published by Omphaloskepsis, USA.

Hess, E.H., (1965), Attitude and pupil size. *Scientific American*, April, 46-54.

Hess, E.H., (1975), The role of pupil size in communication. *Scientific American*, November, 110-119.

Hietanen, E., Bartsch, H., Bereziat, J.C., et al., (1994), Dietary intake and oxidative stress in breast, colon and prostate cancer patients: a case control study.

European Journal of Clinical Nutrition, 48: 575-586.

Hill, K., et al., (2001), Estimates of maternal mortality for 1995. *Bulletin of the World Health Organization*, 79: 182-193.

History of Jerusalem. Article posted on the internet on Wednesday, 20 September 2006: http://www.centuryone.com/hstjrslm.html

Hobbs, A.J., Bush, G.H., Downham, D.Y., (1988), Peri-operative dreaming and awareness in children. *Anaesthesia*, 43: 560-562.

Hoed, van den J., Lucas, E.A., Dement, W.C., (1979), Hallucinatory experiences during cataplexy in patients with narcolepsy. *American Journal of Psychiatry*, 136: 1210-1211.

Hoeper, M.M., Maier, R., Tongers, J., et. al., (1999), Determination of Cardiac Output by the Fick Method, Thermodilution, and Acetylene Rebreathing in Pulmonary Hypertension. *American Journal of Respiratory and Critical Care Medicine*, 160: 535-541.

Huang, G.H., Davidson, A.J., Stargatt, R., (2005), Dreaming during anaesthesia in children: incidence, nature and associations. *Anaesthesia*, 60: 854-861.

Hurovitz, C., Dunn, S., Domhoff, G. W., Fiss, H., (1999), The dreams of blind men and women: A replication and extension of previous findings. *Dreaming*, 9: 183-193.

Isaacson, S.A., Funderburk, M., Yang, J., (2000), Regulation of Proprioceptive Memory by Subarachnoid Regional Anesthesia. *Anesthesiology*, 93:55-61.

Jews in Rome. Article found on the internet on Wednesday, 20 September 2006: http://www.jewishvirtuallibrary.org/jsource/vjw/Rome.html

Kajimura, N., Uchiyama, M., Takayama, Y., et al., (1999), Activity of Midbrain Reticular Formation and Neocortex during the Progression of Human Non-Rapid Eye Movement Sleep. *Journal of Neuroscience*, 19: 10065-10073.

Kennedy, J.M., (1997), How the blind draw. *Scientific American*, January, 76-81.

Kerssens, C., Klein, J., Bonke, B., (2003), Awareness. Monitoring versus remembering what happened. *Anesthesiology*, 99: 570-575.

Kinsella, S.M., Tuckey, J.P., (2001), Perioperative bradycardia and asystole: relationship to vasovagal syncope and the Bezold-Jarisch reflex. *British Journal of Anaesthesia*, 86: 859-868.

Kluger, M.T., (2001), The bispectral index during an anaphylactic circulatory arrest. *Anaesthesia and Intensive Care*, 29: 544-547.

Koch, F., Thompson, J., Chung, R.S., (1991), Giant cerebral aneurysm repair. Incorporating cardiopulmonary bypass and neurosurgery. *Association of periOperative Registered Nurses Journal*, 54: 224-7, 230-3, 236-41.

Koran, translation by Maraduke Pickthall (1875-1936 CE) and first published in 1930 CE. This usually acknowledged to be one of the better English language translations. Unless otherwise specifically noted, this is the source for all passages cited from the Koran.

Koran, (AJA Koran), translation by A.J. Arberry. Passages cited from this translation are specifically marked.

Koran, (MHS Koran), Translation by Mohammad Habib Shakir. Passages cited from this translation are specifically marked.

Koran, (YA Koran), Translation by Yusuf Ali. Passages cited from this translation are specifically marked.

Lai, S.Y., Deffenderfer, O.F., Hanson, W., et al., (2002), Identification of upper respiratory bacterial pathogens with the electronic nose. *Laryngoscope*, 112: 975-979.

Langhelle, A., Sunde, K., Wik, L., Steen, P.A., (2000), Arterial blood-gases with 500- versus 1000-ml tidal volumes during out-of-hospital CPR. *Resuscitation*, 45: 27-33.

Lanier, W.L., Milde, J.H., Michenfelder, J.D., (1986), Cerebral stimulation following Succinylcholine in dogs. *Anesthesiology*, 64: 551-559.

Lanier, W.L., Iaizzo, P.A., Milde, J.H., Sharbrough F.W., (1994), The cerebral and systemic effects of movement in response to a noxious stimulus in lightly anesthetized dogs: Possible modulation of cerebral function by muscle afferents. *Anesthesiology*, 80: 392-401.

Lenggenhager, B., Tadi, T., Metzinger, T., Blanke, O., (2007), Video ergo sum: manipulating bodily self-consciousness. *Science*, 317: 1096-1099.

Liere, van E.J., Stickney, J.C., (1963), *Hypoxia*, published by the University of Chicago Press, U.S.A..

Lommel, P. van, Wees, R. van, Meyers, V., et al., (2001), Near-death experience in survivors of cardiac arrest: a prospective study in the Netherlands. *Lancet*, 358: 2039-2045.

Longstreth, W.T., (1987), The neurological sequelae of cardiac arrest. *Western Journal of Medicine*, 147: 175-180.

Lövblad, K.O., Schindler, K., Jakob, P.M., et al., (2003), Functional imaging of sleep. *Schweizer Archiv fur Neurologie und Psychiatrie*, 154: 324-328.

Machado, R.F., Laskowski, D., Deffenderfer, O., et al., (2005), Detection of lung cancer by sensor array analyses of exhaled breath. *American Journal of Respiratory and Critical Care Medicine*, 171: 1286-1291.

Mack, J.E.., (1994), *Abduction. Human Encounters with aliens*, published by Simon & Schuster, USA, ISBN 0-671-85194-2.

Mainzer, J., (1979), Awareness, muscle relaxants and balanced anaesthesia. *Canadian Anaesthetist's Society Journal*, 26: 386-393.

Mallen, E.A.H., Kashyap, P., Hampson, K.M., (2006), Transient axial length change during the accommodation response in young adults. *Investigative Ophthalmology and Visual Science*, 47:1251-1254.

Maravita, A., Spence, C., Driver, J., (2003), Multisensory Integration and the Body Schema: Close to Hand and Within Reach. *Current Biology*, 13: R531-R539.

McCloskey, D.I., (1978), Kinesthetic sensibility. *Physiological Reviews*, 58: 763-820.

McCulloch, M., Jezierski, T., Broffman, M., et al., (2006), Diagnostic accuracy of canine scent detection in early- and late-stage lung and breast cancers. *Integrative Cancer Therapies*, 5: 30-39.

Mendis, S., Sobotka, P.A., Euler, D.E., (1995), Expired hydrocarbons in patients with acute myocardial infarction. *Free Radical Research*, 23: 117-122.

Moody, R.A., (1976), *Life after Life*, published Bantam, U.S.A., ISBN 0-553-27484-8.

Moore, D.W., (2005), Three in four Americans believe in Paranormal. Little change from 2001. *Gallup Poll News Service.* http://poll.gallup.com/

MORI, (1998), A Paranormal survey conducted for the Sun Newspaper in 1998 by the MORI organisation. www.mori.com

Muldoon, S.J., Carrington, H., *The Projection of the Astral Body*, published by Samuel Weiser Inc., USA, 1989, ISBN 0-87728-069-X.

Munte, S., Schmidt, M., Meyer, M., et al., (2002), Implicit memory for words played during Isoflurane- or Propofol-based anesthesia. The lexical decision task. *Anesthesiology*, 96: 588-594.

Murray, C.J.L., Lopez, A.D., (1997), Mortality by cause for eight regions of the world: Global Burden of Disease Study. *Lancet*, 349: 1269-1276.

Muslim, (Sunnah of Sahih Muslim). This is a collection of the sayings and deeds of Mohammed collected, collated and verified by Abul Husain Muslim bin al-Hajjaj al-Nisapuri, (824-883 CE). This Sunnah enjoys a status equal to that of Bukhari among the Sunni Moslems, a group comprising about 85% of all followers of Islam. This book quotes from the Abdul Hamid Siddiqui translation. The format of the citation is: Muslim Chapter X: Book Y: Number Z, which is shortened to Muslim X:Y:Z.

Natale, C. di., Macagnano, A., Martinelli, E., et al., (2003), Lung cancer identification by the analysis of breath by means of an array of non-selective gas sensors. *Biosensors and Bioelectronics*. 18: 1209-1218.

Neylan, T.C., (1999), Frontal Lobe Function: Mr. Phineas Gage's Famous Injury. *Journal of Neuropsychiatry and Clinical Neurosciences*, 11: 280-283.

Nikolajsen, L., Jensen, T.S. (2001), Phantom limb pain. *British Journal of Anaesthesia*, 87: 107-116.

Olson, E.J., Boeve, B.F., Silber, M.H., (2000), Rapid eye movement sleep behaviour disorder: demographic, clinical and laboratory findings in 93 cases. *Brain*, 123: 331-339.

O'Sullivan, E.P., Childs, D., Bush, G.H., (1988), Peri-operative dreaming in paediatric patients who receive suxamethonium. *Anaesthesia*, 43: 104-106.

Osis, K., Haraldsson, E., (1986), *At the Hour of Death*, published by Hastings House, U.S.A., ISBN 0-8038-9279-9.

Oswald, I., (1959), Sudden bodily jerks on falling asleep. *Brain*, 82: 92-103.

Paqueron, X., Leguen, M., Rosenthal, D., et al., (2003), The phenomenology of body image distortions induced by regional anaesthesia. *Brain*, 126: 702-712.

Parnia, S., Waller, D.G., Yeates, R., et al., (2001), A qualitative and quantitative study of the incidence, features and aetiology of near-death experiences in cardiac arrest survivors. *Resuscitation*, 48: 149-156.

Pasricha, S., Stevenson, I., (1986), Near-death experiences in India. A preliminary report. *Journal of Nervous and Mental Disease*, 174: 165-170.

Penfield, W., Boldrey, E., (1937), Somatic and sensory representation in the sensory cortex of man as studied by electrical stimulation. *Brain*, 60: 389-443.

Penfield, W., (1955), The twenty ninth Maudsley lecture: The role of the temporal cortex in certain psychical phenomena. *Journal of Mental Science*, 101: 451-465.

Penland, H.R., Weder, N., Tampi, R.R., (2006), The catatonic dilemma expanded. *Annals of General Psychiatry*, 5: 14-22.

Personal communication-1. This story is based upon the experiences told me by a woman who underwent repeated anaesthetics. Induction of anaesthesia was with Thiopentone. Each time, just before losing consciousness due to the Thiopentone, she saw a black hole, and felt, as well as saw herself falling into the darkness of this hole.

Personal communication-2: From Nurse Hanneke A. who told me this experience on 19 November 2004.

Personal Note. Several years ago, some café owners in one city of Belgium actually used this tactic to discourage custom in the café of a competitor. The principle was simple. They would pay a particularly repellent beggar to sit outside the café of a competitor with a gaggle of sickly, unattractive, and preferably snotty infants and children. It proved a singularly effective method of deterring pleasure-seekers from entering that café.

Phillips, M., Cataneo, R.N., Greenburg, J., et al., (2003), Breath markers of oxidative stress in patients with unstable angina. *Heart Disease*, 5: 95-99.

Phillips, M., Cataneo, R.N., Cummin, A.R.C., et al., (2003a), Detection of lung cancer with volatile markers in the breath. *Chest*, 123: 2115-2123.

Phillips, M., Cataneo, R.N., Ditkoff, B.A., et al., (2003b), Volatile markers of breast cancer in the breath. *Breast Journal*, 9: 184-191.

Phillips, M., Cataneo, R.N., Cheema, T., et al, (2004), Increased breath biomarkers of oxidative stress in diabetes mellitus. *Clinica Chimica Acta*, 344: 189-194.

Phillips, M., Cataneo, R.N., Condos., R., et al., (2007), Volatile biomarkers of pulmonary tuberculosis in the breath. *Tuberculosis (Edinburgh)*, 87: 44-52.

Poli, D., Carbognani, P., Corradi, M., et al., (2005), Exhaled volatile compounds in patients with non-small cell lung cancer: cross sectional and nested short-term follow-up study. *Respiratory Research*, 6: 71-81.

Prehn, A., Ohrt, A., Sojka, B., et al., (2006), Chemosensory signals augment the startle reflex in humans. *Neuroscience Letters*, 394: 127-130.

Ramachandran, V.S., Hirstein, W., (1998), The perception of phantom limbs. *Brain*, 121: 1603-1630.

Ramachandran, V.S., (1998a), Consciousness and body image: lessons from phantom limbs, Capgras syndrome and pain asymbolia. *Philosophical Transactions of the Royal Society of London*, B353: 1851-1859.

Ramachandran, V.S., Hubbard, E.M., (2003), Hearing colors, tasting shapes. *Scientific American*, May, 52-59.

Rawlings., M., (1979), *Beyond Death's Door*, published by Bantam, New York, U.S.A., ISBN 0-553-22970-2.

Ring, K., Cooper, S., (1999), *Mindsight. Near-Death and Out-of-body Experiences in the Blind.* Published by the William James Center for Consciousness Studies, USA, ISBN 0-9669630-0-8.

Rossen, R., Kabat, H., Anderson, J.P., (1943), Acute arrest of cerebral circulation in man. *Archives of Neurology and Psychiatry*, 50: 510-528.

Sabom, M., (1998), *Light & Death.* published by Zondervan Publishing House, USA, 1998, ISBN 0-310-21992-2.

Safar, P., (1988), Resuscitation from clinical death: Pathophysiologic limits and therapeutic potentials. *Critical Care Medicine*, 16: 923-941.

Saha, M., Muppala, M.R., Castaldo, J.E., et al., (1993), The impact of cardiac index on cerebral hemodynamics. *Stroke*, 24: 1686-1690.

Schenck, C.H., Bundie, S.R., Patterson, R.L., et al., (1987), Rapid eye movement sleep behavior disorder. A treatable parasomnia affecting older adults. *Journal of the American Medical Association*, 257: 1786-1789.

Schipper, M., (2004), Never marry a woman with big feet – world wisdom and development cooperation. Text of lecture given on 27 October 2004 for: Lecture Series on Forgotten Issues of Globalization – Implications for Development Cooperation. See website: http://www.rawoo.nl/pdf/schippers.pdf

Schwartz, S., Maquet, P., (2002), Sleep imaging and the neuropsychological assessment of dreams, *Trends in Cognitive Sciences*, 6: 23-30.

Schwender, D., Kunze-Kronawitter, H., Dietrich, P., et al., (1998), Conscious awareness during general anaesthesia: patients' perceptions, emotions, cognition and reactions. *British Journal of Anaesthesia*, 80: 133-139.

Schwoebel, J., Friedman, R., Duda, N., et al., (2001), Pain and the body schema. Evidence for peripheral effects on mental representations of movement. *Brain*, 124: 2098-2104.

Sedghi, S., Keshavarzian, A., Klamut, M., et al., (1994), Elevated breath ethane levels in active ulcerative colitis: evidence for excessive lipid peroxidation. *American Journal of Gastroenterology*, 89: 2217-2221.

Sharmuta means *bitch* in Arabic.

Shea, J.A., Healey, M.J., Berlin, J.A., et al., (1996), Mortality and complications associated with laparoscopic cholecystectomy. A meta-analysis. *Annals of Surgery*, 224: 609-620.

Smith, N.T., Westover, C.J., Quinn, M., et al., (1986), The effect of muscle movement on the electroencephalogram during anesthesia with alfentanil. *Journal of Clinical Monitoring*, 1: 15-21.

Smith, S.M., Brown, H.O., Toman, J.E.P., Goodman, L.S., (1947), The lack of cerebral effects of d-tubocurarine. *Anesthesiology*, 8: 1-14.

Spence, C., Pavani, F., Maravita, A., et al., (2004), Multisensory contributions to the 3-D representation of visuotactile peripersonal space in humans: evidence from the crossmodal congruency task. *Journal of Physiology – Paris*, 98: 171-189.

Spinoza, B., (1677), *Ethics*. Translated by R.H.M. Elwes, 1883.

Steen-Hansen, J.E., Hansen, N.N., Vagenes, P., et al., (1988), Pupil size and light reactivity during cardiopulmonary resuscitation: A clinical study. *Critical Care Medicine*, 16: 69-70

Stocks, J.M., Taylor, N.A.S., Tipton, M.J., et al., (2004), Human Physiological Responses to Cold Exposure. *Aviation, Space, and Environmental Medicine*, 75: 444-457.

Stone, T.T., (1950), Phantom limb pain and central pain. *Archives of Neurology and Psychiatry*, 63: 739-748.

Strang, R., Wilson, T.M., MacKenzie, T.E., (1977), Choroidal and cerebral blood flow in baboons measured by the external monitoring of radioactive inert gases. *Investigative Ophthalmology & Visual Science*, 16: 571-576.

Summers, M., (1994), *The History of Witchcraft*, published by The Guernsey Press Co. Ltd., U.K., ISBN 8595 0262.

Sundt, T.M., Sharbrough, F.W., Piepgras, D.G., et al., (1981), Correlation of cerebral blood flow and electroencephalographic changes during carotid endarterectomy. With results of surgery and hemodynamics of cerebral ischemia. *May Clinic Proceedings*, 56: 533-543.

Suzuki, M., Hori, S., Nakamura, I., et al., (2004), Long-term survival of Japanese patients transported to an emergency department because of syncope. *Annals of Emergency Medicine*, 44: 215-221.

Szekely, B., Saint-Marc, T., Degremont, A.C., et al., (2002), Value of bispectral index monitoring during cardiopulmonary monitoring. *British Journal of Anaesthesia*, 88: 443-444.

Takatani, S., (2002), Beyond Implantable First Generation Cardiac Prostheses for Treatment of End-stage Cardiac Patients with Clinical Results in a Multicenter. *Annals of Thoracic and Cardiothoracic Surgery*, 8: 253-263.

Taylor, H., (2003), The religious and other beliefs of Americans 2003, *Harris Poll #11*, http://www.harrisinteractive.com/harris_poll/index.asp?PID=359

Tertullian, (Proper name: Quintus Septimius Florens Tertullianus, anglicized as Tertullian, lived 155–230 CE), *A Treatise on the Soul*.

Thornton, C., Sharpe, R.M., (1998), Evoked responses in anaesthesia. *British Journal of Anaesthesia*, 81: 771-781.

Tithe: see Wikipedia, (13 September 2006) http://en.wikipedia.org/wiki/Tithe

Tucker, K.J., Idris A.H., Wenzel, V., et al, (1994), Changes in arterial and mixed venous blood gases during untreated ventricular fibrillation and cardiopulmonary resuscitation. *Resuscitation*, 28: 137-141.

Utts, J., (1991), Replication and meta-analysis in parapsychology. *Statistical Science*, 6: 363-403.

Vignemont, F. de., Ehrsson, H.H., Haggard, P., (2005), Bodily Illusions Modulate Tactile Perception. *Current Biology*, 15: 1286-1290.

Visser, G.H., Wieneke, G.H., Van Huffelen, A.C., et al., (2001), The Development of Spectral EEG Changes During Short Periods of Circulatory Arrest. *Journal of Clinical Neurophysiology*. 18: 169-177.

Weitz, Z.W., Birnbaum, A.J., Sobotka, P.A., et al., (1991), High breath pentane concentrations during acute myocardial infarction. *Lancet*, 337: 933-935.

Williams, M.D., Rainer, W.G., Fieger, H.G., et al., (1991), Cardiopulmonary bypass, profound hypothermia, and circulatory arrest for neurosurgery. *Annals of Thoracic Surgery*, 52: 1069-1074.

Woerlee, G.M., (2003), *Mortal Minds: A Biology of the Soul and the Dying Experience*, published by de Tijdstroom, Utrecht, The Netherlands, ISBN 90 5898 057-X. Also published in the U.S.A. in 2004, by Prometheus Books, U.S.A., 2004, under the title: *Mortal Minds: A Biology of the Near-death Experience*, ISBN 1-59102-283-5.

Yung, G.L., Fedullo, P.F., Kinninger, K., et al., (2004), Comparison of Impedance Cardiography to Direct Fick and Thermodilution Cardiac Output Determination in Pulmonary Arterial Hypertension. *CHF*, 10 (supplement 2): 7-10.

Zampini, M., Moro, V., Aglioti, S.M., (2004), Illusory movements of the contralesional hand in patients with body image disorders. *Journal of Neurology, Neurosurgery and Psychiatry*, 75: 1626-1628.

Zeman, A., (2001), Consciousness, *Brain*, 124: 1263-1289.